A HOUSE IN THE MOUNTAINS

A HOUSE IN THE MOUNTAINS

The Women Who Liberated
Italy from Fascism

CAROLINE MOOREHEAD

Chatto & Windus
LONDON

1 3 5 7 9 10 8 6 4 2

Chatto & Windus, an imprint of Vintage,
20 Vauxhall Bridge Road,
London SW1V 2SA

Chatto & Windus is part of the Penguin Random House group of companies
whose addresses can be found at global.penguinrandomhouse.com.

Penguin
Random House
UK

First published in the United Kingdom by Chatto & Windus in 2019

penguin.co.uk/vintage

A CIP catalogue record for this book is available from the British Library

HB ISBN 9781784741402
TPB ISBN 9781784741419

Typeset in 11/14 pt Sabon LT Std
by Integra Software Services Pvt. Ltd, Pondicherry

Printed and bound in Great Britain by Clays Ltd, Elcograf S.p.A.

Penguin Random House is committed to a sustainable future for
our business, our readers and our planet. This book is made
from Forest Stewardship Council® certified paper.

For Stella

'The hour to resist had arrived; the hour to be men – to die like men and to live like men.'

Pietro Calamandrei, *Uomini e città della Resistenza*, 1955

'We women must now give everything to saving our homeland, our life, our bread. We too must not hesitate. We will show with our actions that we too are capable of every sacrifice.'

Gruppi di difesa della donna e per l'assistenza ai combattenti della libertà, July 1944

Contents

Principal Characters   xi

Chronology   xiii

Maps   xvi

Preface   xix

PART ONE: THE FALL OF ITALY   1

Chapter 1   A Roman coup   3

Chapter 2   Interlude   24

Chapter 3   Bursting into life   37

Chapter 4   A war zone   55

Chapter 5   Making lions   72

Chapter 6   The *piccoli geni*   90

Chapter 7   A little woman   112

PART TWO: A YEAR OF FIRE   133

Chapter 8   Heedless   135

Chapter 9   The hunters and the hunted   156

Chapter 10   A lizard among the rocks   167

Chapter 11   Nesting in kitchens   181

Chapter 12   Summer of flames   198

Chapter 13   Haunted by death   205

Chapter 14   Learning to live better   230

PART THREE: LIBERATION   253

Chapter 15   Mothers of the Resistance   255

Chapter 16   Squashing the cockroaches   270

Chapter 17   Insurrection   289
Chapter 18   Bloodletting   312
Chapter 19   A love of forgetting   330

Afterword   345
Acknowledgements   349
List of Illustrations   351
Bibliography   353
Notes   363
Index   375

Principal Characters

The four women friends

Ada Gobetti, widow of Piero Gobetti and mother of Paolo

Bianca Guidetti Serra, law graduate, companion of Alberto Salmoni

Silvia Pons, doctor, companion of Giorgio Diena and mother of Vittorio

Frida Malan, graduate in literature and sister of Roberto and Gustavo

The staffette

Lisetta Giua, engaged to Vittorio Foa

Lucia Boetta, guide to visiting dignatories

Matilde di Pietrantonio, renowned for kidnapping German officers

Gigliola Spinelli, procurer of weapons

Their Jewish friends

Primo Levi and his sister Anna Maria
Vanda Maestra
Luciana Nissim
Alberto Salmoni
Emanuele Artom
Vittorio Foa
Giorgio, Marisa and Paolo Diena

The partisans

Giorgio Agosti, a Turin magistrate
Dante Livio Bianco, a Turin lawyer, and his *staffetta* wife Pinella
Willy Jervis, liaison with the Allies, and his wife Lucilla
Ettore Marchesini, engineer and Ada's husband
General Perotti, head of the northern Committee of National Liberation
Ferruccio Parri, head of the military wing of the Partito d'Azione
Don Foglia, known as Don Dinamite
Giulio Bolaffi, commander of the Stellina Brigade
Tancredi Galimberti, partisan commander, known as Duccio

The Fascists

Giuseppe Solaro, party secretary in Turin
Valerio Paolo Zerbino, prefect in Turin
Guido Buffarini Guidi, Minister for the Interior in the Salò republic
Renato Ricci, head of the militia in the Salò republic
Alessandro Pavolini, head of the new Partito Fascista Repubblicano

Chronology

1943

10 July–17 August	Allied landings and conquest of Sicily.
25 July	Mussolini deposed, arrested and replaced by Marshal Badoglio. The war continues on the German side.
3 September	Italians sign armistice with Allies, made public on 8 September.
9 September	Allies land in Salerno. Germans begin occupation of Italy. Italy's anti-Semitic laws of 1938 enforced.
	Ada Gobetti starts her war diary.
12 September	Mussolini is rescued from the Gran Sasso by German commandos.
23 September	The new Italian Social Republic is established at Salò with Mussolini at its head.
	Anti-Fascist leaders form clandestine Comitato di Liberazione Nazionale (Committee of National Liberation) in Rome. There are now three Italian governments: Badoglio's, the Roman CLN, and Mussolini's in Salò; and two armies, the German and the Allied.

15 November	First congress of the newly constituted Fascist Party held in Verona. Jews declared enemies of the state. Arrests by Fascists and Germans get underway.
	As do orders for the draft of young men for Salò's army, and for workers for the German war industry.
	The Allied Control Commission set up in the liberated south.
November	Gruppi di difesa della donna e per l'assistenza ai combattenti della libertà – Groups for the protection of women and assistance to fighters for freedom – (GDD) set up.

1944

22 January	Allies land at Anzio, south of Rome.
January–March	Devastating German spring offensive against the partisans in the north.
	Northern Committee of National Liberation sets up unified military command.
April	A Servizio Ausiliario Femminile for women Fascists is set up.
4 June	Rome is liberated by the Allies.
6 June	Normandy landings.
3 August	Florence is liberated.
15 August	Allies land in Provence.
	The Germans establish a new defensive position, the Gothic line, from La Spezia on the west coast to between Ravenna and Pesaro on the east coast.

13 November	General Alexander orders partisans to stand down for the winter months.
	Allies stall on Gothic line. Germans embark on major campaign to crush partisans in the north.

1945

1 February	Italian women get the vote.
18 April	General strike called across the north.
26 April	Insurrection in Turin.
	Capture of Mussolini by the partisans.
27 April	Germans and Fascists retreat as one city after another is liberated.
29 April	Document of surrender by Germans and Fascists in Italy signed in Caserta, to take force on 2 May.
30 April	First Allied soldiers reach Turin.
7 May	Germany surrenders to Allies.
21 June	Ferruccio Parri sworn in as first post-war prime minister.
8 December	The Parri government falls.

1946

2 June	Monarchy replaced by republic after constitutional referendum.
22 June	Widespread amnesty declared for most imprisoned Fascist collaborators.

1947

10 February	Peace Treaty between Italy and Allies formally signed in Paris.

Italy, 1943–45

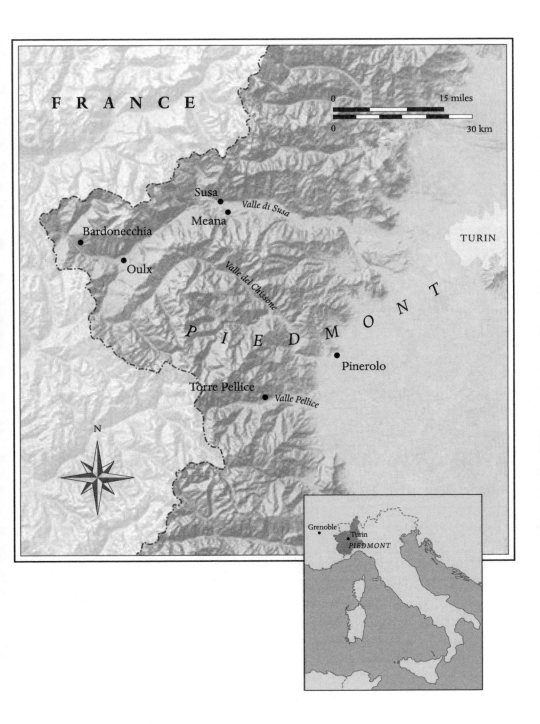

The valleys and mountains of Piedmont

Preface

On the evening of 12 March 1945, soon after dinner, there was a knock on the door at a modest house in one of Turin's northern suburbs, Il Terzo Quartiere, home to many of the workers in the city's vast industrial sector. Teresa Arduino was on the balcony with her youngest daughter, thirteen-year-old Bruna, hanging up the laundry; her six-year-old son, Antonio, was in bed, asleep. Outside were three young men, claiming to be partisans and wanting to be put in touch with a fighting brigade up in the mountains. They were invited to come in. The Arduino family were well regarded locally as long-term members of the Resistance, fighting the Germans and the Fascists, and Teresa's husband, Gaspare, a socialist and steelworker with FIAT, had been arrested eighteen times for his political sympathies. Teresa helped train young men and women serving with the urban partisans. Il Terzo Quartiere was a stronghold for the Resistance.

In the kitchen were Gaspare and Teresa's two older daughters, nineteen-year-old Vera, who had a job in a sweet factory, a young woman who took life and her role as eldest child seriously, and who worked for the Resistance carrying messages between the headquarters of the partisans in the city and those hiding in the mountains; and Libera, sixteen, who, when not at her own job in a mechanics factory, helped the families of imprisoned partisans and regularly gave blood to the Red Cross. With them that evening was another young partisan, 24-year-old Rosa Ghizzone, who, like the Arduino sisters, was a *staffetta* – a runner, a courier, a transporter of weapons, a guide. Rosa was pregnant. Her husband, Libera's fiancé and another partisan had just arrived to move Gaspare to a safe house, on the grounds that he was in increasing danger of arrest.

Once inside the house, the three strangers pulled out guns, said that they belonged to Mussolini's Black Brigades and forced Gaspare and the three girls to follow them out to a car; they also took away the three partisans. The Fascists wanted to take the whole family, but Gaspare persuaded them to leave his wife and younger children at home. The men were taken to the Fascist Party headquarters, the Littorio, in the centre of Turin, where they were separated. While Signora Arduino combed the city for news of her family, her husband and the other men were executed in different parts of the city.

Vera, Libera and Rosa were driven to the banks of the Pellerina canal, where they were shot in the back of the neck. Vera and Libera died immediately, but Rosa was only wounded, managed to get free and threw herself into the canal, where the current carried her to the shadow of a bridge. The young Fascists ran after her, firing into the water and hitting her several times. Believing her to be dead, they left to report their successful executions to the Turin Fascist leader, Giuseppe Solaro. Though badly hurt and covered in blood, Rosa dragged herself out of the water and crawled to a nearby house. Her baby was stillborn. Rosa herself died not long after.

News of the killings travelled rapidly around the city. For a while no one knew where the bodies had been taken or when or where the funerals would take place. But then a man working in the city morgue reported that Vera and Libera were to be buried on the Saturday, three days later, in the central cemetery. Throughout the industrial suburbs, from house to house, from family to family and woman to woman, the word went out: call a strike in your factory, gather the women, come to the funeral. Bring with you something red – a wreath, a scarf, a bunch of carnations.

By 8.30 on the morning of 16 March, more than two thousand women carrying red flowers and wreaths, tricolour flags and placards denouncing Fascist brutality, had gathered at the gates of Turin's main cemetery in Via Catania. Some wore red sweaters; others red scarves. Some were elderly, others little more than children. It was one of the biggest demonstrations by women in the history of Turin. And they were angry. There had been many killings in the previous nineteen months, but the cold-blooded shooting of these girls touched something in their imaginations. When two FIAT cars appeared at 9.15 they were assumed to be bringing representatives from the unions, but the plain-clothes men who got out belonged to Mussolini's crack anti-partisan unit. They fired guns into the air, trampled on the flowers and wreaths, tore up the placards. Reinforcements arrived in lorries. The women scattered, finding hiding places inside the church, behind a florist's booth, between the graves. Some were able to infiltrate themselves among the mourners of another funeral. But a number were caught and lined up facing the cemetery wall, their hands above their heads. One woman, whose son had already been shot by the Fascists, began to curse the men. The Fascists attempted to drag her onto a lorry, but her friends surged around, hiding her. A ninety-year-old woman fainted. More Fascists arrived and set about loading the women onto their lorries, trying to discover where the cursing woman was hidden, so that they could shoot her.

At this moment, two hearses drove up, one each for Vera and Libera. A woman in the crowd called out: 'Let us kneel'. Singing the hymns composed by the Resistance in the months of their war against the Fascists, the women knelt. The coffins passed between them.

Several hundred women were then rounded up and driven away to the grim Fascist barracks in Via Asti. In the following days some were released; others were still there when, six weeks later, Turin was liberated.

All through that Saturday in Turin, the local factories had staged fifteen minute strikes. In the city centre, the trams stopped. At a carpet factory called Paracchi, a woman had climbed out onto the roof and hung a large red flag. And later that day, women went back to the cemetery to gather the wreaths and flowers that had not been too badly crushed and laid them on the new graves. Turin, together with Milan and Genoa, part of Italy's industrial triangle, had seen many strikes and demonstrations since Italy had changed sides in the war and the Germans had first occupied their city in the early autumn of 1943. But there had never been anything quite like this, organised by women, for women, who were neither cowed nor fearful of the consequences.

There were four women in particular, who had been fighting with the Resistance for the previous nineteen months and who were closely connected, each in their own way, with the Arduino sisters. Two attended the funeral; two had been ordered to stay away.

The eldest of the four, Ada, widow of one of the most renowned anti-Fascists in Italian history, Piero Gobetti, and mother of seventeen-year-old Paolo, had just celebrated her forty-first birthday. A well-known translator and teacher, she was a humorous, affectionate, boundlessly energetic woman with dark curly hair, of whom it was said that she prized friendship above nationality, country and ideology. She was a founder of the left-wing Partito d'Azione and a political commissar with Stellina, one of the partisan brigades in the mountains. She had been forbidden to attend the funerals: the partisan leadership considered her life and safety too important to risk.

Bianca Guidetti Serra, twenty-five, a new member of the Communist Party, who had been running action committees against the Fascists in the factories and editing clandestine women's newspapers, was not there either, though she had been one of the event's main organisers, because she too was judged too valuable to the movement to lose. She had spent the previous night going from house to house, giving instructions to the women. Her younger sister Carla, who was still at university, went in her place, was arrested and spent a night in a cell in Via Asti with thirty others reciting poetry to herself to keep her fears at bay. Next day, she told the Fascist police that she had been visiting her father's grave and they released her; but their mother was furious with Bianca, saying: 'You will be the ruin of our family.' Bianca, who had graduated in

Ada Gobetti

the summer of 1943 as a lawyer, a profession then all but closed to women, spent the morning of the funerals in the library.

Bianca Guidetti Serra

One of the two women who did attend the funerals was Frida Malan, twenty-six, the only girl in a Protestant family of militant boys from the valleys to the west of Turin. Headstrong and rebellious, with fair hair and blue eyes and the build of a gymnast, Frida dreamt of a second Risorgimento, an uprising against the German invaders. She was serving as a fighter and *staffetta* with the V Divisione Alpina Val Pellice and was a member of the united regional military command. Seeing the Fascists arrive at the cemetery, Frida took the hand of a little girl standing near her and said: 'Say that you are my daughter.' She managed to avoid arrest.

Frida Malan

As did her closest childhood friend, 26-year-old Silvia Pons, a girl so pretty, with her black hair plaited at her neck, that people were said to stop talking when she came into a room. She was a doctor, another profession with very few women, and had graduated not long before. She also worked as a *staffetta* for the partisan brigades and helped treat wounded fighters.

These four women were friends. By March 1945, they had survived nearly two years of German occupation, Fascist brutality, repeated round-ups and armed battles throughout the city, the suburbs, the valleys and the mountains of the Alps which stretched north and west towards France and Switzerland. Two of them, Frida and Silvia, had been caught and held by the occupiers in prisons notorious for torture and summary executions. How they would fare in the six weeks that lay ahead, as the Allies advanced and the Germans and their Fascist collaborators grew increasingly desperate and embattled, not one of them could imagine.

Silvia Pons

Ada, Frida, Silvia and Bianca were remarkable women. But they were not alone. Between 1943 and 1945 thousands of women throughout occupied Italy rose up, joined the Resistance and fought to liberate their country. What made these women extraordinary was that Fascist Italy under Mussolini's twenty-year-rule had turned them into shadows: they had no rights, no voice, no equality, no say in either their own lives or in the running of the country. That they found the courage, the imagination and the selflessness to fight – and often to suffer arrest, torture, rape and execution – is what made them truly exceptional. Outside Italy, their contribution to the war is barely known. It is a story that deserves to be told.

But then, the story of the Italian Resistance in general is not widely known either. For nineteen months, between September 1943, when Italy surrendered and joined the Allies, and April 1945, when the country was liberated from German occupation, Italy was engaged in a civil war. Italians fought not just their German occupiers, while the Allied campaign moved slowly north through the country after their landings in the south, but also each other: Italians against Italians, partisans against Fascists, in a war of extreme brutality which saw many thousands die. This tragedy, outside Italy, is seldom remembered.

Ada, Frida, Silvia and Bianca were Piedmontese, from the mountains and plains of north-west Italy. Turin and the valleys of

Piedmont lay at the very heart of the northern Resistance. More Piedmontese proportionately fought and died than in any other part of the country.

The civil war and its aftermath brought out all that was best and all that was worst in Italian society. It gave Mussolini's two decades of Fascist rule, which began in the early 1920s, with its corruption, brutality, greed and eventual anti-Semitism, a further eighteen months of life. But it also brought to the fore all the warmth and generosity of the Italian character. The bravery shown by the partisans, both men and women, was exemplary. It is this contrast that makes these years so fascinating.

It is hard to pin down why the Italian partisan war has largely been forgotten. One reason would seem to lie in the complexity of the war itself and the vast array of forces lined up against each other: the American and British Allies, with their very different perceptions and concerns; the Germans intent on slowing the Allied advance while exploiting Italian resources and controlling the Fascists who joined them; the Italian Fascists, trying to position themselves for a future that looked increasingly grim; and the Resistance, with its lofty ideals and often reckless courage. None of this makes for a simple narrative.

But the neglect also comes from the attitude of the Anglo-Saxon world towards the Italians. The Allies were haunted by fears that the Resistance would push Italy into communism, which made them niggardly with their support. Long after the partisans had demonstrated their bravery and commitment, the Allies continued to regard them as unworthy partners, contaminated by the years of Fascism and the country's volte-face in the summer of 1943. Right up until the end of the war, and beyond, the partisans were recognised as necessary for the Italian campaign, but the Allies saw them as neither trustworthy nor ultimately important. The chaos that followed the end of the war only made them feel justified in their suspicions.

As for Ada Gobetti and her friends, whose stories this book tells, the civil war was not simply about ridding Italy of Fascism and the Germans. It was about creating a new, fairer, democratic society, in which women were, by law, to be equal partners, in work and in the family. That it was not to be, that Italy could have changed but did not, is one of the tragedies of what Ada called '*la nostra battaglia*', our battle.

Part One

THE FALL OF ITALY

1

A Roman coup

Almost two years before the Arduino funerals in Turin, at 5.15 on Saturday 24 July 1943, a hot, still, sultry Roman afternoon, the Fascist Grand Council gathered in the Sala del Pappagallo in the Piazza Venezia. This was its first meeting since 1939, after which Mussolini had judged its deliberations unnecessary; and he had resisted convening it now. But his *gerarchi*, the Fascist Party grandees, had insisted. The twenty-seven men present were wearing, on Mussolini's orders, the summer uniform of the militia: black safari jackets and black breeches. Mussolini wore the grey-green colours of the Corporal of Honour.

Ministers, generals, the papacy, the monarchy and the secret services had lost all confidence in Mussolini and for several months now they had been plotting to reduce his powers, though none of them trusted the others. The King's Belgian daughter-in-law, Maria José, an intelligent and shrewd woman Victor Emmanuel did not much like, had been in talks with the Vatican and the anti-Fascist leaders living in secret around the capital. Rome was full of rumours, at least some of them known to Mussolini from his spies and informers.

Italy had remained neutral until the summer of 1940, then joined the Axis powers. But its war had gone badly from the start, with humiliating reversals in Greece, Eritrea, Somalia and Ethiopia, while Mussolini veered between bursts of inspiration and capriciousness and his generals remained myopic and incompetent. It was now deteriorating further, with relations between Hitler and Mussolini increasingly sour. A recent radical reshuffle of the cabinet, with his vain, sly but realistic son-in-law Galeazzo Ciano demoted from Foreign Secretary to Ambassador to the Vatican, had only served to weaken Mussolini's position still further. His rows with his mistress Claretta Petacci, and with the rogues and profiteers who surrounded her, had become a national scandal. Once venerated throughout Italy and obeyed unquestioningly, the dictator was now an isolated and widely despised figure.

After three years of war, Italy's 3.7 million soldiers were ill-equipped and unenthusiastic, with over 350,000 of them prisoners of the Allies in North Africa alone, and nearly half of the 229,000 men dispatched to fight alongside the Germans on the Eastern Front, with outdated weapons, broken radios and boots that let in water, were dead. Letters home told of frostbite and abandonment. A young man described to his mother seeing 'men like larva, emaciated, pale as wax'. The half-million workers who had been sent to German labour camps to contribute to its war economy, were being treated abominably. Italy's air force was pitifully weak; 6,000 planes had already been lost and there were few spare parts for the rest. There was hardly a family, from the top to the toe of Italy, that did not have a son, a father or a husband in Russia, in the Balkans, in a prisoner-of-war camp.

All over the country, people were hungry; in the south, they were starving. The pulling in of belts had become known as the '*foro Mussolini*', a play on the word '*foro*' – belt – and Mussolini's still unfinished forum in Rome. Since the start of the war, Italy had been supplying Germany with rice, tobacco, cheese, fruit and vegetables. There was now no more coffee or tea and on the black market pasta and flour cost ten times what it had in 1940. In the absence of quinine, malaria was spreading. Soap had run low and scabies was sweeping through schools and villages. Since the autumn of 1942, the Allied bombing had left thousands dead and many cities reduced to rubble. There had been a woeful lack of air-raid shelters, sirens or firefighters. Rome itself had just been bombed for the first time, with 166 people killed and many more wounded in the working-class suburb of San Lorenzo. Strikes, a measure of the widespread pessimism and discontent, were paralysing Italian industry for weeks on end.

On 6 June had come a devastating report on the state of the country, a nation with such corrupt leaders, massive tax avoidance and inefficient bureaucrats and military leaders that it was no longer credible. Mussolini had promised the people a quick victory, bringing prestige and booty; what they had got was death, air raids, violence, penury. No one believed any longer in the stories of victorious and heroic battles. Fascism itself had come to feel like a huge trick, parasitic and mendacious. On 10 July, 160,000 Allied soldiers and six hundred tanks had landed in Sicily, and on the day of the Grand Council, Palermo fell into Allied hands. The Italians now wanted peace, at any price. Those in the Grand Council conspiring against Mussolini wanted a war they knew they were losing to end and they wanted the Duce gone.

Mussolini spoke first. For two hours, he rambled on, irritable, obsessive, repeating himself, swinging between accusations and recriminations, railing against the Allies and the 'uncouth, barbarous' Germans, insisting that he was still loved by the Italian people. There were few traces of the former energetic, purposeful leader, with his springy, cat-like step, who had once flown his own plane and been photograped bare-chested with lion cubs; rather he came across to those present as an overweight, ponderous, greying figure, his face shrunken, in considerable pain from a duodenal ulcer. Chief among those plotting for Mussolini's removal was the shrewd and ambitious Minister for Justice, Count Dino Grandi, a man as feline as he was pompous, who proposed that Mussolini hand back command of the armed forces to the King. By turn fawning and attacking, the Fascist Grand Council accused the Duce of being indecisive, of not ridding the government of incompetent bureaucrats, of pursuing a disastrous foreign policy. 'You have imposed a dictatorship on Italy,' Grandi declared, 'which is historically immoral.'

By midnight, the meeting had been going on for almost seven hours. Mussolini asked that it be adjourned until next day. He was granted just ten minutes, but returned refreshed and accusatory. 'I have enough here,' he told the councillors, tapping his briefcase, 'to send you all to the gallows.' Soon after 2 a.m., he called for a vote. It went, overwhelmingly, against him. Nineteen of those present voted for Grandi's resolution; seven abstained; one voted against. Leaving the room, Mussolini said: 'Gentlemen, you have brought about the fall of the regime.' The meeting had lasted a little under 10 hours. In the end, after the years of craven obedience, no senior Fascist had defended him, not even his son-in-law Ciano. It was the speed with which it happened, and the almost unanimous rejection by his formerly slavish followers, that was so shocking.

Next afternoon, apparently heedless of what might logically follow the council meeting, Mussolini went to pay his regular Monday visit to the weak, vacillating but for once resolute King. It was no secret that the two men disliked each other. Before he left for the palace, Mussolini's wife Rachele asked: 'Why didn't you have them all arrested?' When the Duce was shown into the audience room, he was informed, and appeared to accept with little protest or rancour, that he had to resign his command of the army. What he did not realise, as he was led out of the palace to a group of waiting *carabinieri*, and whisked off under cover of an ambulance to their barracks, was that he was being taken away, not for his own protection, but into custody. The following day he was moved to detention on the island of Ponza, off Sicily, where he had once sent many of his own enemies, and where he now passed his sixtieth birthday, in silence, for orders had been given that he was to speak to no one; then on to the still more remote island of La Maddalena, Garibaldi's place of retreat; then on again, to an isolated hotel high in the Abruzzi mountains east of Rome. He pondered writing a memoir about exile, in the style of Napoleon while on St Helena, and told one of the officers guarding him: 'I am politically dead.'

In Rome, meanwhile, the King had asked Marshal Pietro Badoglio, hero of the disastrous Ethiopian war, for which he had been rewarded with a hereditary dukedom, to form a new, non-Fascist government. At 10.45 on the Monday evening, interrupting a programme of popular musical hits, three terse messages were broadcast on the radio. The first said that the King had accepted Mussolini's resignation; the second that Badoglio was now head of government. The last was an announcement that the war, on the side of Germany, would go on: '*la guerra continua*'. Martial law was declared. Rachele Mussolini was put under house arrest. Claretta Petacci and her whole much hated clan, fearing retribution for years of corruption, fled north. The assets of some of the greedier *gerarchi* were seized. A jubilant uncensored *Il Messaggero* newspaper announced: 'Long Live Free Italy'. The Grand Council, the Chamber, the hated Special Tribunals which had over the years summarily sent so many political opponents to the penal colonies on the islands off Sicily, the Fascist Party and its para-military troops were all dissolved. The dreaded secret police, OVRA, was abolished. Ezra Pound, who since 1941 had been delivering regular seven-minute propaganda broadcasts for the Fascists, had time for one final talk before setting out, on foot, for his house in Rapallo.

Both the Allies and the Germans appear to have been taken by surprise at the abruptness of Mussolini's fall. But almost all ordinary Italians greeted it with an explosion of joy. In Rome, as the news spread, there was a frenzy of celebration. The mood was one of gaiety, not revenge, though there were isolated inci-dents of retribution. The houses of senior Fascists were attacked, and known Fascists were spat at, ridiculed and sometimes kicked in the streets, or even forced to drink castor oil, a humiliation they had once forced on their opponents. A much decorated Fascist colonel in the air force, Ettore Muti, famous for his bru-tality, was killed in Fregene. All over Italy, women processed to churches to thank the Madonna; factory workers downed tools and took to the streets, where they held parties. The names of streets were changed, to shed their Fascist connotations. Uniforms, badges, portraits, statues, the visible apparatus of Fascism, disap-peared, with extraordinary speed. Photographs of Mussolini were torn off classroom walls and statues of the dictator were pulled off their plinths and smashed. Prison gates were opened and political detainees released. Italian flags sprouted from every balcony. It was a coup, a bloodless revolution, without a shot fired. The Fascist dictatorship, which for twenty years had imposed a straitjacket of conformity and fear over Italy, was over. That the war would go on was something the revellers chose not to dwell on.

And for the women of Italy, it was indeed a revolution.

One of the key beliefs in Fascist ideology was that men and women were inherently different. In the early days of his rule, Mussolini had expressed some willingness in giving women the vote, at least in local elections. But by 1926 he had come to feel otherwise. Since women were 'not capable of great spiritual ideas', or indeed deep thought of any kind, they were clearly unsuited to politics and to most other intellectual pursuits. In any case, after the 'exceptional' laws brought in that year, which would define the course of the long dictatorship, no one, neither man nor woman, was allowed to vote, except for once, in a plebiscite to endorse his regime.

This was the start of a steady disenfranchisement of Italian women, who, until this moment, had been making steady gains towards equality and emancipation. From his office, high above Piazza Venezia in Rome, Mussolini oversaw the passing of laws to remove 'inferior' women from jobs, professions and activities. Women, he said, were incompatible with machinery: it made them masculine and independent and it castrated the men. A hotchpotch of myths, racial theories, medical chicanery and sophistry poured out from Fascist headquarters to prove that women were biologically lesser beings. Encouraged by the Vatican, which launched a 'crusade for purity', the Fascists decreed in a deluge of orders, speeches, radio programmes and articles that women could own nothing and decide nothing. Year by year they were forced to sit by and face exclusion from teaching literature or philosophy, from being head teachers or senior civil servants. If they wanted to go to university, they had to pay double fees. The penal code of 1930 made it legitimate for a man to kill his wife, daughter or sister in defence of his own honour.

On the other hand, for Mussolini, women did have one essential task: that of being mothers. If work was a 'corrupter of maternal dignity, a perverter . . . of the family', having babies was an obligation, a justification for existence. A woman's mission in life was to turn out great numbers of children for the *patria*, and many little soldiers for the new Italian empire. Nothing was to be allowed to get in the way. Abortion and contraception attracted the harshest punishments. 'He who is not a father,' Mussolini announced, 'is not a man.' Popular songs, sweet and sentimental, celebrated the *donna-angelo* and the *donna-madre*. Widows became symbols of courage, obedience and sacrifice.

In this authoritarian, patriarchal spirit, there was no place for individuality. Fascism was everything: a revolution, a civilising culture, a promise of renewal, a spiritual credo, and it brooked no discussion: 'Believe. Obey. Fight.' The state controlled leisure, textbooks, newspapers, associations and working hours, transmitting its views via slogans, edicts, theatrical spectacles, rituals and announcements. It presented a mishmash of history intended to glorify a certain view of man who acted rather than thought. As the slogans seen all over the walls of Italy put it: 'The Duce is always right.' Those who felt otherwise kept quiet. The men and women who might have taught a different view of the world were in prison, or exiled in the distant penal islands, or abroad, or dead. Dissent, criticism of the regime, even dissatisfaction were treasonable. The very few who persisted in speaking out did so in metaphors and allusions. They were islands, in a great sea of silence.

Fascist boys, according to the Italian Futurist movement, which glorified modernity and sought to liberate Italy from its passive past, should be helped to develop lively bold expressions, sensual mouths (with which to 'command imperiously'), taut muscles, the legs of squirrels (so that they could climb to great heights), and a 'virile, sporty elegance'. In their showy after-school uniforms and fezzes they paraded and goose-stepped, while brandishing wooden rifles and singing rousing martial hymns. Boys – anti-feminist, misogynist and terrified of homosexuality – were to be moulded into little cocks, in coops of subservient hens. Their role was to make Italy great again, as it had been under the Romans, to save the country from Bolshevism and to prove that it was superior to its decadent Western neighbours.

The Sons of the Wolf

In their own after-school classes, girls, in dowdy black and white, danced, skipped, and did callisthenics. At first called Figlie della Lupa (daughters of the wolf which suckled Romulus and Remus), then Piccole Italiane and Giovani Italiane, they were taught the virtues of self-abnegation and were given dolls on which to practise the rearing of Fascist babies. 'Duce! Duce! Duce!' they sang. 'God has sent you to Italy as He sends light.' Girls were told to eschew 'neurotic weakness'. Pale, gaunt, flat-chested career women were branded 'brazen, libertine, sensual, materialistic, egotistic, irreligious', perverted by 'pariginismo' and 'americanismo'. A good Fascist girl was chubby, florid, fecund and had rosy lips, and she was urged to practise 'obedience with joy'.

Stoicism and fecundity, however, did not necessarily mean abandoning modernity and assertiveness; on the contrary, usefulness to the state was much approved of, provided it did not involve politics. What mattered was remembering to be feminine and above all submissive. Hence the particular loathing Mussolini felt for any woman with professed anti-Fascist opinions. During the 1920s and 30s, when he was arresting and sending his opponents to the penal settlements on the islands off Sicily, his secret service kept dossiers on some 5,000 troublesome women picked up for their involvement with communism, socialism or anti-Fascism. Along with their photographs, the dossiers contained notes on the charges against these women, and most referred to them as 'prostitutes', 'unnatural mothers', 'hags' steeped in alcohol and vice, prone to 'tragic exhibitionism'. The vast majority, according to the dossiers, had no real views of their own: they were simply parroting those of their fathers, brothers and husbands.

Throughout the years of Fascism women's salaries were kept at about half those of men. This did not prevent many from taking jobs, especially in the growing number of factories in the northern industrial triangle, where up to a quarter of the workforce in textiles, leather, paper and even engineering was female. And, as air raids, rationing, hunger and fear began to dominate the lives of Italian women, so they began to stir. The strikes that paralysed industry in the north in March 1943, four months before Mussolini's fall, saw women in the front line.

'Better a day as a lion than a hundred years as a sheep,' Mussolini had declared in 1926. On 25 July 1943, all across Italy, in cities and towns and remote country villages, large numbers of Italian women decided that they would be sheep no longer.

Turin, with its majestic, formal eighteenth century palaces, arcades and long straight avenues from which on clear days you can see the snowy Alps stretching away into the distance, was one of the richest cities in Italy, with an ancient feudal aristocracy and strong military traditions. Home to FIAT, which had opened its Lingotto factory, a vast modern hangar of glass and concrete, on the western outskirts in 1923, it had become the heart of Italy's engineering industries, attracting workers from all over the country and especially from its impoverished south. Blasts from factory sirens, some high-pitched, some whistling, others hissing or screeching, marked Turin's working day. FIAT alone employed 46,000 people.

But by the summer of 1943, like much of the country, Turin had been reduced to penury and desolation. And since most of its factories had gone over to producing war material, Turin had been bombed twenty-eight times by the Allies, despite the blackout which kept the city in darkness from dusk to dawn, with the inhabitants riding their bicycles with phosphorescent buttons that glowed in the dark like fireflies. Later, people would remember the sheets of flames and the explosions, and everyone shouting, pushing, trampling over each other to reach safety, and, in winter, the snow dyed red with blood. They felt that they had become hunted animals. Three years of war had seen 430 factories hit, along with the blocks of flats that housed the workers. Fifty churches lay in ruins. The use of gas was banned for weeks on end for fear of explosions.

When, after the air raids, the inhabitants emerged from their cellars and basements, they found a dystopian landscape of deep craters, dangling electricity wires and overturned trams, with faint cries coming from those still trapped inside the crumbling buildings. In some parts of the city, half the houses were no longer standing. On 13 July, two weeks before the coup that brought down Mussolini, Allied planes had dropped

702 tons of explosives, killing 792 people. A cemetery was hit, leaving parts of the bodies of the recently buried scattered about.

Since there were enough air-raid shelters for just 1 per cent of the population, these relentless attacks had driven half of Turin's inhabitants to seek safety in the surrounding valleys or mountain villages, from where some 100,000 people returned to the city each day to work. Those who fled were living in rented rooms, barns, stables, church vestries, whatever they could find or afford. With each new raid, more desperate families could be seen joining the sea of people swarming onto the trains leaving from the Porta Nuova station. There were accidents, when the people clinging onto the roofs fell off as the train went round corners. At night, those without money left the city to sleep in the fields.

But Turin had not given up. By nature independent, conscious that Piedmont was where the impulse for the Risorgimento, the nineteenth-century struggle for Italian unification, was born and where the Enlightenment had taken root, the Piedmontese had been the least swayed by Fascist rhetoric. The old feudal aristocracy, with its interests in justice and finance, looked outwards, towards Europe. Their support for Mussolini had been muted, in spite of the noisy, disputatious Fascist squads that had established themselves in offices and barracks throughout the city centre.

Piedmontese women, angered by the lack of shelters, paucity of food and heating, and the news that their men had been sent to the Eastern Front in shoes made of cardboard, had repeatedly taken to the streets in protest. The strikes in Turin, which had shut down factories at Lancia, Michelin, Mirafiore and FIAT, before spreading across Lombardy and Emilia, were the first significant mass protests in Fascist Italy. There were many women among the strikers, and they were sent to prison or exiled to the penal islands. Shortages of everything, especially salt, had turned women into scavengers and barterers, but in the long queues for food that snaked along the avenues had been born a new kind of comradeship. And their protests had not been altogether in vain. When even factory bosses were forced to recognise that malnutrition was slowing down production, vats of soup were delivered in the middle of the day, to be handed out in mugs along the rows of workers.

Ada, Frida, Silvia and Bianca all came from Turin, formed by Piedmontese culture, schooled in the area's past spirit of independence and rebellion. Long before the war, Turin had been home to some of Italy's leading thinkers and intellectuals and, though decimated by Mussolini's repeated purges, some had managed to escape notice and lie low, carrying on with their own work, especially in medicine, the sciences and the law. In the evenings, defying the legions of spies set to trap them, they had strolled under the arcades, quietly conspiring. It was in Turin in the early 1920s that the Communist theorist Antonio Gramsci called for working-class unity and Soviet-style councils, and here that Ada Gobetti's dazzling, seductive young husband Piero rallied supporters to back a liberal revolution and explore ways to bring about a return to a fairer, more pragmatic democracy, drawing around him a generation of clever rebellious thinkers to write for his magazines *Energie Nuove* and *Rivoluzione Liberale*. He told them that they had to create educated, informed inner selves, with which to confront the evil abroad in Fascist Italy. Piero, said his friends, was a '*condottiere* of ideas'. He embodied courage and hope for a lost generation.

Ada's father, Giacomo Prospero, was a fruit merchant, an immigrant from Switzerland, whose especially delicious melons and peaches had won him royal favour at the turn of the twentieth century. Ada was an only child, slight, with a smiling round face and unruly hair pulled back into a pigtail, excellent at her studies and a promising musician. Her eyes were full of fire and when she was excited they gleamed. She was just sixteen when she met Piero Gobetti, then seventeen, who lived in a flat in the same building in the centre of Turin, and who was about to begin a law degree. Piero was tall, short-sighted, with curly hair and a pointed nose and he smiled a great deal. They started studying Russian together and wrote to each other long letters full of trust and longing. 'I did not know, did not believe one could love like this,' Ada told Piero, 'with so much purity and ardour.' They decided when apart to read the same book at the same time in order to feel always close. She abandoned her music studies to work with Piero on his many publishing and writing ventures, sharing his hatred of Fascism and his passionate desire to rescue Italy from Mussolini's deadening anti-intellectual hand. Ada remained safe, but Piero was repeatedly caught by the blackshirts, the *squadristi*, and beaten up. In 1923, they married and moved into an apartment at 6 Via Fabro. 'For me,' Ada wrote to him, 'this love is not something in my life, it is my life, the air I breathe, the reason why I breathe.' They had a son, Paolo. 'You created me,' Ada told Piero. 'You have given me everything.'

Early in February 1926, fearing that another beating would kill him, Piero left for exile in Paris. It was snowing and they were both in tears. Ada and Paolo were to join him when he had found somewhere for them all to live. On the 16th, weakened by the beatings and with a bad heart, Piero died. Ada was inconsolable. In her diary, she recorded a grief so intense that it is almost too painful to read. 'It isn't possible. It shouldn't be possible. Don't think, don't go mad.' She was twenty-three; Paolo was just six weeks old.

Ada stayed in Turin, earning her living as a teacher and a translator. She spoke and wrote English, French and Russian, when to know foreign languages was in itself a form of rebellion against Fascist conformity. She was quick, shrewd, inventive and clear-headed. She also loved the solitude of the nearby mountains, the chestnut forests and the open meadows, and she found a place to rent for the summer in the hamlet of Meana, in the Val di Susa, on the road to the French border. She never spoke of Piero, but he was always with her. It was in Meana in 1927 that she met Benedetto Croce, the historian, philosopher and life senator, who more than anyone in Fascist Italy was keeping alive a spirit of integrity and anti-Fascism. Croce, said his followers, was a 'living proof of the invincibility of liberty'. On a visit to his own house in the mountains not far away, Croce, who knew Ada slightly from her marriage to Piero, came to see her. She seemed to him, he said later, like a 'wounded animal', hiding herself away. But in Croce Ada rediscovered her curiosity, her desire to learn, and the two became close, spending much of the summer together, walking along the country lanes, discussing projects, books, the state to which Italy had been reduced by the Fascists.

Far left: Benedetta Croce and far right: Ada and Paolo

Croce was then in his sixties and his children, particularly his daughter Elena, became Ada's friends. Relations between the two of them were always formal. They addressed each other as '*Lei*', the polite form of address, and she called him '*Senatore*'. They exchanged proposals for books, plans and ideas. Through his contacts in the publishing world, Ada was offered work translating H. A. L. Fisher, Samuel Johnson and Aldous Huxley. What she loved in Croce was his irony, his understanding, the way he taught her to think through problems rationally, without fear, and to regard 'the exercise of the mind as a moral duty'. In 1928, Croce became leader of the Liberals, but was soon driven away from Rome in disgust at the moribund upper chamber and the feebleness of his fellow senators who, he said, had sold out to the Fascists.

At the end of the 1920s, Ada and Paolo moved to another rented place in Meana, the second floor of a chalet looking directly across the valley to the steep slopes of Rocciamelone, where in winter snow cut them off for weeks at a time and they lived like hermits. In spring, the surrounding meadows were covered in white daisies. There was no running water and no electricity, but Ada could hear a stream running constantly nearby. When Croce came to see her, he brought with him a candle with which to light his way home.

By the 1930s, Croce was living most of the year in Naples, in a sprawling palazzo with 50,000 books. When he read he would almost touch the page with his nose, 'as if he was aspirating the words with his proboscis'. Though his outspokenness – he referred to Fascism as an 'incoherent and bizarre mixture . . . of moth-eaten bric-a-brac, absolutism and Bolshevism . . . toadying to the Catholic church' – earned him disfavour and the banning of his books, he was left in peace, and even allowed to publish his own cultural magazine, *La Critica* – with a provocative ostrich on its cover – perhaps because Mussolini could not quite afford to silence such an internationally renowned academic.

Ada was not Croce's only devoted follower. In Turin, his admirers included a group of exceptional and talented young historians, writers and translators, many of them working for the newly formed publishing house of Giulio Einaudi, where they skirted a delicate line between truth and compromise and spent hours debating Croce's assertion that Fascism was just a 'parenthesis' in history, and that 'evil in the end cannot prevail'. Through painting, writing, talking, promoting culture, putting out cultural and political magazines which were quickly suppressed, these friends went on pretending that they were free and that Fascism had never existed. For their part, the leading Fascists in Rome kept a beady eye on Turin's hostile intellectuals.

Foremost among this group was Leone Ginzburg, whom the others regarded as a natural heir to Gobetti. Ginzburg was a Russian Jew from Odessa, a pale, bow-legged young man with a head a little too big for his body and thick black hair cut *en brosse*. He was phenomenally well read across the European classics, had a prodigious memory, spoke Italian in long, carefully crafted sentences, and had helped Einaudi start his publishing house. To Ada and her circle, Ginzburg's seriousness, moral severity and pleasure in conversation, along with his delight in his friends, were wonderful antidotes to the intellectual stranglehold of Fascism. They called him '*Leoncino*', little lion. Ginzburg seemed to them everything an intellectual should be, full of wisdom and dignity. He spoke of a 'spirit of the catacombs' and assumed that they, like him, would do their duty according to their consciences. Few ever left his company without feeling better about themselves and the world.

As important to this nucleus of intellectually free people in Turin was a historian called Augusto Monti, who had taught many of them – Ginzburg included – at the prestigious Liceo Massimo d'Azeglio, or after school, in a nearby cafe, or wandering along the arcades. Monti, his arms waving, his eyes gleaming with amusement behind thick lenses, never spoke directly about politics. But in coded, 'silent, snake like' allusions and references, there was no mistaking his meaning. His pupils called themselves his '*fraternità*'; he was their 'master of life', an 'aristocratic Jacobin', and they paid little heed to the headmaster, who stood at the school gates insisting that every pupil give the Fascist salute. Monti's disgust at Fascism, his refusal to accept that Italy had been permanently crippled by its strictures, his huge desire to encourage his students to rethink the world they had grown up in, had a profound effect on all who heard him, and no one who sat in on his classes ever forgot him.

As Vittorio Foa, another of his pupils, would say, what Monti taught was not so much against Fascism, as above it. Foa was a short and dark young man, from an old Turin Jewish family. When he laughed, which he did a lot, his face changed shape. He would say that in his home, while he was growing up, Italian politics were all defined by negatives: no liberty, no justice, no democracy. But it had left him curiously optimistic; however bad things were, he spoke as if all could be made well. Foa, Ada and Ginzburg all joined Giustizia e Libertà, Italy's main non-Marxist anti-Fascist party, becoming a close-knit group bound by ties of family and friendship, not easily penetrated by the secret police. In the evenings, Ada typed up flyers telling Italians not to bend to the Fascists, and pasted them around the city to counter the hundreds of bulletins, Fascist decrees and calls to meetings which made of Turin's walls one vast exhibition.

By the mid 1930s, however, this lone liberal pocket in the north was in trouble. Infiltrated by Mussolini's powerful network of spies, many of the group had been arrested, accused of conspiring against the state and sent off to prison or *confino*. Ginzburg was sent to the prison of Regina Coeli in Rome as a 'person dangerous to the safety of the State', and then on to Civitavecchia jail, known to all as 'the cemetery of the living'. Foa was also sent to the Regina Coeli. Their painter doctor friend Carlo Levi went to a village in the Basilicata in the south, where he was soon at work on the memoir that would become the celebrated *Christ Stopped at Eboli*.

Ada escaped arrest. She took a job teaching English in a secondary school and made up parcels of books to send to her imprisoned friends, writing sadly to Croce that Turin had been reduced to 'greyness and almost total isolation'. But Monti was caught. Asked by a Roman prosecutor, before being sent to join Ginzburg in Civitavecchia, what he had told his pupils, he replied: 'I taught them to admire and respect ideas.' But, the prosecutor said, 'what ideas?' 'Their own,' Monti said.

There was another, overlapping group of liberals and anti-Fascists of which Bianca Guidetti Serra was part. These were the sons and daughters of Turin's long-established Jewish community and included Primo Levi and his sister Anna Maria. They, too, had been followers of Piero Gobetti, fighting against '*fascistazione*' and its crippling shadow over intellectual life.

Bianca herself was Catholic, but her family was not religious. Her mother had gone out to work for a dressmaker at the age of ten, and she told her daughter about how she had longed for an education and when sent out on errands had stood at the gates of the local *lycée* and cried with envy. Frida Malan was a childhood friend, and the two girls listened to Bianca's mother as she described life for women in Turin's factories and workshops. Bianca and her younger sister Carla were devoted to each other, but Bianca was the leader. She was a strong, combative girl, though prone to anxiety, and she dropped out of school for a year after the early death of her father. She was filled with what her son Alberto calls 'existential anguish' that she would never be good enough. But she was quick and clever and won a place to study law at Turin University – one of six girls and 134 boys – writing her thesis on juvenile delinquency. She brought in money while studying by working in a law office, and much needed vegetables and fruit by giving private lessons. Her aim in life, she told her friends, was to see the title Avvocato before her name.

Left to right: Frida, Roberto, their parents and Gustavo Malan

It was Mussolini's sudden passing of the anti-Semitic laws, in the summer and autumn of 1938, which closed schools, universities and many jobs to Jews, that drew Bianca and Frida into the Resistance. In Turin alone, fifty-six Jewish university professors were sacked. Bianca's boyfriend was Alberto Salmoni, a bold, charming, eccentric young man with a dreamy, romantic air and a lot of black hair, who came to his classes with Levi on roller skates. Together they went out to the factories in Turin's suburbs on days of strikes and listened as the workers railed against the penury to which Fascism had reduced them. At night, in the blackout, the couple walked around the city's arcades tearing down the posters attacking Jews as 'enemies of the state'. When Bianca graduated, she took a job as a social worker, helping women in the factories with their legal and welfare problems.

Whenever they could get away, Bianca, Alberto, Levi and their circle of friends went climbing, or strapped skis onto their bicycles and rode up into the valleys. The mountains played an important part in all their lives. It was there, Levi would say, that he learned patience, persistence and endurance and to over-come what he regarded as his greatest weakness: his fear of failure, of risk, of fear itself.

In 1938, Ginzburg was freed from detention on condition that he write no more inflammatory articles. He returned to Turin and married another member of the group, Natalia Levi, a girl regarded by the others as very serious-minded, if rather strange, and who was already writing and publishing short stories. Natalia would soon be better known as the novelist Natalia Ginzburg. Because of the racial laws, the couple were sent, with their first child, to *confino* in the village of Pozzoli in the Abruzzi. But the Levi house in Turin remained a meeting place for the city's increasingly anx-ious young Jews and anti-Fascists. Like Ada and Frida, Bianca escaped the notice of the Fascist authorities. Since girls were domestic creatures, destined only for motherhood, they were not expected to harbour political thoughts.

Leone and Natalia Ginzburg

It was on Turin's network of trams, 'rolling cultural centres', that Frida and Bianca met their university friends and rode around the city, talking of rebellion. Bianca had taken to wearing shorts after being told that trousers or anything resembling them were unfascist. Silvia Pons, one of Frida's childhood companions, was part of this group. She had already not only defied Fascist misogyny by insisting on training to be a doctor, but had given birth to a baby out of wedlock, having been forbidden by her parents from marrying the father, a brilliant historian called Giorgio Diena, because he was Jewish. At night, as Carlo Levi wrote, 'the entire city turned into an immense portico', the young walking and talking under the arcades, 'our voices running down the dark corridors of the streets . . . to meet behind the trunks of the plane trees'. It sometimes seemed to him that Turin's very architecture had been purposely designed for these peripatetic talks, 'as if there were no horizons to their words'. Turin, where independent, critical thought flourished, where a taste for liberty was in the air, was a city that Mussolini hated.

When war came to Italy and the air raids started over Turin, Ada told Croce that she had decided to stay in the city, almost as a civic duty, to share the fate of those who could not leave. Her house in Via Fabro had become a regular meeting place for the dissidents. She would have liked to send Paolo, now seventeen and in his last year at school, away but he refused to leave her. She was happy, she said, to watch the way that he was turning from a boy into a man. In 1937 she had married again, an engineer called Ettore Marchesini, a practical, inventive man who had been a childhood friend. One summer's day, hiking with Paolo and Ettore in the mountains above Meana, she suggested writing a story, an allegory about the conformity of life under the Fascists.

Searching for an animal to make her hero, she rejected a dog as 'too pathetic', a horse as 'too detached', a fish as 'too silent', and a swallow as 'too sentimental'. She settled on a rooster and gave him the name Sebastiano. Every Sunday, on their walks above Meana, Ada carried her tale on a little further. The farmyard in which Sebastiano lived included his 'wise, prudent and orderly mother', a hen quite unlike her friend Arcadia who was unruly, absent-minded, fell into puddles and ended up in the pot (a warning to those who did not play by the rules). Serafina the owl stuffed herself on polenta and had to be purged with castor oil (one of the more unpleasant blackshirt punishments). Croce became the model for a wise, elderly rooster called Calusto.

Sebastiano was a contrarian, free, optimistic and humorous. He was the thirteenth chick in a brood and had been born exceptionally ugly, with very thin legs, terrified eyes, ruffled feathers and an absurdly long neck. He muddled his words. His brothers and sisters marched neatly up and down the threshing floor

(Mussolini's famous parades), while he wobbled and fell out of step. When ridiculed by the others, his mother defended him with the 'courage of a lion'. One day, Sebastiano strayed. Everywhere he went, he was rejected by other birds and animals on account of his oddness. Ada gave the birds the surname '*Perbenino*', doing what is right, to describe their slavish attention to conformity. Sebastiano grew sadder until he met a butterfly, who taught him the pleasures of solitude, and a dog who introduced him to the meaning of friendship. When he arrived back at the farmyard, Sebastiano was a different bird: he had seen the world and was no longer afraid.

Ada sent her finished parable to Croce, to amuse his family, and he wrote back full of praise. She decided to use her story as the perfect alibi for frequent visits to anti-Fascist friends in Milan, where the publisher Garzanti, who took the book, was based. The *Storia del Gallo Sebastiano* was published in 1940, under the pseudonym of Margutte. It sold well.

Then came Mussolini's fall. As news of his arrest spread around the city, the people of Turin spilled out of their homes, and the streets were soon filled with music and dancing. Friends told each other that the war would now end, and that the Americans would arrive with food. But years of suppressed fury and submissiveness soon exploded into violence. Crowds set fire to the Fascist Casa Littorio, where Bianca's sister Carla would spend the night in one of the cells after the Arduino funerals, and prevented firemen from putting out the flames. They went on to other Fascist barracks and buildings, looting and desecrating the hated symbols of Fascist power along the way. Those Fascists who failed to remove their party badges fast enough were attacked and beaten. Having freed five hundred political prisoners from Le Nuove, the vast medieval fort that was the city's central jail, into the hands of the hundreds of relations crowded outside and banging on the gates, the people surged on to the German consulate, where they set fire to the German flag and forced the consul, Baron Dirk von Lagen, to come out onto the balcony and hoist an Italian one in its place. Soon, Le Nuove was filling up with arrested Fascists, both men and women.

Within twelve hours, the face of the city had been altered. The sheer delight of the crowd made it clear how hated the Fascist regime had become. But for those who had bought into it, and the young in particular, who had never known anything other than Fascist ideology, whose every day and every action had been subordinated to Fascist dogma, the jubilation was profoundly shocking. They had become, suddenly, outcasts, and all the things of which they had been so proud – the badges, uniforms, medals, honours, prizes – were now a matter for shame. They slunk away and hid.

That night, no one slept. Ada had been at her house in the mountains at Meana when she heard on the radio of Mussolini's fall. She hastened back to her flat in Via Fabro. Soon, friends arrived to celebrate. Their deep pleasure at the end of Mussolini's reign was tempered by wariness. They were not alone in being mystified by Badoglio's pronouncement that '*la guerra continua*'. How would it continue? Who would be fighting whom?

2

Interlude

The events of the forty-five days following Mussolini's fall are among the most confused, dramatic, controversial, remembered and misremembered in the history of Italy.

Marshal Badoglio, the much decorated Italian general appointed prime minister by the King, was faced with three options. He could announce the end of Italy's alliance with Germany, forged in the Pact of Steel between Mussolini and Hitler in May 1939, and switch allegiance to the Allies; he could continue his association with the Germans and hope to persuade them to let Italy sue for peace; or he could secretly pretend to continue the war at the side of the Axis powers, while negotiating clandestinely with the Allies. He chose the last option. In an atmosphere of ambiguity and mistrust and with the desperate hope not to provoke the Germans, whose violent retribution he feared, he dispatched emissaries to Algiers and to Sicily to discuss terms with the Allies. What Badoglio and the King wished for was to parlay a dishonourable surrender for an 'honourable capitulation' and to win Allied support before breaking with the Germans, who had recently increased the number of military divisions stationed in Italy, at Mussolini's request. Throughout the country, clamours for peace were growing louder. Rumours abounded.

At Casablanca, in January 1943, Roosevelt and Churchill had agreed that they would accept nothing but unconditional surrender from any of the Axis powers, and that they would continue operations in the Mediterranean with landings in Sicily, which would mark the start of an Italian campaign. The Wehrmacht still controlled much of continental Europe, but when Stalingrad fell that January, the Red Army began its advance towards Germany. The

Victor Emmanuel III and Marshal Badoglio

Allies made no detailed plans for what would happen next, beyond keeping the Mediterranean open for shipping and controlling airports within reach of targets in Germany, while preparing to open a second front with landings on the French coast. General Eisenhower was put in command of the Mediterranean campaign and there were many talks about British or American supremacy and who would be the senior partner, and how the Italians were to be treated, though no one anticipated Mussolini's abrupt fall. The British ultimately wanted control of the Mediterranean in order to protect its colonies; the United States were concentrating on the defeat of Germany and Japan. Both were extremely nervous that Mussolini's opponents were dominated by Socialists and Communists.

Over the radio in late July, the Allies now promised to enter Italy as liberators – providing the Italians surrendered unconditionally. Neither the Americans nor the British at this point seem to have had much esteem for the Italians. The American press had recently taken to describing Victor Emmanuel as that 'moronic little king'. In a report to London, Harold Macmillan, helping to draw up an agreement with the Italians, noted that the 74-year-old monarch was 'physically infirm, nervous, shaky' and probably not capable of implementing any policy; Marshal Badoglio, who was also in his early seventies, was described as possessing the 'natural shrewdness of the peasant', but was 'clearly without much political sense'. General Roatta, the army chief of staff, was a 'natural coward' who had weaved, ducked and schemed his way through two decades of Fascism, and 'could be bullied if necessary'. Having abstained from bombing for a while, to give the Italians a chance to come up with acceptable terms, the Allies resumed their sorties over the north on 12 August. In Turin, ever in the eye of the air-raid storms, people again fled to the mountains. All over Italy, opposition to Badoglio was mounting, with calls for a 'truly democratic government', particularly after he ordered police to open fire on demonstrators. In Turin, a pregnant woman was shot dead as she led a march calling for peace.

After many tortuous secret meetings and in a spirit of considerable mistrust, a 'short armistice' was drawn up between Badoglio and the Allies, while arguments continued about the forty-two clauses which would go into the final terms, or 'long armistice'. On 3 September 1943, in a tent in an olive grove at Cassibile, near Syracuse in Sicily, the 'short armistice' was signed; the vexed words 'unconditional surrender' were left out. Italy's departure from the war, commented the *Manchester Guardian* drily, was 'as inglorious as its entry'. The Allies undertook to cross the Strait of Messina, land on the Italian mainland south of Naples and make their way speedily to Rome. For their part, the Italians were to protect Rome until the Allies arrived, helped by American airborne troops. At this stage, there was little talk about Italy actually joining the war on the Allied side; but there were many unanswered questions about what should happen next. Since the term armistice usually meant peace, why was the war continuing? Given the impracticality and expense, would it be right for the Allies to take over the administration of the country 'by a system of gauleiters'? And what, precisely, did 'unconditional surrender' mean since Italy remained in a curious limbo, neither ally nor enemy, but suspended without sovereignty and much mistrusted by all sides? An aide-memoire drafted by Churchill and Roosevelt spoke in rather vague terms of the need for Italy to 'work her passage back'. Where the Allies erred was in their underestimation of the German response.

Believing Badoglio's declarations of friendship and commitment, the Allies had been misled over his ability or willingness to act. Terrified at the prospect of German retaliation, Badoglio had spent the month of August doing nothing to prepare for the invasion that was clearly coming. In spite of repeated Allied warnings that the landings on the mainland of Italy were imminent, he continued to sit in Rome and behave as if nothing was about to happen, and at the least certainly not before the middle of September. When he realised that it was being left to the Italian army to neutralise the Germans on both sides of the Tiber, and to help protect the Americans parachuting into the capital, he prevaricated, fearing a rapid occupation of Rome by the Germans stationed around the city, and with it the end of his government. Having learned that the Italians did not intend to secure the Roman airfields, the Allies hardened their own position and decided to make public the armistice.

In any case, the date for both the invasion and the announcement of Italy's surrender had already been set. At 6.30 p.m. on the evening of 8 September, with Badoglio pretending that the Allies had jumped the gun, General Eisenhower announced over Radio Algeri that Italy had signed an armistice. British radio urged the Italian soldiers to resist all attacks from the Germans and for Italian ships to make for neutral ports or scupper themselves. At 7.43 p.m., seeing that he had no alternative, Badoglio told the Italians over the radio about the armistice. Though he had had two weeks to prepare, his message was deeply muddling. On the one hand, he said that the war would still continue; on the other that Italians were not to go on fighting the Allies; but at the same time they were to 'react to any eventual attack, wherever it came from'. He made it sound as if the Germans were withdrawing from Rome: they were, in fact, advancing on the capital. And the next day, 9 September, the Allies landed at Salerno, fifty kilometres south of Naples. It was all the vacillating marshal and weak monarch most dreaded.

Within Italy, Badoglio's message, repeated throughout the night of the 8th, was at first interpreted to mean that the longed-for peace was finally coming. There was a flicker of joy and celebration, but it was very brief. Uncertainty quickly turned to fear and a sense that the Italians had been betrayed by their leaders, which grew sharply as it became known that the King, Badoglio and much of the government had fled Rome, leaving behind them no clear orders, other than to carry on 'for the good of the country'. At 5.10 on the morning of the 9th, a cortège of cars carrying the royal family, Badoglio, the heads of the army and the navy, a number of adjutants, state papers, servants and seventeen suitcases streamed out of the capital on the road to Pescara on the east coast. There the King and his self-serving retinue boarded two corvettes for the south. They reached Brindisi at 2.30 p.m. on the 10th and, on being assured that there were no Germans in the city, disembarked. Badoglio, who arrived by land to join the King, had left crucial state papers on his desk in Rome. His last message, over the radio, was that he was 'absent on military inspections'. The royal family had earlier taken the precaution of moving money, paintings, sculptures, silver and carpets to Switzerland.

With no instructions about who should take charge of the abandoned capital or the army, Rome surrendered without a fight, in spite of having six divisions in and around the city, while the Germans had two. Threatened with bombardments, the remaining Italian senior officers in Rome signed an agreement for the capital to be declared an open city, though open was certainly a misnomer since the city was immediately placed under martial law and was soon full of German soldiers. In just a few hours Italy had collapsed, its navy and air force had 'succumbed and died', and the country had been handed over to the Germans before the Allies had time to muster themselves. 'We had not expected much from the Italians' was the wry British comment. 'Twenty years of Fascist corruption and inefficiency had quenched any speck of patriotic feeling in a not normally warlike people.' Even so, the speed and total disintegration were shocking. Eisenhower spoke of the 'weak and supine Italians . . . of little help and inert'. 8 September 1943, wrote one Italian soldier, became 'the watershed of our memory of things'.

If the Italians had been unprepared for what was coming, the Germans had not. Mussolini's sudden fall in July had left Hitler outraged and vindictive. Orders for the German military to begin assembling were issued as early as the evening of 26 July, according to a plan, code-named Achse, readied for just this eventuality many months before. Four armoured corps and eight divisions were at the Italian border waiting to join those already in the country. Forty-five minutes after Badoglio's announcement on the evening of 8 September, German troops occupied the telephone exchange in Naples. By midnight, train stations had been occupied and railway workers replaced by the 5,000 Germans who were trained and ready to take over. By dawn on the 9th, the Germans were in control of the port of Civitavecchia, north of Rome, and were in the process of occupying Udine, Trento, Alessandria, Genoa, Vicenza, Venice, Verona, Como and Arezzo. Siena Perugia soon followed.

The Germans were extremely well briefed. Armed with excellent maps and detailed drawings about what they would find, they rapidly took over command centres, electricity plants, factories, airports, stations, munition stores and barracks. There was very little opposition. There was some fighting along the coast, and a few Italian Alpine divisions struggled on for a bit by retreating into the mountains, but in the plains they were quickly overrun. Florence held out for a couple of days, but it was then encircled and forced to surrender. Here and there, individual officers, appalled by the ignominy of the army's collapse and the betrayal of their leaders, committed suicide. On some islands in the Aegean, having been kept in the dark about what was happening, the Italian forces resisted. They were massacred, even where they surrendered. In Cephalonia, a week-long battle ended in the deaths of more than 6,000 Italian soldiers, many of them lined up against a wall and shot in groups of four, eight or twelve, over a four-hour period.

Meanwhile, Italy's borders were closed. 'Italy's fate,' Hitler told the Germans on 10 September, 'should be a lesson for all . . . to remain loyal to their allies.' To make his point even more forcefully, the 45,000-ton battleship, the *Roma*, pride of the Italian fleet, was attacked by Junkers and sunk; Admiral Bergamini went down with his ship, along with 1,200 of his men. It was announced that a new 'Italian Fascist government' would now be appointed, and there would be little mercy for the Italian traitors, described by Hermann Göring as a 'gypsy people who will end up putrefying'. In the north, Erwin Rommel was appointed commander of the German forces. The long-contested borderlands of Venezia Giulia and Alto Adige were annexed under German gauleiters.

On 12 September, Field Marshal Albert Kesselring, who held the German command in the centre and south of Italy and was stationed on the outskirts of Rome, declared that Italy was now a 'war zone', a state it would remain in for the next 594 days. All strikes were forbidden; organisers of acts of sabotage were to be shot; attacks on German soldiers would be revenged at a ratio of 100 to 1; all weapons, including hunting rifles, were to be handed in. There would be no more private, uncensored mail and phone conversations were to be monitored. Anyone showing signs of rebellion of any kind would be punished 'with the full severity of German military law'. Communists, and all who shared their opinions, 'be warned!' When Rome Radio came back on air that day, the announcer spoke with a strong German accent. Behind the scenes, the new occupiers helped themselves to the gold reserves in the Bank of Italy. Everywhere, German organisation and efficiency was met by Italian uncertainty and inertia.

On 8 September, the Italian army had had twenty-four divisions stationed in barracks up and down the country, many in poor shape; there were a further thirty-five in the Balkans and the Aegean. Since no orders had been issued by Badoglio, most officers decided to keep the men in their barracks while the situation clarified. Their wavering cost the Italian soldiers dearly. It took only a few days for twenty-six generals to be captured, along with 8,790 officers and 339,000 soldiers. In the north, the Germans took 1,138 pieces of artillery, 536 armoured cars, 236 tanks and 4,053 horses and mules, disarmed the men and helped themselves to everything they needed from the Italian ports, barracks, airports and military offices. Some 45,000 of the 70,000 Allied prisoners of war, men from every ethnic group within the British Empire and the United States who had fallen into Italian hands in North Africa and were being held in seventy-two prisoner-of-war camps around the country, were taken over by the Germans. After 574 ships were lost, what remained of the fleet set off for North Africa, flying a black pennant; they surrendered to the British at Malta.

The Germans wasted no time. Many thousands of captured Italian soldiers were quickly readied for departure over the Brenner Pass to Germany, where they were to be put to work on farms and in mines and factories. Close to half a million more would soon follow. Two hundred captured Italian admirals and generals went with them.

But not every soldier, Italian or Allied prisoner of war, fell into the trap. The shrewder and more prescient, men often disobeying orders from their senior officers, had simply walked out of their barracks and set out for home. A song was composed: 'It was the 8th of September / I thought I had to leave / And I went home to Mother.' Few actually intended to desert. Rather, they believed that the war was in fact over and that a deal had been made with the Germans for a peaceful Italian exit from the war. The hours after Badoglio's announcement saw men streaming along the roads, some in uniform, some in civilian clothes, carrying bags and suitcases, some walking, some on carts, bicycles, milk floats and mules or in stolen military vehicles, which they exchanged for civilian suits. As one man said: 'Anyone trying to find order is insane.' It was the greatest mass escape in modern history and it would be crucial to the Resistance. 'Their odyssey,' wrote the novelist Italo Calvino, 'is the story of all the 8th of Septembers in history: the need to return home by hook or by crook, through lands fraught with enemies.' Their freedom would be essential in the weeks and months to come, and the choices they made that day would split friends and families, just as it would split historians over the meaning of what had taken place.

Turin had passed Badoglio's forty-five days in power uneasily. After Mussolini's fall and the disappearance of the more egregious Fascists from offices and businesses, the main clandestine political parties, all of them left and centre-left, who had spent the thirties trying to keep alive a spirit of resistance, had come together in a coalition. The Fronte Nazionale mirrored the one put together in Rome, proposing a new political order for Italy. Ada was a founder member of one of these parties, the Partito d'Azione, and she and her colleagues made overtures to General Adami-Rossi, senior military leader in Turin, with a view to immediately installing a new non-Fascist city administration, but were rebuffed, with threats of arrest if they pressed too quickly for reform. Various deputations from the factories, asking for better conditions and more food, had also been sent packing. Early in August word came from Rome that General Roatta, the military chief of staff, had issued orders that all demonstrations were to be banned and agitators executed. To show that he meant it, his men shot dead twenty-three strikers in Bari. 'A little bloodshed at the beginning,' he said, 'will save rivers of blood later.'

On 18 August, enraged by the armoured cars surrounding their factory and appalled by the renewed Allied bombing that had taken place the previous night, workers at the FIAT Mirafiori plant had come out en masse and stood talking in the central courtyard. They had been working 48-hour weeks, with their wages frozen, while prices rose steadily. On Adami-Rossi's orders, machine guns opened fire. A young boy was killed and four workers were injured, one of whom died later. The strike leaders were arrested.

The rest of August passed in a state of wary confusion. The Torinesi, like Italians everywhere, watched and waited. The new coalition of left-wing parties, which included the Communists and the Christian Democrats, talked of rising up against the Germans, should Badoglio fail to secure decent peace terms. But without weapons – and knowing nothing of the feverish discussions about an armistice taking place in the south – they felt powerless. Further attempts to meet Adami-Rossi were repeatedly blocked and when the coalition members were finally granted an audience they found him wearing a German Iron Cross.

The opening of Mussolini's prisons after 26 July and the end to the sentences of exile on the penal islands had freed and brought home to Turin the so-called threats to Italy's national security. Monti came back, as did Carlo Levi, Leone Ginzburg and Vittorio Foa. Every day familiar, much missed faces appeared in Ada's house. The men looked gaunt and frail and those who had been forced for many years to wear clogs found walking in shoes hard. Steak was bought on the black market to build up their strength. They were excited, full of plans and optimism. Ginzburg, leaving Natalia and the children in the Abruzzi, planned to go to Rome to open a new office for Einaudi. Time, which had crawled by so miserably in captivity, now accelerated. There was much to be done, books to be written, newspapers to produce, political parties to organise. Ginzburg noted that, after over two decades of dictatorship, sudden liberty made everyone feel disorientated, as if they were still not quite sure what it was that they should be wanting. Among other things, he told Bianca, 'we have to civilise people'. The writer Cesare Pavese wondered how many of them would survive this 'brave new world' which was now facing them.

It took Foa longer than the others to make it back to Turin. Badoglio had dragged his heels about freeing all the political prisoners held in the Regina Coeli in Rome, and it was not until a number of them went on hunger strike that they were at last released. On reaching home he went to call on a fellow ex-prisoner, a chemist called Michele Giua, who had been arrested lest his knowledge of explosives might prove dangerous to the regime, and whose health had suffered in captivity. Giua had a daughter, Lisetta, whom Foa had last seen as a twelve-year-old schoolgirl. Now, revelling in the 'explosion of light, colour, smells' that freedom had brought, he met her again, arriving home on her bicycle, her long fair hair flying in the wind.

Eight years in captivity had made Foa feel old, a survivor, irrelevant. Lisetta's fervour, the rage she felt against the years of Fascism, her optimism and strength, all warmed and charmed him. Now twenty and a law student, intrepid and intense, she told him how the Turin friends had looked after her when both her parents were arrested, leaving her alone with a little brother, and how she had discovered through them what it meant to be part of a 'charmed circle of friendship'. There was never a moment, she said proudly, when she decided to become a '*sovversiva*', a subversive. It had come to her naturally when she looked at the 'hard and hostile faces' of the men who came to arrest her father. She was particularly close to Natalia Ginzburg, and had shared in her family life of concerts and films. On the weekends, when they were young, they had taken their bicycles on long rides out of the city towards the mountains. Like Bianca and her friends, Lisetta was a climber. She had also learned to shoot, taking lessons from a friend doing his military service. Listening to Lisetta's sympathetic questioning and chatter, Foa felt himself come alive again. They fell in love. She told him she wanted six children.

The events of 8 September 1943 took the two of them, as it took all Italians, by surprise. Lisetta's first thought was that the Italians had finally been given the chance to do better.

Two days later, at around four o'clock on the afternoon of 10 September, Ada was standing on the corner of Via Cernaia in the heart of Turin's city centre. With her were her husband Ettore, her son Paolo and Lisetta. They were handing out leaflets calling on the Torinesi to press Badoglio to sue for peace. Rumours of the turmoil in Rome had only just reached the city, and no one yet knew that the King and Badoglio had fled. Ada looked around and saw a column of armoured vehicles making its way up the avenue. Her first thought was that some of the local politicians had confiscated German cars and were now using them for themselves. But behind the cars came lorries mounted with machine guns, and then five tanks, followed by a column of smaller vehicles. They were the veterans of the Eastern Front belonging to an armoured Panzer-Grenadier regiment. And they looked menacing, 'bony and green as lizards', as Cesare Pavese noted. And they were undoubtedly German.

Passers-by, observing Ada with her leaflets and assuming that she would know something, gathered anxiously round. As she wrote a few days later, in the first of the diaries she would keep for the rest of the war, written in pencil, in minuscule letters, using a code fashioned out of English words, the people in the streets looked diminished, afraid, abandoned. A friend appeared and told her that Turin had been turned over to the Germans. 'Leave quickly,' he said.

Ada hurried home to Via Fabro with Lisetta and Ettore while Paolo set off to find out what was happening. On the radio, she listened to a former senior Fascist who confirmed all that she most feared: that the Fascists who had gone into hiding after Mussolini's fall were now re-emerging, calling for revenge, dismissing the forty-five days of Badoglio's reign as a 'carnival' of 'collective drunkeness', and that German troops were indeed in the process of occupying the cities. She began to assemble compromising papers and lit the stove. As she threw the documents onto the flames, friends started arriving at the apartment. Bianca, Lisetta, Foa and Giorgio Agosti, a young magistrate, turned up, as did Giorgio Diena and his sister Marisa.

Paolo soon returned to Via Fabro to report that Adami-Rossi had indeed surrendered the city. A nineteen-year-old boy had thrown a hand grenade at German soldiers from an attic in Via Nizza; he was caught and interrogated, then jumped down the stairwell to his death. The telephone exchange was in German hands, as was the station of Porta Nuova, and the long straight avenues were full of anxious crowds, through which raced the German vehicles, the soldiers shooting low. When the bodies were carried away, they left pools of blood in the streets. Senior local government officers, the non-Fascists who had been put in place after Mussolini's fall, had been removed and were now in custody. Italian soldiers, of which there were several thousand in Turin, had been confined to barracks, outside one of which a group of women had gathered, shouting: 'Go home! Go to your mothers! You don't want to be taken by the Germans.'

In Via Fabro, rapidly becoming the group's headquarters, Ada and her friends held a war council. The weeks of ambiguity were over. Having emerged as vocal opposition leaders since the July coup, they knew they were now in danger. Paolo and Lisetta, the two youngest people present, talked excitedly about resistance. Giorgio said to Foa: 'Look at their eyes.' Indeed, they were sparkling. The older group tried to calm them down. Later, Ada would marvel at their innocence, their belief that they would be able to change things. They were joined by an exhausted young soldier who had escaped from his unit in the south and walked all night to find them. The news he brought with him was terrible: the Germans were everywhere and casualties among Italians were mounting.

Hearing from a friend in the municipal offices that German cars had been dispatched to pick up known anti-Fascists, and that the Partito d'Azione founders were on their list, they agreed to split into three groups, consider their options and reconvene. Already Ada's energy and efficiency were galvanising the others. Foa, Lisetta, Giorgio Agosti and the Dienas would go up to Torre Pellice, a mountain village some forty kilometres to the west of Turin. A second group would set out for Cuneo, long a stronghold of anti-Fascism and from where word had reached them that a flamboyant young soldier friend, Tancredi Galimberti – who went by the name of Duccio – had come out onto a balcony in the main square and called on the people gathered below to rise up against the occupiers. When the officers in the local regiment of Alpini refused to join them, Duccio led a dozen civilian friends, all of them veteran anti-Fascists, among them a lawyer called Dante Livio Bianco, up into the mountains, taking with them two guns, two sacks of flour and one sack of rice. There, they 'dug themselves in like foxes'.

Ada and Paolo in the mountains

Ada, Paolo and Ettore would go up to their house at Meana, in the Val di Susa, to see whether there were any signs of local resistance. As they left, Ettore hid his World War I gun, two Berettas and a hundred cartridges in the cellar. Bianca went home to find that twenty university friends had gathered in her house and were discussing what to do. They talked late into the night and slept on cushions and mattresses on the floor.

Not far away, a seventeen-year-old school boy called Bruno Trentin, son of a famous opponent of Mussolini's, imprisoned under the Fascists, wrote a last entry in his diary: 'Finally, Italy has woken up! The Italian people . . . are on their feet and ready to fight. Lost time – now to work.'

3

Bursting into life

Saturday 11 September 1943 was, in the words of the Pied-montese diarist Carlo Chevallard, a 'day of humiliation and shame'. Chevallard, of French-Swiss descent, was the director of a metal factory and a cool observer of daily events. The streets of Turin were eerily quiet, except for the sounds of sporadic gunfire. There were no newspapers and the radio was silent. The few people who ventured onto the streets wandered about like 'lost souls' trying to find out what was happening. Calls for volunteers to resist the German occupation went unheeded. Italy was now cut in two, the south in the hands of the Allies, the centre and the north occupied by the Germans, and communication between the two virtually ceased. For Ada and the anti-Fascists across Piedmont, Liguria and Emilia-Romagna in the north, it was a question of how to react, what to do next, how to tell friends from enemies and how best to navigate the coming months.

Rommel had been brought back from Salonika to command Armed Group B in northern Italy. He was both feared and disliked by the Italians, who held him responsible for the loss of their colonies; for his part, he did little to conceal his contempt for them. He now dispatched his men, who had been arriving over the last few days from France and the Eastern Front, to Turin, to disarm the Italian soldiers, most of whom were hanging forlornly about their barracks, in Levi's words, 'like a defeated flock of sheep'. Soon, these men were being marched off along the avenues to the trains waiting at Porto Nuova to carry them to a transit camp at Mantova, then on to Germany. Watching these sad, uncertain men, Ada began to cry.

As the barracks emptied, so the looters arrived. In need of almost everything, hungry and angry, the people of Turin bore away flour, salt, blankets, shoes, sheets and pistols, which would soon prove useful, descending on military warehouses like armies of ants, bringing with them wheelbarrows and prams on which to load their loot. Vehicles were dismantled and stripped down to the chassis. At midday, the looting reached a point of frenzy at the main military storeroom on Corso Regina Margherita. But by now the Germans had got wind of what was happening and the soldiers sent to investigate began to shoot. A fire broke out; people ran. When the firemen arrived they found a scene of horror: seventeen dead, their bodies scattered among piles of clothing and torn sacks of wheat.

Then, something extraordinary happened. The 2,000 men of the Nizza Cavalleria regiment stationed in Turin had been ordered by their confused officers to remain in their barracks. German soldiers arrived in tanks, surrounded the building, disarmed the men and lined them up to march to the station. Five hundred of them were told to mount their horses and follow behind. Outside, however, hundreds of women of all ages had gathered, holding stones. As the back half of the mounted troop was suddenly cut off from the front by a passing tram on Corso Sommeiller, these women surged forward shouting: 'Escape!' They pelted the riders in front with the stones, to make the horses panic. The Germans opened fire with machine guns. Chaos followed. Men were pulled or jumped off their horses and were hastily spirited into doorways or down alleyways. The avenues were now full of frantic riderless horses, soon shot dead by the Germans and as soon butchered and picked clean down to their carcasses by Turin's famished citizens.

Later, having been taken in by families, hidden and given civilian clothes, the soldiers were taken to the railway station, walking arm in arm with young women and posing as their fiancés, and put onto local trains heading out of the city in the rainy autumn twilight. Five young women collected five English soldiers who had escaped from their prisoner-of-war camps and were now in hiding, and led them to the station, where they handed them over to two other waiting women. In the countryside, train drivers slowed down to allow wandering soldiers to escape. That day, dozens of young girls, whose Saturdays had been spent singing hymns to the Duce in their neat uniforms, shed their unquestioning obedience to Fascism and were busy pretending to be girlfriends to total strangers. These scenes, in different forms, were taking place all over occupied Italy. 'It was thus,' wrote one woman later, 'that our war began.'

Within Turin itself, the day grew more violent. The looting of other military storerooms, which drew Germans quickly to each scene, left more piles of bodies, including that of a fourteen-year-old girl. At seven in the evening, women and children were shot dead at the abandoned air-force barracks. Another of the dead was a 71-year-old woman, crushed by an armoured car as she pushed home a wheelbarrow full of wood. The killings only served to reinforce a feeling of revulsion towards the Germans, made worse when a rumour went round that their soldiers were cutting off people's arms to steal their watches. The day was not, however, without absurdity: in the afternoon, an open lorry was spotted racing past the Court of Appeal. At the wheel was a young soldier, a huge black iron chest by his side. Behind him sat an Italian general, clasping half a frozen cow.

All through the day, various divisions of Italy's 4th Army, recalled from France in the wake of the armistice, had been arriving in Piedmont, and some 1,500 of these men were quartered at Pinerolo, a town to the west of Turin. Their orders were muddled and contradictory and as the level of uncertainty grew, officers and men decided to slip away. The commanding officer appeared so preoccupied with saving his stamp collection that he took no action. By the time a German column arrived in Pinerolo, they found just one junior officer and fourteen men. By now, the surrounding valleys and hills were full of young soldiers, dressed or partially dressed in civilian clothes, 'looking like a procession of scarecrows'. Abandoned weapons, ammunition and vehicles littered the fields and dusty roads. Mules that had belonged to the army wandered free.

What was completely unexpected was that this initiative to save the soldiers had come largely from women. Other acts followed. Across Piedmont and Liguria, 2,600 Allied prisoners of war, who had disobeyed their senior officers and were making their escape, were also taken in and hidden. Very few spoke any

Italian, and their situation was perilous. At the Porta Nuova station, Lisetta was with a group of friends watching the captives being loaded onto trains, shouted at and bullied by German soldiers with Alsatians. They saw slips of paper being pushed out of windows and through slats, and when the trains pulled out, they gathered them up and made sure they reached their destinations. A few onlookers whistled and jeered at the Germans; machine guns opened fire.

As night fell on the 11th, Rommel's headquarters announced that the Germans were in control of most of northern Italy. However, some 100,000 '*sbanditi*', disbanded soldiers, had got away and were making their way up into the mountains. Simultaneously, without anyone ordering them to do so, without central coordination of any kind, their years of passivity abandoned with astonishing speed, women were taking their first steps into resistance. A group in Modena, covering their faces with scented handkerchiefs, guided a group of young men to safety through the sewers. In just a very few hours, Fascism's mantra – *Credere, Obbedire, Combattere* – had become a thing of the past. As Natalia Ginzburg wrote, 'the "small virtues" of women – their skills at caring for others, their instant responsiveness – were suddenly becoming "big"'.

The Alps that rise above and to the west of Turin, their high peaks disappearing into the distance and for long parts of the year covered in snow, were Waldensian country. It was here that in the sixteenth and seventeenth centuries a Protestant Reform Church, looking spiritually towards England and Switzerland, had resisted troops from Catholic Savoy in a series of valiant confrontations and expulsions, and later established a tight-knit, highly educated spiritual Waldensian community, intent on teaching the Gospels and holding itself apart from the turmoils of political life. Slow to understand the true nature of Fascism, and seduced by Mussolini's insistence on order, the Waldensian Church had weathered the 1930s as an enclave of Calvinism and liberalism, clothed in the 'spiritual armour' of its heroic history and keeping up strong links with foreign Protestantism, while its followers remained Italian citizens, obedient to the laws of the land. Years of unpopularity and persecution had left them proud, rebellious, high-minded and combative for their faith. Their leaders, however, were often timid men, anxious not to invite trouble and in any case not believing that their liberal theology required common positions dictated by them. They advised prudence and docility with which to confront the threats of the world. 'Let us leave it to others the task of speaking out.' It was up to bold individual pastors to interpret their liberty of conscience as they saw fit.

Even after Italian became the obligatory language in schools, the Waldensians spoke French or a Franco-Provençal patois at home. They had a moderator, who presided over a *Table Vaudoise*, made up of seven laymen and clergy, elected by an annual synod. In 1943, most of the Waldensian Church's 30,000 or so followers lived in these valleys above Turin – the Pellice, the Germanasca, the d'Andregna and the Chisone. There was a temple, a boarding school and college – handsome stone buildings with porticos – in the village of Torre Pellice, and a small headquarters and faculty of theology in Rome.

Torre Pellice, said the locals, was '*la Genève italienne*', and over the years it had attracted a number of remarkable theologians and historians. One of these was Jacopo Lombardini, a tall, gangling mystic and republican, a man prone to sudden bursts of exaltation and deep troughs of despair, who converted to evangelical Christianity and made the valleys his home early in the war. During the 1930s the profoundly anti-Fascist Lombardini had been badly beaten by Mussolini's *squadristi*. Around these academics and churchmen, through the late thirties and into the war years, there gathered other young liberals and socialists, Frida Malan's family among them. During summer walks, they told each other that '*pensare Fascista*', to think like a Fascist, was an immoral act. In Torre Pellice's Caffè Italia, Lombardini gave lessons in anti-Fascism to listeners who knew almost nothing about what was going on in the world.

The Waldensian valleys, in which were scattered small mountain villages and hamlets, cut off from the plains by snow for weeks on end during the winter months, were densely forested with chestnut trees. Steep, rocky mountain sides covered in scree and patches of meadow descended precipitously into fast-flowing rivers. Lilies of the valley, convolvulus and juniper grew where the forest gave way to woods, and the village squares, with their Alpine houses and overhanging roofs were planted with elm trees. There were orchards and a few vineyards. Not many of the houses had running water, but it was plentiful in the village wells. Weather and geography encouraged a siege mentality, a gift for survival and a belief in superstition. Raw snails were thought to be good for rickets, and snakeskins helpful for wounds. In the more remote hamlets, bread was made from rye, without yeast, once a year in a communal oven, baked for ten hours then hung from the ceiling until so hard and dry that it had to be broken with a hammer when needed, then soaked in milk. Until cotton and textile factories arrived in the lower valleys in the late nineteeth century, agriculture and a little mining of chalk and graphite had been the villagers' main occupations, but with the Second World War had come new engineering factories to produce ball bearings and vehicle components.

Since the nineteenth century, the more prosperous Torinesi had kept second homes in these cool high valleys, building handsome villas with terraces, balconies and little towers. They gathered here in the summers to climb, walk and camp in the *grange* – huts built by shepherds or charcoal burners. They liked the meticulous attention to the rule of law and considered the locals to be Anglo-Saxon in their seriousness and respectability. A train line to Torre Pellice from Turin had been built in the nineteenth century to cover the thirty-eight kilometres from the city; hotels opened and much was written about the area's bracing moral and spiritual properties. A Club Alpino Italia brought skiers and tourists to an area already criss-crossed by tracks frequented by Italian smugglers and later used for spiriting Mussolini's enemies out of the country to France and Switzerland.

In the late eighteenth century, the French and the Italians had built a line of fortifications on both sides of their border, and in the last years leading up to the war the Italians had added a series of little blockhouses, covered in local stone to make them less visible and sometimes joined together by underground tunnels, all along the 487 kilometres of the western Alpine frontier. Piedmont had become an important reserve of Mussolini's special troops, the Alpini, with their distinctive khaki felt hats with black feathers; many of these soldiers were recruited locally, trained for mountain life in barracks in Pinerolo, Susa and Cuneo, and had families in the valleys. But the Alpini were not the only soldiers stationed in the mountains; there was also a border force, a squadron of cavalry, a section of field artillery and a number of forestry guards.

After the air raids of 1942 drove the people of Turin to flee, many had made their homes in these mountain areas, renting the holiday houses usually left empty in the winter months, or finding refuge in primitive huts and outhouses. The population of Torre Pellice alone rose from five to seven thousand. These refugees were for the most part welcomed, the Waldensians regarding generosity towards strangers as an important part of their faith.

As news of the armistice spread through the mountain villages, the Alpini milled uncertainly around their barracks. After they drifted away, taking weapons, ammunition and even horses to hide on their farms nearby, the locals arrived to carry away anything that had been left behind. That same afternoon, the Waldensian Synod happened to be sitting in Torre Pellice. A young man, a member of a youth Christian movement called Gioventù Cristiana – of which Frida Malan was secretary – proposed that the Church formally condemn the Nazis and the Fascists. The synod conferred and refused. A distinct split was forming. As one of the younger members remarked: 'Our Vaudois Church today doubts, is wary, fears, trembles and buckles and adapts itself, and hides . . .' The individual pastors took note.

Geography, proximity to Turin, the obduracy of religious leaders as well as their attachment to secrecy and silence, along with the presence of independent-minded thinkers and well-armed rebellious young soldiers: the Waldensian valleys were about to become a place in which politics and faith joined forces.

Frida Malan and Silvia Pons became best friends when they spent their childhood summers in Torre Pellice. They were, as the Italians say, 'amiche di pele', skin sisters, so close that nothing came between them. The girls played together in Frida's flat in the centre, where her mother Giulia eventually settled with her three children after the early death of her husband. She was a teacher, in a room above a barn in a village near Torre Pellice, and she played the harmonica. Giulia came from a large local Waldensian family and on fine afternoons the girls would go to the gardens of Frida's grandfather's imposing stone house on the edge of the village, where he was choirmaster, and make up fantastical stories about their lives. Frida, born in 1917, was the eldest; after her came Roberto, born in 1920, and Gustavo, in 1922. There had been other children, who had died at birth or in infancy, their deaths caused, so it was said, by the harsh climate of Catania, where their father was the Waldensian pastor, before the family moved to healthier Pisa.

It was as a twelve-year-old schoolgirl in Pisa that Frida had her epiphany about the Risorgimento leader, Giuseppe Mazzini. One hot day when the sun was streaming through the windows of her classroom, she heard her teacher describe Mazzini as a visionary and a republican. That, she thought, 'sounds right'. Walking home, she spotted a plaque on the wall of the house in which Mazzini had died. 'Everyone,' it said, 'must find his own path in life, and, once they are certain of it, never deviate.' Frida longed to find her true path, but promised to remain obedient to her parents until she reached twenty-one. To fill the time, she resolved to read a book every day. Her father, descended from a long line of pastors and teachers, was serious, studious and strict. No smoking, no dancing, no card games were allowed. But at a time when girls' education was not taken seriously, he treated his three children identically, saying that Frida and Gustavo were equally clever and that Roberto, though slower, was the more practical. Anti-Fascism, though not spelt out, was implicit. Her father's early death, Frida would say, made the three children old before their time.

Obedience did not come naturally to Frida. Attractive, with bright blue eyes that turned purple when she was angry, a high forehead, shoulder-length wavy light brown hair, and strong and athletic in build, Frida could be obstinate, peremptory and capricious. Even Silvia found her difficult. But she was enthusiastic and passionate, with an absolutism inherited from her father, and she was looking for a cause. She was, said her friends, '*pulita*', single-minded, uncompromising. She chattered constantly, starting one story, then taking off in another direction.

Frida studied literature at Turin University, and during the summer holidays of 1937 she went to stay with a cousin in Geneva. Every Sunday afternoon, philosophers, reformers, writers and refugees from Germany and the Soviet Union came to the house to talk. Frida, who already spoke fluent French from her summers in Torre Pellice, listened as they described the Nazi persecution of the Jews. In Turin, she lived in a YMCA hostel and because she was not yet 21, and therefore not allowed out at night, she spent her evenings hearing the stories of her friends' lives. What worried her was that she found the lives of others so much more absorbing than her own.

Frida had made friends with Emanuele Artom and his family, key figures in Turin's Jewish community, and when Italy introduced its anti-Semitic laws in 1938, Emanuele asked her to help him find places to hide Jews. In Rora, a hamlet above Torre Pellice, she was able to persuade peasant families to offer safe houses. Frida called 1938 '*l'anno dell'odio*', the year of hatred. One day after classes, as she walked back to her hostel with Emanuele, who lived nearby, he told her: 'My people will be exterminated, but they don't know it.' Soon after, two much loved Jewish teachers were dismissed from the university, and Frida was active in petitioning on their behalf. She was shaken and frightened, but she had found her cause. Anti-Fascism and all it stood for filled her thoughts. At last, she wrote later, 'I could get on with a life I believed in'.

Emanuele Artom

The very absolutism of her nature and her desires made romantic encounters awkward. During a visit to Florence with Silvia that year, Frida fell in love with a young man called Franco Lattes. But her affection was not reciprocated. 'I don't know how to be a woman,' she wrote forlornly to her aunt. 'I need to learn.' She grew confused, saying of herself that she was 'weak and very easily influenced and spoilt' and that she spent too much time thinking. 'Perhaps if I make myself beautiful I will recover, change, and if I pretend to be indifferent, then he will fall in love with me. I have to do this because it is the most important thing in my life.' But Franco did not fall in love and Frida spoke of killing herself. To Silvia, in a note that was never sent, she wrote: 'Come and see me. I can't go on . . . 5 times I have been on the verge of throwing myself under a train.' She was sent to a clinic, where she was given electric shock treatment, and over time she grew calmer. Franco, she realised, could be nothing but a friend.

Frida graduated from Turin University on 10 June 1940, the day that Italy went to war. Her first teaching job was in Bergamo, which she soon realised was a Fascist stronghold, and moved on to a more congenial school in the Val di Susa, near Ada Gobetti's summer house. Susa, however, was a very Catholic town and the bishop decided that Frida's Waldensian Protestantism was a bad influence; it was suggested that she look for yet another post. She was better suited to a school in Pinerolo, the town from where the Waldensian valleys spread up into the mountains, but here she was denounced by twenty of her pupils' parents for criticising the regime's anti-Semitic policies. There was something strangers found too masculine about her, too impulsive and assertive. Deciding that the life of a school mistress was not for her, she enrolled once again at Turin University, to read law.

She was back in Torre Pellice on 8 September 1943. On hearing the news of the armistice, her instinct was to do what she had always done: take immediate action. She hurried to the local barracks as they emptied of soldiers, to look for weapons and provisions, sensing that these might prove necessary in the struggle she foresaw coming. Her brother Roberto, now twenty-three and a junior officer in Pinerolo, was in his own barracks when instructed by the colonel to wait for the Germans and to hand over their weapons. Roberto leapt onto a wall in the courtyard and shouted out to his comrades: 'Don't listen to what he says . . . don't waste time. Take a mule and a machine gun and . . . disappear as quickly as possible.' He then set off on his bicycle for Torre Pellice.

Frida was pretty; but her friend Silvia was beautiful. With thick black hair pulled back in a knot on her neck, pale skin and dark eyes, she reminded people of a Flemish portrait, vivid against a dull background. She was also exuberant with a cleverness that was said to have been inherited from her renowned mathematician grandfather. Having studied the English feminists, she had strong views about female emancipation and the subjugation of women in Fascist Italy. As she grew up, she wore trousers and smoked, at a time when such things were much frowned upon. Silvia was also good at sports and played the piano but, like Frida, she could be tricky.

Silvia's parents were both Waldensians. Her father Enrico was a small businessman and bank manager, a hard man with a mean streak who married her mother Lily after a ten-year engagement and took her to live in Aosta near the border with France, returning to Torre Pellice for the summer months. Silvia was born in the spring of 1919, her sister Adriana in 1923. During the long hot August afternoons, Lily read English novels to Frida and Silvia as they sat doing embroidery. She was a sad, troubled woman.

In September 1937, Silvia left her family in Aosta and arrived in Turin to study medicine at the university, one of 341 girls and 9,960 boys. She took a room in the Waldensian YMCA hostel, to be near to Frida. Sometime that winter she met Giorgio Diena and his older sister Marisa, who was small and pretty with curly reddish hair. Giorgio had an oval face, brown eyes and a small nose, and he had been drawn into politics as a boy when he visited Ada Gobetti to ask her how to find books censored by the Fascists. Like most young Italians, he had made his way up through the Fascist youth organisations and had even held a Fascist university card; his doubts had come with the Spanish civil war.

Giorgio quickly drew Silvia into his circle of friends, who railed against the straitjacket of conformity and timidity imposed by Fascism and were now searching for some new moral force in their lives. The earlier generation of anti-Fascists, they told each other, had been bold and brave but they had been crushed. 'Politically,' Giorgio wrote to a friend, 'they belong to another world, antiquated, bypassed . . . Fifteen years of waiting has exhausted and embittered them . . . Their hair is white. We need new energy, young people who have not been compromised . . . My temperament needs action.' '*Tutti politici*', everyone for politics, to confront the apathetic indifference created by Fascism, became the order of the day. Whenever they could get away, Giorgio and Silvia climbed in the mountains with the Malans and talked about the new political world that they would forge. To finance their climbing holidays, they wrote a book together, a *giallo* or thriller, and found a small publisher.

Giorgio Diena and Silvia just before the war

Giorgio's father was a printer, specialising in postcards. Some financial irregularity took him briefly into prison and Giorgio, who did not find him easy, joined Lancia rather than the family business. But as a Jew, doors were closing against him. In October 1939, Silvia, still only twenty, found herself pregnant. The new racial laws forbade marriages between Jews and Aryans, and children born out of wedlock were a subject of scandal in Catholic Fascist Italy. Terrified of their families' anger, the couple made a suicide pact. As a medical student, Silvia had access to cyanide. They poured some into two cups. Giorgio swallowed his; Silvia hesitated long enough to change her mind and summon help. Giorgio was rushed to hospital; when he came round they decided to keep the baby.

Silvia's father raged; her mother tried to persuade her to have an abortion, or to give the baby up for adoption, or for Giorgio to convert to Protestantism. Silvia remained defiant. Writing to her parents, in French, the language of her childhood, she said: 'I am not frightened of the future . . . At the moment, I have a lot of confidence.' She refused to leave Giorgio, *'le compagnon de ma vie . . . et bientôt le père de mon enfant'*, and nor would she give the baby away. Vittorio was born in Turin on 30 July 1940. His name, they decided, owed a bit to Queen Victoria, a bit to Silvia's victory over her father, and the rest to the hoped-for victory over Fascism.

Towards the end of August, Silvia's mother Lily, in despair about her husband's infidelities, walked out. Leaving behind her wedding ring, glasses and jewellery, and putting out some money on the table, she threw herself into the river near Massello where the waters become a powerful torrent. It would be two years before two shepherd women found her bones. On the riverbank was a Thermos and bits of material from her dress. Silvia mourned her keenly.

To support his new family, Giorgio left Lancia and took a job in his father's factory in Turin; Silvia struggled on with her medical studies. They moved into Natalia Ginzburg's house in Via Pallamaglia, after Natalia left to join Leone in penal exile at Pizzoli. Both were drawn deeper into clandestine politics, with Giorgio emerging as the theorist for the newly emerging Partito d'Azione, together with Ada Gobetti and Giorgio Agosti. In the autumn of 1942, the party was formally constituted. It brought together the old guard, survivors of the anti-Fascist crackdowns of the 1930s, about whom Giorgio had softened his views, and the young Turks, eager to convert theories into action.

In the summer of 1943 Silvia graduated as a doctor. She, like Frida, was bold and full of resolve, but there was already something uncertain and unhappy in her manner, as if she was constantly looking for something she could not find.

One of the largest and most imposing summer houses on the edge of Torre Pellice, a four-storey building covered in creepers and standing in a large garden and orchard, belonged to Eric Rollier, a Milanese businessman with strong ties to the Waldensians. In its grounds stood a second, smaller villa, 'la casa piccola' or Villa Philadelphia, named after the city in which its former owners had been episcopal Methodists. When not in Ada's house in Turin, the group of anti-Fascist teachers and friends gathered here to discuss how the Partito d'Azione could create a post-war democratic Italy.

After the armistice, the leading thinkers behind the Partito d'Azione began to arrive at the Rollier house. Torre Pellice, it had been decided, was to be their headquarters. Frida and her brothers were there, along with Vittorio Foa and Lisetta, Silvia and Giorgio and his brother Paolo and sister Marisa. Agosti, using his position as public prosecutor in Turin, went to the barracks occupied by the frontier guards near the main piazza and commandeered two cars belonging to the absent general, and used them to carry away machine guns and rifles. Roberto Malan got hold of a mule and with friends loaded it up with the guns to transport them higher up into the mountains to hide in caves in the rocks. They were soon joined by Dante Livio Bianco from Cuneo. No one had any illusions about the brutality of the coming struggle.

A few days later, by which time it was absolutely clear that there would be no resistance to the German occupation on the part of the Italian army, Vittorio and Giorgio went up to the hamlet of Rora. Their plan was to draw up a memorandum for the Partito d'Azione building on their earlier manifesto. Both men had used their time in prison and in exile on the penal islands to reflect.

Giorgio, who was regarded by the others as having an excellent analytical brain, was interested in the larger picture, how and where the Partito d'Azione would fit in with the other political parties, long dormant but now once again emerging from the shadows. Both he and Vittorio agreed that though the Allies would indeed have to provide the military might to expel the Germans from Italy, it was essential that the Italians themselves contribute enough that they could determine their own future once hostilities were over. Resistance, they decided, should also take the form of educating a people for whom political decision-making and independence of thought had been eradicated by the Fascists. But first Italy had to be liberated, and the Italians had to fight. When they returned back down the mountains, they brought with them a programme: cooperation with other political parties, an end to the weak and treacherous monarchy, and preparations, when the moment came, for a new Constituent Assembly and a new constitution. It was Vittorio Foa who first suggested setting up partisan formations in the name of Giustizia e Libertà, the political movement started by Carlo Rosselli before he was murdered on Italian Fascist orders in France in 1937.

The Val Pellice, which would later earn the label of 'cradle of the resistance' was in a ferment of activity and rumours. The refugees from Turin's air raids, the Jews who had sought safety in the valleys, the strikers from the factories in the plains, and the local farmers angry about years of Fascist requisitions, had been joined by the disbanded soldiers arriving by train from Turin or across the mountains from France. It was an explosive mix. What gave it shape was the presence of the Partito d'Azione leaders, men such as Agosti and Foa and Bianco, who were not only thinkers, but men of action, for whom resistance appeared as a crusade, a 'moral imperative', a liberation from a corrupt, equivocating, shoddy past. That they found themselves surrounded by mountain people with a long tradition of soldiering for their faith, determined to translate their disgust at the Fascist years into open rebellion, would be essential in the fight to come. Bianca, Frida and Silvia were not planning to be left out.

Meanwhile the villagers were busy dressing the young disbanded soldiers in civilian clothes and finding places in which to hide them. As Agosti put it to Bianco, 'the road ahead will be long . . . the game is risky, but it is worth playing. For the first time . . . we can distinguish the real men from those who lack courage; there aren't very many of the first, but one of them counts more than a thousand of the others.' The two men had been friends

for many years, part of the group which had climbed and pic-
nicked with Ada and her friends in the 1930s. For both of them,
this was a war for civilisation, to defeat the forces of evil, not
only in Italy but throughout Europe. There was no going back:
no new world was possible without this fight.

Groups of fighters began to form. One, composed of an electri-
cal engineer, an agronomist, a medical student, a barber, a tram
driver, three former Allied prisoners of war, a Russian professor
from Moscow and a shoemaker from Vladivostok, took as their
base a *grange*, clinging like an eagle's nest on a cliff edge high
above Torre Pellice. Another, which made its way over to the
neighbouring Valle dell'Angrogna, was made up of university
students, their professors, a number of factory workers and local
farmers, who had the advantage of being able to go home at
night. The soldiers among them gave the civilians gun practice.
Marisa Diena, whose political sympathies lay to the far left, set
off to join a Communist group nearby. Jacopo Lombardini, the
short-sighted dreamer and apostle of social justice, went to the
valleys with his Bible to urge the villagers to rise up, to fight, to
help each other if they wanted a new Italy of liberty and rights.

By the end of the third week in September, there were twelve
separate groups in these valleys, each with some twelve to twenty
men, calling themselves 'rebels', many but not all of them supporters of the Partito d'Azione. 'The surroundings made us
partisans,' one of the leaders, Antonio Prearo, wrote later. 'You
could say we were born out of chaos.' Roberto Malan volunteered
to organise a group whose job it would be to find food and provisions. Gustavo set up a recruiting office. Agosti and Bianco, busy
putting out leaflets summoning the local people to arms, were
recognised as leaders and coordinators. When food stocks ran
low, they ate the horses taken from the abandoned barracks.

In *L'Italia Libera*, a clandestine paper being produced in Rome,
Leone Ginzburg wrote: 'Hunt down the Germans! Sabotage the
railways! . . . Above all, never allow yourselves to be discouraged!'
Anyone who chose to follow the Germans, he said, was to be
regarded as a traitor and a profiteer and expelled from civilised
society. After twenty years of oppressive Fascism, the partisan war
was 'bursting into life like a miraculous explosion'.

*

Before leaving Turin for Meana on 10 September, Ada had agreed a signal with her concierge Espedita and her neighbour, a lawyer called Cataneo. If it was safe for her to return, and there were no Germans lurking, they would put a canary in its cage on the windowsill. If the canary was not there, she should go elsewhere. Looking out from the train carrying her, Ettore and Paolo up to Susa, she saw hundreds of young soldiers hanging aimlessly about the stations and the sight of their dejected expressions filled her with sadness. Meana seemed to her a 'forgotten paradise'. The sun was setting, its rays falling through the chestnut trees. Smoke rose from the chimneys in the still early-autumn air and carts laden with wheat were being pulled home; from the gardens, she could hear the voices of children playing.

Paolo immediately slipped away and came back two hours later triumphantly clutching two hand grenades and a gun that he had found in a deserted railwayman's cabin. Ada tried to rein in his enthusiasm, but he was impatient. On the 13th, she heard that the Germans, who were now pouring into the valleys, had arrested all the men aged between eighteen and sixty-five in a nearby village, in reprisal for the looting of a military warehouse full of boots. Leaving Paolo at Meana, she and Ettore went back to Turin, thinking that it would be safest if they simply went on with their ordinary lives. They found the canary on the windowsill. Ada resumed her teaching, Ettore returned to his job with a telephone company. They made contact with the other members of the Partito d'Azione and learned that discussions for acts of resistance had started with union organisers and students. Silvia arrived with news of the bands starting up in Val Pellice. 'Initiatives and hopes were born,' Ada wrote in her diary. 'The desire for resistance was taking shape.' Turin was silent and apprehensive; more Germans were arriving and the Italian Fascists, emerging from their hiding places, were already wearing German uniforms. Joy and optimism had given way to weary resignation. The Torinesi had endured air raids, fires, poverty, hunger: they would endure the Germans.

One evening the phone rang in Via Fabro. It was Bianca, who said: 'Have you seen the weather? Let's go for a walk in the mountains.' It was their code that they should return to Meana. Alberto Salmoni, Bianca's boyfriend, had joined Paolo there, and both women were concerned about what the two boys were doing. Next morning they found places in a goods wagon of a train carrying supplies up the mountain. Sitting on the floor, the two women began to talk. For the first time, Ada told Bianca the details of Piero's death. 'It seemed to me at that moment,' she said, 'that the world had gone completely dark.' The train stopped for long periods of time. As dusk fell, they were still talking. It was, Bianca would later say, 'a friendship born in the dark', but that would become 'luminous, cheerful, close'.

They found Paolo and Alberto itching to start sabotaging bridges and the train tracks leading to France, and the two women helped them to hide weapons in a grotto hidden by greenery that they had discovered earlier that summer. The route from Turin to Bardonecchia and the French border went through Susa and it was already clear that the Germans planned to use it to transport men and materials, to bring armoured cars and weapons into Italy, and then to send back looted food, machinery and livestock. Remaining pockets of Italian soldiers were being rounded up; mules were being requisitioned. Ada began sounding out local friends about possible partisan bands in her valley. She felt no fear for herself, but an intense terror for Paolo, for whom she had already obtained false papers, though conscious of how much her fretting would grate on him. When that night he failed to come home, she sat on the terrace, looking up at a 'sky full of incredible stars', waiting, with almost unbearable anxiety.

4

A war zone

In the autumn of 1942, speaking of the war in the East, Hitler had ordered the killing, with no quarter, of all partisans, who he referred to as 'bandits'. Women and children were to be 'shot, or better, hanged' and anyone who hid or helped a bandit risked the confiscation of their property and death. No German soldier who followed these orders was to be held responsible. There was no absence of courage in Ada and her friends, but none had as yet any idea about the brutality they were about to face, nor about the incredible complexity and unpredictability not only of the forces ranged against them, but of those ostensibly on their side.

Towards the Latin races, the Germans felt contempt. They did not understand the Italians, nor did they make any effort to do so. The excessive warmth of their family relations, declared Hitler, robbed them of all 'virility'. Now the armistice had confirmed that its inhabitants were untrustworthy and deceitful, guilty, as Kesselring put it, of the 'basest treachery'. They would be punished accordingly. In the 'total war' being waged by Germany as part of the grand plan to impose its superior might on the continent of Europe, whole populations were to be seen as the enemy; indiscriminate terror would serve to stamp out any form of resistance and 'dominate this pestilence'. Italy, which had been a useless ally, was now occupied by men who had learned in Eastern Europe how to treat useless people. Every day, between 8 September 1943 and liberation in April 1945, an average of 162 people would lose their lives. The bodies of men left hanging on trees as warnings would become a horrible and familiar sight.

After the armistice, there had been some disagreement among the individual German leaders about how to proceed in Italy.

Plans were drawn up to withdraw to various lines and reduce everything left behind to 'scorched earth'. Rommel favoured falling back to the Appenines in Tuscany and Emilia; Hitler and Kesselring wanted to keep the front as far from the Reich as possible. What all agreed was that Italy's resources, its factories, its industry, its food, livestock and manpower would be exploited to the full. All sectors of the German government now dispatched men to further their own interests, whether political, administrative or military, and by favouring sometimes one side and sometimes the other, Hitler kept them in a state of constant rivalry.

Swathes of northern Italy were annexed under two gauleiters. Albert Speer sent his own men, as did Alfred Rosenberg, and the SS arrived on the orders of General Karl Wolff. General Leyers was made responsible for dismantling Italian industry and sending it back to Germany. The despoliation of Italy began. Aping the attitude of their superiors, German soldiers began to loot and sack 'like the predators of the 30 years war'. As a priest in Gaeta observed, overnight the Germans turned from allies into wild animals, intent on death and destruction.

General Sauckel had been given the job of recruiting and deporting manpower for the German war industry. In the chaotic days that followed the armistice, captured Italian soldiers were given the choice of agreeing to cooperate, and thus becoming free workers and being treated decently, or of being rounded up and sent to camps where they would not be recognised as prisoners of war under the Geneva Conventions. Only 36,000 Italians, out of the 547,000 in German hands, often under extreme pressure and fearing retribution against their families, or seduced by leaflets saying 'Leave the traitors, come along with your German comrades', voluntarily signed up to become workers. Those who refused were soon on their way down mines, working in heavy industry or clearing bomb damage. Regarded as traitors, they were humiliated, beaten up, starved. Their camps were enclosed by electric fences.

Plan Achse, the German code name for the occupation of Italy, had foreseen three stages: the military takeover, the release of Mussolini, and the restoration of Fascism in order to give the German presence the veneer of an apparently legal government. After 8 September, many of the *gerarchi*, the senior Fascists who still supported Mussolini and had managed to escape Italy, were in Munich, awaiting the arrival of the Duce. Since he was a closely guarded prisoner in what was still an unknown location, an imaginative and highly unusual rescue plan was put in place.

It had taken the Germans some time to discover exactly where Mussolini was being held. Finally, they learned that he was in a hotel at Gran Sasso high up in the Abruzzi. On the afternoon of Sunday 12 September, twelve German gliders with a hundred commandos and a two-seater Stork reconnaissance plane, commanded by an Austrian captain, Otto Skorzeny, dropped through banks of cloud and landed in the hotel grounds. Minutes later they had freed Mussolini, put him on board the spotter plane and set off, heading first for an airfield near Rome, then on to Hitler's headquarters in Germany. For a moment, the plane seemed to falter, plunging alarmingly towards the rocks. Then it levelled off. In Munich, Mussolini was reunited with Rachele and the children.

Mussolini would have preferred to go back to Rome or even to have Milan as his base. Hitler, who had dismissed suggestions to replace the Duce with another senior Fascist, proposed to settle him near Lake Garda, in the town of Gargnano, ten kilometres from Salò. Here, in exchange for the restoration of Fascist rule, Mussolini was to cede territory to a newly enlarged Austria, supply Italian labour and machinery for the German war effort and sack a few of his more troublesome followers. Salò was chosen as being conveniently near to the German lines of communication. When Mussolini joined the men who had escaped from Rome at the time of the coup and remained faithful to him, they began to plan his new Fascist state, one that would emphasise a return to earlier socialist roots. Revenge was sworn against the 'traitorous and fugitive last king'.

On the night of 18 September, Mussolini broadcast to the Italians. His speech was slurred, flat, sometimes unintelligible; there was no hint of the former boasting or demagoguery. Chevallard, listening from Turin, recorded in his diary that he sounded like a 'finished man'. In *Avanti!*, a newspaper that was about to be suppressed, a journalist referred to Mussolini and the King as having 'dialogues of the dead'. On their first encounter since his fall, Hitler asked Mussolini: 'But what is this Fascism that has dissolved like snow in the sun?'

Mussolini and Hitler

To run his new government, Mussolini appointed Guido Buffarini Guidi as Minister for the Interior, a jowly, cunning and duplicitous intriguer; Renato Ricci, former *squadrista* and head of the youth organisation Balilla, who was now made chief of the new milizia; and a small, pale zealot called Fernando Mezzasoma, who was appointed Minister for Popular Culture. Marshal Rodolfo Graziani, infamous for gassing civilians in Abyssinia, became Minister of National Defence. The establishment of a new party, the Partito Fascista Repubblicano, was put into the hands of Alessandro Pavolini, a fanatical Florentine bully and crony of Galeazzo Ciano's. Mussolini favoured his militia over the army, as more likely to protect his interests, but Graziani had no wish for an alternative and independent force, and certainly not one in the hands of Ricci. As they quarrelled, bartered and jostled for power, Salò began to attract other, competing, militarised groups, each more vicious and chaotic than the last, made up of former secret servicemen, adventurers, thugs, chancers – men who had felt themselves somehow marginalised under the former regime. They spoke of squashing traitors 'like worms'. The *manganello*, a stave studded with metal studs, the blackshirts' weapon of choice in the 1920s, was again seen on the streets, where Fascists, calling themselves 'captain' and 'major', swaggered and sang rousing martial songs. It was as if the clock had turned back twenty years.

One of the many disadvantages of the new Salò government was that its ministries were scattered over a large area. Phone connections between them were appalling, and in any case controlled by German switchboards. Mussolini and his family were in the Villa Feltrinelli, where a permanent guard of SS men – 'always there, like the spots of a leopard' – patrolled the gardens or followed Mussolini in a lorry if he left the grounds. Claretta Petacci was installed in the nearby Villa Fiordaliso; many of their encounters ended in shouting matches and fainting fits. Rachele brooded and complained; Mussolini's daughters-in-law squabbled.

Mussolini hated lakes, saying that the still water seemed to go nowhere. In his office in Palazzo Venezia in Rome, he had reigned over a vast frescoed room in which his desk was always empty, to show that he had all that he needed to know in his head. Here, in a small stuffy study, his desk was a clutter of papers, books, reports, pencils; he compared himself to a 'mad poet' and began to play Beethoven, Wagner and Verdi on the violin, with great verve but little grace. He wore the plain uniform of the Fascist militia, which hung loosely on his thinning frame, and his neck was as 'lined and wrinkled as that of a tortoise'. For hours on end, he read or just sat in a kind of stupor, his silence broken by moments when he talked excitedly about philosophy or religion. At times, he was suddenly bent double with sharp pains from his duodenal ulcer.

To his mortification, the Vatican refused to recognise his new government, claiming that it never recognised an alternative government when a legitimate one was still in existence – in this case that of the King and Badoglio in the south, who were still clinging to at least some kind of legitimacy.

In theory, Mussolini's newly named Repubblica Sociale Italiana (RSI), held sway with its Italian prefects across the whole of German-occupied Italy, except in a small number of 'zones of operation' where German high commissioners were in command. In practice, however, the prefects had at their sides German 'administrative councillors', or minders, who reported back to Berlin and gave orders. In every sector, a biddable Italian had a German minder. To ensure that the Germans were fully in control, Rudolf Rahn, ambassador and plenipotentiary for civilian affairs, set up a group of 'political-cultural' councillors to watch over both the military and the prefects. Those Italians who joined the RSI were known disparagingly as the *'repubblichini'*, the little republicans, to distinguish them from the former genuine members of the Republican Party. The Italian lira was devalued, and the Italians were to pay for the costs of occupation, put at the vast sum of seven milliard lire a month. Mussolini was now effectively a prisoner, a figurehead, a leader with only the semblance of power. Fascism had rested on two myths – a charismatic leader and an invincible army – and both had collapsed. As General Wolff, made responsible for order and security throughout the country, would later say: 'I did not give him orders . . . but in practice he could not decide anything against my will and my advice.'

There was, however, one decision that only Mussolini could take, and that was what to do about the members of the Grand Council who had brought about his downfall. Hitler was insisting on a trial, to be followed by executions. But one of the plotters was Ciano, the husband of his eldest and favourite daughter Edda.

Italy's second government remained in Brindisi, where the King and Badoglio were reigning over their rump state of just four provinces – Bari, Lecce, Brindisi and Taranto. Like Mussolini, they had very little power and no resources. But here the Allies, rather than the Germans, were the masters. The offices of the King, who was the guest of a local admiral, and his *'piccolo Quirinale'*, a disparaging reference to the historical seat of power in Rome, were scattered between warehouses, hotels and barracks. There were no typewriters, no archives and very few civil servants. The south was also desperately poor: its schools were closed, its fountains had run dry and many buildings lay in ruins. Badoglio, the prime minister, who had at times been a good if brutal general, was an incompetent politician who had schemed his way through the years of the dictatorship.

The Allies – behaving towards Badoglio and the King much as the Germans were behaving towards Mussolini – were demanding that the government be 'defascistized', and all former supporters of Mussolini removed. 'No trace of Fascism,' Roosevelt declared, 'will be allowed to remain.' But at the same time they wanted continuity and for the moment favoured the restoration of a democratic monarchy. Badoglio's first dilemma was how to run what remained of monarchical Italy without relying on men who had worked happily for the Fascists for over two decades. He also had to overcome a general feeling of hostility among Italians who thought that, by running away so precipitately from Rome, he and the King had betrayed and abandoned the people, and turned Italy itself into a battlefield. Before he realised the full scale of the disaster he had helped create, Badoglio was reported to be spending his mealtimes 'rosy, smiling, placid, patriarchal', discussing with his ministers their imminent return to Rome.

The Allies faced problems of their own. The people of southern Italy were hungry, homeless and worn down, and the sympathetic voices they had listened to over Radio London, transmitting messages of support and goodwill, had led them to expect warmth and openness as well as supplies of food, fuel and reconstruction projects. Now the cold wariness of the British liberating troops puzzled them. It was, noted Harold Macmillan, 'one vast headache, with all give and no take'. How much money would have to be spent in order to prevent 'disease and unrest'? How much aid was going to be necessary to make the Italians militarily useful in the campaign for liberation? And what was the right approach to take towards a country which was at once a defeated enemy and a co-belligerent which expected to be treated as an ally?

Like the Germans, the Allies were almost totally ignorant about Italy, steeped in prejudice and now about to indulge it. The armistice, they were forced to admit, had been clumsy, on both sides. Cut off from most trustworthy sources of information about the country by twenty-one years of Fascist rule, offered opinions shaped for the most part by misunderstandings, and with little interest in distinguishing between Fascists and anti-Fascists, they were faced with extremely difficult and delicate decisions, none of them made easier by a fundamental difference in the way each of the different players regarded Italy.

Anthony Eden and the British Foreign Office had always disliked and distrusted the Italians and the trickiness of the armistice had done nothing to make them change their minds. Churchill, who had once praised Mussolini as an admirable leader, now referred to him as the 'worst devil of them all'. A Foreign Office report, drawn up in May 1943, had described the Italians as proud, touchy, 'expert at dissimulating and sail trimming, hot tempered and generally more amenable to persuasion than to coercion'. Instinctively not law-abiding, the report went on, the Italians were 'too individualistic to submit to more than outward forms of discipline and too apathetic and fatalistic to break into open revolt'; they were also said to be overly impressed by 'dash and uniforms'.

Churchill dismissed the Italian liberal leaders now emerging from years in hiding as 'political cripples' and warned against any arrangement that meant 'carrying on our shoulders a lot of people who ought to be made to carry themselves'. They needed to work hard before being allowed to join the comity of responsible nations. What the British really wanted was undisputed control of the Mediterranean, and an eventual peace treaty which divested Italy of its colonies. An acronym was coined: KID, keep the Italians down. And since the British expected them to be dishonest, subversive, corrupt and inefficient, this is precisely how they saw them. The Italians, for their part, had been informed by a propaganda report that Englishwomen all had 'big feet, boxers' hands, leathery skins, sharp elbows, the stride of Scottish soldiers and voices that sounded like broken weapons'.

The Americans, who before the war called Mussolini approvingly the 'Latin Cromwell' and a 'Spartan genius', a homely man who could make people chuckle, now took to dismissing him as a 'sawdust Caesar' with his 'Humpty Dumpty regime'. American interests lay in finishing the war and defeating Nazism and Fascism as quickly as possible so that their boys could go home, while keeping an eye on future economic openings. They were not much concerned with the history of the old world, with all its rivalries and betrayals. But, with their own large Italian immigrant population, they were more sympathetic to the Italian character than the British.

The Soviets at this stage were not much interested in Italy at all, except as a useful pawn in the post-war carve-up of Europe. What both the Americans and the British feared, however, was eventual Communist domination, and they had not been very reassured when told by the Marchese d'Ajeta, Ciano's former *chef de cabinet*, that: 'Italy has turned red overnight . . . There remains nothing between the King and the patriots around him, who have control of the situation, and rampant Bolshevism.' The spectre of a red Italy would haunt them for the entire campaign and distort many of their dealings with the Resistance.

An Allied Control Commission was now set up to oversee the transition back to normal life as the fighting moved up towards the north, and Macmillan was sent to Brindisi as political adviser to General Maitland when he took over from Eisenhower as Supreme Allied Commander in the Mediterranean. For all his disparaging comments, Macmillan liked the Italians and provided a sensible counterpoint to the dismissive and belittling Foreign Office. Though even he complained that when Italians came to meetings, they never stopped talking. What no one at this point envisaged was a long campaign.

The Allies expected to race up the mainland towards Rome after the landings at Salerno but encountered tough German resistance and were struggling to reach Naples. They were now confronted with the task of securing the territory they had liberated, restoring order, preventing looting and getting rid of the more egregious Fascists. Convinced that only the heavy bombing of cities would persuade the Italians to reject Mussolini's newly restored Fascist state in the north, they continued to pound Milan, Turin and Genoa. In the House of Commons, Churchill declared that the Italians 'must stew in their own juice a bit'.

In July 1940, in the wake of the fall of France and six weeks after Italy entered the war, the British War Office had approved a new body, a Special Operations Executive, to, in Churchill's words, 'set fire to Europe'. The SOE was to operate, said its first director, Hugh Dalton, on 'ungentlemanly' lines, using subversion and propaganda, encouraging partisans and irregular forces to oppose the Germans with sabotage, boycotts and terrorist attacks. Its Italian section took the name of Special Force Number 1. For the first two years, it achieved little, not least because contacts with Italy were sporadic and superficial; the British agents recruited, for the most part eccentrics and misfits from public schools, the City and the army, were not merely ill-trained but had also been told that it would take them only a couple of weeks to learn everything a sensible Anglo-Saxon would need to know. A small, woefully unprepared SOE team had landed with the invasion force at Brindisi in September 1943.

The Americans had come to this game later. The Office of Strategic Services (OSS) was founded in the early summer of 1942 to overcome the lacunae in information revealed by the Pearl Harbor attack, under the leadership of a lawyer and highly decorated veteran of World War I, William Donovan. As with the SOE, many of the recruits came from business, universities and journalism, in uniform but without ranks; they were soon being described by German propaganda as '50 professors, 20 monkeys, 10 goats, 12 guinea pigs and a group of Jewish scribblers, piloted by an Irish renegade known as Bill the Wild'.

While both the British and Americans were struggling to define their roles and their rivalry in Italy, one of their first joint moves was to rescue Ada's friend Benedetto Croce from where he was living in Sorrento, not far from Salerno. Having been warned that there was a real risk that the elderly academic might be seized at any moment and held hostage by the Germans, they sent a launch to move him and his family to Capri. In the prevailing chaos, Croce was seen as a sane and reliable spokesman for the Italians, even if Churchill referred to him as a '75-year-old professor dwarf'. From Capri, Croce broadcast to the Italians. Listening to him on her radio in Meana, Ada was filled with 'deep emotion'. There had been plans for her and Paolo to spend the summer with him in Sorrento: had they done so, Paolo would now have been safe. 'But these,' she wrote in her diary, 'are useless thoughts.'

With the first wave of the Allied invasion in the south had come a number of prominent Italian exiles who had been waiting in the US for just this moment. They now set about putting in place a body of their own, the Organizzazione della Resistenza Italiana, to act as a bridge between Italian Resistance and the

Allies. One of the key players was Croce's son-in-law, Raimondo Craveri, a Roman lawyer, who cycled from Sorrento to the Allied lines on 13 September and, in fluent English, filled in the SOE and OSS on the political situation in the capital. What was soon clear, however, was that the Allies were deeply sceptical about these anti-Fascists and about any Italian military help to the Allied campaign. Croce was dispatched from Capri to meet Donovan and convince him that a Fronte Nazionale della Liberazione, with himself presiding and Craveri as one of its leaders, be set up and that recruits should be found for a volunteer fighting force. Dozens of young disbanded Italian soldiers, who had managed to escape capture by the Germans, now converged on the south to offer their services.

There was also the further complication of the third Italian government – though not as yet in power – made up of the leading anti-Fascist parties that had been waiting in the wings. In 1942, a first clandestine inter-party committee had been formed, bringing together the six main parties – Liberal, Democratic Labour, Christian Democrat, Socialist, Communist and Partito d'Azione – all of them anxious to break with the past. As the armistice was being signed these parties had come together in Rome as a Committee of National Liberation. Because the city was still in German hands, the CLN met in hiding, in cafes, convents and churches. While they quarrelled and jostled for position, each with very different ideas about what a future Italy should look like, all agreed that Italians must not let slip this 'historic opportunity' to liberate their country for themselves.

By the middle of September, Italy was thus in a state of profound confusion and turmoil with competing governments, disputatious Allied forces, furious Germans, a vacillating and truculent monarchy and many thousands of lost and disbanded soldiers and prisoners of war. There was also an unknown number of Italian civilians, both men and women, who were untrained and largely without weapons, but eager to fight. The Allies were fielding Senegalese, Algerians, Moroccans, Poles, Palestinians and Brazilians, some eleven nations in all; the German forces included Austrians, Czechs and Russians. Each Italian political party was assembling its own partisan force to put into the field, the strongest being that of the Communists and the Partito d'Azione.

As Ada and her friends saw it, it was war, of every kind: between Allies and Axis, between Italians and Italians, between Italians and Germans; a civil war, a war of liberation and a class war, all of which would play into the future and the culture of Italy itself. For the next twenty months, as the Allies moved slowly north through Italy, constantly bogged down by heavy German resistance, Ada, Bianca, Frida, Silvia and their partisan friends would fight them all.

Even the Germans, as they took over Turin, were taken aback by the state of the city: there was barely a house in which the windows had not been blown out, and many were partially or wholly destroyed. The gas had been switched off, and there was no wood, though people had started chopping down the handsome ancient plane trees that lined the city's central avenues and removing the wooden slats from benches along the streets. Fruit and vegetables had all but disappeared. Fearful of what German occupation might bring, the inhabitants continued to stay indoors, watching and waiting. *The ora della passeggiata*, the early-evening hour when Italians normally strolled in the streets, was ghostly.

Piedmont and its valleys were a secondary front for the German forces, but the city of Turin, with its crucial network of factories, was of immense strategic value. It was a question of how the occupiers could best control and exploit it. The military administration for the north, the Militärkommandantur, had set up its headquarters in Milan. A Turin office, MK 1005, covering Piedmont and Aosta, moved into a requisitioned palazzo in the city. The Gestapo command installed itself in another palazzo, on Corso Oporto. In the wake of the occupying forces had come an SS lieutenant, Alois Schmidt, with a first group of secret servicemen. He took over the old Albergo Nazionale and commandeered a wing of Le Nuove prison, filling it with his own guards and issuing orders that no Italian be permitted inside.

Turin had become a war zone, subject to German laws of war. The Militärkommandantur ruled over the SS and the police, and was responsible for safeguarding useful economic and military sites and for enforcing censorship. Since the number of Germans in the city at this stage was very small, the understanding was that, with the help of Mussolini's rump state, they would use local

Italian Fascists, restored to positions of nominal power and thirsting for revenge for the indignities they had recently suffered, for 'daily repression'. For the next twenty months, the German occupiers would wield total power over both private and public life; but they knew they could achieve little without Italian Fascist help, just as the Fascists understood perfectly that they owed their lives and fortunes to their occupiers.

Among the Fascists creeping back out into the open from the prisons to which they had been sent when Mussolini fell, or the hiding places in which they had spent Badoglio's forty-five days of power, the Germans found ready and eager collaborators, angry and humiliated men and women, intent on vengeance. On 16 September, at first incredulous and then jubilant about Mussolini's resurgence, the former Fascist leadership in Turin regrouped, divided the city into twelve local sectors, and looked about for new, younger blood to forge some kind of working relations with the Germans.

They found it in Giuseppe Solaro, a 29-year-old journalist, economist and former volunteer for Franco's forces in the Spanish civil war, and a keen member of GUF, the Fascist university group. Solaro was energetic and venal. Having grown up with the myths of Fascism and blaming its collapse on internal enemies, he was both politically canny and completely ruthless. Soon made party secretary, he began to navigate his way cautiously between the greedy German predators and the industrial Italian strongholds. In due course he was joined as High Fascist Commissioner by a former agrarian scientist and colonial administrator in Italy's conquered Tripolitania, Valerio Paolo Zerbino, a man as resolute as he was ambitious.

For both men, the crucial issues were how to keep in check the Fascist extremists, men reared on violence and eager to use it on those they considered traitors; how to dampen down the ardour of the young recruits now swaggering insolently around the city streets in their black shirts, swinging their clubs; how to adjust to a totally new world, in which former Fascist supremacy was in tatters and Mussolini no longer the sole arbiter of every aspect of daily life; and, perhaps most importantly, how to carve out for themselves positions of power despite the presence of the Germans. Much of Solaro and Zerbino's time was given to mediation and

avoiding schisms, but even so the extremists were not in a concili-
atory mood. Both young and old were rallying to autonomous
squadri, modelled on those that had terrorised Italy during Fascism's
early days, private armies under tough, scheming leaders, eager to
indulge vendettas and make common cause with the Germans. As
Alois Schmidt remarked, not even in Poland, which he considered
a 'country of the third order', had he seen such keenness to give
names and betray neighbours. It was, he said, '*un fangoso spet-
tacolo*', a filthy sight. In Via Asti, a former barracks of the
Bersagliere, the infantry corps with their distinctive feathered hats,
was turned into the Fascist military headquarters, soon to become
infamous for its torture rooms on the second floor. The fury and
violence of these Fascists would mark the months to come.

Rudolf Rahn, Hitler's plenipotentiary, appointed two go-
betweens to help restore order to Turin. One of these was Baron
von Lagen, the long-serving German Consul General, still smarting
from his humiliation at the hands of the anti-Fascists on 26 July.
The other was a journalist called Ludwig Alwens, correspondent
for a German newspaper in Rome at the time of the armistice.
Gas supplies were reconnected, telephone lines restored, schools
reopened. Fascists deemed loyal and reliable were given permits
for their cars and permission to carry weapons. Everyone else, on
pain of death, was to hand in their guns. Orders went out to
industrialists to draw up a comprehensive inventory of the primary
materials they held and the exact uses to which they were being
put. With them went a warning: anyone caught performing an
act of sabotage would be shot.

And, lest anyone think that German occupation might be a
smooth or benign affair, two early incidents of extreme brutality
suggested otherwise.

The small town of Boves lay eight kilometres from Cuneo, in
southern Piedmont. When the Germans arrived in the area, the
young men in Boves gathered and agreed on some kind of resistance. Desultory shots rang out. Two German soldiers were
captured and one was killed. Immediately, German posters went
up threatening reprisals in the case of armed resistance. The
inhabitants hid in their houses.

One of these was 22-year-old Lucia Boetta, a robust, outspoken
young woman, the daughter of a miller, who had spent her youth

helping her ailing parents and looking after her younger brothers. Working at the mill had deprived her of a formal education, but it had made her physically tough and well organised. Anti-Fascism was in the family's blood. When, on 8 September, a group of disbanded Italian soldiers had reached her town, searching for food and somewhere to hide, Lucia had joined with other local women in finding them civilian clothes and something to eat. She was in Boves when the Germans arrived. Finding the municipal offices deserted, she stole a pile of permits lying on a desk, and used a piece of glass to trace the signature of the mayor, rightly sensing that these false documents might prove invaluable in the days to come.

Lucia Boetta

On 19 September, having decided that a show of strength in Boves was required, the Germans went on the attack. It was quickly over: the young men fought bravely, but with their anti-quated rifles, they were no match for artillery and armoured cars. But then the Germans turned on the civilians. Lucia watched as the night was lit up by flames from the burning houses; she smelt burning flesh. Twenty-three people died, among them the parish priest who was doused with petrol and burnt alive, and his curate, who was just twenty-three. Nearly five-hundred houses were destroyed. What shocked everyone was the realisation that the Germans intended to be so murderous. For Lucia, it marked the moment when she became a fighter.

Further proof of German vengeance was not long in coming, this time in the south. Naples had been a target of heavy Allied bombing, but had nevertheless greeted the armistice with euphoria. Even before the Allies arrived, the inhabitants, many of them port workers, cab drivers and waiters, began a series of spontaneous insurrections against the Germans in various different neighbourhoods, and barricaded the city's narrow and twisting streets. Former soldiers, teachers, civil servants and many women joined in. The youngest were twelve-year-old boys.

The local German commander launched a series of reprisals, executing hostages and firing at women queueing for bread. Street by street, the local population fought back. Naples was soon without water, electricity or gas, and food supplies were down to apples. But the street battles continued. The famous Naples Historical Archive went up in flames. By the time the Allies arrived four days later, 665 people, among them children, were dead.

News of the insurrection, Naples' glorious '*quattro giornate*', was broadcast all over Italy by Radio London. What had taken place was not a coordinated operation of resistance. But it had made a point: the Wehrmacht was not invincible and ordinary Italians, women as well as men, were prepared to take to the streets and fight, a message that was lost neither on the Allies nor, perhaps more importantly, on the north, where the Germans were busy digging in. At a moment of profound Italian dejection and shame, the battle for Naples produced a spark of self-respect; and it showed just what partisan warfare could, and could not, achieve.

Kesselring, who had planned to slow the Allied advance with a series of fortified defensive positions, pulled his men back behind the Gustav line, which ran from the bay of Gaeta, past Cassino and to Ortona on the Adriatic, making the most of the high mountain ranges in between, and the fact that this was the narrowest stretch of the Italian peninsula.

By the end of September, Turin had a new map. There was German Turin, its heavily fortified barracks and offices scattered all around the city centre. There was Fascist Turin, with its strongholds sprouting up along the avenues. And there was also Resistance Turin, in which its highly educated inhabitants were joining forces with its many thousands of industrial workers who would prove deaf to the lures of both Germans and Fascists alike. It took most people some time, even those instinctively opposed to the occupiers, to understand that something fundamental was taking place – still formless, uncertain, uncoordinated, but alive. Under the arcades, in cafes and concealed restaurants and church crypts, among Bianca and her friends, in Ada's house in Via Fabro, plans were hatching. Into them played the Italian characteristic of '*arrangiarsi*', to improvise, to make do, to do one's best by fair means or foul, to learn how to show no emotion, give nothing away. Not for them the '*zona grigia*', the grey area of standing back and doing nothing, nor the role of observer, like those known to the anti-Fascists as '*attendisti*' and to the Fascists as 'the people who stand by the window'.

Rather, it was a matter of waking up, even if, for those who had known only Fascism, there was no history, no recent tradition of revolt to model on. As Ada saw it, it was now a fight to rescue Italy from all that had gone before and all that was happening now, a fight that had to be waged, for there was no alternative: ahead lay huge, wide, terrifying horizons, after long years of Fascist littleness.

5

Making lions

As the weather began to turn cold, Bianca and her companion Alberto set off once again for Torre Pellice, where the partisan groups were busy recruiting young fighters. Since the trains were erratic and often closely watched by Fascists hoping to catch any soldiers still on the loose, they decided to cycle the thirty-eight kilometres. Bianca went ahead, singing loudly as she pedalled; if she stopped singing, Alberto would know that there was a German patrol. Young men were in growing danger: the Germans were demanding quotas of workers for their industrial production, and from Salò Mussolini was calling up all men born between 1923 and 1925 for his army and militia.

Bianca had been asked by the Communist Party to work for them in Turin and she had been given a *nom de guerre*, Nerina – a badge of honour in clandestinity. The party decided that it would be best if she kept on with her job as social worker which not only gave her an excuse to move around the factories but also provided her with a German laissez-passer, allowing her to cycle freely around the city. The photograph on her German pass shows her with shoulder-length hair and a wary expression on her face.

From Moscow, the exiled Communist leader Palmiro Togliatti called on party members to join the Resistance and fight the Germans. He had specified a quota: 15 per cent of all card-carrying members and 10 per cent of all cadres. Before long, Bianca gave up her job to work full-time for the party, but not before she had visited several trade union offices and carried away with her, just as Lucia had in Boves, a large quantity of passes and permits of every kind, which she distributed to friends. As the Germans were now circulating the names of suspected anti-Fascists, false documents were becoming essential.

In Torre Pellice much had happened since the meeting of the anti-Fascists on 10 September. Frida's brother Roberto had formed a group from what he mockingly called '*buone famiglie borghesi*', good bourgeois families. Her other brother Gustavo agreed to take charge of propaganda.

Frida had become a *staffetta*, saying of herself laughingly that she was born to be a general. It seemed to her that this explosion of rebellion had been waiting to happen, not just to her but to her whole generation. 'We had,' wrote Roberto later, 'to learn things that no one had taught us, but which were in some sense

Roberto and Frida Malan

already in our surroundings, in our people.' Possible recruits were directed first to Torre Pellice's Caffè Italia under the arcades, where they were told to pick a leaf from a bush outside the door and put it down on the counter with the password '*la rosa è rossa*', the rose is red. They were then vetted, before being sent up into the mountains. Meetings were held in Signora Malan's kitchen.

Alberto decided to join Giorgio Diena in a group composed largely of students, several of them chemists at the university in Turin with him. In mid October they were joined by Jacopo Lombardini, the loping evangelical preacher from the Waldensian community, for whom staying in Torre Pellice, given his well-known and outspoken views on the Fascists, was no longer an option. Wanting to spare the older man too arduous a life, Roberto suggested that he take the position of political commissar, a role somewhere between father figure, confessor, teacher and mentor, originally coined by the Bolsheviks during the Russian civil war. Lombardini walked up and down the mountain paths between the bands, mixing politics with preaching; he was much loved by the young partisans. As Roberto saw it, all bands needed a Socrates, to help them clarify their ideas, and the gentle, studious Lombardini was perfect for the job. All across Piedmont and the north, other groups were forming, with the same mixture of nationalities, backgrounds, ages and skills.

Giorgio Agosti and his friend Dante Livio Bianco, who were emerging as theoreticians and tactical planners, spoke of the '*spirito Piemontese*', the same commitment to patriotism, duty and courage that had once inspired the early members of Italy's Risorgimento. Though both were intensely interested in the shape that Italy would assume once peace came, they agreed that what mattered now was not intellectual dreaming but concerted action. They worried constantly, however, about the safety of the young partisans, for, having subdued Turin, the German soldiers were making their way up the valleys, setting themselves up in the abandoned barracks. In Torre Pellice, they had taken over those that had housed the Alpini, two long brick buildings facing the premises of the printer Gustavo used after dark. They were a constant, menacing presence.

Willy Jervis with Giovanni and Paolo

A friend of Frida's, Willy Jervis, arrived, bringing with him his wife Lucilla and their three children, Giovanni, who was ten, Paola four and the severely handicapped seven-year-old Letizia. Willy was forty-two, with an English grandfather who had served with the East India Company and helped found the War Office's map department in London, but Willy himself had grown up in the Valdesian valleys. He was an engineer by training and had been working in Ivrea, in Aosta, for Adriano Olivetti, son of the inventor of the first Italian typewriters, while at the same time helping escaped Allied prisoners of war cross the Italian border into Switzerland. Under cover of his business, Adriano, who was Jewish and married to Natalia Ginzburg's sister, was issuing false papers to protect people from arrest; Olivetti's was already being spoken of by the Fascists as a 'coven of Jews'. Willy had grown up reading Gobetti and Gramsci and listening to Croce's calls for conscience and intellectual rigour. As a mountaineer, he was fit and knew the passes well. 'I had,' he said later, 'the impression of being alive, after so many years of compromise.' When news reached him that his name was on a list of people the Germans planned to arrest, the family cycled in the night to a house further up the mountains belonging to the Olivettis, from where Willy continued his Resistance activities. But soon this hiding place too seemed perilous.

Next, the Jervis family took rooms in the house of a farmer in the mountains above Torre Pellice. The bedrooms were damp and cold and the fires smoked but they were pleased to be among friends. Willy travelled up and down the valleys, acting as an informal commissar among the groups, and down to Turin where he met Ada and collected posters and flyers for distribution in the mountain villages. He was an excellent organiser. 'We feel calm,' he wrote, 'perhaps blind, but we are not thinking about the future.' Every couple of days, he cycled to a nearby village to fetch milk, which he and Lucilla churned into butter. Both felt free and excited. They were a handsome couple, the half-Swiss, half-Florentine Lucilla, author of a thesis on *The Pilgrim's Progress*, and her tall husband Willy, with his long face and sleek black hair combed back.

Willy and Lucilla Jervis

There was, for a brief moment during this febrile autumn of 1943, a hiatus across northern Italy, a lull of calm, almost a feeling of being safe, inviolable. People were positioning themselves, defining their roles, looking warily about. A young woman working for the municipality started to produce false identity papers; a couple of factories in the plain agreed to ring a bell if a German patrol was spotted; a man taking deliveries to Turin offered to transport partisans along with his daily loads. It was as if everyone was waiting, to see who would move first. There were no maps, no telephones, seldom a radio with which to take a bearing. The partisans' isolation and lack of contact with the rest of Italy was almost total.

What they could not avoid knowing, however, was that the Salò government was planning to call up all fit men, to serve in its militia or volunteer to work for the Germans. This meant that young Italian men were now faced with an impossible choice: they could turn their backs on everything they had been taught to believe, reject the great Fascist mantra of *Credere, Obbedire, Combattere* and recast as enemies the Germans they had only known as allies, and take off up into the mountains in search of others who felt the same. Or, unable to handle the contradictions, they could obey the draft. What they could not do was nothing, however desperately they insisted that all they wanted was to survive the war. As one young man put it, the decision they made demanded an 'extraordinary effort of will, often solitary, to identify, in the midst of so much confusion, the right direction'.

A young boy soldier

Driven by a huge range of emotions – longing for adventure, desire for revenge, class hatred, or simply by a chance meeting with a more decided friend – men were arriving in the mountains above Turin in twos and threes, excited, frightened, alert. They came in shorts, in dungarees, in old First World War uniforms. Some were no older than sixteen. 'Not everyone is born a lion,' one remarked. 'But lions can be made.' Life in the partisan bands quickly pleased them. Huts of canvas and branches were built. They talked, they argued, they recited poetry, they played cards, and they met in groups in stables and clearings in the forest to discuss the war and learn how to handle weapons. When the villagers gave them gifts of food, they celebrated, turning eggs into *zabaglione*, delighted with a change from the endless diet of chestnuts – boiled, dried, roasted or cooked with rice. Lombardini brought them news from the outside world.

Many of the young men were still spending their nights in their own homes, having worked out secret hiding places and escape routes in case of the sudden arrival of an enemy patrol. Sometimes, in the evenings, they went down to the village squares and danced, or found a field and played football. 'We are,' noted one, 'what we are, a mixture of individuals, some selfless and in good faith, some political opportunists, some soldiers on the run from deportation to Germany, some driven by a longing for excitement, some by a desire for loot.' The question, debated for long hours round the fire at night, was what they should call themselves. Someone suggested '*volontari della libertà*' or '*attivisti della libertà*', volunteers or activists for liberty. 'Warriors' was thought to be a bit martial. There were hesitations over 'patriot' and 'partisan', but everyone liked 'bands'. For the intellectuals among them, accustomed to sitting in libraries, there was a sense of freshness, a new language, a different way of looking at life; as one put it, 'we found ourselves with companions made of other flesh and other bones'.

As for the women, it was all rather different. They had no decision to make, for there was no call-up for them. On the other hand, the first heady days of the armistice, when they had been drawn out into the streets to help the fleeing soldiers, had given them a taste for comradeship, for self-assertion. It was not easy to go back. Fascism had trapped them in domesticity and segregation. This new life offered them adventure, the company of boys, intense friendships with other *staffette*, the chance to decide their own fates. Having embarked on resistance with a simple act of kindness, helping escaped prisoners, they were now eager to do more; the role of *staffetta* promised endless opportunities. For the first time in their lives, these young women could imagine having opinions and voicing them, even if they sensed that the very skills they had developed as girls, being biddable, diplomatic and intuitive, might also serve them very well in this extraordinary new world.

A group of young *staffette*

It was out of this rapidly growing inchoate crowd that an army of partisans was now being forged. Its soldiers were untrained, without uniforms, warm clothing or boots, and what weapons they had were for the most part very old. But what it did have, for the moment at least, was the goodwill of the local people, who were prepared to provide food, beds and above all hiding places.

What the Malans and the other partisan leaders now had to decide was how best to conduct this war. The Fascists, trumpeting their new allegiance to Mussolini's RSI, were clearly an obvious target, since it was unlikely that the Germans would demand retribution if they were killed. Another desirable action was sabotage. What the partisans had not yet understood, however, was that though the valleys were perfect guerrilla country, they were also easy for the enemy to drive up, bringing troops and armoured cars. The speed with which this had happened left everyone unprepared. What was happening, thought Agosti, was like a river in spate, bringing down to the plains every kind of detritus which had to be dealt with. It was not enough simply to get rid of the Germans and the Fascists: 'Nazifascism', as the anti-Fascists had begun to call it, had to be annihilated forever. 'When all is said and done,' Agosti wrote to Bianco, in one of the many letters which passed between them over the next twenty months, 'this struggle pleases me, just because it is so stark, so utterly unselfish . . . If we get out of it alive, we'll emerge better people . . . and if we don't, well, we'll know that if only for a few months we lived and obeyed a precise moral imperative.'

Ada's house in the Val di Susa lay just over the mountains from Torre Pellice, but with no buses or trains linking the two valleys, and very few private cars in circulation, it might have been another world. Later, when the war was over and the story of what had taken place was picked over and disputed, Marisa Diena, Giorgio's sister, would say that the partisans in the Val di Susa, compared to those in the Val Pellice, were a timid, cautious bunch. It did not feel that way to Ada.

The valley itself, some hundred kilometres from end to end, running from the plains just west of Turin to the border with France at Bardonecchia, was seen by the locals to fall into three distinct areas. There was the upper valley, an isolated Alpine world, through which the trains ran along viaducts and through tunnels, thickly wooded, with pockets of agriculture and small-holdings. The middle and lower valleys, by contrast, were flatter and more fertile, fed by the fast-flowing River Dora; here many people were employed in one of the cotton mills or factories producing paints and solvents, and as such they had been targets for Allied bombing raids. A large number of these workers were women who had already played an important part in the earlier strikes. This industrial heartland was of great interest to the Germans, but it was of no less interest to the Resistance.

Soon after the armistice, the first groups of disbanded soldiers in the Val di Susa joined forces with local students and factory workers, and began to sabotage the railway line, in order to prevent the Germans moving Italian equipment out and men and weapons in. To provision themselves, they made forays against the factories, carrying away food, clothes and explosives. An electricity plant at Chiomonte went up in flames. The Germans retaliated by stationing three railway carriages in Bussoleno, not far from Susa, to house a full team of engineers to mend the sabotaged tracks.

By early October, much as in the Val Pellice, the Val di Susa had some five hundred partisans scattered in bands around the mountains. In the remote shepherd huts high in the forests they stored requisitioned weapons, sacks of flour and salt. On 24 October, they held up a lorry of Fascists arriving from Turin and took away their weapons before releasing the men; a few days later they attacked a troop of Fascists come to set up a new base in the village of Sant'Antonino. The Germans banned all vehicles in the valley, imposed a curfew and put up placards in the lower valley saying: '*Achtung! Bandengebiet!*' Attention – Bandits. It was a stand-off, but one that was relatively free of casualties. The days passed and the sense of waiting continued.

A young school friend of Paolo's, Cesare Alvazzi, arrived from Oulx, a town in the valley that lay close to the border with France and reported to Ada that the town was full of German soldiers, busily digging themselves in. Cesare was working at Turin's Porta Nuova station while preparing for exams to join the railways as a radio technician. Oulx was renowned for its ardent Fascists and Cesare had been spending his nights painting over the more triumphalist slogans plastered on the town walls. His job on the railways allowed him to travel up and down the valley, and he took with him suitcases stuffed with weapons to deliver to the mountain bands, and clandestine literature which he left in station waiting rooms. Teta, who ran the village shop, offered her cart to transport weapons.

Ada now learned that an English pilot, Major Dennis, wounded in an earlier air raid, was being cared for secretly in a nearby hospital. The Resistance had organised a special group of partisans to help the Allied prisoners of war still on the run. She found him there, with two other POWs. Not one spoke a word of Italian, and though her English was good Ada had trouble understanding Dennis's thick Northumberland accent. Fearing that the men might fall into German hands, she got Ettore to take their photographs for false papers which would get them across the border into Switzerland. Cesare, who often accompanied Ada, was struck by her energy and decisiveness; he thought she looked like a young girl, with her dark hair pulled back into a pigtail, barely older than Paolo and himself. She was a woman who, he said, while appearing simple and straightforward, had a 'soul of fire'.

Ada's enthusiasm and warmth, and the way she made them feel that their views and feelings mattered, were drawing growing numbers of young men in the upper valley to Meana. She was never at rest, never allowing a single minute, a single idea or project go to waste. There was nothing that was not explored or put to use. 'She operated like a general,' Cesare said later. 'She had an enormous network of contacts, she took decisions, she told us what to do. When we got orders, we carried them out.' On 14 November, an expert in explosives appeared. They listened to Radio London together and talked of possible acts of sabotage; Paolo and Cesare joined in, excited. Listening to their plans, Ada felt maternal, sentimental, charmed by their look of 'cagey conspirators in an operetta', but whenever she thought about Paolo, her old terrors returned. She was enchanted by her son, but ever conscious of the risks such love carried.

A local priest, Don Foglia, offered his help. He was a tall man, with a 'fine open face' which made Ada think of an Etruscan mask, and a dark wispy beard. Exchanging his soutane for civilian clothes, Don Foglia would race around the villages, 'enthusing, encouraging, filling their hearts with resolve', Ada wrote, 'always inexhaustible'. The priest had a turbulent past, having been expelled from his seminary in Susa before being ordained in France. He was not long back from service as a military chaplain with the Alpini in the Balkans where he had been wounded and then decorated. There, Don Foglia had learned about explosives; the partisans nicknamed him Don Dinamite. His manner was measured and he exuded authority. Ada loved the precision with which he talked.

It was Don Foglia who proposed their first major act of sabotage, blowing up the bridge above Exilles, which carried cars and trains to the French border. He had managed to collect forty kilos of explosives which he was hiding in the cellars of a hotel not far away. A plan was made for ten partisans, each carrying a suitcase of explosives, to take the train up to Exilles, where they would be joined by twenty others from the surrounding villages. Sergio Bellone, an explosives expert, Paolo and Don Foglia himself were to be in command. The date was set for 17 November. The lull, the stand-off between the Germans and the partisans, was about to end.

Ada, to provide an alibi for her comings and goings, was still teaching at a school in Turin. As she left for the city on the 17th, she felt as if she were being 'physically torn apart' from Paolo. Next morning, Piedmont woke to heavy snow. In Via Fabro, in between classes and meetings with Agosti and Bianco, who were now busy setting up a command structure for the partisan bands, Ada sat worrying. That night she was just in time to catch a train back up to Susa, sitting on the floor of a cattle truck in the dark, listening as the other passengers began to sing. All she could think about was whether she would find Paolo there when she got home. At Susa station, she was met by a young partisan. Of Paolo there was no news.

Ada waited, obsessively playing over in her mind different scenarios. Whenever a dog barked, she rushed outside to stare into the blackness and the falling snow. In the morning, she was obliged to return to Turin and when she got back that night the snow was still falling and piling up in drifts around her house. There was still no word of Paolo. She began to feel that she was losing her mind: had he been killed in an avalanche? frozen to death? Deciding that she was too restless to wait any longer, she set out at first light to find him. In the valley she bumped into Don Foglia, who told her that the mission had been aborted after the snow had fatally dampened the fuses. Paolo, he said, was not far away. Later, in her diary, she wrote that 'chattering with crazy emotion' she had felt, just for a moment, 'entirely happy'. She lit a fire and sat most of the night in front of the flames, correcting the proofs of her most recent translation and then reading a detective story. The snow turned into rain. At nine o'clock next morning she was woken by a dog barking and rushed to the window. She did not recognise the exhausted figure struggling up the hill towards her. When she realised it was Paolo, she started to cry.

Very few of the men and women taking up arms in the north knew anything at all about guerrilla warfare. Italy had no great tradition of partisan life beyond the exploits of Garibaldi's thousand red-shirted followers in the 1860s struggle for unification, which every Italian learned about at school. But among the men now assuming the leadership of the Resistance were some who had fought against Franco in Spain. That civil war, they said, had indeed ended in defeat; but it was a 'glorious defeat', in that it had taught them what irregular forces could achieve.

Soon after the clandestine Committee of National Liberation, the CLN, had formed in Rome in the wake of the armistice, the decision was taken to set up a parallel body for the north, with its headquarters in Milan, a military wing, and sections for finance, supply and propaganda. Among its leaders in Turin was Vittorio Foa, and the members met secretly in small groups, often in the Hotel Canelli in Via San Dalmazio. They had decided to commit as little as possible to paper. Codes were agreed on; names of places and aliases memorised. From the first, reflecting the mood of the CLN in the south, they were united in rejecting both Badoglio's government and the monarchy. Though not always in agreement on other matters, they tried to find a middle ground, dealing mainly with the German occupation and the resurgence of the Italian Fascists, while at the same time laying down markers for a post-war Italy.

The two strongest parties within the six-party coalition remained the Partito d'Azione and the Communists. The Communist ranks in Turin had been decimated during the late twenties and early thirties by Mussolini's purges, so that the active membership in Piedmont now stood at only eight hundred, and they were a disunited spectrum of Trotskyists, Stalinists and anarchists, with many variations in between. But among the men and women returning from years in prison and on the penal islands were efficient Communist organisers, who soon turned their attention to the factories, where the women had been quick to rally and help the disbanded soldiers. Survivors of the bitter March 1943 strikes, these women were fighters; they had tasted power and it had given them strength and resolve.

The Partito d'Azione, which had held many of its first gatherings in Ada's flat in the city, and whose first general assembly in Florence in September had spawned clandestine groups all across German-occupied Italy, now formed a military committee and a war cabinet, under Agosti, Duccio and Bianco. Willy Jervis became one of their first political commissars. These friends, all viscerally anti-Fascist out of disgust at what they saw as the rampant immorality of Mussolini's regime, agreed that what inspired them was a 'passion for liberty always lit up by reason'. None could imagine returning to the 'barbarity and brutishness' of the Mussolini years, or of tolerating the squalor and opportunism of his followers. As Bianco put it, the war in Piedmont would be shaped by the particular character of the men and women who had grown up there, either among the pious Waldensians or as Piedmontese and Savoyards, proud of their past history, their toughness, self-discipline and honesty. The word '*patria*' had been hijacked and debased by the Fascists; he said it had to be reclaimed, made glorious again. Bianco's wife, Pinella, a small, slender, bold woman, had already joined the fight and was carrying messages from the command in Turin up into the mountains.

Relations between the Communists and the Partito d'Azione were for the most part cordial, with occasional fallings-out over resources and territory. The bands in the mountains were carving out their own patches, with Willy Jervis and Jacopo Lombardini moving between them, making peace where friction broke out. Ada, during her encounters with Agosti in Turin, was getting a feel for the differences between the political parties. The Communists, she noted, were effective and realistic; the Partito d'Azione was forward-looking. But the Socialists, though brave and trustworthy, were archaic and made her think of a fine old piece of nineteenth-century lace stowed away in mothballs. The northern CLN, however, was turning into the true government of the valleys, organising everything from supplies of wood for hospitals to distribution of food to the most impoverished families. Ada's dreams of schooling Italians to plan for a new democratic Italy were shared by Agosti, who spoke not just of inspiring the young partisans with the idea of personal sacrifice but of turning them into 'new men', with an 'Italian political mentality'.

Ada had not yet managed to get Major Dennis out to Switzerland, but, now that he had recovered, she was encouraging him to take charge of the remaining Allied prisoners of war. Their presence was not just dangerous for themselves, but for their hosts. Dennis, she remarked with exasperation, possessed a 'typically English slowness and pedantry' and kept making objections. Eventually her combination of charm and firmness wore him down. Some of Ada's time was spent collecting books, medicines and soap for the men in hiding, finding safe houses, getting maps and false papers and setting up a system of messages to be transmitted to the Allies via sympathetic contacts in the Vatican. No one knew how many Allied prisoners of war were still unaccounted for. Twenty thousand men were said to be in enemy hands, and perhaps 3,000 more already in safety either in Switzerland or with the Allied forces. The other 40,000 or so were at large and the Germans had put up posters offering rewards for everyone captured. Maps printed on silk showing routes to the border with Switzerland had been dropped by parachute from Allied planes, but few had actually been retrieved.

Though the Fascists who had been ousted from the factories during Badoglio's forty-five days had returned to their jobs, tougher, triumphant and vengeful, the mood among the workers was greatly changed. Anti-Fascism was in the air, as never before. There was talk of setting up of action committees, to coordinate sabotage and send supplies up to the partisans in the mountains. Young women flocked to join. Visiting factories now, Bianca discovered a new edge of excitement. And mirroring these internal factory groups, young urban commandos were volunteering to take the war into the streets, to sow terror among the Germans and the Fascists. Calling themselves Gruppi di Azione Patriottica (GAP) they got hold of revolvers and hand grenades. Most *gappisti* were very young, some only in their teens. They understood that if caught they could expect no mercy. They operated at night, bringing justice, as they put it, to spies and collaborators and they managed to infiltrate the central telephone exchange in Via Confienza. Ada's husband Ettore, working as an engineer at the Ente

Italiano Radiofoniche, was able to bring them radio transmitters and receivers and spare parts.

After the general assembly of the Partito d'Azione in September, Ferruccio Parri, at fifty-three older than most of the other men, had been sent to organise the Resistance in the north. Parri was a much decorated officer from the First World War, fair, conscientious and greatly loved by his comrades, and he was emerging as a powerful partisan leader. He had a prodigious memory for geography and routes and was a passionate believer in breaking with the tainted monarchy and bringing all Italians together in a new united democracy. Friends called him '*Zio Maurizio*', though his *noms de guerre* would soon include Marsili, Arrigoni, Pasolini, Pozzi and Walter. They teased him about his faith in the ideals of the Risorgimento and said that he was the most 'lay' and least 'Jacobin' of men. For his part, he thought that the Resistance would be a fine test of men and that partisan warfare should be regarded as a 'crucible of character'.

As the autumn wore on, the difference in attitude among the Allies towards any form of Italian resistance was, if anything, growing more pronounced. The British, pointing to the feebleness with which Italy had resisted the German occupation, continued to insist that almost nothing could be expected from its citizens, a tone reflected in the leaflets they dropped over occupied territory, which appeared to regard them as naughty children. Within the British ranks, the schism between Eden and the Foreign Office on one side and the SOE on the other had not been resolved. Eden wanted no concessions, the SOE would concede almost anything as long as it led to valuable cooperation. One general suggested that the best use for the disbanded Italian soldiers would be as slave labour. The Americans, who thought the British attitude smacked of neocolonialism, tended to side with the SOE. None of this was made easier by the fact that the offices of the two nations' competing secret services lay far to the south, many hundreds of miles from the partisans in the north, and that at every level they too were awash with prejudice and misunderstanding, much of it to do with the spectre of communism. News of the groups of partisans forming in Piedmont and across Tuscany was greeted with extreme wariness. Reluctantly, a decision was now taken to send military advisers to the 'larger and more virile groups'.

A steady stream of idealistic Italian former prisoners, who had escaped from German-held territory across enemy lines, was continuing to arrive in the south, often famished and exhausted, describing inhuman treatment by their captors. What they asked now was to be allowed to fight alongside the Allies. The first attempts to set up an Italian volunteer army foundered through distrust and inefficiency, and Raimondo Craveri suggested to the Americans that he might be allowed to set up a select, secret organisation, the Organizzazione della Resistenza Italiana (ORI) to drop agents behind enemy lines to gather much needed military information, which could then be transmitted to the south.

Volunteers were recruited, then trained by the Allies in sabotage, spying, explosives, mines, map reading, investigation techniques, German insignia and unarmed combat. Like their leader Craveri, they were republicans and democrats, a curious assortment of men, some veterans of the Spanish civil war, others long-time Italian exiles in the United States. One was a Piedmontese judge from Detroit. A first mission was dropped into Liguria; a second made contact with a clandestine intelligence group just forming in Genoa.

At a more senior level, a first meeting was arranged between on the one side Parri and a former exiled anti-Fascist, Leo Valiani, speaking for the CLN and the northern partisans, and on the other the Allied leadership. Berne had been chosen as the headquarters for the Allied missions, and the meeting was conducted by Allen W. Dulles on behalf of the Americans, and John McCaffery for the British. The two Italians were spirited over the Swiss border.

What was instantly clear was that a vast gap separated their two visions of the war. The Allies made it plain that all they wanted from the Italians was 'useful guerrilla work and sabotage', while Parri was planning for nothing less than a united partisan insurrectionary army, a *democrazia armata*, which would wage such convincing war against the Germans that it would be impossible to deny Italy a proper seat at any post-war negotiations. The talks were cautious. The British in particular were disconcerted by the idea of a national uprising, and displeased to hear the

Partito d'Azione described as a 'revolutionary movement'. However, both Parri and Valiani personally impressed the Allied representatives. The Italians came away with less support than they had hoped for, but a promise of at least some financial assistance and supplies of weapons. In return, they undertook to provide assistance to the Allied prisoners of war in hiding and to gather and transmit information about the Germans to the south.

By early November, at least some of the clouds of chaos left by the armistice had cleared. The Allies were stalled behind the Gustav line, and none of the rivalries between Badoglio's government in Brindisi and the CLN in Rome had been overcome. But in the north, Piedmont's partisans were getting more organised every day, with acts of sabotage – bridges blown up, trains derailed, German supplies looted – taking place with increasing frequency. It was no longer, one man remarked, a question of playing blind man's buff, searching hopefully in the mountains for hidden bands of friends: they had secure links via the *staffette*, as Frida, Bianca and Silvia and their friends flitted across the valleys. Turin was their capital. In the mountains, Communists, Partito d'Azione and Autonomi – men and women of no particular political affiliation – were finding their feet, agreeing to put aside their differences and quarrels over territory in the face of common foes and to hit hardest at the Fascists. It had been decided that Willy Jervis would liaise with the Allies over drops of weapons and supplies. 'Have courage,' Leone Ginzburg, who was still in hiding in Rome, urged in the pages of *L'Italia Libera*. 'Hunt down the Germans, sabotage their means of communication. Don't believe in alarmist rumours. And, above all, do not be discouraged.'

6

The *piccoli geni*

It is possible that Bianca, Frida and Silvia would have taken longer to join the Resistance had it not been for their Jewish friends. For them, as for Turin's close-knit Jewish community of some 4,000 people, the 1938 racial laws, with their assertion that Jews were not true Italians, had come as a shock, a sudden and appalling realisation that the simmering racism that had started with victory in Ethiopia and Mussolini's obsession with miscegenation, had become real and menacing.

There had, of course, been signs: speeches about the parasitic and self-interested '*borghesia*', the reviled bourgeoisie of which the Jews were an integral part; references to Judaeo-Bolshevik conspiracies; talk of persecutions in Germany. But these were only rumours and most people preferred not to believe them. To proclaim their own trust in the Fascist regime, a group of anxious Jews in Turin had started a paper, *La Nostra Bandiera*, Our Flag, in which they reminded their readers that Italy had in fact had the first Jewish prime minister in Europe, and at least five of the 119 founders of the Fascist Party in Milan's Piazza San Sepolcro in March 1919 had been Jewish. If anything, Mussolini's position towards Italy's small and highly assimilated Jewish communities – some twenty-six in different cities and not many more than 45,000 people all told in the late 1930s – had been marked more by ambiguity than hostility. At first highly critical of Hitler's racial tirades, his attacks on the Jews became harsher only with his need to cement ties with Germany.

But the racial laws were something different. They brought expulsion from schools, jobs and professions, the sequestration of properties and businesses. They forbade Jews to employ Aryans as maids and reduced the acreage of property they were allowed to own. When Italy went to war, and was doing badly, Mussolini's newspapers were full of articles about Jews spreading defeatism and 'assassinating the Patria'. Those who defended them were branded '*ebrei onorari*', honorary Jews. A column in a Cremona paper, under the heading '*Occhio Agli Ebrei*', an eye on Jews, published reports on transgressions, amply fed by anonymous tips about undeclared properties, war profiteers and illegal marriages with Aryans, whose purity they would corrupt.

Nowhere had this campaign been more vicious than in the universities, and nowhere more so than among Bianca, Frida and Silvia's fellow students in Turin. GUF, the Gruppi Universitari Fascisti, to which all students were obliged to belong, in their special green tricorn hats and toggled blue kerchiefs, had been quick to seize on the slogan that Jewish culture was incompatible with true Fascism. Only the purest of the pure, which by defin-ition excluded the Jews, they maintained, were worthy of carrying forward the great cleansing Fascist revolution. In the wake of a *manifesto della razza*, a hotchpotch of phoney science and in-accurate statistics, had come special demographic and racial sections attached to every branch of GUF.

One of Italian anti-Semitism's most fanatical exponents was *Il Lambello*, GUF's paper in Turin, which instructed its readers to 'hate the Jew and all he stands for till death: destroy him'. Jews, it suggested, should, like rabid dogs, be forced to wear brightly coloured bracelets to warn others against the 'peril of infection'. When Italy went to war, the young Gufini, as they were called, were the first to enrol. Peace, they declared, was 'satanic': it eroded energy, enfeebled the body and crushed the soul. War would serve to put an end to all compromise and corruption, peel away para-sites and spongers, and hone heroic new men for the Duce's revived '*squadrismo*'.

After the racial laws of 1938 banned young Jews not already enrolled in a university from all further education, a group of recent graduates had come together in the library of the Jewish school in Turin, near the synagogue in Via Sant'Anselmo. No longer was it possible, they agreed, to remain in what Levi called a 'white limbo of anaesthesia': they would now act to help others and set up a *scuola ebraica*. The group included Giorgio

Diena and Alberto Salmoni, Bianca's boyfriend, along with Levi and his sister Anna Maria, Luciana Nissim, Vanda Maestra and Franco Momigliano, as well as Sandro Delmastro, a Catholic, two years older than the others, strong, stubborn, passionate and with a taste for practical jokes and a cocker spaniel called Virginia Woolf. Jewish identity, strong feelings about the Risorgimento, a shared understanding that they were different and under threat: it was a heady mix and made them cling together.

From left: Primo Levi, Bianca, Alberto Salmoni and two friends

Levi, Sandro and Alberto were old climbing friends. Franco was a lawyer, a tall, gloomy intellectual who was passionate about politics, and he was attached to Luciana, a medical student, daughter of a textile merchant in Biella. Vanda was small, thin and frail, with deep green eyes and curly hair, and she wore a brace to correct a slight curvature of the spine. She was a gifted mathematician but her mother had persuaded her to study industrial chemistry, believing it would lead to a better career. Vanda was terrified in the bombing raids and told the others that she dreaded illness and pain. In the group there were three chemists,

Levi, Alberto and herself. Luciana called them the '*piccoli geni*', the little geniuses. The *scuola ebraica* became a place of safety for them all, teachers and students alike, somewhere they could talk, argue, learn and make intense friendships. None of them ever forgot it.

In the evenings, after her work in a lawyer's office, Bianca joined the group to rip the anti-Semitic slogans off the walls along Via Roma. One had a cartoon showing a Jew with his tongue cut out with scissors. Another spoke of Jews as 'manipulators of the stock exchange, traitors, hoarders, homosexuals', whose only passion was money, and asked: 'Shall we finish them off once and for all, not in concentration camps but with flame throwers?' The young friends took it in turns to guard the *scuola ebraica* after the nearby synagogue was set on fire by Fascists throwing petrol against the walls. It was not long before police began to arrest foreign Jews and send them off to camps in the south – though not Italian Jews, unless they were also deemed to be 'officially dangerous'. There were no plans, at first, for pogroms; simply a hope that the Jewish population would leave the country. True Italians, said Mussolini, had to learn to be less 'friendly'; they had to become 'hard, implacable, odious. In other words, masters.'

Frida's particular friend in the Jewish group was a slender, precocious mathematician with black hair and a mournful, quizzical expression called Emanuele Artom. He had been a student at the Liceo d'Azeglio under Augusto Monti and was drawing closer to Judaism, exploring his sense that it was neither a religion nor a homeland but rather a 'moral tradition'. Luciana thought he had a very ugly, strange face but that he was exceptionally clever and kind. Emanuele and his younger brother Ennio, a high-spirited and laughing boy, were the star teachers of the classes that took place in the library on Wednesdays for those of their younger friends who were now denied an education, and the Artom house in Via Sacchi, presided over by their brilliant mathematician father Emilio, was regarded as one of the city's most important Jewish cultural centres.

Ennio had been a child prodigy, a boy who could read and write at the age of three, who worked as a translator for the publisher Einaudi at fourteen and had gone to university at sixteen. The two brothers were very close. But in the summer of 1940, climbing in the mountains with his father and friends, Ennio had slipped two hundred metres down a mountain face. At first he appeared unharmed; but by the time the doctor arrived he was dead. He was twenty. Ennio's death plunged his parents into acute misery: he had been their favourite son.

Emanuele forever tried to live up to his brother and win his parents' affection, but it was an impossible task. He refused to join his friends in removing the anti-Semitic posters from Turin's walls, saying that it was a job for all the city's inhabitants, not just for the Jews, for surely everyone must find their sentiments offensive. He started to keep a diary, and was thinking about Kafka and the way that the Jews had become the 'other', the stranger, the 'parthenogenic element', tranformed overnight into insects.

'We were a group of rather exclusive friends,' wrote Levi in a short story later, 'We were bound together, men and women, by a serious and profound feeling . . . that comes from having lived through important years together, and for having lived them without too much weakness.' In 1942 came a decree that Italian Jews were to be mobilised for forced labour. Emanuele was one of 476 Jewish men in Turin assigned to roadworks and building sites.

That summer, Levi went to Milan to work for a Swiss pharmaceutical company: despite the racial laws, there was a need for chemists to replace those who had gone off to the war. Milan was bigger, less parochial, more open than enclosed and secretive Turin, where its Jewish community had, as Levi wrote, like molluscs, found a 'reef on which to attach themselves, grow a shell and never move again'. He took lodgings with his cousin, Ada della Torre, who had been working for a publisher but, having been tracked down and uncovered as a Jew, had been forced into compulsory labour sewing canvas covers for water bottles for Italian troops in Africa. Vanda Maestra had come to join them, and Anna Maria Levi was not far away.

In the evenings, Ada della Torre's large flat became a meeting place for the group of friends, many of whose families were already in hiding in the mountains behind Turin and Milan. They were determinedly cheerful and talkative, but after reading aloud the stories and poetry they had written, they would quietly slip away into the night, to meet their contacts in the clandestine political world. They listened to the forbidden Radio London, and heard reports about what was happening to Jews across German-occupied Europe, but they only half believed them. However, after the fall of Stalingrad in February 1943, 'we understood', wrote Levi later, 'that the war was getting closer and that history was on the march once again. In just a few weeks, each one of us matured.' Their friendship, they agreed, was something that was 'divine', though it needed neither temples nor altars. It existed 'only in the hearts of men'.

After the 'khaki serpent' of German soldiers marched into Italy, 'brutally awakening' the group of young Jewish friends, they scattered. Levi, Anna Maria and their mother went to a rented flat in Saint-Vincent, a village in the mountains. Vanda and Luciana travelled up to Brusson in the Val d'Aosta, where Allied prisoners of war who had escaped from a camp at Vercellese were trying to reach the Swiss border, and where a regiment of disbanded Alpini, in borrowed clothes and with borrowed identity papers, were looking for ways to get home. Ada della Torre, whose flat had been destroyed in an air raid, went underground and joined the Partito d'Azione full-time, becoming a *staffetta* and carrying messages between Milan, Turin and Novara. 'Against a background of defeated and divided Italy,' wrote Levi, 'we descended into the ring to prove ourselves . . . We separated to pursue our destinies, each in a different valley.'

With the German occupation, any sense of safety that the Italian Jews might have possessed was quickly dispelled. Within days, two platoons from a German regiment stationed at Chivasso near Turin were dispatched to Lake Maggiore, where they began to search for Jews. Some they arrested at a hotel in Meina; others in Stresa. Fifty-four were taken. Soon, their bodies were seen surfacing in the lake, hands bound behind their backs and bullet holes in their necks. Some were children, drowned by oars keeping them below the water. Posters went up offering L5,000, roughly £2,000 in today's money, for information leading to the arrest of Italian Jews. In Turin, the *scuola ebraica*'s library was vandalised. On 16 September, a train left from Merano bearing Jews to the German camps in the east. Alongside the military, a dense network of police and spies, both German and Italian, began to identify and arrest civilians 'for reasons of security'. From this moment, no Jew in central or northern Italy was safe.

In Rora, the village above Torre Pellice, Frida had by now found places for twenty-five Jews from Turin. Together with Rora's small Waldensian community, she persuaded the Jewish refugees not to stay hidden indoors, but to join the other villagers, in the market and the central square, and wear the same rough country clothes. That way, she thought, they would not be spotted.

On 15 October Badoglio and the King had finally been persuaded by the insistent Allies to go further and actually declare war on Germany. Beyond increasing the anger and contempt the Germans already felt towards the Italians, this changed little. The British and the Americans were still stalled on the Gustav line. In November, General Alfred Jodl reported that the German army had captured 1.25 million weapons, 67,000 mules and horses, and enough military clothing for half a million men. Six hundred thousand Italian soldiers had been rounded up, along with over 34,000 British prisoners of war. In the north, German troops had installed themselves in garrisons along the strategic valleys and Alpine passes.

Some of their invincibility was, however, illusory: they were in fact short of men and fighting against a larger and better equipped army. This made them merciless towards the country they were occupying, marking their every step with a *scia di sangue*, a wake of blood and atrocities. These were carried out not only by the SS but by the Wehrmacht, especially by men who had been fighting on the Eastern Front. Villages were burnt, civilians press-ganged into building defences or deported as slave labour; when they tried to hide they were treated as spies and shot. Winter had come and the Italians were hungry, frightened, miserable and still subject to ferocious Allied air raids. A Piedmontese girl, just ten years old when the Germans occupied her village, would remember all her life being forced to watch the execution of a group of partisans, then seeing the bodies left swinging from lamp posts.

By this stage, the European territories occupied by the Germans were providing almost a quarter of its war economy and rather more in primary resources, a matter of growing importance as the Soviet army was advancing steadily from the east, and the Allied aerial bombing of Germany was intensifying day and night. Beyond its heavy contribution to the costs of occupation – feeding, housing and transporting the German troops – Italy's industry continued to be regarded as legitimate war booty. But the steady spoliation could not have worked without the active help of the Italian industrialists and the managers of the major state concerns.

Agostino Rocca, the Fascist head of the Ansaldo and Dalmine steelworks, became one of the main contacts for the Germans over armaments and war material. In September, observing the German destruction of rebellious Naples, he had realised that to prevent the same happening in the north, industrialists would have to collaborate, become, as he put it, 'apolitical' and do the Germans' bidding, which would serve to protect both the factories and the men and women who worked in them. At the same time, surreptitiously, he – and the workers – would lend a hand to the Resistance, with an eye to positioning themselves advantageously for the end of the war and the reconstruction of Italy.

It was not, however, easy to control the vast body of northern workers whose sense of solidarity had grown more pronounced during the Fascist years. High levels of absenteeism and strikes against food shortages, low wages and spiralling costs, which had started long before the armistice, continued. In mid November, FIAT was faced with insufficient raw materials and no liquidity. When they announced a delay in paying wages, 70,000 workers went on strike, demanding a 100 per cent increase in pay. Since what was at stake was the war economy, and since the Germans were desperate to reach an understanding with both bosses and workers, a 30 per cent pay increase was offered, along with more food and the distribution of five hundred kilos of salt, now totally absent from the shops.

But where FIAT led, others followed, and a spiral of demands and concessions ensued. At the end of November, a special representative of the SS, Paul Zimmermann, was dispatched from Germany to 'repress strikes'. The system of stick and carrot, threats, arrests and concessions, continued. Looting was made a capital offence and bosses were informed that unless they cooperated life would become harder for everyone. But the strikes did not stop. And in the factories – Lancia, Westinghouse, Raselli, Nebbiolo and FIAT itself – little groups of partisans were entrenching. Bianca, on her regular visits to the factories, found the mood of the women angrier and more defiant.

Mussolini's new Repubblica Sociale Italiana, meanwhile, was stumbling into life. On 15 November, the freshly reconstituted Fascist Party held its first congress in Verona. The Duce hoped to orient the RSI towards the left, blaming the collapse of the original party on profiteering 'plutocrats' and the treacherous monarchy. New Fascism was to be proletarian, Jacobin and pitiless. The 18-point programme agreed on by the *gerarchi* promised a Constituent Assembly of trade unionists, magistrates, scholars and soldiers, nominated rather than elected, who would become the custodians of the new revolution. The economy would be made collective and 'socialised'. There were to be death sentences for black marketeers. Religions other than Catholicism were to be respected, though Jews were to be regarded as enemies of the state. Workers were promised a greater say in management.

In the event, it was all talk. The Constitutent Assembly was never convened. But Verona was the site of a first ugly manifestation of rekindled Fascist *squadrismo*. After the Fascist Party secretary in nearby Ferrara was shot by partisans, eleven citizens, none of whom had anything to do with the killing, were hacked to death in the streets and their bodies left on display to act as a warning to others. The Germans did not become involved. Hearing of the massacre, the Committee of National Liberation in Rome declared that Mussolini had unleashed a 'civil war', a 'crazed, criminal and desperate attempt to avoid the end' that the Fascists surely deserved.

Salò was rapidly becoming a state in which the rule of law had little meaning. Ruling by carrot and stick, it was a place where double crossing, opportunism and greed became the order of the day. To prove that it was indeed a valid state, Mussolini needed a police force and an army, men so moved by the grandeur and power of the Fascist dream that they would serve selflessly right up to the moment of a 'beautiful death'. With most twenty- to forty-year-old Italian men prisoners in German camps or trapped in the Balkans, unreachable in the south or hiding out in the north, just finding men to serve was the first hurdle. Mussolini's call to arms had been answered by veteran blackshirts, adventurers, thugs, men on the make, baying for the blood of traitors, with a few intellectuals, such as the educational reformer Giovanni Gentile and the outrageous Futurist F. T. Marinelli to lend some kind of legitimacy.

A second draft produced derisory numbers, many young men getting hold of false documents they called Kesselrings that claimed they were working for the Germans and were therefore exempt. The Germans, for their part, refused to release anyone working on war production. Renato Ricci, the head of the new militia, was liked by the Germans and had links to Himmler, but even he struggled to gather an initial force of a few thousand men, and many of these were boys of fifteen and sixteen, with a single pair of shoes between three, and one machine gun for every fifty.

Graziani, the only Italian marshal to remain loyal to Mussolini, was hoping to recruit at least twenty-five divisions – half a million men – drawn from Italian soldiers now being held in German prisoner-of-war camps. With such an army, Mussolini told Hitler, any 'crisis' would definitely be over. After much haggling, with Hitler declaring the defeated soldiers – '*Badogliotruppen*' – to be totally unreliable, permission was reluctantly given for 12,000 men to be returned to Italy, to act as instructors for those recruited locally, making up just four divisions. Sauckel, working directly under Göring and in charge of controlling labour across occupied Europe, said he needed at least one and a half million men for his labour force.

Alongside the militia and Graziani's men was a third force, that of Renato Pavolini, a Florentine writer of poetry and comedies, former Minister for Popular Culture and a crony of Ciano's, a man of considerable vanity, who wore his black tunic zipped up to his neck under a fur coat, and kept a pistol prominently on his hip. Pavolini's plan was to set up a Fascist federal police force, completely independent of the Germans, housed in the local Fascist headquarters.

There was also a fourth body, a new volunteer force of Italian SS. These men were given basic training in Germany, then sent back to Italy, wearing kit looted by the Wehrmacht from the former Italian army, but they were not much trusted by the real German SS, who tried to school them in Nazi discipline and gave them antiquated weapons. A first battalion of these men was sent to Turin where they were met with 'icy indifference'. 'We see ourselves,' they declared defiantly in their newspaper *Onore* – Honour – as 'volunteers for death, determined to wash away with our own blood the shame of Italy's betrayal.'

Added to these rivalrous, disputatious bodies, each slyly competing for weapons and for the largely non-existent recruits, were the rather more successful private armies. Prince Valerio Julio Borghese had converted the sailors under his command into a land unit called Decima Mas. Young men flocked to his call. And in Milan, by now a magnet for disaffected former Fascists, there was the Legione Muti, raised by a veteran *squadrista* called Franco Colombo, who had been militant in Fascist trade unionism since the age of fifteen, then spent time in prison for murder. Muti was the name of a Fascist martyr who had swaggered around Rome in military uniform with a large pistol threatening mayhem until shot dead by a nervous policeman. Colombo's men regarded themselves as specialists in violence, with fist, revolver, bomb and dagger. Mussolini's Ministry of the Interior helpfully provided them with weapons.

Though Pavolini's police force lasted barely a month, and Ricci's militia soon turned into the Guardia Nazionale Repubblicana (GNR), recruiting *carabinieri* and young soldiers from the army in Africa, and Graziani's army took many months even to begin assembling, by late autumn the north of Italy was awash with vengeful, agitated men over whom no one, least of all Mussolini, had much control. Many looked like gangsters, with leather boots, shaven heads and grenades strapped to their belts. They had been 'vilely betrayed' and they wanted revenge. Since they could not fight the Germans, ostensibly their friends and protectors, and since the Allies were still far away in the south, they happily turned their attention to the enemies within, the anti-Fascists, the partisans, the strikers and the Jews and all who supported them. For these people, the German invaders were indeed deeply alarming, with their chilly alien efficiency; but there was something about the anarchical frenzied Italian Fascists – their countrymen – that was truly terrifying.

*

Winter came early to the Alpine valleys that year. Snow settled on the passes, then piled up in the mountain villages. The cold was bitter. Ada and Ettore continued to travel up and down between Turin and Meana, often with Bianca, who wanted to visit Alberto in his mountain hideout. While the weather remained clear, they cycled, two bicycles between the three of them, the women taking it in turns to ride on the handlebars. To pass the time, they played a game, dividing the people they knew into the '*simpatici*' and the '*antipatici*', and imagined parties at which they would again eat delicious food.

Giorgio Diena had asked Bianca to look after his manuscript on the future of the Partito d'Azione, which he believed should unite with all the parties of the left, expressing the needs of all Italians and of all classes. Bianca hid it under a stone in a wall near Susa, but she was nervous about checking up on it too often, in case she was spotted. The precariousness of her life made her moods swing between explosions of laughter and sudden tears. 'We grew accustomed,' she said later, 'to living in uncertainty.' Silvia, working hard as a *staffetta* and doctor for the partisans, said much the same in a grimmer way, putting it in verse:

'The water is cloudy tonight / black with blood that slips slowly away / blood that flows and does not coagulate / the bitter blood of tears . . . this is our night: / footsteps in the dark dense with blood / for us, tonight, the vigil is over.'

Ada had become a maternal figure for the young partisans, loving, concerned, coaxing them to tell their own stories. She was a natural teacher, and taught them to be critical of everything, to take nothing on trust, to be thirsty, always, for more knowledge. Life, she would say, had to be treated seriously, and they had political and moral duties they must not ignore. Freedom and liberty were precious. 'I don't have political ideas,' she said, 'only moral certainties.'

While she talked, Paolo studied the insignia of German soldiers and their uniforms and badges, and Ettore mended anything that needed attending to. When the hour for a transmission from Radio London came round, they all sat and listened. One day, Lisetta appeared and told them that she and Foa were engaged. Lisetta reminded Ada of a 'wicked little angel', full of youthful enthusiasm, and at first she was not sure that she quite believed her. But then Foa appeared and confirmed it. 'I felt,' Ada wrote in her diary, 'my eyes fill with tears and my heart with joy . . . I think that this affirmation of faith, of life, is a good omen for all of us . . . Yes, every now and then, there is something truly wonderful.' Sandro Delmastro also brought his fiancée, Esther, to see Ada. She had, Ada thought, a particularly sweet expression. Sandro – 'Ferro' in Levi's *The Periodic Table* – was setting up citizen squads of partisans in Turin. He teased Ada about possible acts of sabotage to be carried out with Paolo. Ada wrote in her diary: 'I ended up laughing too. If I cannot laugh at these matters, I will end up by going crazy.'

She was continuing her work arranging for Allied prisoners of war still at large to get to the safety of Switzerland and had joined forces with Professor Paolo Braccini, a lecturer in the Veterinary Institute at Turin University. She reflected on the way that the Resistance was drawing in the most unexpected collaborators, very ordinary men and women who were discovering in themselves strengths and qualities they had never known they possessed. Her telephone calls with Braccini, on a line they suspected to be bugged, were all about animals. 'Do you know, signora,' he said one day, 'I found another dog of the same breed as the one you had me see yesterday . . . It would be interesting if we met, all the more because mine has to leave quickly, for a warmer climate . . . By the way, did you see the horses I sent you?' 'Which ones, the ones from last week?' 'No, two other horses.' Braccini then brought round his 'dog'. This turned out to be Johnny, an Allied soldier, whose daredevil nature seemed to her to be dangerous for them all. She had come to appreciate the plodding, pedantic Major Dennis. The CLN had promised L100 for every Allied prisoner of war conveyed to safety: the smugglers were given chits, to be signed by the men once they reached the border, and then redeemed in Turin.

Ferruccio Parri also came to see Ada, and to meet Braccini. He was now commander of all the Partito d'Azione forces in northern Italy, and she found him as sweet-natured and overworked as ever. The entire general staff were reorganising in Turin and she suspected that the movement was entering a new and more structured phase, which part of her could not help regretting. For Bianco, this 'war cabinet' of Agosti, Parri, Galimberti and Diena contained all that was best of old Piedmont: fine soldiers and able administrators, complementing each other, discovering in themselves, as one man wrote, 'the moral strength to disobey, quickly, before the false lures of heroism ensnared you'. Bianco was turning into an impressive guerrilla leader, tough, self-disciplined and scrupulously honest. Giorgio Diena was putting together clandestine material, saying that it was an important political tool for a party which had no hinterland. Ada left the men talking, having decided that she preferred not to know too much, in case she was captured and tortured, and might compromise them all.

Capture, for all of them, had become a constant possibility. In early December, General Zimmermann launched a major offensive against the valleys. A regional command had been set up, with a special unit dedicated to finding the partisans. News came from the nearby Canavese that the occupiers had sent in three hundred men who, in two days, had caught and shot nineteen partisans, lining them up in a village square in front of the forcibly assembled population. A friend of Ada's in Turin was arrested and beaten up, but managed to escape, pulling the brim of his hat down over his badly bruised face. In Susa, German troops were now installed in the station hotel. In nearby Bussolino, four companies of White Russians, acting as German auxiliaries, had carried out a raid, burnt down a number of houses and, led by a spy, seized, tortured and then killed three partisans who had refused to divulge where they kept their weapons and stores. Several women had been raped.

In ones and twos, and sometimes in whole bands, partisans were dying. Most painful, Ada's close friend Sergio Diena had been wounded in a badly prepared raid on a Fascist barracks. His leg was amputated but he died two days later. The whole town turned out for his funeral, despite German and Fascist threats. Sergio was the first young partisan to die in the Val Pellice.

Another young Jew, a brilliant translator of Rilke called Giaime Pintor, had just trodden on a mine and been killed as he crossed the lines to join the partisans. The last letter he wrote, to his brother, became one of the Resistance's founding documents. Without the war, he said, he would never have been anything but a translator and a diplomat. Resistance for him was the only possible step now. 'Today Italians can once again unite behind the Risorgimento . . . If I should not return, do not be inconsolable. One of the few certainties that experience has taught me is that there are no irreplaceable individuals and no irreparable losses.'

On 8 December, Don Foglia decided to hold a religious meeting for the five hundred or so fighters gathered around the valleys of western Piedmont. It was to be a '*giuramento partigiano*', an oath of fealty to the Resistance. Snow lay on the ground, and the trees were bare. Don Foglia set up an altar in a clearing in the forest and the men, in every kind of uniform and dress, came up to swear and salute the Italian flag. 'We have to defend liberty,' he told them. 'That is the most important thing.' After the ceremony, the partisans were given gnocchi for lunch.

But Don Foglia, still smarting from his earlier failure at Exilles, had more bellicose plans. He, Paolo and some others had inspected the bridges on the railway line between Turin and Modane. A first attack, blowing up a bridge not far away, had taken the Germans just two weeks to repair. They decided that what they needed was somewhere more rugged, more inaccessible. They settled on the viaduct of Anodera, not far from Meana, where the water coursed down the riverbed in a rushing torrent and the single railway line curved as it entered the tunnel. Four mules and a horse were used to pull carts carrying 3,000 kilos of explosives, lifted from the depot of the Nobel factory. Where the track ran out, the explosives were loaded, in baskets weighing 35 to 40 kilos each, to be carried by the men walking single file along a narrow, icy path; when they swore, Don Foglia gently chided them.

On the night of 28 December, having cut the nearby telephone lines, the men spent three hours in total darkness chiselling out seven holes in the viaduct in which to pack the explosives. Most of them then retreated, leaving Don Foglia and a couple of other experts to set fuses and detonators along a 62-metre stretch. The resulting explosion was heard fifteen kilometres away. All traffic on the Turin–Modane route was halted for three months. Even the furious German command admitted that, as an act of sabotage, it had been a 'work of art'. But it left the valley vulnerable. Ten thousand men, Fascists as well as Germans, were sent in to prevent further such attacks. Warned that retribution would be pitiless, the partisan leaders decided that one group would go to the upper valley and hide there, while another would go down into Turin to join the urban guerrillas. Liaison between the various men would be put into the hands of *staffette*.

Ada, Ettore and Paolo spent New Year's Eve in Meana, sitting around the stove, with the snow deep outside. Paolo had just celebrated his eighteenth birthday, 'not very old', noted Ada, 'for what he must face'. He was bold, a great climber and full of energy, neither quite a boy nor yet a man, very conscious of the responsibility of his father's legacy. Ada thought back to a similar evening, nine years earlier, when Paolo was a little boy, asleep in his bed in a white woolly cap with a tassel. 'Now,' she wrote sadly, 'I cannot do anything more for him, or practically anything . . . I can only try not to stifle his initiative, and his vital force.' Sometimes, she felt a 'desperate nostalgia' for the innocent, long-dead past of her childhood.

From the late 1930s, right up until the armistice, the western Alps had been a place of refuge for Europe's Jews. The advance of the German troops after 8 September had driven some 3,700 of them, including a number of Turin's Jewish families, to cross into Switzerland. '*I sentieri del sale*' – the mountain routes used by smugglers to bring desperately needed salt into Italy, and to carry out butter, cheeses, rice and stockings – now saw Allied prisoners of war and Jewish families conveyed to safety. But as the weather grew colder, and snow came to the mountains, the journeys became more hazardous, not least because of the increasing greed of the smugglers, who suspected that the Jews carried money and so made extortionate demands, but then often turned them over to the border police even once they had paid. Switzerland, which had closed its borders to French Jews in July 1942, proved little more welcoming to Italian ones.

Though the Fascist newspapers in northern Italy had led a crusade against the 'cancerous scab' settled on healthy Italy by its small Jewish population, it was not until the Congress of Vienna in mid-November 1943 that the part of Italy ruled by Mussolini became an active collaborator in Hitler's Final Solution. In October, 1,022 Jews had been rounded up in Rome, despite the Jewish community having acceded to German demands to hand over fifty kilos of gold to the Gestapo. But this was a German operation. Loaded onto cattle trucks on the 18th, in Auschwitz on the 22nd, over eight hundred of them were by now dead.

At their conference in Verona, the RSI had agreed to provide Italian police to find Jews for deportation. Giovanni Preziosi, an eager anti-Semite, met Hitler, described to him Mussolini's inability to deal with Italy's Jews and had himself appointed the RSI's Inspector General for Race. With the support of Theodor Dannecker, sent by Eichmann from Berlin, Preziosi embarked on an enthusiastic hunt for Jews, his men taking the name of 'counsellors for the Jewish question'. For a while, the sick and those over seventy were spared; but not for long. Italian prisons became way stations to the Polish camps. In Milan, the self-styled militia men drove around in search of prey. It was said that while a Jewish man fetched L5,000, and a Jewish woman or child L2–3,000, a rabbi could net as much as L10,000 or more.

There was silence from the Vatican. As one German official wrote: 'As to the protest from the Pope over the arrest of the Jews, there is no word at all.' Individual priests, meanwhile, were putting in place rescue operations. In and around Rome there were already more than 4,000 Jews in hiding, many of them in convents, and some within the Vatican itself.

Before Mussolini's fall, Fossoli, just outside Carpi, had been an internment camp for Allied prisoners of war. Now, with Mussolini's undertaking to supply the Germans with Jews, it was turned into a holding camp for those the Fascists caught. It was not the only one. In Bolzano, Jews and gypsies were put into a former military warehouse. In Trieste, an industrial complex, the Risiera di San Sabba, was made into a *Polizeihaftlager*, a police detention camp. It had a crematorium, converted from an existing dryer for crops by Erwin Lambert, the SS officer who had helped set up Treblinka. The Risiera, which held Croatians, Slovenes, civilian hostages and partisans as well as Jews, had the only crematorium in Italy. Between 3,000 and 4,000 people would eventually be gassed, shot or beaten to death there.

For young Jewish men, the options had shrunk to almost nothing. They could hide, but Italy was awash with informers; or they could join the partisans. In the valleys above Turin, Giorgio Diena, Alberto Salmoni and Emanuele Artom were now only three out of dozens of young Jewish partisans. There would be no '*resistenza ebraica*' as a separate force, but many young Jews joined existing bands, most finding a congenial home within the Partito d'Azione.

As Foa said, they were drawn not so much on account of their faith as for the fact that the Partito d'Azione talked so clearly about the need to build a new Italy, the old one having lost its way.

Emanuele had been seconded as a political commissar by his Partito d'Azione band in the Val Pellice to one of the Communist groups, now known as the Garibaldini. Most of its members, young Waldensians and disbanded soldiers, were little educated and not greatly interested in politics. With his gentle city manners, Emanuele had trouble making himself heard. They called him, not unkindly, 'politruk' and listened with varying degrees of impatience to his lectures on the need for responsible citizens for a better, united Italy. Fascism, he told them, was not a brick dropped onto their heads, and they now needed to think for themselves. Both Frida and Bianca, who were making regular trips as *staffette* up to his band in the mountains, brought him books and letters from his family and Emanuele asked them to look after the diary he was keeping on scraps of paper. He had taken a *nom de guerre*, Eugenio Ansaldi, and had made friends with a partisan girl, who was not Jewish, and he worried about what effect this would have on his parents. After a successful raid by his band on an airfield, in which a number of enemy planes were destroyed and much material taken, he ate salami with his friends, and rejoiced in feeling no guilt. 'I now realise,' he told his companions, 'that I wasn't born to be a professor but a gangster.'

In his diary, Emanuele reflected on the partisan war and the nature of those now fighting in the mountains. The Communists, he noted, 'have faith and enthusiasm'; they were orderly, dedicated, admirable and seldom swore. But as true believers, willing to sacrifice themselves, they were also 'terrifying'. They made him think of the early Christians. The Partito d'Azione followers, like himself, were far more sceptical, but also more sympathetic. As for those who arrived in the mountains with no politics beyond a desire to survive the war, he found them shockingly lazy and deplored the way that they had allowed their brains to be addled by Fascist propaganda. He wrote irritably in his diary that they were 'grubby, crude, ignorant'.

One of Emanuele's duties as political commissar was to distribute money to the families of the partisans; another was to write reports on the daily activities of his band. He forced himself to take on physical chores that lay at the very edge of his strength so as to merge in better with his companions. For all his attempts to fit in, so averse was he to every form of violence that he refused to set traps for the mice which plagued his quarters. Towards the end of November, his father came up into the mountains to see him and they discussed a problem much on Emanuele's mind: what should be done with captured spies. Emilio told him that according to the Talmud, a tribunal which passed a death sentence once in every hundred years was considered very severe.

On 10 December, faced with the problem of a spy captured by the Garibaldini, Emanuele recorded in his diary that the best thing would be to remind the spy that the Germans killed the partisans they caught. They should then take him out to be shot, and at the very last minute pardon him. If he went back to the Fascists, well, little was lost. But there was a chance that the spy would take note of the fact that he had been spared, and perhaps deal more kindly with the partisans in the future. Emanuele himself had painfully established this man's guilt, feeling like a fisherman inexorably pulling in a net. When his band decided that the man had to die, he recorded with horror the captive's last minutes when he was refused permission to finish his cigarette and told that no message from him would be relayed to his wife. This was a man like himself, he kept thinking, with a family.

Every day now brought news of German and Fascist ambushes, and in the cold December air he could smell the smoke from burning houses. 'War proceeds very slowly and very heavily,' he wrote in his diary. 'Like a monstrous great snail, leaving behind it a trail of blood.'

Soon after the band of Jewish friends in Milan had moved up to the Val d'Aosta in search of a hiding place, the CLN in Turin sent someone to see if partisan bands could be organised in the area. With the Germans advancing up the valleys, Levi, Anna Maria and their mother Esther had retreated further up into the mountains, to the hamlet of Amay in the Colle di Joux. It was remote, surrounded by dense chestnut forests and meadows of dandelion. The Albergo Ristoro was reached along a mule track: more Alpine refuge than hotel, with owners who had never made any secret of their anti-Fascist views, it offered basic food, running water and immense views over the snowy mountains and the plains below. It felt deceptively safe.

Another mule track through the forest led to Brusson, where Luciana Nissim and Vanda Maestra had found shelter and were now knitting socks for the partisans. Vanda had tried to cross into Switzerland but she had been turned back at the border. Hearing that Levi had joined forces with a dozen young men affiliated to the Partito d'Azione, and increasingly conscious that Brusson was full of Fascists on the lookout for suspicious strangers, the two girls walked up to Amay. Anna Maria had meanwhile decided that the village was too unsafe for her mother, and had persuaded a reluctant Esther to move further away, under a false name. She herself had gone back to Turin, to work with Ada, preparing and distributing clandestine literature for the Partito d'Azione. Anna Maria, said her friends, was a 'motor boat', frenetically active and determined. When her bicycle was stolen, she went straight to the gates of a factory as the workers were leaving and stopped the first woman who emerged with a bicycle. 'In the name of Italy,' she told her, 'you must give me your bicycle. When the war is over, I will return it.' To make her point, she pretended that the visible bulge in her raincoat was a pistol.

Luciana Nissim and Vanda Maestra

Though this new band had a leader, Guido Bachi, slightly older than the others, it was, as Levi said, 'totally in the dark, without contacts, without military experience'. Forays into the surrounding valleys in search of weapons and provisions netted almost nothing and the group lived on handouts from generous local anti-Fascists. Levi had never fired a gun; Bachi, who possessed just six bullets, spared him one with which to practise. They were, said a friend later, 'playing at being partisans'. Vanda and Luciana were *staffette* for the young men, and went down to nearby Saint-Vincent, where they talked and danced with some German soldiers and returned to Amay with useful information for the CLN in Turin.

Not far away, there was a larger, less innocent, better equipped band – more bandits than partisans – with whom Levi's group was on fractious terms. Spies and informers milled around its fringes and the day came when Bachi and his men took the decision to execute two renegade boys who had been preying on the local peasants and throwing their weight around, thereby endangering them all. Like Emanuele, Levi found the prospect of killing extremely disturbing. He emerged from the experience 'destroyed, destitute, desiring that everything be finished and to be finished ourselves'.

There was a new prefect in Aosta, Cesare Augusto Carnazzi, and he was eager to prove his Fascist credentials with a quick raid on the troublesome marauders. On Monday 13 December, having marshalled together 297 men from various militias, along with a few Germans, he sent them in search of the larger band, which had recently made off with a considerable haul from a barracks in Ivrea. Fifty of his men were also detailed to climb stealthily up the path to Amay. They had dogs and were not anticipating any trouble, having been informed by a spy that Bachi's band was hopelessly ill-prepared and living in a hotel.

Just as it was getting light, Luciana looked out of her window to see men surrounding the inn. Before she could rouse the others, the door was broken down. Levi was slapped in the face and roughed up but in the confusion he was able to slip two revolvers into the ashes of the stove, hoping that the embers would not trigger an explosion. He, Luciana and Vanda were marched for two hours through the snow down to a barracks outside Aosta, Levi successfully managing to chew through his false identity papers and get rid of a diary containing incriminating addresses. The militia were in high spirits, singing war songs, shooting at rabbits with their machine guns and throwing grenades into the streams to catch trout. When the party crossed with Bachi, who had been absent from the inn, he pretended not to know them; but the militia arrested him just the same. The rest of the band, who had not been captured, followed them down the mountains, hiding behind the trees.

Bianca, hearing of the arrests, left Milan and returned to Turin where, with Anna Maria, she helped distribute Ada's Partito d'Azione flyers while desperately trying to get news of her friends. One day she was stopped and when her bag was found to contain a packet of partisan literature she was taken to a police station and interrogated. Bianca kept her head; she insisted that it had been given to her by a stranger in a bar and that she knew nothing of its contents. That night, given permission to use the toilet, she slipped out between the bars of the window and disappeared into the night. Then she made her way up the Val Germanasca to look for Alberto. Neither Germans nor Fascists were yet much aware of the roles being taken by young women in the Resistance. But the incident brought the danger closer to home for all of them.

A month later, Levi, Vanda and Luciana were moved to the camp at Fossoli. One of the guards in Aosta had proposed to Luciana that she sleep with him in return for her freedom. 'With a Fascist?' she told him. 'Never.' What was most telling about how little was still known in Italy about the killing of the Jews in the east was that they each separately decided that it was safer to admit to being Jews – which they thought would simply land them in custody – than to say that they were partisans, for which they knew they risked a military tribunal and possibly a sentence of death. For the moment, they were not particularly apprehensive. As Levi would write, many years later, in *The Drowned and the Saved*, no one knows how and when the soul will break.

7

A little woman

'I am a woman,' wrote Ada in one of Piedmont's clandestine partisan papers. 'An insignificant little woman, who has revolutionised her private life, a traditionally female one with the needle and the broom as her emblems, to transform herself . . . into a bandit. Partisans! I am not alone. With me, I am certain, there are thousands and thousands of women, who have my faith, my enthusiasm, my courage, my thirst to act. We too are organising. We too share your dream.' Ada was right. Across the whole of German occupied Italy there were indeed thousands of women who were moving steadily into the Resistance. What had started as a spontaneous movement to help the disbanded Italian soldiers had turned into something more purposeful, idealistic and politically aware. Later, the role played by Italian women during this time would be belittled as a *'resistenza passiva'*, as opposed to the *'resistenza armata'* waged by men. But the reality was that women performed all the same activities as the men and spent the twenty months of occupation and civil war in precisely the same danger. 'I hate neutrality in all its forms,' Ada would write later. 'I think you have to believe in something and then fight for it, not impersonally but with the greatest passion.' In 1943 many Italian women discovered that they too hated neutrality.

Drawn into the partisan world as they witnessed the desperate young soldiers trying to hide, or because they had seen their fathers and brothers come home covered in blood from Fascist beatings, or because they felt a need to win back a sense of freedom lost during twenty years of dictatorship, by the time the Germans and the Fascists had entrenched themselves in the northern cities and the mountain valleys, the women were already fighters.

Staffette discovering new skills

The speed with which it happened surprised even the women themselves. Almost all had started life in a generation moulded by Mussolini's misogynist views. Few had questioned his diktat that the function of a woman was to marry and produce children, preferably boys, for the *patria*. Overnight, twenty years of servitude simply vanished into thin air. In a groundswell that had no obvious leaders, a great number of women decided that '*patria*' had a totally new meaning: it meant not allegiance to a feeble king and a dictator, but a different kind of Italy, and to achieve it they would need first to rid the country not only of the occupiers but of the Fascists.

Few regarded themselves as heroines; rather, they saw themselves as neither better nor worse than the men, but complementary to them. And they were beginning to enjoy the subterfuge, the need to learn new skills quickly, to be wily and inventive. They discovered that they could barter salt for bread with farmers, and they went out into the fields that had already been harvested to dig for potatoes that had been overlooked, and they learned how to make liqueur out of apricot stones.

The word '*staffetta*' has many meanings in Italian. It is a clamp, a bar, a small bolt, a kind of engine. It is also a courier, a dispatch rider. In sport, it means a relay race. The very lack of precision perfectly mirrors the great spectrum of activities, and kinds of women, drawn into the Resistance. *Staffette* carried messages, transported weapons, nursed, acted as lookouts, became political commissars, arranged escape routes, stole explosives, and occasionally became commanders of bands. They strolled around the towns, writing down the numbers of German and Fascist soldiers. They collected the bodies of executed partisans and washed them, and noted the names of those thrown into unmarked graves by the Fascists so that they could later show their families, though some were too disfigured to identify. They learned to shoot, most preferring revolvers to machine guns, and those who chose not to were given little pipes and shown how to hold them in such a way that they looked like pistols. Up in the mountains, they were learning how to become mechanics and carpenters. Before long, most partisan units had as many as ten *staffette* attached to them.

Some, with their pigtails and white socks, were absurdly young. The writer Oriana Fallaci was fourteen when she started delivering messages for her father on her bicycle. Some were mothers, who took their babies along with them as cover. There were housewives, peasants, teachers, university professors, secretaries, Jews, Catholics and non-believers. That, said Ada, was the miracle of it all; they looked so ordinary, so unremarkable, yet they had 'spirits of fire'. And there were grandmothers, who looked after the young fighters and called what they were doing '*maternage*', being motherly. When, in 1949, Renata Viganò decided to fictionalise her own experiences in the Resistance, she chose as her heroine Agnese, a sturdy washerwoman in her fifties, a shapeless, 'fat, ill and almost old' woman with a hard voice and ugly muscular legs, whose husband had been killed by the Fascists. The young fighters called her an 'armoured car', but welcomed her as a mother figure who mended their clothes and made them eat properly. That, observed Agnese, repeating Ada's words, was the strength of the Resistance: you could be anybody. You were a fire without smoke or a flame. Only when the enemy got burnt did they realise it was you.

Oriana Fallaci

But the real revolution lay with the younger women. Traditional Catholic Italy had been happy to go along with Mussolini's segregation of the sexes. Girls were brought up to feel inferior. They did not talk to boys, walk home from school with them, or meet them unless closely chaperoned. 'We were,' wrote one, 'quite terrifyingly ignorant.' Bianca had never been out on her own at night until the war came. The freedoms that came so suddenly with a *staffetta*'s life were overwhelming. The girls found themselves alone, independent, entrusted with tasks that took them up into the mountains and into parts of their cities that they had never visited, to have discussions with strange men, then to spend nights sleeping in huts with them. Having been spotlessly clean and neat, they became grubby, wore the same chaotic array of clothes as the boys did, and ate whatever they could find because they were permanently hungry. Alberto gave Bianca slices of blood cake from his father's slaughterhouse; often she was so starving that she ate them raw.

Parents had trouble recognising their daughters as they stumbled home after days in the mountains, their clothes torn, their hair filthy. Even family relations changed, as mothers, long perceived by their daughters as timid and browbeaten, became resourceful and imaginative foragers and turned their houses into hiding places, their terraces into coops for rabbits and chickens, their attics into storerooms for weapons. Lisetta was busy printing and distributing underground newspapers and carrying weapons, and as she put it later, this entirely new way of living, nomadic and full of adventure, soon seemed perfectly normal. She knew a little German and had taken to dressing up as smartly as the poverty of the times allowed, asking German soldiers to carry her heavy bags full of pistols and hand grenades, confident that they would assume they contained her dirty washing or her shopping. Conformity had been grey, pallid, depressing. Freedom was an explosion of colour.

What all would remember was the walking, the sore feet, the chilblains, the exhaustion, struggling through mud and snow lugging huge baskets, often in unsuitable shoes. A few of the luckier ones had bicycles. Marisa Ombra, who became a *staffetta* with the Communist Garibaldini at the age of eighteen, later described eighty-kilometre walks, mainly by night because it was safer, carrying heavy knapsacks of provisions on her back, living on chestnuts, boiled with rice and cabbage. She was often covered in fleas and scabies. You needed, she would say, to be quick on your feet, inventive and cool-headed, 'running and thinking, running and thinking'. You needed to learn the lie of the land in incredible detail, for behind every wall and every tree could be an enemy. You needed to listen for the bark of a dog, for it meant someone was nearby, and that someone could be an enemy. Marisa was a country girl, who grew up in a world in which houses had no running water and lavatories were holes over a ditch, and where it was so cold that in winter windowsills were sealed with strips of ice and were defrosted in the spring with flaming branches.

With the freedom came new perceptions. Girls were encouraged to use their looks, to flirt, to ask Germans brazenly for lifts in their lorries in order to find out what they were doing and where they were going. They learned to disguise themselves, with wigs, scarves, spectacles, and they sewed deep pockets into their dresses in which to carry papers and weapons. They were instructed to approach roadblocks boldly, swinging their heavy bags full of weapons, and to say: 'You'll never guess what I've got in my bag!' confident that the German or Fascist soldier would answer: 'I bet you've been stealing potatoes!' and wave them through. They had been hungry and afraid for a long time. Now they felt themselves to be actresses and brave.

A young partisan meeting with the enemy

Recognition by the men and boys did not come at once. They too had grown up in a divided world and some were far from sure that they wanted their sisters and girlfriends, let alone their mothers, to share their rugged lives. In some bands, the *staffette* slept apart, or under the protection of the older men. Very quickly, a code of behaviour was imposed: partisan women were not to be molested, and anyone caught propositioning them would be severely punished. In a very few bands, strict segregation prevailed. In one Garibaldi brigade, a detachment of *staffette* was set up, most of them the sisters, wives and mothers of the men. 'They work continually,' noted a smug report circulated to other Garibaldi formations, 'almost as a chain,' ironing, sewing, mending, making trousers, shirts and underpants, from seven in the morning until noon, and from two to six in the evening, 'supervised by two elderly women and under the command of a Garibaldino who was a tailor in civilian life'. From seven to ten in the evening, they were free to go out, but forbidden to have any contact with civilians. A weekly medical visit was arranged, to prevent 'more or less contagious illnesses'. Just occasionally, some of the more old-fashioned men banned women altogether, saying that they did not want them 'underfoot'. But they seldom held out for long.

These were the exceptions. For the vast majority of the female partisans, it was a question of imposing recognition and expecting respect. A story did the rounds: when one partisan leader greeted the arrival of a young woman recruit with the words 'thank heavens you've arrived, look at this tear in my trousers', the girl handed him a needle and thread. The sister of one prominent partisan leader, who had successfully crossed behind German lines bearing a message from the Allies after two male couriers had been killed trying to deliver it, snapped at the partisan commander who greeted her patronisingly, 'I am not a *donnetta*' – a little woman – 'I am a *donna*.'

All partisan groups set much store on written communications. Early on, the Garibaldini drew up instructions for their *staffette*. You are indispensable, they told them, and we could not function without you, for how else will we send out messages? Tell no one what you are doing or where you are going, be punctual and prudent, be vigilant, and if you should be caught, you must be worthy of the trust we put in you. 'Keep quiet, whatever the cost . . . accept death rather than cause harm to the party by becoming a spy. Do not sully your name forever.'

As winter set in, Frida took increasing charge of collecting information and carrying messages for the Partito d'Azione in the Val Pellice. To make it safer for them all, she was not told the whereabouts of Roberto and Gustavo, her two brothers, now rising through the partisan ranks. Marisa, Giorgio Diena's sister, was doing much the same for the Garibaldini, covering many kilometres on her bicycle to attend meetings that took place in riverbeds, deserted farmhouses and clearings in the forest, at which *staffette* from the whole area would come together to receive orders. She moved house every night. Since there were no maps, she was frequently lost. For days on end she lived on vegetable soup, salad, and polenta soaked in warm milk, given to her by friendly farmers.

Hot baths were an unimaginable luxury. She washed at pumps, in the open, in front of everyone. Having felt oppressed all her childhood by the rules and regulations of middle-class Turin life, she felt deliriously free. She loved being a 'vagabond'.

One of the oldest Piedmontese *staffette* was tiny Emma Sacerdote, who was almost sixty and only 1 metre 50 tall. Emma, one of thirty Jewish women with the regional command of the Partito d'Azione, wore a flat hat like the one Garibaldi had worn and a skirt down to her ankles. Every fortnight she went up into the mountains to see her son Ugo. She had a warm sweet smile and steely authority. Though Ugo and his friends complained that she controlled them and behaved as if she were the inspector of a military unit at the front, they secretly enjoyed the sense of reality that she imparted, bringing them down to earth after the heady excitement of partisan actions.

One of the boldest was 21-year-old Matilde di Pietrantonio, who rose to be commander of a brigade in the hills above Cumiano. Matilde specialised in kidnapping prominent civilians and even German officers to use later as hostages in prisoner exchanges. Wearing a neat blue coat with a white collar, short socks and carrying a bag in which she had hidden a pistol, Matilde would position her men at a distance, home in on her target and begin a conversation, while the partisans stealthily closed in and bundled him away in a car. If caught with a weapon, as she well knew, she risked instant execution.

Though small and frail-looking, Pinella, wife of Bianco, was indomitable; Ada called her the 'most capable woman I have ever met'. Together with her cousin Alda, Pinella trudged up and down the mountains bearing toothpaste, flea powder and pencils for the partisans, all the little things she thought they lacked. Stopped one day by the Fascist police and taken into custody, she so fooled the commander with her light-hearted chatter that he let her go, only realising later that he had had in his hands a '*pezzo grosso*', a big cheese. Pinella and Bianco were devoted to each other and worried constantly about the danger the other was in.

Gigliola Spinelli, who later married Bianco's great friend Franco Venturi, joined the partisans in the Val Pellice. Gigliola too had a specialisation. She was a procurer of weapons, of which the partisan bands never had enough. Going into restaurants where

German officers were eating, she would drape her coat casually over the holsters they had hung from the coat hooks, remove the revolvers and slip them into her bag before strolling casually back out again. One day, a call went out for leather with which to make desperately needed winter shoes. Gigliola took a razor blade from her cupboard, entered a smart hotel in the centre of Turin, sat down in a large leather armchair and carefully cut out the seat from under her and bore it away.

Rosetta Solaro left a memoir of her time with the partisans. It had been the brutality of the Germans, their violence and destructiveness, that had freed her from any doubt as to what she should do. 'We felt tied to those who had fallen, to prisoners, to all the blood spilt by innocent people.' So eager was she to join the Resistance that she overlooked the fact that she was terrified of the dark. At night, returning alone through the dense chestnut forests from a mission, she fancied she saw 'in the silent penumbra, as if I were walking on the sea bed' ghosts and werewolves behind every tree. But all her life she would remember standing on a high ridge watching through her binoculars the lives of the people unfolding in the villages far below, and the particular smell of the remote peasant huts, a smell, she wrote, of emptiness, of freezing floors and a lingering odour of apples, cheese, fat, old clothes and cats. In the meadows, she came across small children, alone with their flocks. The leather of her shoes became as hard as bark in the constant rain and mud and her socks froze to her feet, until she felt herself to be 'part of the earth, the mountains, seasoned by the wind and the sun'.

It took some time for the Germans to realise that the laughing girls whose heavy bags they helped to carry and the bent old women to whom they gave their seats on trams were laden down not with vegetables and dirty washing but with guns. The freedom to move around Turin and the valleys unmolested had made the women bolder and drew others into the movement. But once the Germans understood that they were being duped, the mood turned sour. Partisan women, when arrested, were slapped about and taken to the Fascist headquarters in Via Asti, or to the German interrogation centre in the Hotel Nazionale, where they would be interrogated and, often, tortured. Many were raped. In Le Nuove prison, which had become a holding pen for partisans and Jews from the whole of Piedmont, there was a women's section, run by nuns. Its director was a remarkable woman called Suor Giuseppina de Muro.

From the moment that the Germans occupied Italy, the attitude of the Catholic Church towards the war was deeply ambivalent. On the one hand, the Vatican refused to recognise Mussolini's Salò republic; on the other, it refused to condemn it, or to welcome any form of resistance. The Pope urged the faithful to concentrate on prayer and good works. Catholic women were enjoined to spread 'calm, serenity, faith in God, in the army and its leaders', but just who all these leaders were was not entirely clear. The war itself was presented as divine justice and there was very little said about the Germans at all.

Turin, traditionally fiercely monarchist, considered Mussolini's loud condemnation of the King distasteful. Its senior clergy, under the prudent but humane Archbishop Maurilio Fossati, could not afford to totally reject the Salò republic; instead, it retreated into cool and eloquent silence. Fossati's message, at least on the surface, was clear: discipline and prayer, obedience and the law. 'We will never tire,' he told his parishioners, 'of resolutely condemning every form of hatred, vendetta, reprisal and violence, whatever form it takes and however justified it appears to be.' Behind the scenes, however, in churches and convents and sacristies, room was left for manoeuvre. Fossati instructed that food be given to those in hiding, and that any of his priests who chose to 'hide fugitives and not to turn in wanderers' were not to be censured. Don Foglia was not the only priest to throw in his lot with the partisans without criticism from his superiors, though most took a somewhat more cautious line. Outwardly, the Turin curia preached silence and discipline; but as the war progressed, the city's churches and their cellars became places of safety for many partisans. And in Le Nuove, Suor Giuseppina intended to push Church complicity to its very limits.

Until the 1860s, Turin had no prison. The vast red-brick structure that went up in 1862, looking like a forbidding medieval fortress and extending along several blocks of the Corso Vittorio Emanuele II, was designed to reflect Turin's position as capital of Italy. Modelled on Pentonville in London, it had two observation towers and a series of wings around an open central courtyard, five of them for men and one for women. In the basement were fifteen punishment cells. During the 1920s and 30s, hundreds of anti-Fascists had been locked up here, many of them en route to the penal colonies. Suor Giuseppina of the Figlie della Carità, the Daughters of Charity, arrived here as a 24-year-old in the mid 1920s, just as Mussolini's Special Tribunals were sending the first Piedmontese women to jail for defying his regime.

Suor Giuseppina was round, forceful and full of charm. Her deep-set eyes gleamed from beneath her white wimple. The second of nine children in an affluent Sardinian family with a wine, almond and pecorino cheese business, she had been drawn to an order that insisted on the dignity of women prisoners. From the first, the nuns shared their lives with the prisoners, sleeping and eating alongside them. Suor Giuseppina was an excellent organiser, brisk, friendly and tenacious, and in 1942 she was chosen by the Figlie della Carità to become the mother superior and director of Le Nuove's female section. It was at the height of the bombing raids on Turin, and after two prisoners died, she insisted on moving the others to the safety of the cellars. Under her rule, the prisoners thrived.

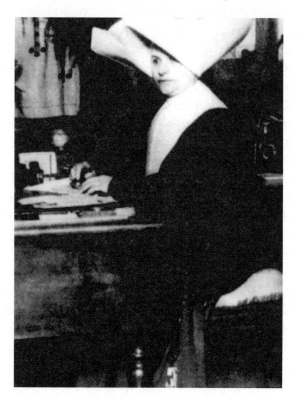

When the Germans commandeered part of Le Nuove, declaring it to be their private wing, to which all Italians were forbidden access, they announced that the Jewish and partisan women detainees would reside with them. Suor Giuseppina, with a mixture of guile and determination, dissuaded them. She convinced the commandant, an SS officer called Siegel, to let the women live in her own wing, returning there after interrogations, on the understanding that they would be kept separate from the criminal prisoners. She offered to do his laundry, then to have her nuns keep his office clean. Siegel was seduced. When his men demanded the keys to the cells of the prettier women, a furious Suor Giuseppina clipped the keys to her belt and defied them to come and get them.

Rumours about the horror of the German wing spread around Le Nuove. It took Suor Giuseppina a while, but the day came when she wormed her way past the guards. She found sick, injured, ravenous men – partisans, Jews and Allied prisoners of war – kept either in solitary confinement in humid cells into which no light penetrated, or crowded ten to a cell with room for only two or three to lie down at any one time. Misdemeanours were punished with the 'letto di ferro', an iron-and-canvas frame to which prisoners were tied in such a way that they could not move, with a hole cut in the canvas through which to urinate. The men were forbidden to leave their cells, to read, to attend Mass or to speak. Two friends, in adjoining cells, risked punishment by shouting out each day 'I want to die', so that the other would know that they were still alive. Suor Giuseppina and her nuns set about improving their lives.

Common criminals had food brought in by their families, but since this right was denied to the political detainees, many were slowly starving to death. Suor Giuseppina made contact with the partisan networks and the Catholic charities in Turin and arranged for secret deliveries of fruit. She told Siegel that it was for the pigs being reared in an inner courtyard, asking him whether a little of it could go to his prisoners. Siegel, who was not heartless, agreed. After this came eggs, tins of cream and broth, and letters, hidden under medicines and fruit. Suor Giuseppina used her deliveries to learn the names of those detained, so that she could tell the partisans in the city. When a leading partisan was brought in, badly wounded, she arranged for his X-rays to be swapped with those of a man who had just died of tuberculosis; the partisan was moved to a hospital, from which he was soon rescued. Nothing was ever written down. The Germans were watchful and suspicious, but could find no proof of wrongdoing.

The women's section held, at any one time, some 150 political prisoners, the Germans occasionally freeing one of them in order to follow her to see who her contacts were before rearresting her. As the months passed, and the round-ups of Piedmont's Jews intensified, so the cells filled up with Turin's long-established Jewish families, many of the women elderly and frail. There were also babies and small children, all destined for deportation to the camps in the east. Suor Giuseppina hated the idea of women being in prison at all, but she particularly resisted having small children there. Then the day came when two-year-old Massimo Foa arrived with his parents. His father disappeared into the German wing, but Massimo and his mother came under Suor Giuseppina's jurisdiction.

Once a week a washerwoman came to Le Nuove with a large wheelbarrow to collect the dirty laundry. One day Suor Giuseppina decided to help the laundress push her load back into the city, after which Massimo was seen no more. Other small Jewish children were passed off as her nieces and nephews and sent out into the care of Catholic families. Siegel decided not to notice.

Suor Giuseppina had other, sadder, tasks. She was forced to see her Jewish female prisoners depart on convoys bound for Auschwitz, providing them with as much food as she could muster for their journeys. And she arranged for the men facing execution in Le Nuove's grim internal courtyard to have a nun at their side for their final hours. She never let up. With every small victory, every small concession, she pushed for more. From the outside, Archbishop Fossati observed and took note.

One winter day, a partisan from the leadership in Turin came to ask Ada if she would take part in a new drive to recruit women. He told her that a movement was taking shape in Milan, with representatives from all of the main political parties in waiting, and he wanted her to promote the idea in Turin and the Piedmontese valleys. Its name, he told her, was Gruppi di difesa della donna e per l'assistenza ai combattenti della libertà – Groups for the protection of women and for assistance to fighters for freedom (GDD). Her first thought was to refuse. She had never been greatly interested in feminist issues, believing it a foregone conclusion that Italian women would finally get the vote once the war was won, and that men and women were essentially different but certainly equal. She also thought the name cumbersome and absurd, both too general and reductive: who was being defended? the women? or were they doing the defending?

But then he showed her their manifesto and she was intrigued. 'The barbarians steal and lay waste, ravage and kill,' it said. 'We cannot give in. We must fight for liberation.' More importantly, it laid down plans for a fairer, more equal future, in which Italian women not only voted, but had an actual say in their own working conditions, and in drafting a new constitution for a country that had been ground down and ruined by Fascism. It would be a battle 'not against men, but with them', to build a new society under 'the sign of liberty, love and progress'. Ada was still deliberating when a woman, a stranger, came to call on her. It turned out to be Ada della Torre, Levi's friend. Ada della Torre was calling herself Ariane, and she struck Ada Gobetti as having a very particular expression, at once witty and bashful. She still had no news of Levi, Vanda and Luciana, beyond the fact that they had been moved from Aosta to the camp at Fossoli where, the Italians still being in charge, they were being treated relatively well.

The two Adas became friends, wrote a pamphlet together and set about forming a separate committee in Turin. As in Milan, they took as their symbol the yellow mimosa, adopted in Germany for International Women's Day in 1910. Other friends joined them. One of the volunteers was Pinella Bianco, with 'two bright eyes perennially open wide', as Ada described her; when her face 'hardened and became decisive' and obstinate, she reminded Ada of Bette Davis. Then a rich acquaintance, Maria Daviso di Charvensod, offered them her seventeenth-century villa at Borello on the outskirts of Turin, where they could meet and hide weapons. As they talked, the full extent of the backwardness of Italian women, the years of misogyny and discrimination, began to seem to Ada issues that would in fact not go away on their own. What joining the Resistance could offer was a chance for women to act for themselves, to learn and to set forth their grievances. She proposed inviting women to knit socks and make clothes for the young men in the mountains: knitting today, she thought, would make it easier to confront bigger tasks tomorrow. The fight for the liberation of Italy would be a fight for the liberation of women.

Turin was the perfect recruiting ground. Italy was still a country of tight-knit communities and nowhere more so than in the neighbourhoods surrounding the factories, where eight-storey apartment buildings were clustered around open central court-yards, ideal places to meet and talk, and where almost every adult worked in one factory or another. At dawn, alarm clocks could be heard going off all at the same time, from one block to the next.

The women had already endured four years of air raids, food shortages, hunger, the absence of their men and a constant, daily, nagging battle to keep their children safe and fed. But their sense of injustice went back much further, to the time when, as girls of eleven and twelve – or younger if their parents had good contacts – they had been in charge of feeding thread to weavers six days a week, or getting up at four in the morning to light the boilers, or having their hands plunged in water dyeing fabrics for eleven hours a day, readily punished if they were too slow. They had been known as '*le piccole*', the little ones, and many had arms permanently stained with dye, or deformed bones, or respiratory diseases, as proof of their years of labour. These were the women who had seen fathers and brothers hauled away by Mussolini's *squadristi*, returning unrecognisable and covered in blood, and who had marched in the successful factory strikes in March 1943 and seen that determination and unity could produce results. The need to beg, barter and scavenge had made them resourceful. Now, they were angry, and afraid, for their sons. To harness these emotions to the Resistance, thought Ada, would be a first step; education, learning would surely follow.

Bianca, Frida and Silvia were ideal recruiters. They were young, energetic and desperate to be distracted from the terror of what might be happening to the men they loved. Determined to play her part and understanding that she needed to be free to do it, Silvia had placed three-year-old Vittorio with a wicker-maker's family in Torre Pellice. It was a measure of her commitment – as it was for many young women – that faced with the choice of looking after her child or joining the fight, she did not hesitate. She struck her friends as being fearless to the point of absurdity, but also, perhaps for the first time in her life, happy; it was, they said, as if something 'had blossomed in her'. As a recently qualified doctor, she was providing medical help to the bands, but she was also carrying messages, calling on families of absent men and standing outside factory gates to intercept the women as they came off their shifts. She could not forget seeing an older woman, an unskilled cleaner, whose job it was to wash down the toilets, arrested and then loaded onto a lorry, with dozens of others, for her part in a strike. This woman had stood silently for a while, upright and stiff, with an old grey scarf wound around her neck. Then, suddenly, she had begun to laugh, a clear, youthful, almost girlish laugh, and she called out to her companions 'Let's show these pigs we're not afraid!' and then she began to sing, songs of the Resistance, until knocked over by a blow with the butt of a rifle. As she fell silent, the other women took up her song, and it could be heard long after the lorry disappeared from sight.

Silvia was shrewd and tireless and she had discovered ways of getting advance news of impending German and Fascist round-ups, which gave her time to reach families and warn them. In her talks with Ada, she said that she wanted to include material about working conditions for women in the pamphlets put out by the GDD. Frida, meanwhile, had come up with a scheme for holding meetings. Since large gatherings were banned, she turned them into fake weddings, arriving herself as the bride in a wedding dress. She was a great talker and full of passion. Bianca was liaising with the Communist women, keeping notes in her diary in the shape of Greek letters, shorthand symbols and squiggles of her own invention. At a meeting with Silvia and Ada one day, up in the Val Germanasca, she held forth on the subject of equality, and what the new fairer Italy would look like. Was this shared 'spirit of the resistance', wondered Ada in her diary, something for which you really 'could sacrifice your mortal life'?

It was not only in Turin's vast factories that the GDD attracted a following. To her job of gathering information for the Garibaldi bands, Marisa Diena had now added that of recruiting the women in Piedmont's remote mountain villages. Her brothers were fighting in the mountains, doubly at risk, as she was, by virtue of being both partisans and Jews. Their parents were living under false identities in Turin. Arriving one morning in the small village of Bibiana, Marisa saw a group of women talking agitatedly. It was nine o'clock, and they would normally have been at work in the fields. She learned that, during the night, a lorry carrying partisan fighters had passed through the village on its way up the mountains, but that it had failed to return. They now feared that the young men had been captured. Though it turned out they were safe, the episode made Marisa realise the extent to which these mountain women were already involved with the Resistance, and when she went from house to house to talk about the GDD and the war, she found ready listeners and eager recruits. Having been isolated in the high valleys, their horizons had been opened by the refugees from Turin and now they were full of curiosity. They kept asking questions, 'the meaning of which they themselves did not yet understand'.

By early 1944, the GDD were growing at an extraordinary rate. There were twenty-four groups in Milan and as many in Turin, with new ones opening throughout Tuscany and the Veneto. In the Turin factories, cells of five to six women, usually friends, were coming together to sew, to distribute clandestine literature, to discuss strikes and plan small acts of sabotage, such as introducing imperceptible faults into the pieces of equipment they were making. They used the privacy of the women's toilets to transmit what they called 'radio FIAT', and they took first-aid courses from friendly doctors so that they would be able to treat wounds. When they heard that the Germans were going to collect a consignment of finished goods, they alerted the partisans, so that the lorries could be ambushed, and they changed the road signs to confuse the drivers.

On 8 March, International Women's Day, they celebrated with sprays of mimosa. Frida, Bianca and Silvia sped from factory to factory, on foot and on their bicycles, bringing leaflets in baskets under salad and celery sticks. They conducted their meetings walking along, as the women set out for home at the end of their working day, explaining the tasks that needed doing and the importance of being organised, or on Sunday mornings, when the men could look after the children. The women told themselves that it was a '*discorso per il futuro*', and they called themselves '*battagliere*'.

For all of them in Turin, Ada's house in Via Fabro had become somewhere to pick up news, receive orders, rest and have something to eat. One day, Ada recorded that, between dawn and dusk, fifty-four people had passed through. From her lookout in the hallway, the concierge Espedita kept a beady eye on the street and the surrounding square. Over and above the presence of a canary, she and Ada had devised a series of signals: a finger pulled slowly under the nose meant immediate danger, a white cloth hung from the balcony that the house was under surveillance. Ada came and went, dressed in a mothy fur coat several sizes too large for her, with a scarf wound round her face, trying to look like an arthritic old woman bringing her washing in.

They all knew what they risked. Cesarina Carletti was the daughter of an anarchist electrician who had been kicked to death by the Fascists in the 1930s, his body thrown out of a car like a sack. A striking-looking woman, with slanting eyes, high cheekbones and a full mouth, her hair pulled tightly into a bun, she had already spent long spells in jail for writing angry letters to Mussolini about his betrayal of socialism. The armistice and the arrival of the Germans had turned her into an immediate volunteer for the Resistance, bearing messages up into the mountains, a pistol hidden in the sleeve of her coat. At night, she painted anti-Fascist slogans onto the walls.

Just as the GDD were taking shape, Cesarina was caught and held in a barracks in the city, from which she escaped, only to be wounded and captured again in a Fascist round-up. This time she was taken to Via Asti and then to Le Nuove and tortured. She refused to give names; her teeth were knocked out. Sometimes, when the screams from tortured prisoners were very loud, Suor Giuseppina played Schubert's 'Ave Maria' on an ancient creaky piano in the central hall to drown out the sounds. One day, Cesarina was handed over to the SS in the Albergo Nazionale. Here the torture took the form of making her sit with her back against the wall, and firing bullets all around her, while asking her for the real names of the partisans she served with. She said nothing. When she was returned to Le Nuove and to Suor Giuseppina, she fainted.

There was another entirely different group of Italian women active across the north, with dreams and convictions of quite another kind. These were Mussolini's Fascist supporters, and their contempt for the girls who joined the Resistance was ferocious. 'Only little creatures, without personality or character,' wrote the actress and journalist Fulvia Giuliani, 'not <u>women</u>, but spoilt and hungry little animals, that every society carries within itself as the germs of a disgusting illness.' Giuliani was an ardent supporter of the Fascists, one of the many society women who rallied, during the 1920s and 30s, to Mussolini's call for '*la vera donna Italiana*', the true Italian woman, young, patriotic, brave and '*essentialmente madre*', willing to sacrifice herself for the grandeur of ancient Rome.

But as war took men from factories and agriculture, so the ideal Fascist woman became one who could combine motherhood with making herself useful; and after the arrival of the Germans, she needed also to be a '*donna soldato*', able to lay aside her mission as mother in order to save Fascism from civil war and the threat of partisan victory. She was to be imbued with 'moral energy, pride in the *patria*, disregard for all danger' and to be strong enough to combine love of country with the safeguarding of family values. Though taught to handle firearms she was not, at least at first, expected to fire them; with or without a pistol in her hand, however, she was never, ever, to lose her femininity. She would be a little mother, vigilant and attentive, looking after her sons. Or she would be a little wife who 'will have a good hot soup waiting for him when her man comes back from battle'. '*La donna soldato*' became another aspect of Italy's civil war, Italian women fighting Italian women, women soldiers versus women partisans.

Mussolini's new soldiers had another job. He needed them to stem the tide of deserters disappearing in their hundreds into the mountains to escape his drafts. At the Verona Congress in November, the new Fascist party had called on women 'in this hour of torment' to cosset and steer their men, not, heaven forbid, by entering politics, but by showing them their duty, leading them out from the 'mist of uncertainties and perplexity' into which they had strayed.

To call these errant men to their senses, to restore their pride and dignity, *La Stampa* newspaper floated the idea of forming a battalion of women, auxiliaries to the armed forces, to help with propaganda, nursing, office work and supplies. The suggestion brought immediate results. Women from all over Italy, professing adoration for the Duce, pressed to join up. They wanted, they said, just like the partisan women, to have parity with men, but in their case it was another kind of parity, not one of rights and equal pay, but of courage and self-sacrifice. They, too, wanted to die for the *patria*. Soon, every female student at Venice University was reported to be offering her services.

Mussolini had always liked to see his Fasci Femminili filled with aristocrats. He asked a Tuscan countess, Piera Gatteschi Fondelli, to found a Servizio Ausiliario Femminile (SAF). Gatteschi had been a founder member of the FF in 1921 and had joined the march on Rome that had brought Mussolini to power in 1922. She was made a General – the only woman to become one – and announced that she would exclude from her ranks all 'adventuresses and fanatics', and that only Ayran Italians between the ages of eighteen and forty could apply. A headquarters opened on Lake Como. By late spring of 1944, there were 6,000 women on the books, many of them graduates from Orvieto's sports academy where young girls had swum, danced, sung, acted and learned to fence to acquire *'bellezza superiore'*.

As the general saw it, her auxiliaries were to be an elite, above reproach, ruled by her as if in an enclosed religious order. Their uniforms were severe: a dark skirt that fell to four centimetres below the knee, a white shirt with its collar folded curiously at an angle round the neck, thick khaki stockings, heavy shoes, gloves and a beret with a red flash. There was to be no make-up and no smoking, and they were to address their superiors at all times with the polite Fascist *'Voi'*. The first volunteers included a well-known popular singer. Whether secretary, laundress or liaison officer, however, the auxiliaries were to keep in mind the need to be 'virile', never forgetting for a moment that they were serving an ideal far greater than simply that of being a woman. Such was the adulation for Mussolini, even at this late stage in the war, that very young girls took to lying about their ages to serve him. A first group was dispatched to the Lido in Venice to begin training.

Not to be outdone, Prince Borghese began to recruit auxiliaries for his Decima Mas militia and though he too tried to screen out the 'overly sentimental and emotional', many zealous young women found places there. They were instructed to 'eschew all luxury and parasitical snobbery', and forbidden to wear trousers, except when jumping onto a motorcycle or into an armoured car, because trousers were 'amoral' and offensive to male sensitivities.

For a while at least no one intended that Salò's female auxiliaries should actually fight. It was enough that they were a counterpoint to the 'emancipated, sly and treacherous' young women who joined the partisans and who, for their part, had taken to calling their Fascist sisters *puttane*, whores. There was never any suggestion that once the war was over they would not immediately go back to being 'exemplary wives and mothers'. Political views and aspirations were deemed 'useless, if not actually harmful'.

It was as cheerleaders that the auxiliaries now took up their posts, waving off the male colleagues from the barracks, comforting those that returned bloodied and dishevelled, honouring the bodies of those who had sacrificed their lives. Everywhere they went, they sang hymns to Mussolini and to the Fascist dream: 'Death does not frighten us,' they chanted, 'We woo it as fiancées and lovers.' On the walls of their dormitories in the barracks they pinned up photographs of Mussolini. Some brought small stuffed animals to keep on their beds. Describing the fever of exaltation that gripped her as she enrolled, the sense of needing to redeem the honour of a 'betrayed' Italy, a young woman called Zelmira Marazio later wrote: 'We were young, persecuted and happy.'

Part Two

A YEAR OF FIRE

8

Heedless

In the middle of January 1944, the Allied forces reached the sixth-century Benedictine monastery at Monte Cassino; and here they stopped. Kesselring's defensive Gustav line was proving stronger than expected and the advance on Rome continued to stall. In an attempt to break the deadlock, on 22 January, an extra 36,000 Allied soldiers landed further up the coast between Anzio and Nettuno. The Germans were caught unprepared, but while the Allied command delayed in advancing from the beachhead, Kesselring hastily brought up German units. What was to have been a 'lightning thrust' turned into a protracted battle against strong German forces trying to push the Allies back into the sea. The weather was terrible and the Allies were no closer to Rome. 'I expected to see a wild cat roaring into the mountains,' Churchill said to General Alexander. 'And what do I find? A whale wallowing on the beaches.'

All through the autumn disagreements had raged, between the Badoglio government in the south and the Allies, between the Americans and the British, as well as between the members of the six-party CLN coalition in Rome, over the future government and the fate of the monarchy. Benedetto Croce, regarded generally as part of a conservative wing, spoke of the twenty-year Fascist dictatorship as a 'parenthesis' in the long history of Italy, an accident that would leave no trace on the country's national identity. Others disagreed, rejecting any suggestion of a return to the Liberal politics of pre-Fascist Italy. What needed to emerge now, they insisted, was a totally new kind of government, fairer and more equal, much along the lines favoured by Ada and her friends in the north. Having at first thought that the monarchy might be retained, Croce now argued that, on the contrary, Italy needed to be freed from this 'supremely guilty King'. Some agreed; others fought against it. However, by 1944 an acceptable solution seemed to be in reach. The King would abdicate and hand over to his son, Prince Umberto, as Lieutenant General of the Realm. The King refused. The quarrels continued.

A proposed congress of anti-Fascist leaders was cancelled, on Allied orders, then reinstated. Finally, on 28 January, hemmed in by restrictions and in total secrecy, twenty representatives from the CLN parties in Rome – still in German hands – crossed the enemy lines to attend a meeting in Bari. It was the first official democratic assembly to meet anywhere in Europe since the Germans had overrun the continent, and the first to take place in Italy for twenty years. The heated debates continued.

The Allies were still vacillating, unsure how to treat the Italians as both foes and friends, and in any case they had other more pressing concerns. The Russians were making steady gains in the east, preparations for a seaborne invasion of occupied France were progressing, and the war in Italy was sinking down their list of priorities. Though both the British and Americans saw the Badoglio government as essentially hopeless, 'ill-conceived, ill-staffed and ill-equipped for purpose', the British wanted all decisions about the future of Italy to wait until after the liberation of Rome, while the Americans thought that it was up to the Italians to choose and in any case preferred the idea of supporting the six-party CLN politicians in Rome. As Churchill told Macmillan, Badoglio was at least 'tame . . . well-meaning, honest and very friendly' and probably the best bet until someone more inspiring were found to replace the 'ambitious windbags now agitating behind our front'.

On one thing, however, the British and Americans did agree: that with the Italian economy in the liberated areas in the south still in chaos, with high inflation, hoarding farmers, hungry people and rampant crime, the eventual reconstruction of Italy would have to start from scratch; and that until Italy was totally liberated, the Allies needed to remain in charge. Such was the chaos in liberated Naples, as Norman Lewis recorded in his diary, that 65 per cent of the income of the Neapolitans came from dealing in stolen Allied supplies, and that one in three women, their families destitute, had, regularly or occasionally, worked as prostitutes.

After more days of wrangling in Bari the King was once again invited to abdicate. Once again, he did nothing. The six parties of the CLN discussed, protested, disagreed. Little was achieved beyond getting fractious northerners and southerners to begin talking to each other. Just what shape the new Italy would take was going to have to wait, at least until Rome was liberated.

On 9 November 1943 Goebbels had written in his diary that he did not believe Mussolini would dare to kill Galeazzo Ciano, his own son-in-law. Considerable pressure was put on Mussolini to bring to trial the conspirators who had brought him down in the July plot, with Hitler insisting on death sentences but demanding that the Italians, rather than the Germans, see them through. Of the thirteen men who had voted against him, seven had already found ways of escaping abroad or gone into hiding.

Ciano declared himself surprised to find himself included among the guilty conspirators, maintaining that he had never been disloyal either to the state or to the monarchy, but had been simply opposed to Mussolini's continuing rule, not in itself a treasonable act. Believing himself to be safe, he returned voluntarily to Italy from Germany, where he had been a virtual prisoner for some months. When he landed at Verona he was arrested, taken first to a cloister at Scalzi, then to prison. What Mussolini thought about encountering the son-in-law who had betrayed him no one knew. They met just once, a short, uncomfortable interview in which Mussolini looked at Ciano with cold dislike. Edda, who shared her father's hypnotic intensity and many of the same mannerisms, came to beg him for her husband's life. Mussolini told her that he could never forgive Ciano, for the sake of Italy. Rachele added that Ciano was a second Brutus and deserved to die.

The trial of the six men opened on Saturday 8 January 1944 in the hall of the Castelvecchio in Verona. It was snowing hard. The members of the tribunal, in their black Fascist uniforms, had the night before each received an anonymous gift of a miniature coffin, a warning that they would do well to show no mercy. In the dock, the 78-year-old Marshal de Bono was in full military uniform, with medals. Giovanni Marinelli, long-time treasurer of the Fascist Party, pleaded innocence on account of his extreme deafness, which meant, he said, that he had never heard the Grand Council's deliberations. Throughout the trial, Ciano was addressed as 'conte'. All denied there had been a plot to overthrow Mussolini in order to sue for peace with the Allies behind his back.

The first day ended with the prosecuting counsel unable to prove even a hint of a conspiracy. But next morning, they produced a document, apparently written by the former chief of staff, General Ugo Cavallero, who had mysteriously been found dead on a garden bench some months earlier. The paper laid out, in great detail, a number of plots against Mussolini going back to November 1942. Though there was some doubt as to its authenticity, it was enough to condemn to death the men in the dock. Only Tullio Cianetti, former Minister of Corporations, who had prudently written a grovelling apology to Mussolini, was absolved. On hearing the verdict, Marinelli fainted.

Edda possessed secret documents of her own. These were Ciano's diaries, thought to contain potentially damaging descriptions of Italian–German relations, which she now hoped to use as barter in exchange for her husband's life. She beseeched, stormed, and wrote letters to Mussolini and Hitler. When it was clear that Ciano's life would not be spared, Edda took her children and fled to Switzerland, the diaries hidden under her skirt. She never saw or spoke to her father again.

As traitors, the conspirators were denied the right to be shot facing their executioners. Five school chairs were placed by a wall at Forte Procolo outside Verona. The militia squad was nervous and untrained, and the executions were a grisly affair. One of the condemned men became hysterical and had to be tied down. At the last moment, Ciano managed to turn round, so that he faced the rifles, and shouted '*Viva l'Italia!*', but he did not die until an officer put a bullet through his head.

Most of the Mussolini clan was now gathered in the Villa Feltrinelli, with Vittorio, the eldest son, proving an incompetent and high-handed secretary, much disliked by everyone. Mussolini's daughters-in-law bickered, his grandchildren ran wild. With Claretta just up the road in Gabriele d'Annunzio's theatrical Villa Fiordaliso, a mansion full of mirrors, coloured glass and

Doric columns topped with sculptures in the shape of bowls of fruit and pumpkins, Rachele fumed. One day she paid Claretta a visit and called her a whore. Mussolini, gloomy, ailing, was even further estranged from the daily political struggles of his new state, but he remained obsessed with the refusal of the Vatican to recognise his government. He talked of putting in place a new authoritarian socialism, and occasionally roused himself to rail against his German allies, calling them 'barbaric vandals . . . violent and rapacious'.

Nothing Mussolini said carried weight any longer. He was never anything but subject to the Germans, who tolerated him as a useful figurehead in helping run and police Italy, maintaining order and exploiting resources. Under pressure, he wavered, retreated, compromised, thereby allowing the more violent men around him to operate unchecked. In the streets of the northern cities young men, '*i ragazzi di Salò*', strode around the streets singing '*Battaglioni del Duce, della morte e della vita, ricomincia la partita*'. (Battalions of the Duce, of death and life, now the game recommences.)

Salò was a mass of conflicting interests, of bullies and profiteers, of civil servants too lazy or too venal to challenge the rampant corruption, with just a few idealistic individuals who sincerely believed that the new state might yet salvage something of Fascism's former glory. With the Fascist government in control of 57 daily papers, 214 periodicals and several radio stations, repeating again and again the message that Germany and Italy were as one, only those brave enough to listen to Radio London had any true idea of what was going on. With the country still under its three governments – Salò in the north-east, Badoglio in Brindisi and the six-party underground coalition in Rome – and four fighting forces – Allies, Germans, Salò and the partisans – most of Italy was a battlefield. Its inhabitants lived in what was described as 'agnostic *attendismo*', waiting and seeing, or in Levi's grey zone, somewhere between the territory of good and the territory of evil.

In Milan, Renato Ricci was recruiting hard for his new Guardia Nazionale Repubblicana, drawing in a mixture of former *carabinieri* and misguided young Fascists, setting up regional inspectorates and provincial commands, with the job of countering the growing number of partisan attacks. By the end of January 1944, with considerable difficulty, he had nevertheless assembled over 100,000 men, but lost some to the Germans, who forced them onto trains bound for labour in Germany.

In Turin, where over 5,000 GNR men had been mustered, the new Fascist leaders were tough, violent men, veterans of the wars in Ethiopia and Spain and survivors of the horrors of the Eastern Front. Though the Germans insisted that they wanted 'normal' life to resume, the city was anything but normal. An attack on two local Fascist Party leaders led to the arrest and execution of three men, all married with children, deemed 'morally responsible'. Explosions, assassinations, arrests and reprisals were now daily events. The Fascists had turned their headquarters in Via Asti into an 'inferno' where torturers, dressed up in false wigs and beards in order not to be recognised, had commandeered the second floor for their nightly sessions.

Around them gathered spies and informers, who visited families of suspected partisans to loot their houses and blackmail them. Even the Germans admitted that the degree of 'depravation and corruption' by the Italian 'legal Fascist functionaries' was extremely high. Scattered in buildings all around the city, there were seven hundred German SS men. Every German and Fascist centre had become a fort. Every wall had become a display of competing messages, the partisans declaring 'Death to the German invader, death to the Fascist traitor', the Fascists presenting distorted images of 'Bolsheviks, Jews and negroes', putting them behind glass, to stop them from being torn down. It was a new kind of violence, in graphic form. In this cold and hungry winter, where a bar of soap had to last for two months, where women were driving trams and growing zucchini in their window boxes, the state of mind of the Torinesi, according to one of the Militärkommandantur's monthly reports to its superiors in Germany, had reached the depths of despair.

On the other hand, day by day, the partisan war was evolving, its numbers growing steeply, their acts of sabotage multiplying. Everyone needed men – the Germans to send home as labour, Salò for its militias and its army. Early in 1944, Mussolini – who had himself gone to prison as a young man for failing to turn up for military service – widened the age bracket of compulsory service to include both younger and older men. The response was muted. More than half of those eligible, 57 per cent, did not show up. On 18 February came a decree threatening the death penalty for those who continued to stay away and Special Tribunals worked overtime to reinforce the message. Families of young men were threatened with confiscation of their livestock and withdrawal of ration books, and fathers were taken hostage.

Before the war, Italy had well over two million boys enrolled in the after-school Balilla and Avanguardista Fascist organisations. Almost every boy in Italy had grown up preparing for war and military service and chanting, 'If, one day, a battle sets mountains and seas on fire, we will be the rifles of sainted Liberty.' The first virtue of the good young Fascist was 'Obedience. The second? Yet more obedience.' Who, now, were these young men to obey? If the legal government, which one? And who was the real enemy? The British and the Americans, at one and the same time old enemies and new allies? Or the Germans? As Emanuele Artom wrote in his diary, what made it so confusing was that it was 'in Italy's interest to be defeated'. Dragooned into barracks, many more young men, disgusted by the lack of uniforms and blankets, by the insufficient food and the brutishness of their recruiters, began to turn their backs on their Fascist childhoods and desert to the partisans. Groups of women descended on the recruiting centres, shouting and crying, come to liberate their sons.

The draft was proving an unrivalled recruiting agent for the Resistance. The northern partisan army drew in not only these young resisters, but also their parents, priests, friends, shopkeepers, bank tellers, even children. 'Deluded, disoriented', bitter young men were finding that they had the courage to disobey, particularly when they read the posters the partisans had plastered on the walls of every town and village: 'We are expecting you . . . We will greet you with the happiness of finding a lost brother.'

Ada, still working at her school in Turin, received a circular for teachers to declare whether they had sons born in the call-up years. Ada went to see the headmaster. 'I know I am speaking with a gentleman,' she started. Then she told him that she had just such a son and that he had not presented himself. The headmaster, 'an annoying stuffed shirt, full of his own authority', fiddled with his papers, but she saw that his hand was trembling. 'Where is he?' 'I do not know,' replied Ada, perfectly truthfully, for she had not seen him for some days. Then, said the headmaster with relief, we shall say that he was in the south when the Allies arrived and that you have lost touch with him. She left, appreciating his inventiveness. But over the next few days, her classes began to empty, the boys of draft age disappearing, one after the other. With Lisetta, she had written a flyer, explaining why young men should refuse to work for the Salò republic, and the two women, Lisetta with a scarf concealing her very identifiable blonde hair, and Ada in an old hat which covered much of her face, stood outside the gates of two of Turin's largest schools, handing them out, then hastening away before they could be caught.

A further event now brought more men and women into the Resistance. The factories of the northern triangle had been in a state of suppressed mutiny since the end of 1943 and with food becoming ever more expensive and severely rationed the mood was getting angrier. Fritz Sauckel, chief commissioner for manpower, rounded up the black marketeers, settled on fixed prices and issued threats but was unable, as one German report put it, 'to eliminate the black market altogether, given the mentality of the Latins'. All he could do was to make sure that people who agreed to work for the Germans were fed, while issuing menaces that the others 'will not eat'.

The CLN had been making solid gains among factory workers, and early in February 1944 it called for a general strike to demand better conditions for workers and a halt to deportations of manpower and machinery to Germany. On 1 March, 'all work for Hitler' ceased. It was the first such strike in occupied Europe and what were later estimated at well over a million people stopped work in factories, offices and shops. In Turin the strikers were backed up by the partisan bands in the mountains who descended into the plains to block trains and trams. Marisa Diena and another *staffetta* boarded the early train carrying workers down from the valleys to the city: their task was to identify Fascist spies so that other partisans could 'neutralise' them.

The Germans and Fascists had done surprisingly little to prepare. But on the second day, the arrests began. The workers continued to stay away. Hitler sent a message demanding that 20 per cent of the strikers be arrested and deported. Determined to make no concessions, the Germans rounded up troublemakers, their leaders identified for them by Fascist spies. By the time the strike was called off by the CLN four days later, some 1,100 people had been put on trains from Turin's Porta Nuova station, bound for the concentration camp of Mauthausen.

Even so, the strike had sent out a powerful message: that ordinary Italian men and women, whatever their politics, were prepared to risk a great deal to defy the occupiers, and that strike action could effectively paralyse German plans. The strikers felt proud. Salò and the Fascists became yet more unpopular. The Communist partisans, already emerging as the strongest force in the factories, grew stronger and began to recruit more seriously for further confrontations. As for the Germans, the strike convinced them of the need for a tougher hand. Salò was clearly incapable of policing its recalcitrant citizens: a regime of terror would be needed. The partisan war was about to become a great deal more brutal.

The first time Ada heard the word 'rastrellamento' – roundup – she was in Turin. Ettore rang to say: 'Aunt Ada is sick.' This was their code for danger. Until this moment, attacks by both Germans and Fascists had been little coordinated. But the rastrellamenti – blocking off roads in order to carry out house-to-house searches – were something new. This word would grow horribly familiar to them all.

Early one morning, a rastrellamento conducted by German and Italian police, fanning out and acting together, descended on Via Fabro. Two Italian policemen banged on Ada's door at seven. It was too late for anyone to hide. Paolo, just back from the mountains, ran a bath and got into it. Ada and Ettore took the policemen slowly round each room rather, as Ada noted later in her diary, as if they were showing prospective tenants a property. Ettore flung open the bathroom door, but the policemen merely glanced in, failing to detect Paolo in his bath. As the men left, they asked the concierge Espedita whether there was anything that they should have noticed. 'Certainly not,' she replied with an offended air. 'Only honest, peaceful people live here. But did you see anything suspicious?' No, they replied, 'but even if there was something we didn't see it'. They left, recommending that she tell any German who might come to ask that the house had been most thoroughly searched. Not all Italian police, it seemed, had been corrupted.

Ada, Ettore and Paolo were often up in Meana, where Paolo spent his days scouting for explosives in abandoned military bases, bringing back dynamite for Ettore to experiment with. To distract herself from the acute anxiety she felt every time Paolo disappeared, one evening Ada turned her old fur coat inside out, put on dirty trousers and a dark hat, and went down into Susa with a glass jam jar full of glue and a pile of leaflets urging young men to refuse the draft. These she plastered on every available surface, including the church, the local brothel and the hotel used by the Germans. Though she came home with the lining of her coat smeared in glue, she noted in her diary that she felt she had truly done a good job. 'If only all underground work were like this.'

Paolo had been hoping to establish a new band of partisans in the upper valley, but decided instead to cross over to the Val Germanasca to join forces with Roberto Malan, Frida's brother. Ada, ever reluctant to let him out of her sight, went with him. Roberto had set up his base in an abandoned talc-graphite plant in Gianna. The valley was peaceful, the Germans and partisans circling warily around each other. Frida was there meeting local teachers with a view to revising the Fascist textbooks for the schools. In the early-spring sun, the young partisans, tanned and fit, looked to Ada as if they were enjoying a holiday in a hotel. A *carabiniere* stationed in Torre Pellice had agreed to act as a lookout, sending up news almost daily of German and Fascist movements in the valley, while *staffette* walked the hills, bringing information from other valleys.

Roberto greeted his visitors courteously and suggested that Paolo join Emanuele Artom as political commissar. Emanuele was still keeping his daily diary, writing that he feared that the partisan forces remained dangerously weak, 'like water spilt on the sand', in comparison with the might of the Germans. He slept fitfully, worried endlessly and was often irritated by the quarrels of the bands he visited, the undisciplined boys 'racing towards their own ruin', resisting his attempts to teach them something of the history of their own country. 'I navigate between Scylla and Charybdis,' he wrote mournfully. 'On my right are the Badoglio officers, on my left the Communist officers . . . in the middle me,' with the 'grey, deaf' young soldiers beneath him and Roberto Malan 'squashing' him from above. He noted: 'I feel as if I am swimming blindly in a pond of dirty water.'

Another occasional visitor to the Val Germanasca was Willy Jervis, known to the others as the 'Alpine academic', busy carrying messages between Piedmont and the Allies based in Berne. Willy's mission to persuade the British and the Americans to drop supplies and weapons was at last beginning to pay off, though the Allies remained openly sceptical about the usefulness of the partisans in the liberation of Italy.

Weapons were still in painfully short supply, particularly revolvers, machine guns and grenades; at best the partisans had old hunting rifles, and some had no weapons at all. What many of the Allied officers had trouble understanding was that there were Italians willing to risk their lives for what was essentially the defeat of their own country. Since the invasion of the south, the whole of northern Italy lay within reach of Allied planes, but there were other calls on their resources, notably in the Balkans. Drops were rapidly becoming the crucial ingredient in all dealings between partisans and Allies, and it was an issue beset by disagreements, disappointments and recriminations. Willy spent many long cold nights at agreed sites, waiting for drops that never came. As Ferruccio Parri later drily noted: 'Neither the zeal nor the commitment of the Allies match the temperature of our anxieties.'

However, drops of another kind had started. In Brindisi, Raimondo Craveri had been working hard to gather together volunteers to parachute into the north, to coordinate the activities of the partisans and the Allies, to arrange drops of supplies and to train the partisans in sabotage and guerrilla warfare. By early 1944 he had recruited and trained thirty-seven men, eleven of them as radio operators. The Americans, through the OSS, had agreed to support the volunteers and provide each mission with $10,000. Early in March, Ada was asked by Agosti to verify the identity of a man from the south who had arrived with a message from Craveri, accompanied by a photograph of Craveri's small son, Piero. She looked at the picture, recognised the child, and was struck by how much he looked like his grandfather, Benedetto Croce. The messenger confirmed a first drop of three men, code name Orange Gobi, and soon after, an engineer, a radio operator and a team leader trained in explosives were parachuted onto a field near the border with France. They waited in a cave until a partisan band led them down to Torre Pellice.

Micki Cesan was a fourteen-year-old schoolgirl, from a large family who were friends of the Malans in the close-knit Waldensian community. The Cesans volunteered to help the three agents set up a radio transmitter in a beehive. Micki became their *staffetta*, carrying the coded messages that came through from Brindisi on her bicycle, stuffed into a secret opening in the handlebars, down to nearby Luserna, where an engineer working for a large industrial complex couriered them on to Turin.

When the message contained the words 'free and open', she knew that a drop was imminent, which meant that the fabric from the parachutes would be available for the village women to make into dresses, swathes of bright green, yellow or red material, wonderfully gaudy after so much greyness and rationing. Micki, like everyone else, was always hungry and the agents fed her with their rations of cheese. Micki told no one, not even her closest school friends, what she was doing. Only after the war ended did she discover that several of them had been doing the same thing. 'I didn't feel frightened at the time,' she says. 'I had grown up with guns. But later, thinking back on it, I was terrified.' She talks of the total disregard with which her family seemed to treat the surrounding danger, saying they were *'incoscienti'*, heedless; but also very lucky. None of them were ever caught.

As Emanuele noted in his diary, by the spring of 1944 a few bands, such as Roberto Malan's, were disciplined and effective, exploring ways to turn the whole area into a free zone. But the partisans generally were young, unpredictable and inexperienced, in their many different pieces of uniform and colours, the Communists sporting scarves, headbands and even shawls in red, with their fringes trailing down to the ground. Some wore berets covered in red stars, the tips falling over their faces, which made one officer think that they looked like squids, drooped over their heads. The young men had all taken *noms de guerre*, some opting for extreme weather conditions – Thunderbolt, Lightning, Tornado – others for classical heroes – Hercules, Gracchus – or for animals – Wolf, Leopard, Tiger. The women too took names, sometimes masculine ones, but more often those of goddesses.

Ada herself was reflecting that since she was now performing all the duties of a political commissar, she would like to have her role made official, 'to consolidate my authority'. She and Bianca had more meetings with friends in the women's GDD but were encountering resistance to their suggestions. Not everyone, they were discovering, shared their instinctive belief in a natural solidarity between women, and Ada herself was still struggling with ideas that even to her felt very new.

By now, there was almost no valley in Piedmont that had not been touched by the violence. Remote hamlets and villages that had seen no fighting since Napoleon's army swept down over the Alpine passes were losing sons and daughters to the partisans, while finding themselves in the middle of firefights, round-ups and reprisals. There were incessant demands on their diminishing supplies of food, and a constant fear of being taken hostage. The ebullient and excitable young partisans brought with them levity, drinking, dancing in the squares. The Germans and Fascists brought terror.

Despite the ferocious cold and thick snow which lasted well into April, there were repeated partisan attacks on militia barracks, police stations, electricity pylons and railway tracks, with bold stunts such as unhitching and diverting wagons from goods trains carrying weapons into Italy. Often with inside help, the bands were making daily forays to the lower valleys and the plains, to raid factories for food, shoes, blankets and warm clothes. They were not always successful, and there were casualties. Sometimes the intelligence was wrong, or the target was too heavily guarded, or the bands themselves made mistakes. But the raids were enough to attract counter-attacks, and for the Germans and the Fascists to estimate partisan numbers considerably higher than they actually were.

An early act of sabotage

The dynamiting priest, Don Foglia, was an early casualty. After a number of partisans in his flock were taken prisoner, he went down to Turin to see if he could negotiate their release. The Gestapo were waiting. They took him to their barracks and asked him to collaborate: he spat in their faces. He was moved to Le Nuove, where Suor Giuseppina managed to get him a blanket and some books. Cardinal Fossati sent Monsignor Garneri to try to broker a prisoner exchange, but Don Foglia would not hear of it, and nor would he sign a document saying that he would have nothing more to do with the partisans. One morning, when Suor Giuseppina brought him his food, his cell was empty.

The Germans were losing patience with the disruptive and increasingly effective partisans. In view of the rumours of an imminent Allied landing on a Mediterranean shore, and because of the strategic importance of the Alpine passes, General Wolff decided that the moment had come to concentrate his forces on crushing the northern Resistance. His plan was to annihilate them in carefully targeted assaults, lasting not hours but weeks, cutting off entire areas and blasting them, moving from one village to the next. The horror was about to get worse. Before the snows melted, a division of the Alpenjäger, not long back from the Eastern Front, bringing with them newly trained Italian SS, flooded the valleys, shooting the partisans they captured and forcing the villagers to watch the executions, setting fire to barns and farms and standing by while the Germans' White Russian auxiliaries looted and raped.

After a partisan band attacked a barracks of frontier guards in Bobbio, the Fascists, who had a radio, summoned help and 140 soldiers arrived from Pinerolo, in an armoured car and three lorries. Though vastly outnumbered and having between them only rifles and one machine gun, the partisans managed to kill twelve Fascists and wound many others. The battle lasted all afternoon. Believing there to be many reserves of partisans, the enemy withdrew, leaving behind prisoners and useful ammunition and mortars. But in Torre Pellice they took forty hostages, among them the Catholic priest, the Waldensian pastor and several professors from the college, announcing that they would be released only if their own men were freed. Malan negotiated a deal; the prisoners were exchanged. At the day's end, there was just one dead partisan, but several civilians had lost their lives in the battle.

In a separate attack, Fascist reprisals took the form of setting fire to seventy village houses, while the villagers sheltered in cellars. In Rozello, a partisan was trapped in his house and burnt to death. Nearby, four peasants working in their fields were accused of concealing weapons and executed. A parish priest went to see six boys who knew that they were about to be shot and wrote later that they 'shrieked like wild beasts, because they were dying so young'. At the edge of the village of Sangone, twenty-three captured partisans were ordered to dig ditches and then shot, after which earth was piled on their bodies. Not all died at once, and for several hours faint cries could be heard coming from the ground. The Germans hoped that this might lure other partisans, desperate to save their friends, into the open. In one of their daily reports, the Italian militia described how, after the Italians refused to carry out executions, a German lieutenant drank a bottle of cognac and shot fifty-four hostages himself, one by one.

While the mountain tops were still covered in snow, the Germans launched yet another blitz to dislodge the 'rebels'. This time they poured not just men and weapons through the valleys, but Tiger tanks and armoured cars supported by artillery, intending to remain until the area had been swept clean. The partisans fought back hard, blowing up roads, and then slipping away into the forest to avoid capture, but the Germans cut down trees, took hostages, set fire to houses and lined up captives against village walls, saying that they would shoot ten for every German killed. One victim was an 85-year-old grandmother. The villagers, who had at first so willingly sheltered and cared for the partisans, were growing anxious, particularly after the Germans called them all together and told them that henceforth they, the civilians, would be held responsible for partisan actions. Later, the memory of these weeks of hell would haunt them all, a time of horror, terror and confusion, the survivors crouching in the forests watching their homes go up in smoke, creeping down afterwards to find the rooms used by the Germans to hold their prisoners were covered in blood.

*

On 11 March, a beautiful spring day, mild and sunny, Lucilla Jervis walked into Torre Pellice to get bread for her three children. The valley was at last peaceful and she felt cheerful and relieved. She found Giorgio Agosti waiting for her. He told her that Willy had been stopped at a Fascist roadblock, while returning on his motorcycle to the Val Pellice, and found not to possess a licence. He had tried but failed to hide the messages that he was carrying about guiding Allied prisoners of war over the Alps to safety. The Fascists had beaten him up and there was a rumour that he had been taken to the barracks at Luserna to be hanged. Lucilla forced herself to remain calm. She packed up some belongings and prepared to move the children to greater safety higher up the mountains. Before she left, Agosti returned with better news. Willy had been taken down to Turin and there were plans to exchange him for a high-ranking German official.

Two weeks after Willy's capture – a measure of the isolation of the valleys and how long it took for news to circulate – word reached Ada in Turin that there had been a major *rastrellamento* in the Germanasca, Pellice and Chisone valleys, where Malan had posted Paolo. 'Alarming news,' she wrote in her diary, 'and we do not know the outcome.' On 24 March, she and Ettore set off to look for him. On the little train carrying them up from the plains, the conductor confirmed that the Germans had indeed occupied the valleys and that many partisans had died in the fighting. The first village they reached was full of soldiers, with radios and cannons. They had been driving women and children before them as they combed the valleys, to shield them from partisan fire. Ada and Ettore continued up the valley, passing smouldering mountain barns. The sun shone brightly but to Ada there was an unmistakable aura of death. They met a group of boys who told them that there was a dead partisan on the road above. All around lay peaceful meadows and snowy peaks: all she could see was a 'gelid and empty abyss'. This, she thought, 'must be hell'.

Round a corner they came across a group of women gathered by the corpse of a badly mutilated boy. It was not Paolo, but Ada began to cry, thinking of the boy's mother, and other mothers like herself. The women told them that the boy had been called Davide and that he had insisted on trying to block the road while his friends retreated. The Germans had forbidden them to move his body. Later, Ada and Ettore went back, and after Ettore made a cross, she decorated it with wild flowers and a branch of pine.

There was no sign of Paolo. As they walked higher, they came across burnt-out cars, bombed bridges, smoking houses. A girl told them that a partisan band had passed this way, pursued by the Germans, using the help of a spotter plane. Ada listened to a cuckoo and was assailed by a sweet smell of resin. She thought about all the young boys 'tired, famished, threatened and pursued on every side, like hunted beasts'. She feared that she would go mad.

They returned to Turin to wait for news. Ada remembered how her first husband Piero had spoken of 'volunteers for death' when writing about the early anti-Fascists, and she wondered whether this was not precisely what these young men were doing, volunteering to die for their ideals. She clung to the thought that even if their actions seemed on the surface futile, they still had an 'inevitable and profound significance'. 'I do not want to be, I cannot be, shipwrecked.'

And then a letter came. Though Ada was crying so much that she could not immediately decipher the words, she saw that it was in Paolo's handwriting. He wrote that he and Alberto were both safe and in Meana. After a series of skirmishes, and narrowly avoiding being hit by a German tank, they had wandered in the mountains for three days, hungry and in a state of constant alarm, never knowing from which direction the Germans might come, hiding from a spotter plane with a machine gun which swooped low over the valleys. She felt giddy with relief, as if she had been drinking brandy, and immediately set out for Meana with Bianca. Walking the last bit of the road up towards the house, Ada saw a shadow coming towards her. She opened her arms but could not speak. That night she wrote in her diary: 'I did not even know how to be happy any more . . . The miraculous nearness to my son seemed to me a privilege for which sooner or later I would have to atone.'

The *rastrellamento* had spared Paolo, Alberto and the two Malan brothers. But others had not been as lucky.

While searching the mountains, Ada had been told that 'an old man' with the partisans had been taken by the Germans. It turned out to be Jacopo Lombardini, the much loved preacher, stopped by militiamen as he struggled to reach Torre Pellice. Not long before he had written that 'we are free up here in the mountains, and we have no wish at all to be made slaves again'. Gustavo Malan had been with him but had managed to escape. He had slipped on an icy rock and broken his leg, but had been rescued by his friends and hidden in a pit until it was safe to take him to his mother's village. Now came news that Emanuele Artom, the ungainly '*professorino*', had also been arrested and that he had been identified as both a Jew and a partisan by a spy whose life Emanuele had recently forced his partisan band to spare. A few days earlier, he had asked Bianca to bring him some books to help him teach democracy to the young partisans, 'otherwise we risk that it will all return to what it was before'. By the time Bianca had got hold of the books, the *rastrellamento* was underway and she was forced to turn back.

Jacopo Lombardini

Never very strong and exhausted by too many nights without sleep, Emanuele had decided he could go no further, and while the others escaped, he allowed himself to be caught. As they fled, his friends heard him say '*Io non posso*', I can't.

Like Lombardini, Emanuele was taken down to Bobbio, then to the prison in the barracks at Luserna. For five days, he was tortured but said nothing. Then he was put on an ass, back to front, and ridiculed by the militiamen. He was plunged into baths of freezing water, deprived of sleep and given no food. His nails were pulled out. A fellow partisan called Oscar, held in the barracks at the same time, later described how Emanuele was made to lift a very heavy beam, while his tormentors taunted him, saying 'and this is the man who is meant to teach you'. Emanuele replied that he was a teacher of moral education, not of gymnastics. He was then beaten again until he collapsed. But he said nothing until he believed that any information he gave would no longer be relevant; and then he told his tormentors about the Malans, Giorgio Agosti and Willy Jervis, providing details about Willy's place in the leadership and his negotiations with the Allies over the drops.

When, soon after, a small shard of glass was found hidden in his cell, Emanuele was told that if he killed himself, all the other partisans held with him would be shot. He gave up the idea of suicide. A partisan with the Garibaldi brigades, in the same cell, later reported seeing Emanuele so disfigured as to be almost unrecognisable, with a Fascist military chaplain egging on his tormentors with the words: 'Hit him! Hit him hard, boys!' Emanuele and Lombardini, whose teeth had been knocked out, were then turned over to the Germans and taken down to Le Nuove in Turin. Here, Emanuele dictated a will to one of the guards.

At times now, it seemed to Ada and her friends that none of them would be alive to see Italy liberated. Bianca had just received a card, slipped out through the slats of a cattle truck and posted by a sympathetic passer-by, from Levi. Since January, Levi, Luciana and Vanda had been in Fossoli, the former prisoner-of-war camp. While it was still in Italian hands, conditions remained bearable; food parcels and letters were allowed in and in the evenings the prisoners read and played cards. They could use their own money to order in supplies, which were pooled in a common mess. Franco, one of their friends, had got hold of a tin of Nestlé's milk and they made zabaglione with some eggs. Vanda and Luciana were even allowed out to visit the public baths and the hairdresser.

But when the German SS took over the camp in the middle of February 1944, they cut the food rations dramatically and announced that all Jews, without exception, would be leaving immediately for an unknown destination. That night, Vanda had tried and failed to cut her wrists. Defying an order to assemble in alphabetical order, Levi, Vanda and Luciana had managed to stay together. Among those deported were thirty-one children and 118 elderly people. The journey lasted four days and four nights, without water. On the few occasions they were allowed off the train, the guards revelled in taking pictures of the 'Jews with their trousers unbuttoned'. One man died on the journey. By the time they reached Auschwitz, Levi would later write, 'the demolition' of the people had begun. In their note posted to Bianca from the train, the friends had written: 'Greetings to all. The baton passes to you. Ciao, Bianca, we love you.' To Franco Momigliano, her fiancé, Luciana wrote: 'Thank you for being you. I am leaving . . . Ciao, ciao, ciao.'

9

The hunters and the hunted

March 1944 ended in a renewed explosion of violence in Turin and throughout the valleys. Partisan attacks and acts of sabotage were met with more *rastrellamenti*, reprisals and executions. Mongolian and Russian auxiliaries joined German SS and Fascist militia in terrorising the mountain villages, intending to make the local people blame the partisans for the violence and so turn against them. Then, on 31 March, the Germans pulled off a major coup. Two partisans were caught trying to smuggle weapons into Turin. Under torture they revealed plans for a secret meeting of the partisan leadership in the sacristy of the Duomo. The entire northern military command was there, fifteen men, including their most senior officer, General Giuseppe Perotti, and Ada's friend, Professor Braccini. The Duomo was surrounded. The men were taken with vital and incriminating documents.

Orders came from Mussolini and Salò to set up a Special Tribunal to hear their case immediately, with the maximum publicity, under the Minister for the Interior, Buffarini Guidi, and Turin's two leading Fascist officials, Zerbino and Solaro, and the German consul, Baron Von Lagen. Defence lawyers, braving retaliation, hastened to offer their services; frantic efforts for prisoner exchanges were made and rebuffed. The men in the dock who had no children tried to take full responsibility for the entire northern partisan war; but in the end, after a trial of dubious legality, eight of the fifteen were sentenced to death. As the verdicts were read out, Perotti, the youngest general in the pre-war Italian army, called his friends to attention and all shouted: '*Viva l'Italia!*'

That night, Perotti wrote to his wife: 'It has been given to me, unlike the vast majority of mortals, to know that in a few hours

I will die and I can assure you that it does not terrify me. I would never have believed it so easy to adapt oneself to the idea of one's death . . . I die, as I have said, calm . . . I consider myself a casualty of war, because we are at war, and in war death is a common risk.' His daughter was allowed to visit him. When she arrived at the barracks where he was held, she found the Fascists celebrating, laughing, rejoicing. She was shown into Perotti's cell, where she knelt down and kissed him.

Ada was in Meana with Ettore and Paolo and had not yet heard the news of the tribunal. On Palm Sunday, 2 April, a soft spring day, with sun and gusts of wind, they walked along a lane between hedges covered in white briars and past a stream; the birch trees were sprouting new green leaves which were 'quivering in the sun'. But Ada was finding it ever harder to keep the encircling violence from her thoughts. Earlier in the day she had been visited by Giorgio Diena's mother, whose husband had just been taken away. 'I am happy that my boys are in the mountains,' she told Ada. 'They must continue to fight.' Ada wondered how long she would be able to endure the terrible anxiety that filled her days. Then she heard about the capture of Perotti and the Resistance leaders.

At dawn on 5 April, the eight men were tied to chairs and shot in the back of the head, as befitted traitors. In the nearby streets, people stood horrified, listening and counting the shots. It was indeed a catastrophe for the northern partisans. The executed men had represented the full political spectrum of the Resistance and among them had been distinguished university professors, lawyers and career officers. A scramble began to replace them.

Matilde di Pietrantonio, the intrepid young specialist in hostage-taking, tried to pull off a spectacular kidnapping to use as barter with the Fascists. She trapped the clerk of the Special Tribunal which had tried the men. Her colleagues wanted to shoot him on the spot, but she persuaded them to let her try for an exchange. Telling her prisoner that she would not hesitate to put a bullet through his head if he gave any trouble, she borrowed a car, locked up her captive in his underpants in a friend's house, then went to the Duomo to negotiate. She was too late to save Perotti, Braccini and their friends, but she secured the release of six other imprisoned partisans. Matilde was finding partisan life intoxicating.

In a separate operation, the daughter of the German consul, Usci von Lagen, was also kidnapped. Usci was treated kindly, but her captors held firm when violent retribution was threatened. After much blustering, the Germans reluctantly released a partisan commander and a number of *staffette*, and Usci was let go.

Early April brought new blows to the northern Resistance. After a leading Turin Fascist called Ather Capelli was assassinated, thirty-two prisoners, several of whom had never had anything to do with the Resistance, were taken out of Le Nuove, led to a public square and shot, their bodies left lying there as a warning.

Then on the 7th, guards in Le Nuove found Emanuele dead in his cell, his body covered in blood. News of his death was greeted with horror. The idea of the *professorino*, who had worried so constantly about his friends, being battered to death was unbearable; and, physically frail, he should never really have been in the mountains at all. Four fellow partisans were detailed to bury him in the woods at Stupinigi, on the edge of the city. Around the same time Sandro Delmastro, his chemist friend, who had risen to join the northern military command but avoided capture with Perotti, was caught and shot in a volley of machine-gun fire as he tried to escape from the truck carrying him to prison.

On hearing of these deaths, Ada thought of their tragedy and meaninglessness and of the overwhelming grief of Esther, Delmastro's fiancée. 'They are more like heroes,' she wrote, 'because they do not want to be one. They do not even know that they are one.' Braccini too, she reflected, had been a man who 'understood the significance of the hour in which he lived', and she kept hearing in her head, over and over again, his words: 'Signora, how is your dog?' And Emanuele had been little more than a boy. She, Lisetta and Vittorio clung together, feeling a 'desire to fight that bordered on fury', telling each other that they understood as never before what it meant to want to 'vindicate the dead'. The sun was shining, the poppies were out and the fields were covered in daisies and violets; but it was as if, wrote Ada, everything was covered in a thick veil of sadness.

Italy's Jewish population was shrinking fast. Friedrich Bosshammer, from Eichmann's staff, was in the process of organising the last convoys from Fossoli to Auschwitz and Bergen-Belsen. In Salò, Giovanni Preziosi, Inspector General for Race, was calling for the 'total elimination' of all Jews, including the 'half-breeds'. Ada and her friends thought of Germans as the hunters; the Italian spies and informers as their dogs. Fascist headquarters were inundated with anonymous tips, not only of hidden Jews but of those who helped them, and Alpine guides were making good money from the groups they had offered to take to safety over the mountains, paid first by the Jewish families and then a second time by the Fascists when they turned them in. Betrayal of the remaining Jews was bringing handsome rewards. At the Risiera di San Sabba in Trieste, Odilo Globocnik was gassing his last Jewish prisoners, often in a special van.

Towards the end of March, a group of partisans in Rome, most of them students, had attacked a platoon of German SS police marching down Via Raselli in the centre of the city, using a rubbish cart filled with explosives. Thirty-three were killed, together with two Italian civilians. Hitler was incensed and ordered thirty hostages to be executed for each of the dead Germans, which had to be reduced to ten for every one after the German command in Rome said that they did not have enough hostages. On the night of the 24th, 335 Italians, 176 of them Jewish, were taken from Rome's prisons, put into sealed meat trucks and driven to a labyrinth of tunnels in the Christian catacombs on the Appian Way. Inside the Ardeatine caves, SS men shot them, five at a time, in the back of the head as they knelt in the dust. The murdered men included diplomats, professors, postmen, generals, waiters, clerks, doctors and bankers. One was a Catholic priest. When they were all dead the Germans blew up the entrance to the caves, hoping to seal their contents forever.

Giaime Pintor, the young Turin intellectual killed crossing the lines, had spoken in the days before he died of there being no irreplaceable individuals. For Ada and the small group of Turin friends, there was one whose place could not be filled. This was Leone Ginzburg, the very clever, much loved translator and writer about whom it was said that his moral world seemed like a 'tranquil port', and that when with him you felt at peace with yourself and with the world. All through the turbulent years of Fascism, Ginzburg had provided his friends with a steady point of reference, a certainty in the right of what they believed in and the necessity of acting in a certain way; no amount of imprisonment or persecution had altered his fundamental kindness and love for his friends, nor his quickness to detect falsehood and equivocation.

After the armistice and the German occupation of Rome, Ginzburg had continued to live in the city under the name of Leonida Gianturco, helping edit the foremost clandestine paper, *L'Italia Libera*. In the autumn, during a round-up of suspect printers, he had been caught by the Fascists and taken to the prison of Regina Coeli. Not knowing who he was, they put him in the Italian wing. The inmates called it the '*carcere allegro*', the cheerful jail, because the doors to the cells had been smashed in an air raid and in the evenings the prisoners talked to each other, while those who could gave lessons. Ginzburg spoke about Tolstoy and Dostoevsky, Mazzini and the Risorgimento. The Italian wing held whole families, black marketeers, prostitutes, uncooperative priests.

One afternoon in early December a group of SS men had descended on the prison. The Germans had discovered not only Ginzburg's identity but also the fact that he was Jewish. They took him to their own grim section of the jail, where they tortured him. Word reached his friends that his jaw had been broken, and he was glimpsed, bloody, almost unrecognisable, and heard to say: 'Shame on us if in the future we do not hate the entire German people.' In February, his friends managed to have him transferred to the infirmary and plans were made to rescue him. The nurse refused to call a doctor. Ginzburg was found dead at dawn on 5 February. It seemed that his heart had given out.

Leone Ginzburg

On the night of the 4th, he had written to Natalia. He reminded her that it was almost their sixth wedding anniversary. 'Goodbye, my love . . . kiss the children. I bless all four of you and thank you for being in this world. I love you, I kiss you, my love.' Think of me, he told her, as a prisoner of war 'most of whom return home. Let us hope that I am among them, isn't that right, Natalia? I kiss you again and again and again. Be brave.' Natalia took the children to Florence, but feeling that to be unsafe, she placed one of them with her sister, another in a convent and, with her eldest child and her mother, went to a hotel in Vallombrosa. 'Either you go mad,' she said, 'or you kill yourself, or you stop being frightened.' Later she wrote a poem called 'Memory'.

'When you used to cry there was his calm voice; / When you used to laugh, there was his quiet laugh. / But the gate that once opened in the evenings will now remain closed forever; / And your youth is a desert, the fire gone out, the house empty.'

Ada's world, the once exceptional Turin of intellectuals, thinkers and writers, was crumbling. Artom, Ginzburg, Delmastro all dead; Levi in Auschwitz; Lombardini and Don Foglia in Le Nuove; Monti in hiding; Agosti and Foa in constant danger. The women resisters were becoming ever more crucial.

The Italian Churches, faced with violence coming from all sides, continued to equivocate. The Waldensian elders in Torre Pellice and the surrounding valleys were resisting all entreaties for a firm stand against the draft and support for those who refused it, preferring to concentrate instead on condemning reprisals and acting as intermediaries between Fascists and partisans.

The Catholics, who refused to recognise the Salò government, took a line that was not much clearer. However, after the executions in the Ardeatine caves, the bishops of Piedmont issued an Episcopal Easter Letter, in which they condemned excesses of every kind, whether carried out by the Germans, the Fascists or the partisans. It exhorted the priests in the province's 324 parishes to eschew politics, vendettas, hatred and reprisals, and to concentrate on caring for their flocks. The 'bloody war' was deplored, as were deportations, torture and the 'barbarity' into which Italy had fallen. And behind the scenes, the cool and measured Cardinal Fossati was urging his priests and nuns to hide people on the run, especially the Jews. Attacks on the Church in general, and on the cardinal in particular, multiplied, with Salò accusing the clergy of complicity with the Resistance. How could the Church *not* support them, the Fascists asked, since they too were fighting Freemasons, Bolsheviks, atheism and anarchy? The louder the attacks became, the more the younger priests did to help the partisans.

High up in the Piedmontese valleys, another Catholic priest, Don Marabotto, followed Don Foglia's example and threw in his lot with the partisans. Thures was a village of 124 inhabitants, clinging to the edge of a hillside almost 2,000 metres above the town of Cesana, near the border with France. Its houses were built half in stone and half in larch, and during the long snowy winters, which lasted from September to May, the children went to school by ski or sledge. Don Marabotto had arrived here as a young priest in 1943. Even in his clerical clothes, he had a military look, with rather pointed features and a full dark beard. News of the burning of Boves in September had transformed his life. 'A scintilla of that fire entered my heart,' he said, 'and lit a flame.'

When he got to Thures he agreed with the partisan leadership in Turin to take charge of counter-espionage along the border, where the abandoned military forts were providing a rich supply of weapons. The village teacher, Ines Barone, volunteered to carry them down to the plains on Sundays, when she visited her parents, and 22-year-old Maria Teresa Gorlier, who had grown up in Thures and knew every inch of its mountain paths, became Don Marabotto's *staffetta*. Not far away, his sister, who worked as the director of a small enterprise of women making uniforms for the Fascists, also became a *staffetta* and began squirrelling away material from her supplies for the partisans. Whenever she could, she hitched rides with the Germans, hoping to learn their plans. By the late spring of 1944, Don Marabotto and his three women helpers were in touch with Ada and Ettore in the valleys far below. It was a measure of the ambivalence of the Church towards the partisans that Cardinal Fossati did nothing to curb the activities of his warrior priest.

From right: Maria Gorlier, Don Marabotto and friend

If they had been hoping to deal the northern Resistance a death blow with the trial and execution of General Perotti and his colleagues, the Germans soon discovered their mistake. What became known as '*il processo Perotti*' was a decisive moment for the partisans. Until then, for all the attacks and reprisals, the sabotage and the *rastrellamenti*, there had been a feeling that some at least were only playing at warfare. Perotti himself had been pressing for a tighter military structure and more discipline. In the wake of his death, plans were urgently put in place to identify, coordinate and unify the galaxy of different groups, individuals and movements across Piedmont. Since the partisans regarded the Fascists as traitors, and since paying off scores and vendettas lay close to the surface, guidelines were needed. Fascists and Germans were merged into '*neofascisti*', not human beings at all, and certainly not citizens, but rather symbols of evil. They had to be identified and fought, and the battle against them was one of liberation from an incubus. As Livio Bianco wrote: 'We have to start over again, adapt ourselves to conditions ever harder than those that went before.'

Duccio, '*il nostro Trotsky*', took Braccini's place at the head of all the Partito d'Azione formations; Agosti, '*il piccolo padre*', became its political chief in Turin. Bianco took charge of partisan warfare. He was an admirable leader, Agosti told him, because he considered shoes more important that political debates and because he argued not on the basis of ideology, but of morality, which everyone could understand. Augusto Monti, the much loved and respected teacher from the Liceo d'Azeglio, the 'aristocratic Jacobin', was made adviser for schools in which the partisans were trying to shed Fascist ideology. He had refused to hide, saying that he was too old to be of interest to the Fascists, but Agosti decided otherwise. 'Kidnap him if you must,' he instructed one of the bands. 'This man is too important for our future.' Monti was given half an hour to pack a suitcase, and whisked away into the mountains. Giorgio Diena was setting up a committee to study trade unionism; Vittorio Foa was acting as liaison. The other political parties appointed new leaders of their own. Realising how lax security had become, stricter rules were now put in place to ensure safety.

In the bands themselves, 'the tepid, the uncertain, the dilettanti' were eased out, as were the '*pazzi esaltati*', the overexcited young men who threw their weight about. Those who remained had to be 'hard and determined', '*pocchi ma buoni*', few but good, as Emanuele had written in his diary. Though there was much talk of limiting guerrilla warfare to small bands and quick actions, not least because ammunition was in such short supply, the new leaders continued to see in a large-scale military uprising the best hope for Italy's future. There were no proper uniforms, but the partisans were instructed to wear something distinctive, a beret with insignia or a coloured kerchief. Saluting became fashionable; the clenched fist became a greeting. Partisans were asked to swear oaths of fealty. Duccio wanted his Partito d'Azione men and women to be '*partigiani per bene*', respectable, with style and confidence, preying on no one, brave and full of *esprit de corps*. He was a lively speaker, calm, decisive and efficient, and people found him fascinating. His *staffette*, he said, were the best guarantee that the fight they were waging was a truly popular one. When Ada bumped into him on a tram one day, she noted that he had grown a splendid beard; but they took care not to recognise each other.

And the numbers of partisans were rising, in a vast arc that stretched across the Apennines, from coast to coast, through valleys and mountains, cities and villages, in the marshes round Ravenna and throughout the Veneto. Estimated at around 10,000 in Piedmont alone at the beginning of 1944, a combination of the call-ups by Salò and growing dislike of the Fascists and the Germans were driving many thousands more into the mountains. By late spring the figure had risen to 50–60,000, perhaps one in six of them women. According to a survey carried out later, the largest number were factory workers, followed by peasants and farmers, artisans and students. Most of the women referred to themselves as 'housewives' but the factories were providing ever more recruits for Ada's GDD.

While almost half of the partisans listed themselves as Communists, the members of the Partito d'Azione were not far behind and the Autonomi were gathering momentum. The Socialists were setting up their own bands, named Matteotti after the murdered Socialist deputy. A tight military framework was devised: a basic unit of ten was a *squadra*; three *squadre* made a detachment; three detachments a battalion, three battalions a brigade, three brigades a division. Flying squads, more flexible, less vulnerable, were to replace the static formations that could never be a match for the larger enemy forces. It was agreed that the partisan war should not be solely a military affair, and as two decades of Fascism had sapped Italy's moral conscience, a political commissar would be attached to each band to teach the young about justice, equality and liberal democracy, so that in the future it would be harder to take refuge in political ignorance.

All through the late spring and early summer discussions continued between the various partisan forces, each jostling for power and territory. With immense difficulty, it was finally decided to split the north into seven commands, shared out to reflect the political nature of each, with Garibaldini in one valley, Partito d'Azione in another, each jealously guarding their autonomy. But for all the professed unity, in practice the bands – splitting up, re-forming, moving, splitting again – remained an anarchical and extraordinary mixture of people, some highly political, some recently emerging from prison and bursting out of years of repression, some uncertain whether to stay or go, some terrified, some viscerally hostile to authority of any kind, some filled with youthful passion, some resentful about class, some lazy, and a considerable number of them unfit, ungainly, having spent their lives in the cities and never having seen a weapon. Many were little more than boys and girls, their minds formed on snippets of Fascist ideology and remnants of village culture. It was like an earthquake, threatening the roots of Italian society, dangerous, intoxicating, calling on reserves of imagination and character few knew they possessed and the need to reinvent the very fabric of their lives. They grew up fast.

Speaking every dialect from Sicilian to Piedmontese, their leaders elected not on the basis of experience so much as being able to prove that they were good at guerrilla warfare, the partisans were told that they had to earn their positions. There were quarrels. There was everything to learn, to understand, to try out. And not everyone welcomed the new discipline, preferring the gypsy-like attitude of the early days. It was the question of how to forge these disparate people into a well-drilled and equipped army, how to solve the myriad inherent and internal contradictions, how to put together all the values and norms which they believed should form the basis of a new society, that Agosti, Duccio, Ada and Bianco now had to address.

10

A lizard among the rocks

The four friends were pursuing their own adventures. Frida, who had grown very close to the *professorino*, had been crushed by Emanuele's death. When, after much searching, she discovered that his friend Jacopo Lombardini was still alive, but had been moved from Le Nuove to the camp at Fossoli to await deportation to the east, she set out to see him. She had always been fearless: the deaths of people she loved had only made her more so. Jewish friends, who had made contact with Fossoli's prisoners, told her to go to the best local hotel, which was known to be full of spies and informers of every kind, and to explain loudly that she was there to do research for a thesis on the area. Then she was to hire a bicycle and cycle around the town, making herself very visible.

In due course, a man approached her and offered to introduce her to a bricklayer who worked at the camp. She said that she was Lombardini's daughter and gave him some money and some clothes. He took her to the edge of the camp and she was able to talk to Lombardini through the fence. He told her that he knew that he was shortly to be deported, and asked for a Bible and a suitcase with a change of clothes. Frida made several journeys between Turin and Fossoli, bringing things not just for Lombardini but also for the other Jewish prisoners. She got lifts, sometimes from German soldiers, and spent the nights in haylofts, avoiding the curfew.

One day, Lombardini said to her that when the war was over, and he had come home, he planned to go into politics. 'I'll continue to –' he began, but was then stopped by a guard, ordering him away from the fence. Frida did not see him again.

*

Crucial to the partisan war was practical survival. The bands still lacked everything: shoes, warm clothes, medicines, false identity papers and driving licences, tinned meat, tobacco and, always, salt. At one point a hundred kilos of salt could buy a machine gun. A third of a typical partisan day was said to be spent on finding food, and there were many days when all there was to eat were potatoes and mushrooms. A partisan section called L'Intendenza, formed of some twenty men and women, was detailed to scour the countryside for food. Horses stolen from barracks were eaten or exchanged for food with the farmers. With the new structure to the northern Resistance came strict rules: everything taken from the farmers was to be paid for, either immediately or very soon. To win over the local people, who were increasingly angry at losing what little they had and cross when, after butchering a cow, the young partisans threw away what they considered to be edible pieces of meat, convoys of animals requisitioned by the Germans were hijacked when on their way through the valleys and shared out with the villagers and farmers. Local support was too essential to risk and the partisan leaders were conscious of the extent to which their high spirits, dancing and drinking were unsettling to the traditional life of the remote valleys. As reprisals threatened their lives, many villagers began to urge the young partisans to give themselves up and volunteer to work for the Germans.

In the towns, factories were given promissory notes for things taken against redemption at the end of the war. Several of the *staffette* were becoming skilled at negotiating with industrialists, using a mixture of charm and threat against recalcitrant factory owners. In this ever-evolving Resistance, women were exploring their own talents. Some chose to do what they had always done, act as cooks, providers and housekeepers for the bands. Others, such as Silvia, found that they were good at liaising between the partisans and their families. Very few seemed aware of the danger they were in, even after the Germans started executing the *staffette* they managed to catch. For every active fighting man, it was said, there were fifteen people behind him, and many of these were women. The advice 'Do not fear, women of occupied Italy, to sacrifice your femininity' was broadcast on *Italia Combatte* to the partisans in the north. 'By helping you will be like the sweetest, most generous women of the Risorgimento.'

In the early days, bandits had menaced the partisan dream. Crooks, adventurers and Fascist cowboys, seeing how easy it was to bully people sympathetic to the partisan cause into parting with food and clothes, carried out raids on the mountain villages, stealing cattle and selling it on the black market. Anxious not to be perceived as outlaws but as the creators of a new society, the Resistance devised a disciplinary code and set about crushing these roaming bandits and dealing with the informers and spies who circled around. Minor misdemeanours were punished by tying the culprit to a stake, with his feet balancing on a rock, or by expelling him from the band. Treachery, pillaging and collaboration with the enemy were made capital offences.

In time, formal partisan tribunals were set up, with four judges, a president and a defender, chosen by the person on trial. Those executed were shot in the back as traitors. These trials were grisly affairs for many of the young partisans, assembled in mountain clearings to decide the fate of people who often did not believe themselves to be traitors, and when taken away to be shot still could not understand why. As one partisan put it: 'Not to punish them for what they did would be to doubt the very basis of the reasons for which we were fighting.' Still, it was hard to be clear, in a conflict which day by day was more obviously a civil war. Even the senior Fascists in Salò now spoke openly of it as a 'civil war, with all its horrors' that seemed to 'have been unleashed'.

No one, now, was safe. In mid April, a partisan in Florence shot the corpulent, ageing Giovanni Gentile, architect of Fascism's educational programmes and one of its best-known intellectual supporters, shouting out as he did so: 'I am not killing the man, but the idea.' On hearing of the assassination, Benedetto Croce asked: 'Who shot him?' His son-in-law, Raimondo Craveri, replied: 'The partisans.' 'Ah,' said Croce, 'now they are killing philosophers too.'

When a spy in Roberto Malan's band was caught with a loaded revolver, clearly intent on trouble, the decision was taken to shoot him. Paolo came to tell Ada what had happened. Fearing that his expression would be one of satisfaction or indifference, she watched his face closely and was intensely relieved to see him disturbed. 'It can be necessary to kill,' she wrote in her diary, 'but troublesome if we find it simple and natural.' Among the messages carried up and down the mountains by the *staffette* was often the question: 'Who do we need to execute?' Some of the partisans found execution duties impossible.

Prisoner exchanges were also codified: one SS sergeant major, for example, could be swapped for two partisans with military experience. But the Fascists were worth nothing, since the Germans did not consider them worth bartering for. The system never worked well, as the partisans often refrained from carrying out their threats because of fear of reprisals against local civilians.

Women who consorted with the Fascists or the Germans were judged severely. The records kept meticulously by the partisan groups include painful accounts of young mothers executed for 'general nazifascist mentality and acts of anti partisan espionage'. Irma P., the mother of a new baby daughter, caught giving her German lover information that led to the death of several partisans, pleaded for her life, saying that if they spared her, she would become a prostitute for the partisans. She was shot. Flyers were circulated with the words: 'Italian girl, not one look, not one smile, for the German occupiers.' *Staffette* were also often in danger of being suspected by their own side. And many bands prohibited relations between men and women, either because the men still thought of girls as temptresses, or because they believed that their innate weakness would make them chatter and give away secrets to the enemy. Those who dallied with the *staffette* found themselves punished with hours at the stake. And many of the young men, reared on Fascism's '*donna-madre*' and '*donna-sorella*', continued to find the notion of a '*donna compagna d'armi*' too revolutionary.

Money was always a problem. In January, General Raffaello Operti, from the disbanded 4th Army in Piedmont, had revealed that he was still holding the equivalent of some 200 million lire in funds and that he was prepared to distribute it to the partisans in return for an undertaking to limit warfare to sabotage and for himself to be appointed as the head of a unified command. Operti was neither much liked nor trusted, and there were rumours that he had made deals with the Salò government, but his family were Waldensians and Foa went to meet him. After many negotiations, Operti was offered the role of coordinator of the military wing, but not before he had handed over most of the money, and he was soon marginalised.

Consorting with the Fascists

In Turin, Agosti and Ada became involved in elaborate schemes to exchange the part of the money that was in French francs into lire. Ada found herself lugging a suitcase full of thousand-lire notes to the Hotel Canelli, where the leaders continued to meet, while Agosti arrived with a packet 'the size of a table' wrapped up in newspapers. Neither one of them was stopped along the way. For a while, the partisans lived well. After Operti's money was spent, a well-respected local banker called Alfredo Pizzoni was dispatched to Switzerland to negotiate with the Allies and cash was funnelled into Italy through Swiss banks, until the Germans succeeded in halting Swiss cooperation. But finances were always precarious; and the partisans were often hungry.

To boost morale, clarity and unity, an underground press was beginning to take shape, simultaneously all over occupied Italy. It started slowly, with a few cyclostyled or stencilled news sheets and flyers; but then it took fire. In all shapes and sizes, on paper of terrible quality, with ink that smudged, information poured out, typed, handwritten, copied, printed. There were calls for strikes and protests; careful explanations about responsibility and thought; disquisitions on liberty. There were flyers addressed to teachers, to villagers in the mountains, to young people, to the families of partisans and to the widows of victims of Fascist attacks. Italy had never seen such an outpouring of urgent and exhortatory words. Records would later show that there had been 2,357 separate newspaper titles, a few of them printing up to 10,000 copies every fortnight.

In Torre Pellice, the Tipografia Alpina, founded in the 1880s by one of the Malan family, passed into the hands of a supporter of the Partito d'Azione, Pier Luigi Pagliai. By day, Pagliai printed wedding invitations, biblical circulars and local history. By night, he turned his presses over to the partisans, and Gustavo Malan and four local boys put together a broadsheet containing news of the different local bands, melting the lead immediately after printing to remove all traces before the day staff arrived. What made the Tipografia Alpina stand out was the fact that it was situated opposite German and Fascist barracks. When it seemed that the Germans were growing suspicious, the four boys moved up the mountains to a shepherd's hut, which had an earth floor and was built into the rocks, and began to cyclostyle material on an ancient machine they had carried up with them. It was often very cold and the rocks oozed damp. The ink froze and the type became almost illegible. When the pages were printed, they took it in turns to carry the bundles down to Torre Pellice for the *staffette* to distribute. They went to great lengths never to be seen, moving only at night or under the shelter of the surrounding forests. Sometimes they heard German and Fascist patrols trawling through the nearby valleys.

The underground press was expanding too rapidly to rely on such a primitive system and Gustavo's helpers returned to Torre Pellice to use Pagliai's presses. All the different formations of partisans, and some of the individual bands, now wanted to put out their own papers, full of war news, plans, obituaries of dead friends, instructions on how to dress and behave, on weapons and tactics. After *L'Italia Libera* and *La Baili*, a Garibaldino paper, came *Il Partigiano Alpino*. As the months went by, partisans began to contribute poems and short stories and accounts of their own acts of sabotage, in which they had bravely duped and seen off the treacherous Fascists. Names of collaborators were printed, along with their addresses. 'We are fighting,' the various writers repeated, again and again, in different ways, 'so that we may be forgiven our 20 years of inertia, during which the Italian people supinely and tepidly accepted Fascism.'

Gustavo's *Il Pioniere* was one of the most widely circulated papers, and became a mouthpiece for the Partito d'Azione. Once printed, the finished copies were hidden in a Catholic graveyard. The Fascists grew suspicious and took to raiding the premises. The young partisans were never caught, but one employee, hauled away and brutally questioned, lost an eye. *Il Pioniere* appeared fortnightly, four pages of broadsheet, Gustavo putting out digests about the progress of the war, drawing on transmissions from Radio London and other illicit radio stations. Soon, the demand was such that the print run was increased to 15,000 copies, many of them carried down to the plains by the *staffette* in their bicycle baskets. The paper gave its readers a sense of optimism and of a shared fight, and Gustavo used its columns as a springboard for ideas for the political future of Italy.

Distribution of the written material, which was becoming more and more crucial to the partisans, would not have been possible without the *staffette*. In their bags, as they flitted up and down the valleys, young girls like Micki Cesan carried the papers alongside the messages and weapons. Micki took great pride in being called the 'bravest girl in the valley', but even her calm, buoyant nature was buffeted by the killings and arrests she witnessed every day. The articles in the papers she ferried around were often aimed at girls like herself: the *staffette* in every corner of Piedmont and the north were instructed to use the Germans to help them carry their heavy bags because 'the Nazis understand almost nothing . . . your smile, if combined with a careless manner and discretion will certainly fool them'. They were urged to take their babies with them on their journeys, hiding the papers in the prams. Agosti, drafting his articles at his office in Turin, put the pages inside milk churns, covering the paper with a plastic lining, before the milk was poured in and they were borne away to the hidden printers.

In Turin, Bianca, Frida and Silvia were all turning their hands to the secret press. Bianca was friends with a concierge, who gave her a key to an abandoned flat. Here she and two friends installed a cumbersome and very ancient cyclostyle machine and at night churned out material brought to them from the partisan leadership. One evening, very late, they heard footsteps; then a key in the lock. It was the owner of the flat, returned unexpectedly, to the utter terror both of himself and of Bianca and her friends, covered in ink and cowering in a corner. The *portinaia* explained that they were students, working on a photography project.

Bianca was constantly on the lookout for new hiding places and better, newer machines. One day, she calculated that she had collected enough money to buy a new printer. Together with a couple of friends, also *staffette*, she went to a shop that sold printers, and while two of them entered, the third stayed in the street to keep watch. 'Where shall we deliver it?' asked the sales assistant. 'Oh, we'll take it with us,' Bianca replied. The assistant looked sceptical but the girls wrapped the machine up in a piece of tarpaulin and staggered out into the street. They had not reckoned on its weight. They heaved it onto a tram, and since it was unsafe for them to sit together, Bianca took the machine on her own to one end. She was too flustered to note where they were going. Her two friends, from the other end, realising that she was making no move to get off, shouted very loudly to each other: 'Signorina, I think this is your stop.' Afterwards, they laughed at their audacity.

And along with this outpouring of writing came songs, composed by the partisans as they walked the mountain paths, and then cyclostyled and circulated by the *staffette*. School teachers in the mountains got their pupils to copy them out, under the guise of practising their handwriting. Sitting by their fires at night, roasting chestnuts, looking down at the dark and silent valleys far below, the partisans sang: 'The partisan fights his battle, Germans and Fascists, get out of Italy . . . We shout out as loudly as we can: Pity is dead!' These last words, 'Pity is dead', became a rallying cry, a catchword among the bands. 'The Fascists do not move in the dark,' wrote one young man. 'The night belongs to the partisans.' The Val di Susa in particular was famous for its nostalgic songs.

One of the problems faced by the partisans was what to do with their wounded and dead. Falls in the mountains left fractured bones and gunshots needed surgery. With penicillin only newly discovered and almost impossible to come by, there were many deaths from septicaemia. To prevent the Germans from desecrating the bodies of dead partisans, villagers buried them temporarily under snow or in the forests, coming to collect them later. Silvia had only just completed her medical degree when war took her into hiding, but she joined others with medical knowledge in setting up first-aid centres. When her friends talked about her later, they said that even as life became more dangerous, day by day, Silvia seemed fearless, often absurdly so. Her small son Vittorio remained in Torre Pellice while she and Giorgio were living secretly in Natalia Ginzburg's house in the centre of Turin. Both were often away, Silvia on her medical rounds, Giorgio on Partito d'Azione business. They had little time with their child.

In the early days, much of the medical care was carried out in people's homes, and Silvia and her doctor friends would be summoned after dark. In Turin, Dr Bersano Begey put his surgery in Via San Francisco d'Assisi at the disposal of the Resistance and it quickly became a place where Allied prisoners of war on the run could make contact with the partisans. But Dr Bersano Begey was betrayed and forced to go into hiding. After the spring drafts drove more young men up into the mountains, and the *rastrellamenti* caused ever greater numbers of casualties, Dr Bersano Begey was asked to set up a clandestine health service for the Resistance across Piedmont.

Dr Bersano Begey's first secret hospital was in a large abandoned villa in Margone. He turned the former billiard room into a ward; the first floor became an isolation unit. *Staffette*, with considerable ingenuity, borrowed, bought, stole and bartered medical supplies; local women did the laundry, but never so much at any one time as to attract attention. Patients arrived hidden in coffins or delivered after dark on the backs of mules. When the Fascists were closing in, Dr Bersano Begey moved his hospital up into the mountains above Torre Pellice, to a disused hydroelectric building perched on the edge of a bleak and treeless escarpment. The wounded were carried up on stretchers or on the *téléphérique*. When there were too many of them, or their wounds were too serious, Dr Bersano Begey sent his patients over the mountain passes to France, lines of stretcher-bearers tramping through the snow, *staffette* going on ahead.

Dr Begey's hospital in the mountains

In the plains around Turin the badly injured were smuggled into general hospitals by sympathetic doctors. The hospital at Riva was not only kept under constant surveillance by the Fascists but was often obliged to take in and treat wounded Germans. It was an old building, with cellars beneath the mortuary, reached by a series of underground passages, the entrance behind a wood-pile. Here, two resident doctors set up a ward for partisan casualties. Nuns did the nursing. When captured wounded partisans, held by the Germans and the Fascists in the hospital above, were due to be shot, the nurses injected them with something to make their temperatures rise, as the Fascists did not execute seriously ill prisoners, while they arranged their escape. In this world of death and injury and a lack of almost every basic medical supply, Silvia and her doctor friends, like the young partisans in the bands, grew up fast.

The warm weather came slowly to the high valleys. When Ada went up to Meana, she found the meadows dotted with yellow and violet and the briars covered in white flowers. Repairs were finally being carried out to the flat in Via Fabro, which had suffered a number of near hits in the winter bombing. Walls had cracked and several of the windows had lost their glass, but Ada felt totally detached from the damage, as she did from Piero's library and her parents' crystal glasses; in the grimness of the struggle they seemed to her to have shed all meaning.

A young friend of Paolo's, Pillo, whom she had known since he was a little boy, had been caught and beaten up by the Fascists and he was now in Le Nuove. Ada baked a cake to be taken in to him by a regular visitor to the prison. Visiting Le Nuove, despite Suor Giuseppina's helpfulness, was a long and agonising process: the families of captured partisans had first to apply for permission at the German headquarters in the Hotel Nazionale, then, on Thursdays, queue to put food and clean clothes onto a revolving tray which was pulled round inside the prison walls. Sometimes, the dirty clothes came back covered in blood. When the tray reappeared empty, it meant that the prisoner had been either deported or executed. One day, the mother of a young partisan found a scrap of paper in her son's dirty clothes. 'Mother,' it said, 'I am dying. I won't see you again.' The women who gathered silently each Thursday clung together, waiting, tearful.

In the middle of May, Ada met her young friend Cesare Alvazzi on the train coming down the Val di Susa to Turin. All such encounters between partisans were risky affairs on account of the spies who haunted the trains. But Cesare was with his father, his hands swathed in bandages and his face riddled with tiny holes. Crossly, his father explained that his foolish son, fishing in the Dora, had seen and picked up a strange object, which had then exploded in his hands. Cesare gave Ada a look indicating that she should say nothing. Later, he told her that he had in fact been up in the mountains salvaging detonators from German hand grenades and that one had gone off, taking with it the tip of one of his fingers. The bleeding had been such that he had only just made it back home. Without antibiotics, the wound had gone septic. As a last resort, fearing that part of his hand would have to be amputated, Cesare's mother had forced him to plunge it into a bowl of bleach, causing him extreme pain but effectively curing the infection. Cesare and Paolo were making plans to form a new band high in Susa's upper valley.

Ada was still not officially a political commissar, but her friendship with Agosti and the rest of the Partito d'Azione leadership meant that she was taking decisions and making plans. Agosti was working out of a derelict building in Turin's old centre, where bombs had turned the surrounding streets into piles of rubble, and where the cornices from the fine eighteenth-century palazzi hung down over windows blackened by fire. He was grey and taut with anxiety and fatigue, unlike Ada, who struck all who saw her with her energy and decisiveness. Those who met her for the first time said that she seemed to them like a girl, brisk, affectionate, tireless. She was trying to persuade Duccio to take an interest in unifying the different bands in the Val di Susa. After a successful meeting in Via Fabro, where Espedita and the canary continued to function as lookouts, Ada decided that she should put in place an escape route, in case of the sudden arrival of the Germans. Under cover of a violent thunderstorm, she, Ettore and Paolo explored crossing from their balcony to that of the bomb-damaged and empty house next door, and from there out into the street at the back. At any moment, as she put it, the flat could 'burn'. None of her friends could understand why or how she was still safe. She was, wrote one, 'like a lizard among the rocks'.

Every day brought news of fresh arrests. But the partisans, increasingly conscious of danger and ever more resourceful, were not without ideas. Franco Momigliano, Emanuele Artom and Levi's friend from the *scuola ebraica* and Luciana Nissim's fiancé, had worked briefly with Leone Ginzburg on a paper in Rome after the fall of Mussolini, and then acted as liaison in Piedmont between factories and the unions, before escaping the *rastrellamento* in the valleys above Torre Pellice in which Emanuele was caught. He was in Milan, transporting clandestine material, messages and weapons, when he was spotted by a spy whose life he had previously spared. He was turned over to the Fascists and taken to the San Vittore prison. Its director was a blacksmith, an imaginative torturer, a 'hyena with the face of an angelic child'. It took several weeks of interrogation and torture before they discovered his true identity and the fact that he was Jewish. The message he got out to his friends was bleak: 'They have caught me. I have little hope. They have too much evidence against me'.

Franco's sister Mila met up with Ada, Silvia and Giorgio Diena, Lisetta and Vittorio Foa and they set about planning a rescue. Foa was a very reassuring figure, listening carefully, discarding all irrelevant information, then speaking as if nothing was impossible. Even so, he said to Mila that getting a prisoner out of San Vittore was like catching the moon.

San Vittore was surrounded by the shells of bombed-out houses and darkened, deserted streets. Mila wandered around the area, 'like a sleepwalker', imagining herself bombing the prison, poisoning the guards or seducing and corrupting them. The days passed. Then another note was smuggled out. 'I won't escape execution,' Franco wrote. 'Save yourselves.' He asked Mila for poison, fearing that he would not be able to stand up to the torture and might betray his friends. Mila managed to get hold of a cyanide pill.

But Foa had already bribed a guard to lend him his pass to the prison, had it copied by an artist friend in Brescia, and arranged with two members of Parri's squad of *gappisti* – the urban partisans – to go into the jail and get Franco out. Learning that he was about to be handed over to the Germans, and most likely shot, Foa bribed another guard and sent Lisetta in as a visitor to tell Franco the plan. Franco told her that it was impossible and forbade it. Just the same, soon after, Franco was conducted from his cell to the main hall of the prison by a guard who whispered in his ear 'Parri sends his greetings'. There he found the youngest of the *gappisti*, a student, waiting with false papers ordering Franco's immediate release. He had brought with him a revolver and a grenade in case they had to fight their way out. The false papers were duly countersigned and stamped and the two men, having briefly got lost in the maze of corridors, walked out through the prison gates, casually watched by policemen. When they were out of sight they began to run. Foa, wrote Mila later, 'gave us back, my mother and myself, our lives'.

She had found a derelict cottage on the edge of Turin and here Franco was hidden while the Fascists launched a manhunt to recapture him. It was bitterly cold but too dangerous to light a fire in case the smoke attracted attention. A 'vocabulary of sounds' was established for visitors. Franco's mother rang the bell once, then tapped a few times. Silvia and Giorgio Diena rang twice, paused, then rang again. Ada della Torre rang twice, very fast. Franco's rescue gave them all hope.

11

Nesting in kitchens

Day after day, all through the spring and early summer of 1944, Allied bombs fell on Italian cities. With so few air-raid shelters and sirens that sounded only when the planes were visible, families took it in turn to stay awake and listen. In April, 438 cities and industrial centres were hit. In May, 661 bridges, railway lines, viaducts and oil depots were destroyed. In Treviso, 1,600 civilians died. In Milan, placards were put up on bombed homes: 'This house was destroyed by our liberators.' But the Allies were finally advancing.

The Italian campaign was turning into one of the hardest fought of the whole war. The Apennine mountains, with peaks, rivers and gorges and the surrounding plains dominated by defensive positions on the high ground, made the Allied progress slow and treacherous. Casualties were mounting. While the campaign itself was increasingly marginal to the Allies, for the Germans it was a way of using comparatively few divisions to hold back the Allies, thereby preventing them from being deployed elsewhere.

From Turin, the diarist Chevallard followed the Allied progress on his clandestine radio. On 18 May he noted that, after fierce fighting and the almost total destruction of the Benedictine monastery by British and Polish forces and 55,000 Allied casualties, the Germans were at last pulling out of Monte Cassino. Three days later, he recorded that the Allies had reached the town of Sperlunga. Leaving the plains of Latina, the Germans broke the dams, allowing mosquitoes and malaria to return. By 2 June, the Allies were less than twenty kilometres from Rome; the Germans had dug in and were fighting hard round the Alban hills. Then, at 9.30 on the morning of 4 June, came the news all of Italy had been waiting for. Rome was free. That afternoon the Americans reached the Piazza Venezia. There were cheering crowds and a flag was dipped in salute before the Pope's window in the Vatican. Radio Tevere played Bing Crosby and Louis Armstrong, interspersed with messages from Roosevelt and Churchill.

Realising that the capital was lost, Kesselring ordered his troops to withdraw. The bridges were left standing and the German evacuation was orderly. That day, Turin was bombed for the thirty-fourth time. It was the fifth summer of war and all over Italy people were longing for peace. Suddenly it seemed as if the end were near. Piero Calamandrei, a leading anti-Fascist, spoke of a 'sort of beatific stupefaction of happiness'. Ada did not share his delight. She thought of Leone Ginzburg, dead before this day, and said that no one should become too excited. 'I cannot forget,' she wrote in her diary, 'that inevitably every large scale action of war is accompanied by destruction and massacre.'

What the Allies discovered in the capital was far from peaceful. All through the late spring the anti-Fascist coalition had been bickering as to who should form a government and whether the King, still clinging on to power in Brindisi, should go. At the end of March, the Communists had dropped a destabilising bomb of their own. Palmiro Togliatti, co-founder with Gramsci of the Italian Communist Party in 1921, had returned from exile in Moscow saying that he saw no difficulty in collaborating both with the King and with the by now widely reviled Badoglio. What mattered was defeating the Germans; the rest could wait. What became known as 'la svolta di Salerno', the about-turn, was a clever move by Moscow to counter British and American hegemony in Italy, and a reflection of a new vision for a post-war less sectarian, more popular, Communist Party, one which would work not outside but within the system. But its immediate effect was to sow consternation and further discord within the six-party coalition.

After splits, recriminations and much ill-tempered horse trading, a solution of sorts was reached. The King, after forty-six years on the throne, was forced to honour the promise that he had made to step down the day that Rome was liberated. His son Umberto became Lieutenant General of the Kingdom. Badoglio was flown to Rome and met the CLN leadership in a testy encounter at the Grand Hotel. Since what he stood for and what he proposed were acceptable to no one, he crossly and reluctantly bowed out of government. The CLN, paying no heed to the exasperated Allies, appointed the elderly but uncorrupted Ivanoe Bonomi to head a new government, naming seven 'ministers without portfolios', among them Ada's friend and mentor Benedetto Croce, to reflect all regions and all parties. They were sworn in with an oath not to the monarchy but to the nation. There were now just two Italian governments, one in Rome, the other in Salò.

Once Italy was finally liberated, a Constituent Assembly would be elected by universal, direct, secret ballot and a new constitution drawn up to replace the Fascist one. Women would get the vote. A referendum would decide the fate of the monarchy. Churchill, railing against the new 'cluster of aged and hungry politicians', would have preferred to keep Badoglio as a bulwark against the left, and pointed out that since Italy had surrendered unconditionally, it had no right to name a government without Allied authority. Stalin, with his eye on his own push into Eastern Europe, was accommodating to the Italians. The Americans supported their plan. A High Commission for Sanctions against Fascism was set up, but with at least a quarter of all Italians being former members of Fascist organisations, the task of punishing them was soon mired in political squabbling. Though the commission announced that it would be lenient with those who had joined the Fascist Party out of 'family necessity' and draconian with the 'big shots', there was outrage among former Fascists, who argued that their only sin was to have been 'patriots'.

Political interference, shifts to the left and the right, jostling for position and power and endless deals marked the first weeks of Rome's liberation. Even as Churchill arrived on a visit, during which he pointed out that a nation that had allowed itself to be taken over by a dictator could not expect to be immediately absolved of its crimes, the new cabinet was buffeted by one crisis after another. In any case, the part of Italy that had already been liberated was in a state of chaos and penury. Seven million people were homeless, there was very little electricity, a third of all roads were impassable and the black market flourished. Looting, of everything, was endemic. And most people were very hungry.

The rift between liberated south and occupied north widened, exacerbated by Togliatti's political about-turn, which effectively put paid to the northern partisans' dream of Resistance as revolution. Since both the Allies and the Bonomi government were dragging their heels over recognising the northern command, Parri and the other leaders in Piedmont and Lombardy pressed on with their plans to unify the entire northern Resistance and create a pyramid of local liberation committees. Rome now appointed a general, Raffaele Cadorna, as military counsellor for the north, in essence to bring the conservatives and the Autonomi into the fold, but the move did little to solve the schism between the south and the north. Nor did the Allies do much to help, not least because Anthony Eden and the Foreign Office remained hostile to the Italians and wished at all costs to isolate the Resistance, which they continued to regard as dangerously communist.

On 6 June, 156,000 Allied troops landed on the coast of Normandy: the invasion of occupied Europe had begun. The next day, General Alexander called for the partisans in northern and central Italy to rise up, to sabotage the enemy's communication lines and to hinder their efforts to withdraw northwards from Rome. But with the Normandy landings had come an Allied decision to reduce their concentration on the Italian theatre of war. Troops and resources were to be diverted to France. But this the Northern partisans, convinced that their task would soon be over, did not yet know.

Every stage of the Germans' slow retreat north was marked by atrocities, carried out not only by violent SS detachments but by the men of the Wehrmacht. In the early months of occupation, Kesselring had dismissed the Resistance as bandits, from whom he did not have much to fear. He considered guerrilla warfare a 'degenerate form of war . . . contradicting every principle of clear soldierly fighting . . . an example of the southern temperament run riot'. With the fall of Rome, and ever-increasing partisan attacks, he was forced, as he wrote later, to recognise that they posed a 'very real danger and their elimination [was] an objective of capital importance'. Given command over an all-out war against the partisans in Italy, he spelt out to his soldiers how it was to be conducted. There was to be no mercy. Partisans were, in Hitler's words, to be 'massacred, killed, annihilated'. Hangings, burnings, pillage, slaughter of every kind was legitimate and no soldier would later pay the penalty for his actions.

As the twenty German divisions retreated up through Umbria, Le Marche and Tuscany, they left behind them towns and villages without food, electricity or water, destroying everything as they went. When they reached Pesaro, they ordered the city to be evacuated. Homeless families, clutching a few precious belongings, drifted around the countryside, while the German forces plundered and dispatched their loot home.

Kesselring had been perfectly clear about the need to sow terror. If no partisan was found to pay for attacks and acts of sabotage, then a civilian would be punished instead. Ada had been right. The liberation of Rome spelt not the end of the war but an explosion of bloodshed. Fuelled by their losses and the constant harassment of the partisans, the Germans lashed out. 'Raiding detachments' were formed. They had been 'too mild' up till now; but they would be mild no longer. Even women and children could be executed.

Many acts of savagery are still remembered today. But the attack on Civitella in the Val di Chiana was exceptional for its brutality. A medieval walled town, Civitella had a fine tower and a palace with a terracotta by Della Robbia. The Germans reached the town on the morning of 18 June. They hung about all day, playing cards, menacing the local people and getting drunk, but it was only towards dusk that trouble broke out. Four partisans entered a bar where soldiers were drinking and shots were exchanged. Two Germans were killed. The partisans disappeared.

At dawn next morning, in pouring rain, the terrified inhabitants, fearful of reprisals, took to the surrounding woods. A few days later, they crept out of hiding and went home to find the Germans still in Civitella, still looting and still drunk. They had failed to find the guilty partisans but seemed prepared to leave it at that. They pulled out. But on the 29th, they returned. One woman, trying to protect a small son and her husband, saw them both killed. Buildings were set on fire. The people who had taken refuge in the church were driven out into the square, where machine guns had been set up. The men were lined up, in fives, and shot, their bodies flung into the flames. Covered in blood, in their nightdresses, the women, clutching their children, were marched out to the nearby fields, from where they stood watching the flames consume their town. Later, they were taken further away; but the surviving men were held. Towards evening, the Germans left. The women crept back to search for their husbands and sons. The scene that confronted them was the stuff of nightmares: mutilated bodies strewn everywhere, houses burnt to the ground.

One of the now familiar Fascist massacres

After Civitella, the massacres went on. In Caprara, three girls were tied to trees and stakes pushed through their bodies; not far away two pregnant women had their stomachs ripped open. In Pinerolo a young girl watched as a farmer, hoping to save his cows from the looting Germans, drove them towards a wood.

Before he got there, soldiers with flamethrowers chased them back inside a barn together with the farmer and his family and set fire to it. In Marzabotto in the Appenines, partisans – of which ninety were women – had formed a band called the Stella Rossa. They attacked a barracks full of German and Italian soldiers and made forays against the retreating troops. Retribution came swiftly. This was the most brutal massacre to date. At dawn, the area was sealed off and attacked from all sides. Among the estimated nine hundred people who died were 155 children under the age of ten, as well as five priests. A woman in a wheelchair was slaughtered in the cemetery. In the days after the killings, the area was eerily silent; there were only cows, wandering about. The Germans lost seven men and twenty-nine were wounded.

One of the stories that stayed long in people's minds was that of Cleonice Tomassetti, known to everyone as Nice. She was a 32-year-old *staffetta*, a brown-haired, slender woman with a flirtatious manner, and she had worked as a maid and a shop assistant in Milan until her anti-Fascist boyfriend died and she joined the partisans in Valdossola. Cleonice had not been with them many weeks when she was caught in a *rastrellamento* of the area. The Germans put a rope around her neck and tied it to a branch, pulling it up and down, releasing the pressure when she fainted. Later, she was taken to a barracks and put in a cellar with a group of hostages and partisans. She was quiet and dignified. When she saw the German soldiers adjusting their uniforms and getting out their weapons, she said to the others: 'Don't be afraid. Remember that it's better to die as Italians, than to live as spies and servants of the Germans.' One of the soldiers, who understood Italian, slapped her.

But what everyone remembers is the picture of Cleonice, beneath a banner with the words 'Are these people the liberators of Italy or are they bandits?', leading a line of forty-two men – she was the only woman – many with bloodied faces, very slowly along a deserted street. She looks calm. They walked for five kilometres. At the place of execution, Cleonice was one of the first to die. The local priest and the families were forbidden to collect the bodies. One eighteen-year-old boy survived. Later he took the name 'Quarantadue', in memory of his forty-two friends.

Cleonice Tomassetti leading partisans to their execution

The Germans were not alone in terrorising Italy. At their side, and often despised by them, were the Fascist militias and vigilantes. Soon after the fall of Rome, profiting from the evident corruption and inefficiency of Ricci's Guardia Nazionale Repubblicana and the fear that the Allies were advancing rapidly on the north, Pavolini, the strutting, vain, fanatical follower of Hitler, persuaded Mussolini to allow him to militarise the Fascist Party, thereby creating yet another new fighting force, the Brigate Nere. All existing male Fascist Party members aged eighteen to sixty were ordered to join and told that if they failed to do so they would forfeit their party membership. Their main task, they were informed, was to counter the 'partisan poison' which was afflicting Italy, 'without mercy . . . let it be a total vendetta'. There would be no taking of prisoners, only executions. Their uniform was to be a black shirt or sweater, khaki jodhpurs, knee-high boots and a skull and crossbones as insignia.

Italy's northern cities were full of unkempt, slovenly, violent young men hanging around the streets, cigarettes dangling from their mouths. They found the idea of the brigade very appealing.

Recruits flocked. Some were just thirteen, others men in their seventies, harking back to the heroic days of punitive expeditions. The oldest was eighty-three. The Germans nicknamed them '*i neri*', which pleased Pavolini. 'We like this,' he declared. 'We are black, that lugubrious and unforgiving colour.'

Since no checks were made on military ranks, former sergeants restyled themselves as majors. Pavolini made himself a colonel. He set up his headquarters on Lake Garda, with its own press corps, military tribunal and post office. Like the Roman legions, he divided his men into threes – three squadrons, three companies, three battalions forming brigades, which were named after martyrs fallen in the cause of Fascism. Though they lacked almost every-thing – money, petrol, vehicles, uniforms and above all weapons, which the Germans dragged their heels over providing – by the end of June, Pavolini was able to inspect his new force, baptised in showers of flowers and cigarettes by the women auxiliaries at the parades so beloved by the Fascists. Among his recruits were a number of priests, soon known as the Cappellani Neri, who fought and prayed with their men and were disowned by the Vatican.

Turin got the Ather Capelli Brigade, which at its peak consisted of 6,000 men, under the local Fascist federal commissioner, Giuseppe Solaro. They set up their base in a former *carabiniere* barracks and began hunting for partisans, taking suspects back for interrogations, mostly at night, in rooms full of heavily armed men, their guns menacingly drawn. Since the Ather Capelli was as impoverished as all the other Fascist organisations, raiding parties were sent out to requisition what was needed, even irons for their uniforms and dominoes and dice. Farmers in the coun-tryside around Turin took to burying anything they valued. The Brigate Nere were soon known as the Briganti Neri, the black brigands. In Turin, the inhabitants crossed the road to avoid walking near the barracks. A radio transmitter was installed and former journalists and writers recruited. Fourteen Fascist women joined as auxiliaries, in their khaki trousers and black shirts, causing Chevallard to remark that they looked like 'a species of virago', barely recognisable as women. Piedmont, Mussolini declared, had to be 'pacified' before the other provinces because it was the 'very heart of Monarchical, Reactionary, Bolshevik conspiracy'. Bicycles were now banned for civilians in Turin, making the lives of the *staffette* still harder.

'*I neri*' were not, of course, the only hunters and predators. The spring and early summer of 1944 had seen a new slew of competing Fascist paramilitary forces across the north. Operating in heavily armed marauding gangs, they seemed to thrive on the excitement of killing. In the Legione Muti militia, the ex-convict Colombo had commandeered a magnificent Lancia car. Fifty-eight of his followers were women and the hangers-on included twenty-three chefs, fifty waiters and a masseur. One in ten members of the legion had a criminal record. Colombo had also requisitioned two old biplanes, a cinema, a library and an armoured train. A dairy with a looted herd of twenty cows provided them with milk and butter. 'Pederasts', and a few Jews, saved from deportation, were press-ganged into service.

A small group of excessively brutal Fascists had been operating under a thug called Pietro Koch in Rome, and after the capital fell to the Allies they followed him to Milan. Here Koch installed himself in a luxurious villa, where expensively dressed men and women, often drunk and high on drugs, tortured the captured partisans in the basement. In various corners of Piedmont, a Battaglione Lupo, composed mainly of very young men, some still teenagers, indoctrinated since early childhood in the cult of the Duce, alternated manhunts for partisans with deep debates about the nature of Fascism and the future of Italy. The Germans found these youths useful when they had particularly dangerous jobs to do.

The forces lining up against the partisans were growing, in a great confusing jumble of military, legal, semi-legal, autonomous and renegade groups, some German, some Italian, all violent and vindictive and all, one way or another, looking over their shoulders at the advancing Allied forces and wondering what would become of them, once Italy was liberated. Few had any illusions that they would thrive. The civil war, as Ada had feared, was becoming more confusing and more brutal.

Against this background of constant menace, in which at any moment any one of them could be spotted, arrested and taken to the cellars of the German and Fascist torture centres, women, in their dozens, were joining Ada's Gruppi *di difesa della donna e per l'assistenza ai combattenti della libertà*. Though she had taken a while to work out for herself what they could actually achieve, Ada was increasingly excited by the possibilities that lay ahead. These *gruppi*, she decided, could indeed become the basis of a whole new Italian society. As she wrote later, explaining their cumbersome name, 'Why "defence"? Precisely because as the specific creator of life, woman is more prone, even more than man, to defend it. Why "assistance"? Because . . . fundamentally maternal, woman sees in the field of assistance one of her principal expressions. And why "woman"? Because woman has in herself qualities, virtues and possibilities . . . that until then she was not aware of and that instead had to be developed in the great creative virtues of a different world.'

Ever energetic, impatient for things to happen, Ada hastened around Turin talking, explaining, persuading; her enthusiasm was infectious. For her much younger friends, Frida, Bianca and Silvia, all three of them children during Fascism's oppressive years, the ideas now put forward seemed revolutionary, intoxicating; perhaps most especially so for Frida and Silvia, whose Waldensian upbringing had conceded only minor roles to girls. In Ada's house, the women met, planned, dreamt, talked about the future while organising the delivery of packages to Turin's many hundreds of political prisoners, without which they would starve. It was companionable, and it felt safe, a bulwark against the surrounding chaos.

The defining premise behind the GDD was that they would be open to all women, regardless of politics, class, age or religion. The four friends agreed that, as the war entered its painfully slow closing stages, their task was to promote active, physical resistance to the occupying Germans, by means of strikes and protests in factories, schools and offices. The list of things to accomplish was long. Money would have to be raised and acts of sabotage thought out. Strikes would have to be arranged to demand better and more equal pay, more help in looking after children, more rations, paid maternity leave, and an end to night-time work and dangerous factory conditions. This was for now. After Italy was free again, the horizon looked boundless.

All Italian women were invited to join in this 'profound revolution', not as pale or poor imitations of men, but as individuals worthy of 'complete parity'. 'Get together,' they were urged, 'encourage your more diffident friends to join you, tear your sons and your husbands and your fellow citizens from the clutches of the Germans!' Women of Italy, 'Do not reject, out of laziness, indifference or fear the responsibilities that are being offered you.' Ask yourselves: 'How do we want to live tomorrow?'

Sitting round Ada's table, the four women and their friends wrote. It was a war, noted one, 'nested in kitchens'. They put together pamphlets, flyers, posters, the tone urgent and declamatory. Silvia discovered that she had a talent for clear, concise sentences. A newspaper, *Noi Donne*, We Women, took shape, borrowing its title from an earlier paper written among the Italian exiles in Paris in the 1930s, informing readers about voting, working conditions, education and, again and again, about the need to build a new Italy. Copies travelled secretly to the liberated south and all over the occupied north.

Bianca had become a skilled printer and set up a paper for factory women called *La Difesa della Lavoratrice*, the Defence of Women Workers, also mirroring an earlier publication. A ruined building off the Piazza Statuto became a storeroom. Here *staffette* came to collect the latest papers, carrying away bundles to hand on to other *staffette* in the different sectors. In the afternoons, the four women stood outside factory gates and schools and offices, handing out what they had written to the women leaving for home, one eye constantly on the lookout for danger. Esther Valabrega, crushed by the death of her fiancé Sandro Delmastro, flung herself into the work with a recklessness that worried the others. When she was picked up by the Fascists with lists of names, they feared for their own safety; but there were no repercussions and she was freed in a prisoner exchange.

Not all the new recruits were content simply to read and talk. To match the male partisans, who had formed themselves into *volontari per la libertà*, the women set up their own matching formations, *volontarie*, specifically to carry out acts of sabotage and to mobilise other women. Bianca, who had remained closely involved with Turin's industrial belt, was one of the young women who went into the factories to explain the steps they should take. The *volontarie* took on a structure: thirty women, under a commander, a deputy and a political commissar – 'young, brave, audacious . . . unconditionally devoted to the cause of liberty' – split into *squadre* of five, modelled on what they imagined Russian fighters to be. It was hard at first to take on tasks that had only ever fallen to men; but they learned fast. Politics, they were discovering, was exciting. Later, many would speak about a feeling of exultation when they discovered what they were capable of. Danger, remarked Ada, had turned discontent into a mass movement. '*Guerra alla guerra*' became their rallying cry. A decision was taken to split Turin into five zones, each with its own leadership.

The movement was spreading, catching fire, moving from town to town, province to province. Soon, the women of Modena and Parma, Alessandria and Genoa were staging strikes. They were attacked by the Fascist militias, and casualties and deportations followed, but they kept going. The first to die was a mother of five young children, in a factory in Forlì. Since it was all so risky, many learned to use revolvers. The factory women were instructed in small acts of sabotage, like sewing military boots so poorly that they fell apart. Successes were followed by further protests. In Carrara, when ordered to evacuate the town by the Germans, the women staged an enormous demonstration and the Germans backed down. In Schio, after drunken militiamen assaulted three young girls, the GDD organised a two-day strike, which spread and paralysed the area. And the women became imaginative, resourceful. Faced with the perennial shortage of salt, they arranged for those living near the sea to boil up vast vats of seawater, from which they distilled salt, which could be used as barter. Carrying it over the mountains, the bearers called themselves '*formichine*', little ants. They invented codes, *noms de guerre* and found safe houses. 'Oh women of Italy,' they sang, 'oh women, oh girls, / Rise up and gather, for in every piazza / The Fascist is back, to oppress us yet more / The hour has sounded – to war!'

As the movement gathered pace through Piedmont, Liguria and Emilia, so Ada found herself in meetings with other emerging women leaders, travelling up and down between Meana and the valleys to Turin and to Milan. Often, these journeys were interminable, the trains halted by air raids, during which the passengers got out and ran across the fields into the forests. At a full gathering of the northern GDD in Milan, she was amused to find herself one of only two women who had not dressed as if going to a party. One wore a fox coat, another an elegant hat with a red feather, a third fine embroidered gloves. The discussions, she noted wryly in her diary, were a bit like the clothes, 'many compliments, many abstract statements, and many concerns for each other's feelings'. Very little of importance was actually concluded but she came away pleased that all the women seemed disposed to 'work together fairly'. Ada herself was always resolutely scruffy.

From the first, the GDD were dominated by the more active and vocal communists. Ada had nothing against the communists, but had been irritated by the sectarian and dogmatic attitude of one of its leaders who informed her that she would not be welcome in their ranks unless she espoused their principles. What she proposed now was a separate organisation for the women of her own party, the Partito d'Azione, and at her kitchen table the four friends mapped out the Movimento Femminile Giustizia e Libertà.

Ada's idea was that each of the six political groups that made up the northern CLN, which all had their own partisan formations, would equally have their own women's sectors, collaborating, remaining distinct but collegiate. She was therefore cross and nonplussed when the CLN abruptly decided to keep them all together under the umbrella of the GDD. But she agreed to join its secretariat, while promoting the independence of her own group. Silvia's imagination was taking flight in an outpouring of communiqués, and she took on the job of producing a paper especially aimed at Partito d'Azione women. They decided to call it *La Nuova Realtà*, the New Reality, which, as Ada pointed out, was a better reflection of what they had in mind than *Noi Donne*. Late at night, they talked about this new Italy, in which men and women would be equal. But alone, Ada wondered how realistic it really was. 'Will we ever be able to do it?'

It was not easy, as the Germans moved north, and the Fascists grew more vicious, conscious that their time in power was limited, to remain free and safe. Early in the summer, Bianca received a message from Auschwitz. It was from Levi, but was signed by his friend Lorenzo Perone, a fellow Piemontese working as an indentured labourer in the factory in Auschwitz to which Levi had been assigned. Lorenzo was providing Levi with an army mess tin of soup every day and occasional bits of clothing, handing them over surreptitiously when their paths crossed. He would accept nothing in return, not even money for his family. The message told Bianca that Levi was alive and well, if thin. She passed it on to Levi's mother and sister and they in turn were able to use Lorenzo as a conduit for messages back. Levi later wrote that, because of Lorenzo's selflessness and generosity, his 'pure and uncontaminated humanity . . . I did not forget that I was myself a man'. But soon after the note arrived, Bianca herself was very nearly caught.

One evening, delivering letters and messages high in the mountains above Susa, in the little village of Fenestrelle, she heard the unmistakable sound of an approaching *rastrellamento*, the grinding gears of military vehicles making their way up the single steep mountain road, effectively cutting off all escape. The partisans she had come to see faded away into the forests. The villagers hastily put up their shutters and retired into darkened rooms. Total silence fell, while the sounds of the German vehicles grew louder.

Bianca knew no one in the village. It was, she wrote later, as if time itself had stopped. Thinking that her only course of action was to behave as if entirely innocent, she went into an old inn, the Tre Re, and ordered a bowl of soup. When the Germans arrived, they burst in, dragged her over to a wall and shouted that they knew that she was a partisan. At this point the proprietor, emerging from the back, calmly told them that Bianca worked for him, helping him out from time to time. He gave her an apron, and she retreated behind the counter. For the next three days, while the Germans remained in Fenestrelle, she served them. Later she would say that vanity had made her leave her glasses behind, and that she had great difficulty reading the labels on the bottles when they gave her their orders. The German soldiers watched her closely, suspiciously, but made no move. When they left, she leapt gratefully onto her bicycle and headed down the mountain road, where she was immediately caught in the crossfire between the departing soldiers and the partisans, who had returned to harass the enemy. Only by flinging herself into a ditch did she emerge unscathed.

But it was Frida, excitable, voluble, impulsive, obstinate Frida, who very nearly lost her life. She was now living in hiding with her mother Giulia in a rented flat in Turin. With all three of her children wanted partisans – Gustavo as editor of *Il Pioniere*, and Roberto as commander of the V Alpine GL Division – it had been decided that Giulia was no longer safe in Torre Pellice. Frida was working undercover in a car factory in the city and in two other factories in the valleys, recruiting for the GDD, when she was asked to accompany a partisan up into the mountains. Soon after, the young man was picked up by the Fascists. Under interrogation, he gave her name. Cycling down to Pinerolo to catch her train back to Turin, she was followed by a militia patrol, stopped, arrested and taken back to their barracks. Left on her own in a room with an open stove, she shredded the documents she was carrying and threw them onto the flames.

One of the Brigate Nere was a boyhood contemporary of Roberto's, a hard and angry young man who had sworn that if he caught him, he would personally pull out Roberto's nails, one by one. This militiaman had once been caught by the partisans, and condemned to death, but had escaped, thanks, it was thought, to the tender-hearted Jacopo Lombardini. He now came to interrogate Frida. His manner was cheerful, almost merry. He asked her about a flyer found on her which spoke of revolution. She explained that she was writing a paper on the French Revolution. She was apprehensive, but felt somewhat reassured by the fact that the room was full of other Fascists from the Brigate Nere, who seemed to be competing against each other for her favours. No one touched her. Would she prefer, they asked, to be sent to prison or deported to a concentration camp? Prison, she replied.

In due course, they moved her to their barracks in Turin, where they left her for thirty-six hours without food. From the window, she could just see out into the street; she waved wildly at the passers-by, some of whom she recognised; but no one did anything. Indeed, what could they do? After three weeks, menstruating and her clothes filthy, she was allowed to communicate with the wife of a Waldensian pastor. She was then transferred to the much feared Fascist headquarters in Via Asti. She was hungry, dirty and now very afraid. She could hear the shots when partisans were taken out into the courtyard and executed. She had got hold of a piece of paper and a pencil and tried to make a note of their names as they passed her cell. In the evenings, guards sometimes came to slap her about.

Then, suddenly, Frida's fortunes turned. A captain in the Brigate Nere came to her cell one night and said to her: 'Listen carefully. We know everything about you. But I am going to let you go. Walk quickly away and don't look back. Your brother saved my woman from a difficult situation in Torre Pellice.' Frida left, went straight home, put milk on to boil, then fell asleep, with the gas on. When she was found, she was almost unconscious. She was taken to hospital. Later, she learned that the captain's fiancée had been caught by Roberto's partisans who, knowing of her involvement with the Fascists, were intending to execute her. Roberto stopped them, saying that they had no proof, and in any case, as honourable men, there were things that should not be done. The girl had been freed.

Though it had been a terrifying experience, Frida refused to slow down. A sort of frenzy now possessed the women, as if only unremitting action could save them. She dyed her blonde hair black, cut her fringe, discarded her casual clothes and bought a fur coat and a flamboyant hat. It made her, she thought, look like a tart. She changed her name again, this time to Giovanna Malaspina. Now, in the factories, women stared at her. One asked: 'How can you bear to go around like that, dressed like a capitalist?' But she felt safe.

The flat she shared with her mother became the meeting place for the secret factory committee, with Giulia keeping watch from the balcony. Incriminating documents were hidden under the potatoes. *Staffette* came from Turin's factories – there were two attached to each committee – with information about what they were doing, and Frida compiled it into reports, which she then delivered to the leadership of the Partito d'Azione. Nothing made her pause, not even a sudden encounter in the street with one of the Fascists from Via Asti, who recognised her and made to approach. She just had time to flee into a nearby cafe which had a back entrance. She got away.

12

Summer of flames

The summer of 1944 in Piedmont became known throughout the north as the 'glorious summer', or, sometimes, the 'summer of fire'. German flames did indeed consume swathes of village houses, and German and Fascist soldiers slaughtered partisans and civilians alike, but after the Normandy landings and the fall of Rome in June, the northern Resistance was riding high. The partisans had been much encouraged by General Alexander's call for a 'violent and sustained assault' on the enemy. They obeyed, with some 2,000 acts of sabotage in a month. No longer feeling isolated, they believed the end to be near. For all their setbacks, the number of fighters had risen to some 25,000 across Piedmont. But the violence was not over.

After scoring successes and then suffering defeats in the valleys of Chisone, Germanasca and Pellice, the Germans turned their attention to the all-important Val di Susa which, in view of the suspected imminent Allied landings in the South of France or the Ligurian coast, they could not afford to lose. Ada was overwhelmingly busy with the rapidly proliferating women's groups, but she was also trying to bring unity to the disparate bands fighting in the lower, middle and upper valleys.

She was in Meana towards the end of June when the Communist Garibaldini attacked the nearby village of Bussoleno and blew up its railway bridge. Orders had gone out from the partisan command to concentrate on sabotaging electricity pylons, bridges and railway lines. Bussoleno, with its large railway depot, was a crucial German stronghold. Hearing from a neighbour about a German counter-attack, Ada walked down the hill to see Teta in the village shop, where she learned that soldiers were now advancing rapidly towards Meana and Susa. Most of the local men had time to disappear into the forests; but the families who had come up for the summer, scornful of the idea that the *rastrellamento* might include them, declined to hide.

Having carried food up the mountain for the hidden men, Ada returned to see a mournful procession of outsiders, press-ganged by the Germans as porters. Later all the men and boys found still in the village were locked into the local school, while the women crowded outside, herded by German soldiers shouting 'Raus! Raus!' They seemed to Ada not so much cruel as 'impassive and mechanical'. Two days later, leaving the women in tears, the men were loaded onto trucks, destined for deportation as slave labourers to Germany.

The attack prompted Ada to act. She set off in search of Marcellin, a former sergeant and ski champion who she had heard was leading a band of some thousand men and women, to see if he would join forces and set up a command for the upper valley. Climbing the mountain tracks, she found the pink rhododendrons in flower. In the fields, the poppies were out. Marcellin greeted her warmly. She was impressed by the orderliness of his camp, the guards at the checkpoints, the fit young partisans with their goatee beards and sunburnt shoulders. What she admired in Marcellin, she thought, was his heroism, nostalgia for the past, concern for the future, all traits she considered ideally suited for 'this war of ours'. For his part, Marcellin noted that the meeting with Ada had been pleasant and cordial. 'I have always had a weakness for positive people,' he wrote. 'She won me over.' Together, they drafted a number of contracts between the various valleys, agreed to meetings with other bands, and talked of setting up a joint partisan radio station, which Ettore would help put in place.

Before she left, Marcellin gave her a pass, stamped and signed with his *nom de guerre*, Bluter. Ada studied the various names and aliases of his men and hid the list in a little sack tied to her belt. Descending the valley, she walked beside a stream under pine trees and passed a woman with goats and their kids grazing in a meadow. In the villages of Chiomonte and Gravere, she paused to note down the registration numbers of the German and Fascist vehicles and to assess the strength of the troops. She arrived back in Meana exhausted and soaked through by a sudden shower. In the village shop, Teta fed her and put her to bed.

Later, going on down to Turin, she felt impatient with a group of women she encountered behaving girlishly over having to cross the makeshift bridge strung up to replace the one blown up at Bussoleno. Ada had little time for frivolities. She called on Agosti in the courthouse and arranged to meet him in the park; they sat on a bench and made plans for the valleys. Duccio, now commander-in-chief for the Partito d'Azione across the whole of Piedmont, agreed to drive back with her up into the mountains to visit the different formations. Both had watertight false identification papers. When they were stopped at a German checkpoint, Duccio took a haughty line and they were saluted through. There was good news waiting for them: a large detachment of Czech soldiers had come over to the Resistance from the Germans, bringing with them blankets, equipment, uniforms and weapons. And Ettore had managed to establish working radio transmissions in the valleys. It went out under the name of Radio General Perotti, after the executed leader.

Ada was back in her house in Meana when, on 17 July, the Fascists attacked a partisan base at Triplex, not far from the French border, and Germans and Fascists arrived from the plains and began to move steadily up the valley. This was Marcellin territory and his men patrolled the passes. Fierce fighting continued all day, with six of his men killed. The valleys rang with the sound of gunfire. At dusk, the outnumbered Germans were forced to withdraw, leaving a considerable cache of weapons. Among their casualties was a German lieutenant, who was badly injured. Marcellin ordered him to be taken to the nearest partisan hospital and, when he died soon after, had his body, covered in an Italian flag, borne to the German command, with a letter expressing admiration for the fallen man's courage. Later, it would be said that Marcellin's gesture had effectively stopped reprisals against local civilians. One of his men, Momo, who was also a friend of Ada's, miraculously survived by feigning death and allowing himself to be buried under a pile of stones, later to be rescued after dark by his companions. The wounded were carried up the mountain on mules to Dr Bersano Begey's hospital eyrie. To prove themselves unbeaten, Marcellin immediately sent his men to blow up three electric pylons, two stretches of railway line and a main road, and to lay mines in the tunnels.

The battle for Triplex was merely a prelude for a more brutal attack. Karl Wolff, commander of the SS in the North, now unleashed what became known as Operation Nachtigall, sending up into the valleys above Turin some 4,000 Wehrmacht, SS, Ukrainians, Georgians, Brigate Nere and assorted Fascist units, along with a few tanks, heavy artillery and armoured vehicles, declaring that he intended to clear, once and for all, all partisan 'infestations' from the border regions. For days, partisans and occupiers fought, advanced, fell back, regrouped, advanced again. There were massacres and executions; hostages were rounded up; houses were set on fire. Day after day, trains pulled out of Porta Nuova in Turin, bearing partisan prisoners bound for Germany.

One young boy proposed rolling boulders down the steep mountain slopes onto the German troops below, and this was done, with considerable success. A captured partisan called Pietro was strapped to the top of a field gun on a bluff to prevent his comrades from advancing. He shouted out 'Shoot! Go ahead and shoot!' which they did. Pietro died, but the Germans were beaten back. After suffering heavy casualties, Marcellin ordered his men to retreat further up into the mountains, and the Germans advanced again, securing whole villages. Though they had lost many men, they now set up fortified garrisons, from where they were able to control the whole of the Val Chisone as well as the upper Susa valley. Unable to move around by day, the partisans came out at night, 'like nocturnal animals'. It was a painful setback.

Maria Gorlier, the young girl whose intimate knowledge of the mountain paths had helped Don Marabotto navigate his acts of sabotage from Thures, was one of the *staffette* caught by the Fascists in this summer of fire. Marabotto had been betrayed by a fellow priest, arrested and taken to the Fascist barracks in Cesana, where he was stripped of his habit and tortured, his hair, ears and neck singed with matches. But he did not give names. Maria's capture was a matter of extreme bad luck. One evening, coming down the mountains with a donkey, she neglected to observe the curfew. A Fascist militia picked her up and put her in a room opposite the one in which Don Marabotto was being held. The priest was forced to listen while the men stroked and mocked the girl. He could hear her praying and crying. At night, the door to her room was left open and the men returned repeatedly to molest her. After Don Marabotto protested, the officer in charge agreed to keep her cell door locked. But the soldiers had a second key.

One evening, while he was dozing, he heard Maria shout out: 'Better to die. I would rather die.' Then came the sound of a window opening, followed by a thud. She had managed to jump out of the window and had landed in the courtyard. The sergeant, alerted, shouted: 'Give me a gun.' There was a rattle of bullets. Later, at a trial of the Brigate Nere of Cesana after the war, he admitted that he could easily have taken her alive, but 'I wanted to kill her with my own hands, that was what I wanted'. At the time, her parents were told that she had been shot as she tried to escape, had reached the River Dora and drowned. But in court a doctor produced evidence that Maria had broken her leg in her fall, and could never have run anywhere. She was twenty-three. One of the last photographs taken of her was at a picnic in the mountains, sitting on an ancient cannon, with her brother, sister and Don Marabotto and the vast mountains all around.

Two weeks later, Don Marabotto was moved to Le Nuove. Instructions about the sabotage of an electricity plant had been found on him, and he was brought before a military tribunal and sentenced to death. Cardinal Fossati appealed directly to Mussolini, who neither freed Marabotto nor upheld the sentence. Don Marabotto stayed in Le Nuove, where Suor Giuseppina looked after him, listening, night after night, to the footsteps of prisoners taken out to be shot.

In Meana, during these terrible days, Ada brought home a sick eighteen-year-old-partisan and put him to bed. Before he went to sleep he put his arms around her; she kissed his forehead and stroked his hair. That night, she took the first watch; Paolo came to relieve her at three. She had become conscious, with a kind of 'forlorn sobriety', of the inevitability and tragedy of it all, the fact that the 'masses and crowds have become an army', an educated army, having learned things about politics that years of schooling had not taught them, and that there was no escaping the certainty that anyone caught would be deported or shot. She was not frightened for herself or for Ettore, but the panic she felt for her son tormented her.

Something of this stark reality was brought home when Fascist militia captured a young partisan from the Val Chisone who had come down to see his family. Stefano was sixteen, and the soldiers hanged him from the balcony of the municipal building in Meana, then left a squad of men to prevent the villagers from cutting him down. That night, passing silently along shuttered and deserted streets, Ada heard the young militiamen talking softly in a Venetian accent, as they stood guard. It filled her with intense sadness and a sense of futility. She had picked flowers in an abandoned garden and, after the soldiers left to return to their barracks, she touched the feet and the rigid cold hand of the dead boy, and laid the flowers at his feet. Weeping, she thought that nothing mattered any more, whatever anyone did to her.

On 7 August, the Germans came to Meana. Paolo just had time to escape to the forests through the vegetable patch. Ada walked down to Teta's shop in search of news, on the way giving wrong directions to four Germans who were looking for the quarry. She returned to find soldiers combing through her flat, flinging the papers from Paolo's desk onto the floor, and rifling through the pages of her diary which she had written in English. Calmly, she explained that she was a teacher. Graziella, her land-lady Esterina's fourteen-year-old daughter, was in tears, terrified and furious because one of the men, having been scratched by her cat, had thrown him over the balcony. When they finally left, writing the letter K in chalk on the wall, Ada was intensely relieved that they had overlooked a cartridge in a pocket of a jacket and various items of military clothing.

Flames were rising from her neighbours' houses. While Esterina began to dismantle the knitting machine which was her livelihood, and Ettore packed a knapsack with a precious dinner service, Ada carried out winter clothes and blankets and dragged them to the forest. She decided to abandon the translations she had been working on. Graziella was darting feverishly about trying to save her things. From the fields, Ada could hear the terrified bellowing of cattle. When a German soldier appeared and asked for a glass of water, Ada asked him what the K meant. K is all right, he told her; the houses marked F – *Feuer*, fire – would all be burnt.

Seeing the tearful Graziella, he asked what was wrong with her. Ada was sharp. 'Do you think that these are sights that children should witness?' For a moment, the soldier looked stricken. Sitting on the doorstep he said that he too had children and that he hated what was happening. Ada asked him to stay with them for a bit, to protect them. He did so, but in silence, his face 'cold, passive and lifeless'. When the last of the Germans pulled out from the village, he followed them; he did not say goodbye.

Ada went to inspect the damage. Seventy houses had been burnt as an act of terror. The village animals had been rounded up to drive away, but one of the older mules kept trying to get back to its master, until beaten into submission. There was a moment when Ettore was going to be forced by the Germans to drive the animals to the station but a canny villager volunteered to do so himself. Along the way, yelling and shouting, he managed to scatter them in the nearby forest. Ettore's papers had been scrutinised, but as a state employee, he was safe.

A few days later, the Germans returned. This time they came with a list of people to arrest, evidently provided by a spy. A naive and very young local priest, who had been looking after an injured partisan, made the fatal mistake of persuading the boy to give himself up to the Germans, believing the captain to be a friend. They hanged him from the balcony of his own house. As in the Middle Ages, bodies were to be seen hanging from trees, balconies, lamp posts.

Later that night, listening to her radio, Ada heard that the Allies had liberated Florence.

13

Haunted by death

On the night of Saturday 5 August, the Germans hanged Willy Jervis. He was already dead, having been shot earlier in the day with five other men in Villar Pellice, in reprisal for soldiers killed during the recent *rastrellamento* of the valleys. His body was found by villagers next morning, hanging from the lamp post closest to the church. Covered in mud from being dragged along the ground, he would not have been identified had the pastor not found a Bible lying by a wall next to him, protected from the rain. Inside the back cover, in pencil and capital letters, Willy had written a last letter to Lucilla. 'My dear love, as things have turned out I fear there is no longer any hope. God's will be done. I will have faith until the last. I am calm, God comforts me. I am certain that you too will find consolation . . . I will always think of you. Kiss the children for me, poor little things, be strong for them.'

During the 147 days of his captivity, Lucilla and their friends had believed that Willy might be saved. His colleagues at Olivetti offered ransom money, partisan groups worked on possible escapes, and there was repeatedly talk of a prisoner exchange or an eventual transfer to a labour camp in Germany. Twice, Willy was led out to be shot; both times he was taken back to his cell. But his jailers were not in the mood for leniency. The failed July plot against Hitler had resulted in orders for increased brutality throughout the occupied territories, and, combined with the Normandy landings and the growing numbers of German casualties in Piedmont, this sealed Willy's fate.

After his capture in February, Willy had been held in solitary confinement in Le Nuove and never allowed to leave his cell. Opposite him were a number of Jewish prisoners, awaiting

deportation to Germany. Permitted no books, and fighting a losing battle against fleas and lice, he spent his days doing exercises,
thinking, praying and singing hymns as he walked backwards and
forwards in the small space. His faith, he said, became an interior
'free zone' where he could isolate his thoughts. For a while, Lucilla
was allowed to bring in food and tobacco for his pipe; he craved
sugar. Then she was told that she could deliver only medicines,
soap and clean linen. He asked for, and was allowed, his Bible.
Two weeks after Emanuele's confession, Willy gave one of his
own; like Emanuele he gave names, but he denied all knowledge
of the partisans' activities or their whereabouts. He said that
Roberto Malan was a '*capo banda*', one of the military leaders.

Agosti had managed to bribe one of the Italian guards to carry
messages in and out of the prison. Willy scribbled his, with the
stub of a pencil three centimetres long, on tiny scraps of paper.
The ones Lucilla sent back, sometimes sewn into the lining of the
clean linen delivered with all the other mothers and wives on
Thursdays, were calm, loving, uncomplaining. 'This trial which
we are undergoing, together and separate,' she wrote, 'will serve
to cement still more the already strong love we have for each
other.' When Willy had been there for six weeks, she reminded
him that this was the longest they had ever been apart. Their
daughter Paola had just turned five. 'Don't pity me and don't call
me "poor",' he told her. And if he were to die, he would prefer
her not to wear mourning. On 20 July, returned to his cell after
his second false execution, he wrote: 'I live, by a miracle. Help!'

Behind the scenes, the entire remaining leadership of the Partito
d'Azione were doing all they could: they bribed, they negotiated,
they bartered. In April, it seemed that Willy was about to be
released: Lucilla looked for a hotel where they could go to be
together. Later, she wondered whether had she done more, made
more fuss, thrown herself at the feet of the Germans, it might
have ended differently. But when Emanuele, having stayed silent
for days under vicious torture, finally gave Willy's name as one
of the Partito d'Azione's senior organisers, responsible for liaising
with the Allies, there was very little anyone could do, particularly
after partisans executed a German officer who might have been
used in a swap. Signing the death warrant, the German in charge
wrote: 'Engineer Jervis must be considered an extremely

dangerous element.' What agonised Lucilla was that Willy had spent his last night in the barracks in Torre Pellice, very close to her, and that she had not known he was there.

On the morning of 6 August, Lucilla noticed that the people around her seemed to be behaving strangely. She glimpsed Agosti, but he pretended not to see her. Then, as she was preparing lunch, she saw Willy's parents and his sister Laura walking slowly up the hill towards her. She did not need to be told that Willy was dead. They stopped her from seeing his body, but they gave her his Bible and the letters found in his pocket; some were covered in blood. At the time she had no wish to see him, but later she minded that she had not touched his face and his hands one last time. Giovanni, her son, 'behaved like a man'. She only saw him cry once, when she and the children were allowed to go to the cemetery where Willy had been hastily buried. That night, *staffette* placed a huge poster recording his death, its edges painted in the colours of the Italian flag, in the middle of the village.

For Agosti, who had not known Willy long but had grown very close to him, and who had persuaded him to join the struggle and act as go-between with the Allied missions, Willy's death was terrible. 'I lose a dear friend,' he wrote sadly to Bianco. 'He had a rare moral strength.' Even if the Resistance won, the best men would have disappeared. Italy had become medieval in its horror, and at the end there would be nothing left 'for men of conscience and heart other than suicide or the cloisters'. Only 'little men' would be left alive to rebuild Italy. Today, he went on, 'I don't want to think about anything except for vendetta, vendetta that will be just, but which must be merciless.' He felt that he had neither the will nor the physical strength to go on, but clung to a belief that what mattered was acting, doing, keeping faith with one's beliefs and so reaching the end with nothing to reproach oneself with. When he told Ada about Willy's death, his voice, she wrote in her diary, 'usually so firm and ironic, was trembling'.

Towards the middle of August, a *staffetta* came to find Ada to take her to an elusive partisan commander called Giulio Bolaffi. She had been wanting to meet him for some time, having heard that he had recently occupied the slopes of the Rocciamelone mountain opposite her house at Meana with thirty-two followers, brought across from the Val Chisone after a fallout with the Garibaldi Communists. Bolaffi was rumoured to be profoundly wary of alliances and deeply averse to political control. Still in pursuit of a unified command of the valleys, Ada hoped to win him over. Others had tried and failed to woo him, but behind Ada's charm and sweet nature lay dogged determination.

Bolaffi was an interesting man. He was Jewish, the descendant of merchants in precious stones and ostrich feathers from Gibraltar, with a grandfather who had been an unsuccessful theatre impresario. His father had grown up in Turin where, at the age of nineteen, he had bought an important stamp collection and been asked by Queen Elena of Savoy to curate her own valuable stamps. Bolaffi had a law degree but his passion too lay with stamps. When in due course his father turned the business over to him he rapidly built it up into one of the most renowned collections in Europe. Politics meant little to him until the anti-Semitic laws of 1938; before then he had happily spent the Fascist years as a party member, described by the secret services as a 'mediocre Fascist', one who neither supported nor opposed Mussolini.

Seeing his friends lose their jobs and finding himself increasingly marginalised, Bolaffi had helped set up a network of hiding places in the valleys above Turin for Jews who could not afford to emigrate, drawing in local hotel owners, priests and *carabinieri*, and often paying for them out of his own money. In 1942, under the anti-Semitic laws, he had been forced to hand over his main stock of stamps to an Aryan colleague. The following year his wife died and, with a warrant out for his arrest, he moved his two young children, Stella and Paolo, up into the mountains to hide with a schoolteacher under false names, buried his most valuable stamps in a box in the garden and joined the Resistance. There was nothing martial or athletic about Bolaffi's appearance. He was forty, stocky, plump, round-faced with a rather sharp nose and beady eyes and he had never strayed far from his desk. But he was an exceptional organiser, solicitous about those around him, and the men who joined him in the early days loved him, and followed him to the Rocciamelone.

Ada met him in the woods and came away impressed. Bolaffi, she wrote in her diary, was 'a good man', even if he had a 'most bourgeois' view of politics. She noted that he treated his men with a mixture of good-humoured kindness and authoritarianism, 'a bit like a priest, a bit like a teacher'. Evidently won over by her charm and determination, Bolaffi agreed to meet Duccio and the Turin leadership. Though the encounter lasted five tedious hours, during which Bolaffi kept asking for guarantees that he would be allowed to remain autonomous, a deal was struck and ten days later he and his men became a brigade under the unified command, with Bolaffi himself appointed military commander in the area. He showed Ada a photograph of his children, and proposed calling his brigade the Stellina, after his daughter, and also after a small goat adopted by the band as mascot. 'And why not?' Ada wrote in her diary. 'The name is not only dear to him, but it is a lucky one.' Bolaffi now took the code name Aldo Laghi, and gave Ada, who promised to be his link with the other bands, that of Ulisse. Towards her, he remained very respectful, heading his letters 'Caro Signor Ulisse'.

A week later, the Stellina went into battle. On 26 August, 180 Italian Fascists, under German officers, were spotted climbing the slopes of the Rocciamelone, evidently believing themselves undetected. Bolaffi led a force of a hundred partisans and took them by surprise. At the Grange Sevina, the enemy retreated into mountain huts, taking with them twenty elderly people and children as hostages. After seven hours, during which time he had forbidden anyone to fire on the grounds that it might endanger the lives of the hostages, Bolaffi decided to broker a truce. He would free the Germans, together with their weapons, provided the Fascists surrendered unconditionally. There was much discussion and much talk of dishonour, but the Germans capitulated. They left, the Fascist militiamen were taken prisoner and distributed into the custody of various bands, and the civilians were released unharmed.

For a while, Bolaffi's decision was severely criticised. Duccio reprimanded him for allowing the Germans to go free, rather than using them as hostages. But the battle had been an overwhelming success. Bolaffi had lost just one man, a Russian lieutenant who had joined the Garibaldini, and he had come away with 150 rifles, forty automatic weapons and two machine guns. To her great pleasure, Ada was promised a revolver for herself and given a tommy gun to take to Paolo. Carrying it to him, in pieces, dismantled by Ettore, and hidden under her Loden coat, she passed in front of a cafe full of Germans, then slipped in the mud, tearing her coat and exposing the barrel. No one saw. Her luck held.

News of the victory spread around the valleys, and other volunteers arrived. Soon, Bolaffi had six hundred men under his command. In the way that partisan exploits were often celebrated in verse, a song of Grange Sevina was written.

'We are soldiers of the Stellina, the little stars please us / Do not be fooled if our name sounds mild / Because we are Alpini of Italy.'

Still determined to prove his autonomy, Bolaffi set about binding his men into a coherent and united group. Getting a friend in the stamp business to dig up the box in his garden and sell his most valuable items, he established a fund for his partisans' families, made certain that there was always enough food, and insisted on good relations with the nearby villagers, ordering his men never to take anything without giving a receipt for it. Local women agreed to knit socks for his men. In his diary he recorded his daily acquisitions of cheese, rubber-soled boots, tobacco, sausage, salt and traps to keep down the mice. He found a doctor for his men in Bussoleno, got hold of a large supply of surgical instruments and drugs, and arranged for a captured SS nurse to help. Most days, he inundated the command of the Partito d'Azione in Turin with letters, debating, protesting, demanding; Agosti and his colleagues complained that Bolaffi was stubborn, dictatorial and a nuisance and called him 'the most undisciplined commander' in the field, but admitted to admiring his results. Ada had grown fond of him but it took all of her tact to keep the peace. Together they talked about the need to create an army of experienced mountaineers and skiers, willing to prove themselves in the 'battle of the spirit'. Though passionately opposed to the idea of a political commissar, Bolaffi finally allowed her to take the position with his men. And he grew fit, no longer the 'pale Jewish philatelist', but a fighter, lean, younger-looking in his military kit.

A squad of alpine partisans

Locally, the partisans were at last making progress. The FIAT factory in Susa's lower valley was making fighter planes under German control. News came that the Allies were intending to bomb it. The partisans had other plans. A Garibaldi brigade sent a man disguised as a worker to map the inside of the factory and bring back details of the number of soldiers and guards and their shifts. Late one night, 170 partisans from different bands descended silently from the mountains and attacked. Ten soldiers were taken prisoner and the entire factory was occupied. By the time the partisans pulled out, three hours later, without casualties on either side, they had destroyed the planes in production, sabotaged the machinery and made off with an exceptional haul of desperately needed weapons, including 240 machine guns, as well as ammunition, petrol and vehicles.

Fifty of the attackers were Georgians, caught by the Germans in Russia, press-ganged into the army and brought to Italy, and who had recently defected to the partisans. They were country men, hunters, and they were much admired by the Italians for their intrepid ways and their willingness to volunteer for the most arduous missions. Soon after, another group drove a lorry into a cigarette factory, locked up the workers and made off with 1,200 kilos of tobacco, which they took back into the mountains to distribute, preceded by a *staffetta* on a moped. It was a summer of daring exploits, of armed raids, stunts, hold-ups and ambushes, and Bolaffi and his men were behind many of them.

On 15 August 1944, 86,575 Allied troops and 12,250 vehicles were landed from boats on the coast of Provence, near Le Lavandou. Within days they had taken the strategic ports of Marseilles and Toulon. Hindered by Allied air supremacy and attacks by the French Resistance, the German forces withdrew through the Rhône Valley. Between June and the end of August, they lost some 600,000 men. An Allied border now faced Germany, all the way from the Swiss frontier to the Channel.

Having rapidly liberated the French side of the western Alps, the Allies were in a position to operate from France and Switzerland into northern Italy. The Germans had been expecting a landing in Liguria, and now scrambled to dispatch all possible reserves to stem the Allied advance. Ada heard the boom of cannons from the other side of the mountains. It took a while for it to become clear that the Allies, pressing on towards Berlin, had no intention of taking the Alps: the men landed in Provence were directed across France towards the German border. But Turin was in the very eye of the storm of war, with four German divisions, eleven Fascist divisions and 10,000 men from the Brigate Nere occupying Piedmont. They quickly secured a new Alpine front, but the partisans held many of the valleys.

The strategy of terror, reprisals, killings and hostage-taking intensified. Listening on her radio to the accounts of the Allied victories in France, her heart swelling with 'a joy that was almost painful' at the thought of the liberation of Paris, Ada worried about how, when and if peace came, she would cope with the 'new order', how she would remake herself, 'blood, instincts, thoughts and dreams', so as not to feel 'like a nostalgic, forlorn survivor'. 'I am afraid,' she wrote, 'this tomorrow will be so different, so hostile perhaps to too many things I had believed in.' The end, suddenly, seemed very near. When airplanes swooped low over the road down which she was cycling towards Turin, dropping their bombs around her, she carried on. 'As always,' she wrote, 'when I do not pay attention to something dangerous, I arrived in Turin unharmed.'

The attitude of the Allies towards the Italian partisans had, if anything, become more ambivalent. The British, increasingly fearful of a Communist takeover, continued to favour the Autonomi and the Monarchists; they wanted to isolate the Garibaldini and the Partito d'Azione formations and thereby weaken the Committee of National Liberation. What they feared most was a popular uprising and for the north to form its own separate government. Neither Churchill nor Eden had softened their hostility. The Americans, and in particular Allen Dulles at OSS, with their eye on a post-war Europe dominated by the Russians, saw Italy as an indispensable ally, and envisaged a grand epilogue for the partisans, in which they would expunge the ignominy of the armistice. Neither one of the Allies, nor the Bonomi government in Rome, however, wished the Resistance to be treated as regular soldiers and had only grudgingly permitted 5,000 Italian soldiers of the former army to take part in the final battle for Monte Cassino.

When General Cadorna, viewed as a peacemaker and organiser, was parachuted into Milan in the late summer, he brought with him directions from General Alexander to make certain that, in exchange for military support, 'combat should not be paralysed by political interference'. Since Cadorna was fervently anti-Communist, initial meetings with the CLN were awkward. The recently formed Psychological Warfare Branch, in charge of Allied propaganda, was instructed to 'play down very gradually the activities of patriots'. The Resistance was indeed acknowledged to be useful, but the Allies wanted small, biddable, trained groups of saboteurs and spies. The partisans wanted an army. And recognition of the Committee of National Liberation in the north continued to stall, as the Allies and the Bonomi government in Rome procrastinated, quarrelled and failed to get to grips with purging the more egregious Fascists.

This divided and often contradictory strategy played itself out in the endlessly vexed questions of missions and air drops. The Resistance in the north was desperate for weapons, ammunition, clothes and supplies. The early parsimonious and grudging deliveries of weapons brokered by Willy Jervis continued erratically. By the summer of 1944, 129 landing fields had been prepared in the north, but in practice only one drop in every two or three reached its target, either because of bad weather in the mountains or because rival groups, and even the Germans, had advance warning and lit decoys and made off with material intended for others. Provisioning the partisan formations had in part passed from the RAF to the more generous Americans, and B17 Flying Fortresses were taking over from some of the Halifaxes. The coded messages over the radio ranged from the prosaic to the literary, Dante's 'Nel mezzo del cammin di nostra vita' being popular. The supplies that did get through shaped many of the partisans' activities. When gelignite was dropped, a new Gruppo Dinamite was formed, which descended into the plains and carried out a series of operations designed to paralyse German communications and factories working for them. Even so, the drops remained a source of constant resentment, disappointments and bitterness.

Much the same mood plagued the missions of the Allied agents parachuted into the north. Though the attitude of the individual agents was considerably warmer towards the Italians than that expressed at headquarters, and became warmer the longer they stayed, few of them spoke much Italian and all found the labyrinthine politics on the ground almost impossible to comprehend. Given the rank of major or lieutenant colonel, they were instructed to wear uniforms, told to paint the British as mighty, invincible and reliable, and to remember that Italians had 'a keen sense of humour', and were by nature 'jealous, vain and theatrical'. They were warned that if captured by the Germans or Fascists they had 'only the slenderest chance of survival'. Given their tendency to be high-handed with the partisans, it was perhaps not surprising that sometimes, when the agents woke in the morning, they found that the band they had thought they were leading had slipped away during the night.

Raimondo Craveri, still running the Italian information service and in close touch with the OSS, was constantly on the move, between the Allied bases in the south, Switzerland and Algiers, and the north, juggling demands and arrangements with the party militants, the factory strikers and the leadership in Milan and Turin. He was fixing points for drops, and briefing agents on how to work with the vast network of existing and competing formations, coming together and disbanding in response to attacks. What he knew perfectly well, and what the Allies preferred not to see, was that in the north people regarded themselves as representatives of the future Italy, and that, having taken on the Fascists and the Germans, and scored many successes, they felt entitled to be taken seriously. 'In this partisan war,' noted Agosti irritably, 'we are allies of the Anglo-Americans, not their tools.' The question was how to persuade the Allies to recognise and use them sensibly. As Craveri wrote later, much more could have been achieved and much faster, and many more Germans defeated, had the Allies enabled the partisans to have a stronger, well-equipped network. In the summer of 1944, this was not on the cards.

No single Italian fought harder for his dream of an Italy liberating itself in a glorious insurrection than the by now exhausted Ferruccio Parri. In the middle of August, he went to Switzerland to meet John McCaffery, to put to him his plans for a revolutionary army for which he would need more weapons and supplies. McCaffery's reply, in the form of a letter, laid out the Allied view with disconcerting clarity. Italy, he wrote, had entered the war on the German side, at great cost to the Allies. If things had not turned out better for the Italian anti-Fascists then they had only their own quarrelsomeness to blame. 'Now,' he went on, 'you have the chance to find your feet again and to end up on the side of those to whom you caused so much damage. No one is more willing than we are to see this happen; no one is readier to help you. But, for God's sake, don't tell us how to conduct the military operation in the place of Eisenhower and Alexander! A long time ago, I said that the greatest contribution you could make to the Allied cause was sabotage, continuous, everywhere, on a large scale. You wanted partisan formations. I agreed, because I saw what moral value they offered . . . Then you wanted an army. Who asked you for this? Not us. You wanted it for political reasons . . . Do not complain if our generals are more concerned with military goals.'

When the letter was made public, a 'tempest of anger' spread around the Italian anti-Fascist leadership. Here was clear proof that the Allies intended to place obstacles to their plans for post-war Italy and that the partisans were regarded as peripheral and subordinate to their own war. As Parri observed later: 'What did the Allies think? They knew neither Italy nor us well.' The fact that the Allies were focused on defeating the Germans, and had little time, money or logistical support to help set up such an army, and that the liberation of Italy was far down their list of priorities, was not considered by the Resistance.

Having witnessed the massacre in Boves in September 1943, and watched the town burn, Lucia Boetta had spent the early part of the occupation guiding deserters from the army up into the mountains, stealing documents from municipal offices to serve as false identity papers, taking food to Jews awaiting deportation and making her house into a way station for people looking for hiding places. Returning one day from carrying funds from Duccio up into the mountains, she found a woman waiting for her at the end of her road to prevent her going home. A local boy had given her name to the Germans. Her fiancé, Renato Testori, hiding in an alleyway nearby, told her that soldiers were looking for her. Lucia was taken in by a priest, dyed her hair blonde, put on glasses and got new identity papers in the name of Laura Bianca, a refugee from Genova, where she had supposedly lost her mother in the bombing. She was resolute, contemptuous of cowardice.

When the British began dropping agents into Piedmont, Lucia became a specialist at conducting them around the mountains. She also persuaded one of them to train her in the use of explosives, so that she could train others. On her rounds, she stuffed detonators into the fingers of her gloves and wound fuses and wires around her stomach, and she showed railwaymen how to soften the explosive and then pack it into the wheels of carriages full of loot waiting to be sent back to Germany.

Lucia Boetta on her rounds

An early Allied arrival was an Irish captain, Patrick O'Regan, who came with instructions to coordinate the partisans in the Susa, Sangone and Chisone valleys. He was twenty-four, the son of a history master at Marlborough, and had started the war as a conscientious objector. Given a room by a local doctor, O'Regan was jovial, easy-going and much liked, cycling up and down the valleys and to Turin to meet Duccio. He had some battles with the bands over his insistence on distributing the dropped weapons and supplies himself, and had to deal with the disappointments and irritation that followed deliveries of guns and clothing destined not for the partisans but for the Allied prisoners of war still hiding out in the mountains, particularly when they were labelled '*Vietato agli Italiani*', forbidden to the Italians. O'Regan chose a landing strip in the plains, and set up a reception squad. With each drop came a packet reserved only for him, with tea, sugar and chocolate. In his reports home, O'Regan noted that the partisans seemed more concerned with politics than warfare, that they did not always tell him their plans, and that the political commissars were 'of nuisance value only'. During a brush with some Moroccans who had joined the partisans and were stealing from the villagers, he was slapped in the face. O'Regan's picture of the Allied missions was not encouraging: infinite confusion, a sort of blind man's buff, with uncoordinated agents wandering about, requesting drops that never came, and wireless operators who had their equipment stolen.

After O'Regan came Neville Darewski, who went by the name of Major Temple and whose father was a well-known Polish music-hall writer of sketches. Lucia considered Temple's false documents just about adequate but she was appalled by his obviously English clothes, forced him to take them all off and then burnt them. One day she led him through fourteen separate road blocks. For a while, they operated out of an abandoned castle and Lucia, who had grown up in a household in which girls led sheltered lives, found herself for the first time living in close proximity to a group of young men. The castle's housekeeper made up a bed for her on a sofa, and the boys treated her with respect. Later, she felt that this had been her rite of passage into a new Italian society. Like many of the *staffette*, she felt released by the war. She loved travelling around the valleys and up into the mountains, away from the cities where she never knew whom she could trust, and where every encounter could be a trap. 'Up there,' she said later, 'you breathed another air: an air of liberty, of fraternity. It felt as if you were living in another world.'

Journeys, for all of them, had, however, become extremely hazardous. After cycling was forbidden to all civilians in and around Turin, Ada was forced to put her bicycle onto a handcart and wheel it for fifteen kilometres across the plains to catch her train to Meana. Paolo and Alberto were making plans to derail a train along the Val di Susa and Ada joined them late one night, standing guard while they reconnoitred a section of the line. Later the boys came back to the house in Meana to sleep. When it was still dark, she was woken by sounds of German voices. Looking out of the window, she saw shapes in the meadow below the house: a German detachment was setting up camp. Terrified that someone would knock at her door and discover the house to be full of partisans, detonators and hand grenades, she alerted the boys and made them spend the rest of the night in a *grangia* further up the mountains. That day, Susa was bombed for the first time by the Allies. On meeting up with Bolaffi, Ada was given the revolver that she had been promised. His men had thoughtfully made a leather holster for her.

Ada's young friend Cesare was putting together a new band, under Bolaffi's orders, in the upper valley, bringing together partisans scattered by the earlier *rastrellamenti*. Paolo and Alberto joined him, and Ada and Bianca travelled up the valley on their bicycles to look for them, riding 25 kilometres in the hot sunshine, Bianca perched on Ettore's handlebars, keeping the others happy with stories and songs as they pedalled, sweating under heavy knapsacks.

The entry in Ada's diary on 13 September was bleak. 'Terrible news. Lisetta was taken in Milan by the Koch band . . . Knowing that she is in their hands is frightful.' Ada was especially fond of the charming young Lisetta, and had just received a happy postcard from her, saying how much she was looking forward to the birth of her baby and how many cigarettes Vittorio was smoking. Ada had watched with maternal approval her love affair with Vittorio and was constantly pleased to see how such happiness could flourish in these uncertain times. To distract herself from the anguish she now felt, and her own inability to help, she plunged herself into a frenetic round of new activities.

Despite her advanced pregnancy Lisetta had continued her work as a *staffetta*, moving between Milan and Turin and the valleys. She had just returned from a mission to Lecco and thought she would call on friends who lived not far from Milan's central station. It was, she said later, a moment of fatal imprudence. She had barely arrived when there were bangs on the door. Outside were militiamen, not from the usual Fascist squads, who might conceivably have treated a heavily pregnant woman with some respect, but from the infamous Koch band who respected no one.

Pietro Koch was in his late twenties and had a German father. He had a small head, a full moustache that fell over his lips and he kept his black hair neatly parted. He had trained as an accountant but had spent the early part of the war developing his skills as a trafficker and a fraudster. The arrival of the Germans had turned him into a keen persecutor of 'subversives' and he had helped the SS select the victims for the massacre in the Ardeatine caves. Early in 1944 Koch had joined forces with Tullio Tamburini, head of Salò's police, to set up a unit specifically to hunt down the partisans. By the time he settled in Milan he had gathered around him a collection of greedy, amoral, sadistic men – and ten women – who called themselves the flower of *squadrismo*.

What Koch and his unit specialised in was torture. In two town houses in Via Paolo Uccello – known as the Villa Triste, the Sad Villa – surrounded by high walls, covered in barbed wire, and with searchlights kept permanently lit, they kept their captives in underground cellars, decked out, survivors revealed later, like surgeries, with rows of instruments of torture. The floors were cement and the ceilings of the cells were too low for the prisoners to stand up. Two of the keenest members of the group were well-known actors, Luisa Ferida and Osvaldo Valenti, at the peak of their success and among the highest paid in Italy, who, when drunk or high on cocaine, would come down to the cellars to watch the torturers at work. Valenti treated the spectacle like a piece of theatre and Luisa, half naked under a transparent dress-ing gown, danced provocatively around the torture room. Teeth were knocked out or drilled down to the nerve and arms and legs broken. Several inmates tried to kill themselves. Koch prided himself on being a 'scientific torturer' and was constantly thinking up new variations. The two actors were useful go-betweens with senior Fascists.

Koch believed in treating his men well, saying that they could not be expected to do their jobs unless they were properly fed. A deal was made with a local restaurant, Da Giannino, which Koch kept supplied with black-market meat, oil, butter and wine. From their cells in the basements, the starving prisoners, often kept for days without food or water, could see through the bars of the window giant roasts of meat, fish, millefeuilles and bottles of wine and champagne carried past for the feasts.

Koch was protected not just by the Salò Minister for the Inter-ior, Buffarini Guidi, but by the German SS, who appreciated his results. In less than a year, he had extracted confessions and information that had led to some six hundred arrests, many of them leading partisans. He had also managed to track down a number of the remaining Jews in hiding. By the beginning of August 1944, the camp at Fossoli had been closed and the Jews caught by Koch and others were already in Auschwitz, Bergen-Belsen, Ravensbrück and Buchenwald. Families who came to the Villa Triste in search of news were told that if they showed up again they too would be thrown into the cells.

By the time Lisetta was taken to the Villa Triste, Koch was at the peak of his success. Increasingly dissatisfied with the results of their *rastrellamenti*, the Germans had come to see that spies and confessions under torture, especially in the hands of such able practitioners as Koch, yielded far higher numbers of partisan arrests. They were also spending considerable sums of money on informers: the capture of a prominent partisan was worth up to L10,000 and ten kilos of salt; that of a saboteur, L25,000; while a leader yielded as much as L100,000. Posters all over the walls of the northern cities and towns specified the exact amounts. The partisan press, meanwhile, had taken to publishing lists of the 'secret friends of the Germans', and when these Italian spies were caught, they were shot, with placards hung around their necks with the words: 'The Germans pay with money, we partisans with bullets.'

Koch and his men went about their work with relish. When Lisetta was brought in she was roughed up and a female guard dealt her a blow to her head. Later she would say that the fifteen days she passed in the cellars of the Villa Triste were a blur in her mind, as she had spent them not on observing her surroundings but on concentrating on survival. 'You had to keep your wits sharp in order to avoid being tortured, give away just enough plausible information which you knew would harm no one, live one moment at a time, thinking of nothing else.' For three days, under interrogation, Lisetta gave nothing away. It was only once she decided that Vittorio and her friends would have moved, changed names and identities, that she began to talk. Her life was made more bearable by the presence of another pregnant woman, the wife of a partisan, already in the Villa Triste. They clung together.

Ada, who could no longer bear being so far away from Lisetta, went to Milan to be with Vittorio. They agreed that there was probably nothing to be done: the next move was likely to be deportation, and the chances of survival for a pregnant woman in a concentration camp were negligible. Then one morning Koch, evidently anxious about the inevitable Allied victory, released two partisans, telling them to go to the Resistance and propose a truce: the release of Villa Triste's prisoners in exchange for a safe passage for himself to Switzerland. They were to return before nightfall, or all the inmates would be executed. The two men, bruised and ragged from torture, went to see Foa. The most agonising part of it was that it fell to him to tell them that no deal was possible: the decision had been taken by the CLN never to negotiate. Lisetta could not be saved. 'With hyenas,' Foa said, 'we do not deal.' In despair, he went to find an old friend who lived in Milan. She saw his face, said nothing and put Beethoven's 'Eroica' on her gramophone. They listened to it in silence.

Then came an extraordinary piece of luck. The Wehrmacht in Milan had been growing increasingly uneasy about the stories of depravity and bestiality coming out of the Villa Triste. When the CLN leadership asked Cardinal Schuster to intervene, and he in turn went to the German command to say that it was scandalous that two pregnant women were being tortured, the Wehrmacht decided to act. Though the SS protested, they ordered the arrest of Koch and his followers, and sent his bitter rivals, the Mutti legion, to apprehend them. Forty-three of Koch's men and women were detained, though Koch himself was allowed to go free. Lisetta and the other prisoners were rescued from the cellars and she and her friend were sent to the women's section of the San Vittore prison, in an old convent. Forty-four prisoners had been killed in the Villa Triste, and thirty-three of those who had survived were in an appalling state. Despite rations of food in the San Vittore that were slowly starving the prisoners to death, Lisetta felt better there, though she could hear constant screams coming from the men's section, and soon witnessed the departure of inmates for the camps in Germany.

Lisetta might have remained in San Vittore until she herself was put on a train for the camps, had it not been for the fact that a doctor, a prominent gynaecologist who served in the prison as an auxiliary, was also a secret supporter of the partisans. He schooled the two young women into how to fake complications to their pregnancies. He also contacted Vittorio to tell him precisely where they were being held. Lisetta would say later that one of the worst moments was having to pretend to faint while in a filthy latrine, and to stay there feigning unconsciousness until found and removed to a maternity clinic. Though still closely guarded, the two women were more comfortable. The director of the clinic, whose brother was a leading Fascist, appeared every day to say that the two young women looked to him perfectly healthy enough to return to prison, but his assistants managed to counter his orders. Sympathetic nurses brought them sandwiches, which they ate under the bedclothes, hidden from the guards.

It was now that Gigliola Spinelli, the bold planner of improbable stunts, came to Milan. At two o'clock one afternoon, during siesta hour, she arrived at the clinic dressed as a Red Cross nurse, bringing with her four young partisans. They disarmed the guards and locked them up, then hurried the two women, barefoot and in their nightdresses, down the stairs to a waiting car. A doctor, encountered in the corridor and seeing what was happening, said: 'Good, good, you're getting away.' Looking back up at the windows, Lisetta expected to see policemen with guns; instead there were nurses and nuns, waving their handkerchiefs. Lisetta was given a Red Cross uniform and she and Gigliola boarded a train for Turin. There was a further scare when, having reached the safe house, they were woken by police. Gigliola escaped by jumping out of the window and Lisetta hid in a cupboard before getting away over the roof.

A few days later, Lisetta went to see Ada. She had dyed her hair and was wearing glasses which gave her, Ada noted, a rather distinguished air. Recounting her story, she was both 'amused and proud'. Like Frida and Bianca, she had had a miraculous escape. The Resistance, Lisetta said later, took friendship to a new height, and it was something she had never encountered before nor would ever again. Ada, seeing her young friend safe, thought with tenderness about the child soon to be born.

In between visits to Turin to work with Silvia and Frida on articles for *Noi Donne* and *La Nuova Realtà*, and trying to recruit some nuns to join her GDD, Ada continued to travel around the Val di Susa, usually on her bicycle, to regular meetings with Bolaffi. Cycling one day with Bianca and two other women, she felt pleased to note that the four of them looked absolutely 'insignificant', 'neither blond nor brown haired, neither tall nor short, neither fat nor thin, neither pretty nor ugly'. Their very ordinariness would, she felt, protect them.

In October, an uneasy truce in the valleys – cessation of reprisals and the sparing of a number of captured partisans – brokered by Bolaffi with the Germans came to an abrupt end when a meeting which he had agreed to attend turned into a trap and he only just escaped in time. The partisans whose lives he had hoped to save were executed. Warfare resumed. Streams of tracer bullets fired by the Germans left long arcs of light which lit up the valleys. Walking down from Meana to Susa one day, Ada and Paolo failed to notice until too late that lorries full of Fascists were parked in the main square. A quick-witted *staffetta*, seeing them arrive, called out to say that she needed their help picking grapes; they followed her into the vineyard and slipped away.

Bolaffi decided to move his men further up the mountains. One night, after leaving his camp late and refusing an escort, Ada tripped, scrambled through thorn bushes, lost her footing and fell twenty metres down a slope. She was shaken but unhurt. In the distance she could hear shots. When the moon rose she saw that she had miraculously avoided falling down a rocky escarpment. She set off, crossed a stream, found the road, then, feeling too exposed in the bright moonlight, ducked back into the chestnut woods. Susa seemed to her almost as bright as day. Beyond it, she could see her house gleaming white.

She took off her boots, crouched down and began dashing 'like a cat' from shadow to shadow through the town. When she reached a street in plain view of the German anti-aircraft battery she crawled on all fours. Suddenly, out of the shadows, a German soldier appeared. They both stopped. For a minute they stood looking at each other in total silence. Then Ada calmly turned round and made her way back into the woods. The German never moved. Once out of sight, she began to run.

Paolo and his two friends Cesare and Alberto had thought to name their new partisan band at Beaulard, not far from the French border, after Franco Dusi, a school friend who had recently been killed. Local partisans came to help them build a log cabin, deep in the forest, well concealed by trees, and Ada drew up a rota of *staffette*. She had made contacts with women in the Christian Democratic Party, who had until now been wary of the Communist-dominated GDD, and felt that this was a good omen for the future. She was very conscious of how dishevelled she had let herself become, how careless about her appearance, compared to the neat and tidy women she was recruiting.

Ada and Bianca paid frequent visits to the cabin, worrying about the boys' comfort and its nearness to German positions. When the first snows came the fine traces of white on Paolo's eyelashes reminded her of his first long-distance ski run. She travelled home that day perched perilously on Cesare's sister's handlebars, through ice and rain, snowflakes whirling around them. She was never able to leave Paolo without a sense of desolation. In the early dawn, she had sat watching him sleep and seen that Bianca too was awake, looking at the sleeping Alberto and softly stroking his black hair.

Bianca was once again very nearly caught when she was talking to a partisan in a stable and a German patrol arrived. The two young people threw themselves on the straw and pretended they were making love. The Germans passed on. The women had no choice now but to be bold. Unable to find any other way of getting down from Susa to Turin, Ada hitched a lift with a German truck loaded with weapons. She travelled sitting on the barrel of a small cannon. Her own bag was full of explosives, which made her laugh.

In mid October, it fell to Ada to carry bad news to Bolaffi. His father, whom he had not seen for nine months, had died. Bolaffi was an emotional man. That night, he filled his diary with an outpouring of grief: 'My best friend, my comforter, my twin soul is dead! Why didn't I stay close to you? . . . I will be sad until the day I die . . .' Ada and his men did their best to soothe him. When she left, he read and reread all his father's letters, as well as those from his children, still hiding in the mountains.

Death haunted them all. They lived with it, thought about it, imagined it. Ada's terrors about Paolo filled her waking hours. The next family to be hit was that of Silvia Pons. She was still based in Turin, working as a doctor, *staffetta* and editor of the clandestine papers, going up to Torre Pellice whenever she could to see her small son, when news came of the death of Giorgio's younger brother. Nineteen-year-old Paolo Diena had only recently returned to the front line in the partisan war, having been held back by a commander who complained that he was too rash and heedless of danger. His sister Marisa, travelling up to the valleys, learned that two Garibaldini partisans had been killed in a skirmish after three lorries carrying Fascist militiamen suddenly appeared as they were stringing barbed wire across a road. It was open country, and there had been nowhere to hide. Not until the next day was she told that one of them was her brother, shot dead as he was throwing a grenade at one of the lorries. 'I fell to the ground,' she wrote later. 'I rolled on the grass, shouting, again and again, "it isn't possible, it isn't possible".'

The area where Paolo Diena had fallen was in enemy hands. Marisa was informed that her brother's body had been taken by his partisan friends to a cemetery and left there. The local priest, reluctant to become involved, gave her the keys to the cemetery gates but refused to accompany her. She found Paolo's body, covered in newspapers, on a narrow bench. He looked calm, she thought, handsome, with his black curly hair. Three days later, he was buried. Marisa returned to Turin to tell their parents. Marisa had always felt very protective towards Paolo, and now threw herself manically back into the war. Cycling furiously round the valleys, she found herself saying, out loud, again and again: 'Paquito is dead, Paquito is dead.' This had been his childhood nickname. Another light, Ada thought, has been extinguished.

Later, Marisa would marvel that her Jewish parents survived. For months they had refused to leave Turin, even after her father was briefly arrested and her mother's brother was caught, sent to the camp at Fossoli and then deported to Dachau, and after two elderly great uncles, identified as Jews at a hotel in the mountains, were also rounded up and put on trains for Germany. The most they would agree to was to move house from time to time, and her father agreed to grow a beard and wear glasses, saying that he thought it made him look less Jewish. One day, not long before Paolo's death, two young men in Fascist uniform had come looking for them and Marisa's mother explained that it was a case of mistaken identity. Realising that danger was growing closer, they had finally agreed to move to a small village not far away.

The day they arrived coincided with a surprise visit by a Fascist official from Pinerolo. As the villagers fled to hide, the two of them sat calmly in the village square, at a table in a cafe, while the locals wondered whether they were spies. Then Marisa had taken them up the mountains to see Paolo, going ahead with her bicycle, while they followed behind, stopping every now and again to pick peaches or apricots in the orchards. It had been a very happy reunion. But Marisa's parents soon grew restless and insisted on returning to their house in Turin. They remained safe, but they never saw their younger son again.

During the late summer and early autumn of 1944, the northern partisans felt that they had come of age. They had proved themselves as fighters and their leaders were at least partly united. Even schoolchildren were volunteering to help, carry messages and support strikes. And a remarkable experiment in democracy was starting across the north. After intense battles, a number of places were now under total partisan occupation and in these 'free republics' at Ossola, Carnia and Montefiorino, schools had been set up, mayors appointed, taxes collected, hospitals opened and newspapers printed. 'Popular administrative juntas', composed of men and women from the different parties, were organising courts and experimenting with a democracy that many of the people were too young ever to have known. In all of them, women occupied senior positions, doing things that for the last twenty years had been forbidden.

When the Germans laid siege around Carnia, blocking all the roads leading to the area, and starving its 90,000 inhabitants, 150 strong young women slipped between the lines on foot, walked to Emilia, and came back carrying baskets of wheat and cereals on their backs. Nineteen separate republics were set up, some lasting no more than a few days before being overrun by the Germans and Fascists, but the fact that they happened, and that they had given the inhabitants a taste of democracy, enchanted them all. The partisans, noted Chevallard in his diary, 'are spreading like a puddle of oil, slowly taking over, bit by bit, the whole countryside'.

The liberation of Florence in August had provided a model for what the partisans hoped would happen in the north. Bands of partisans had come down from the surrounding mountains to join in the freeing of the city. As Iris Origo wrote in her diary, 'destruction and death have united us . . . there is hope in the air'. But it had also presented the Allies with a new and not altogether reassuring situation. When they finally entered Florence, they found that the Tuscan Committee of National Liberation had taken over the municipal offices, installed a new mayor and city council, and regarded itself as the legitimate representative of the Italian government. They had consulted neither the Allies nor Rome before doing so. The Allies took a high-handed line and installed a prefect of their own, who was immediately challenged. While various accommodations, some cordial, some disputatious, were put in place, it was made perfectly clear that the anti-Fascists had no intention of yielding power to the Allies. It did not make the Allied command easy.

In the cities and plains of Piedmont, boys and girls, some no older than fifteen and sixteen, had formed themselves into Gioventù d'Azione and were carrying out acts of sabotage alongside the urban *gappisti* and *sappisti*, the fighters within the cities, whose attacks on the enemy were now everyday events. As the paper of their movement put it, these young people were acquiring a 'profound moral sense . . . and a consciousness of honesty, a feeling that they too can participate actively in the reconstruction of Italy'. A second 'Risorgimento' was invoked on all sides and in the Veneto 32 out of 112 bands had taken the names of Garibaldi, Mazzini or Cavour. Meanwhile, the Allies were advancing up the spine of Italy, and the Germans were falling back. Liberation was in the air. 'War has reached its epilogue,' wrote one young partisan. 'We will return singing to our homes, with the joy of victory in our eyes.'

Then, on 13 November, General Alexander broadcast a devastating message to the partisans. It went out on public radio, on *Italia Combatte*. In view of the 'seasonal barrier', of the 'rains and mud', and of the difficulty of keeping up regular drops during the winter snows, the partisans should, he announced, immediately halt all large-scale military operations, save their 'munitions and matériel until further orders' and 'prepare for a new phase of the struggle, against a new enemy, winter'.

Whether Alexander understood what his words meant to the 82,000 'rebels' stretched out across the north, 25,000 of them in Piedmont, clinging on day by day in the belief that the end of the war was near, no one knows. Certainly, like Eden, he had made his lack of respect for them clear, telling an emissary sent by Parri: 'These partisans bother me a great deal.' It was perfectly true that the main thrust of the war was now elsewhere and that the Allied drive, so confidently launched by Churchill in August and so bravely supported by the partisans, had become bogged down not far from Bologna in a sea of torrential rain and mud. And the Germans were defending Kesselring's last major line of defence, the Gothic line, which ran along the northern Apennines from south of Spezia to the Adriatic sea between Pesaro and Ravenna, with great tenaciousness. The Allied decision was, nonetheless, a catastrophe, and made more so by the public way in which it had been announced.

What Alexander was proposing was that the partisans hibernate, go home, preserve their strength for the spring. But this was precisely what they could not do. They had survived a first terrible winter because it was all so new and the enemy was not organised. But their names and identities were now known to the Fascists and they were wanted men. Their only option was to hide, to save both themselves and their families. A second winter lay ahead, as cold and hungry but considerably more dangerous than the first. Despair spread around the valleys.

As for the Germans, their delight at Alexander's broadcast was palpable. Major *rastrellamenti* were immediately planned across the north, using not only all their own men, together with Georgians, Mongols and Cossacks, but all the various legal and semi-legal Italian Fascist militias. Soon, more bodies were swinging from lamp posts and the bare branches of trees, which had shed their leaves with the arrival of winter. The free republic of Carnia was quickly wiped out, seven of its communes destroyed and 15,000 partisans made prisoners. As Marisa said: 'Suddenly we were frightened, very frightened indeed.'

14

Learning to live better

Not everyone was confident that the Allies had really intended to break through the Gothic line and press on towards the north. Ada, following events on her radio, had increasingly sensed that the Italian campaign had become a sideshow and that the British and the Americans had lost interest in their Resistance. 'As if,' Ada wrote bitterly in her diary, 'surrounded, harassed, pursued as we are, we can wait without doing anything . . . We will fend for ourselves,' she went on. 'I am more and more convinced that we must not rely on foreign help, but on our own forces.' Bolaffi, conscious of his dwindling resources and the coming snow, of his men without warm winter clothes, dressed in shirts made from Allied nylon parachutes, many of them sick, had already been making plans to form his best fighters and those who could ski into small groups in the mountains. Those who could safely do so, he sent home to spend the coldest months with their families. But he was not a man who easily gave up. When Salò sensibly chose the moment to offer an amnesty to partisans who turned themselves in, and the Germans assured them that there would be no repercussions for men volunteering for civilian service, Ada and Bolaffi sped around the valleys, trying to instil strength and determination into their men. Now weary and very angry, there were many who did not listen to them. There were defections, but not many.

Both Agosti, now political commissar for the Partito d'Azione for the whole of Piedmont, and Duccio, its military commander and in charge of 10,000 men, were exhausted and overworked. They worried that unless they acted quickly and firmly the partisan forces across the north would splinter and weaken. The CLN's reply to General Alexander was dignified, but utterly firm. The partisan war was not, it said, 'a mere whim, an idle caprice to be refrained from at will'. On the contrary, it was about defending the patrimony and 'moral heritage' of Italy, and every partisan was fighting for 'his individual freedom, his right to live'. Their war would therefore go on, with 'no relaxation, no weakening'. In fact, it would be intensified.

The orders that went out to the men in the mountains were clear: '*Durare*', endure, do not weaken. 'We who are responsible for the lives of the men who gave us their trust,' noted one circular, 'owe them explanations.' For the coming winter campaign, those who wished to do so should go home and resume their lives, volunteer for civilian service under the Germans or cross the border into Switzerland, but they should hold their heads high and feel no shame, for they had demonstrated the courage to rebel against the Fascists. If they chose to stay, they would be issued with false identity papers. Small mobile groups of five to six saboteurs would carry out quick attacks in the plains. Others would work as policemen, ignoring the Germans but concentrating on eliminating Fascist spies. Courses in sabotage would be arranged, and the partisans helped to think for themselves about the kind of Italy they wanted after liberation. The fight was not over. The moment would come when they would again be needed. Meanwhile they should dig in. It marked another moment in the partisan war, when they came down from the mountains and into the plains. But it was a low one, and the numbers of partisans across the north rapidly dropped from 80,000 to 50,000. As Livio Bianco wrote to his friend Agosti, his energy and his morale were shattered. If they should both, by some miracle, survive, it would be as white-haired old men, leaning on sticks, wanting only to sleep, to rest, in their slippers, among friends. 'But will we still be capable of friendship?'

With the Allied landings in Provence, and the Free French now in control of their side of the Alps, there was growing interest among the Italian Resistance in making contact with France. Even before Alexander's proclamation, Paolo and Alberto, both mountaineers and extremely fit, had volunteered to make the crossing over the Passo dell'Orso. Bolaffi, desperate for a new supply of weapons, and intrigued by their proposal for a joint action with the French Maquis against the Germans stationed on the passes, agreed. For Ada, it spelt more anguish, more dread.

Having waited for a full moon, the boys set out. Alberto was in charge; Paolo called him '*il mio commandante*'. They expected to be away less than a week. To fill the days, Ada went down to Turin then to Milan where, under the guise of having talks with her publishers, she spent time with her Milanese colleagues in the GDD, coming away newly impressed by the speed and enthusiasm with which women were joining. It was as if the twenty years of enforced Fascist intellectual slumber had suddenly exploded into a ferocious hunger for knowledge and responsibility.

Later that week, Ada returned to their cabin above Oulx. She expected to find Paolo; instead she found thick snow, which was worrying but also reassuring as it meant that any tracks made by the boys would have been obliterated. For almost four hours, she struggled back through the snow to Meana on foot, since the Germans, having miscalculated the effects of moisture on their explosives, had inadvertently blown up a crucial railway bridge. 'I am,' she wrote in her diary, 'terribly unhappy.' More days passed. It was now almost two weeks since Paolo's departure. Long after, she wondered how she had endured the growing sensation that she was spiralling into madness. 'When alone, I howled like a wounded beast.' In their coded telephone calls, even Bianca, usually so calm and optimistic, sounded flat and tense. Ada wrote reports – on politics, on women, on military plans – went to meetings, and visited Bolaffi. One day she bought a small pocket copy of Ariosto, which she thought Paolo might like.

Then, one electric-blue morning, when the sun gleamed on the high peaks, Paolo and Alberto returned. 'Absolute happiness,' Ada wrote, 'like absolute pain, has no beginning and no end.' They brought with them new weapons, some packets of Nescafé, which Ada had never seen, and military combat rations of eggs, cheese, ham and chocolate, all neatly packed so that she marvelled at the efficiency. Their story tumbled out: how they had been caught in blizzards and slipped and fumbled through unfamiliar snowy landscapes, how the mission to capture the Germans on the passes had been aborted, how the French had first been hostile and then friendly, and how they had now undertaken to provide the Free French with information about German movements along the

Alps. What really annoyed them was that they had been forced to throw away a knapsack full of new French gramophone records. Ada wrote: 'I continued to navigate in an unreal euphoria . . . miraculously detached from the sadness of the universe and miraculously illuminated by the sun of happiness.'

The euphoria was dazzling, but it did not last. In Paolo and Alberto's absence, a local girl, suspected of being a spy for the Fascists, had been taken to their cabin by their companions and questioned, but had then escaped. Should they catch and 'eliminate' her before she gave away their whereabouts? No one had the heart for murder. Paolo and Alberto set off further up into the mountains, to build a new hut.

Later, the partisans would talk about the winter of 1944 as 'tragic'. Even as they were trying to come to terms with Alexander's orders to stand down, the Germans acted. Using the same tactics as they had deployed in the spring – major assaults with several thousand soldiers, blocking off the valleys, then penning the partisans into ever smaller areas and pulling the net in – Germans and Fascists surged out of their bases. The country roads shook with the rumble of tanks and armoured cars. There was a constant smell of burning from houses which had been looted and set fire to. Civilians were caught in the crossfire or taken away as hostages. The violence became gratuitous, vicious, as if the German soldiers, freed by Kesselring's promises of impunity, were trying to rival each other in barbarity. A six-year-old girl was casually shot as she played; a seventeen-year-old, washing clothes at a well, was crushed by a lorry full of soldiers. Rape, by both German and Italian gangs, was common. Kesselring's contempt for the partisans had grown stronger. They were 'criminal elements', he said, 'riffraff who murdered and pillaged wherever and whenever they could', using the Resistance as a 'cloak for the release of baser instincts'.

When partisans exploded a bomb under a German lorry on the outskirts of Milan and five civilians were killed and eleven wounded, one of them the German driver, Kesselring pressed for exemplary measures. Milan's Cardinal Schuster intervened and in the end fifteen partisans were shot in the Piazzale Loreto by a firing squad from the Fascist militia. The Fascists were untrained and it was a messy and painful business. The bodies, covered in blood, were then posed in horrible positions for passers-by to witness.

German reports spoke of 2,700 dead partisans in a single month, along with 5,000 captured, and put their own losses at 103 dead and just over 100 wounded. General Wolff put in place a deadly new tactic he called 'excursions', sudden forays by small groups of killers, among them the newly formed Italian SS. They and members of the Fascist Arditi, the crack soldiers, united in their 'limitless love of Italy', were instructed to 'pursue the enemy to death'. When the decision was taken to make the Italian SS 'more German', they were issued with better weapons, discipline was tightened up and the officers were sent off for further training in Prussia and Pomerania. After Kesselring called for a *settimana antifascista*, a week dedicated to hunting down the partisans, they set about their duties with great willing. They called it *ripulitura*, recleansing.

The partisans, driven up into the furthest reaches of the frozen mountains, were now facing a losing battle against the crippling cold, and they needed constant vigilance against these silent patrols, many of them led by sniffer dogs. They had fought valiantly for thirteen months and were now dejected and ill. The songs they composed were all about hunger, ice, fear. Like stray dogs, wrote Calvino later, 'they dreamt of bones, gnawed and buried underground'. The snow kept falling, the fires smoked, shoes never got dry. The men scribbled notes to their families on scraps of paper and waited for one of the rare visits by a *staffetta* to take them down into the plains. 'The only thing that tortures me,' wrote a boy to his mother, 'is the distance from you, from everyone, the disappearance of my old life, in which, even if I do return, I will never again find myself.'

Villagers and farmers had made huge efforts to help, but they too were exhausted, their livestock looted, their food stocks depleted, and they were always fearful of reprisals. Forbidden by their leaders to requisition food, how were the partisans to eat? And there were still three months until spring and the promised Allied advance arrived. Cesare escaped a round-up and came to Meana to hide with Ada. She sent his parents a postcard – 'The boy is well' – and they came to see him. The mood in the bands had become tense, with individuals bickering and making plays for power. When Cesare's band decided to vote for a new leader, Cesare lost out to a rival who entertained them with dirty stories rather than enforcing discipline.

But the partisans were not entirely without resources. After seizing a cache of fifty kilos of papers, containing secret information from Kesselring to the German army, along with lists of the names and identities of spies, agents and collaborators, the partisans launched their own manhunts. November was, according to a doleful German report, a 'phenomenal' month for spy catching by the Resistance. Fifty German agents, the youngest just fifteen – and all but two of them men – were caught, often with messages written in invisible ink onto white handkerchiefs. Many of these men were not hard to track down, being invariably well dressed, with new shoes and suitcases. There was 'Trinca', a well-known Roman lawyer, aged forty-five, fat and pallid, with scars on his forehead; 'Koffi', an Italian of German descent, with a little moustache, who was a known morphine addict; and the Marchese Cairella, a movie producer, who had taken the name of Oscar de Toledo and spoke fluent Spanish and German. If these men were in danger from the partisans, they were no safer from their German masters. As a secret memorandum to the Wehrmacht put it, any Italian agent with access to confidential German documents was to be considered completely untrustworthy and, when the right moment came, 'liquidated' as rapidly and discreetly as possible.

In Salò, Mussolini's Repubblica Sociale Italiana was beginning to disintegrate. It was impossible, now, not to realise what had been lost or given away to the Germans: almost all of Italy's gold reserves, most of its mercury and other minerals, its entire radio network. Much needed food, equipment, spare parts, everything useful to their war, had gone on trains to the Reich. Men and women, in their tens of thousands, had been put to work making materiel for the German war effort. As a state, Salò was barely functioning. The party faithful, the civil servants, the adventurers, mercenaries and opportunists, were all quarrelling among themselves, while looking anxiously over their shoulders and wondering what awaited them. Conscious of German defeats in the east, of the steady Allied advance across occupied Europe, few believed that the war could still be won, or that Hitler's rumoured secret weapon could save them. Wives and families were making escape plans. There were rumours that General Graziani was meeting with other senior Fascists behind Mussolini's back to plan for the restoration of some kind of Fascism in a new Italy after liberation. Mussolini, remote and fretful, was rarely seen. Prefects around the country reported a mood of 'grey hostility'.

If the Germans despised the Italian SS regiments they had spawned, they despised Pavolini's Black Brigades more. Though they needed both groups of men for their war against the 'rebels', they considered them ill-disciplined and unreliable. As the months passed, so the ill-equipped and disorderly recruits became ever more lawless, drunken and corrupt, living well and looting ferociously, smuggling and trafficking at will. They were merciless, sullen, afraid of the future.

Plans to recruit a million and a half Italian workers to send to Germany had come to almost nothing. By the autumn of 1944 only 23,000 men and women had volunteered, and successive call-ups, accompanied by threats, had met with every kind of resistance and succeeded mainly in driving more men to join the partisans, even if some stayed only briefly and then faded away into hiding. This stubborn resistance to German and Fascist blandishments was, it would later be said, another facet of the partisan war: without the Resistance many young Italians would never have discovered in themselves a taste for rebellion, nor an interest in the political and cultural education denied them during twenty years of Fascism. This, as Agosti and Bianco saw it, was one of the Resistance's major challenges: that of instilling a new form of obedience in young people who had finally rejected Fascism and broken free of absolute submission and the cult of the regime.

No other European country suffered as much military desertion as Italy. Some 45,000 men deserted from the Italian SS, from the Littorio, San Marco, Monterosa and Italia brigades – trained in Germany and sent back to Italy – from the Black Brigades and from the Salò army, in spite of threats that if caught they would be shot (they were) and menaces to their families. In an effort to protect those who came over to them, the Resistance took to intimidating and threatening the families of the Fascists. The civil war grew darker. Villages and communities split, some going to the Fascists, some to the partisans, some backing away, putting their heads down, waiting grimly for liberation. Those who went over to Salò out of necessity were spoken of as '*poveracci*', poor things; but those who did so for gain became pariahs.

Yet most of the women did not desert. Often more fanatical about Fascism than the men, some of the women auxiliaries were now demanding guns and asking to be sent out on *rastrellamenti* in the valleys. 'Let them go where they want,' Mussolini replied to an officer asking for guidance. 'They give a better example than the men.' Zelmira Marazio, who later wrote a memoir of her time with the Black Brigades, described a state of exaltation, of total veneration for the Duce, of crying over the coffins of comrades and singing hymns in praise of '*la bella morte*'. She was told, and believed, that she was both a saint and a heroine, a '*cittadina-soldato*', pure in habits and staunch in 'personal morality'. Since women partisans were obviously brazen and manly, auxiliaries were told to practise 'feminine virtues' and to eschew all 'luxury and parasitical snobbery'. Like the partisans, these young women were growing up, learning about a world they had known nothing of, even if their political indoctrination led them in a totally different direction. When it became known that women would get the vote in liberated France, the idea was greeted by the Fascist women auxiliaries with mockery and derision.

The Allies in Italy spent the winter of 1944 building up their supplies for a major spring offensive. They were still dug in behind the Gothic line, with the German leadership intent on keeping them as far from Germany as possible, having used over 15,000 Italian slave labourers to shore up their line. They had lost 100,000 men in the Ardennes, along with eight hundred tanks, but Hitler was showing no signs of the Germans capitulating. As a result of their relentless brutality, hostility towards the Germans and their Fascist collaborators had intensified among ordinary Italians. In order to lessen it, it was clear that something would have to be done for the Italians in captivity in the German camps, who were said to have lost thirty kilos or more from hunger and misery. The letters that got through to their families back in Italy described working conditions reminiscent of Dickensian England. All efforts by Mussolini and the Salò government to have the captives returned to Italy and recruited into the Salò army had yielded almost nothing. The Germans needed, not unreliable and untrustworthy soldiers, but slave labour.

After sustained pressure, these half-million surviving men – 20,000 had already died – had finally passed out of the hands of the German military and into those of the civilian administration. Even the Germans admitted they would work better if they were not actually starving to death. Officially they were now free workers, but they were allowed to leave the camps only on condition that they agreed to work for the Reich in Germany until the end of the war. Those who refused stayed inside, where they continued to die from malnutrition and violence. But even those who accepted the German offer found that as civilian workers they were treated little better than prisoners, and regardless of their own individual contributions, their food rations remained the same. There were fights and much resentment.

And in Italy itself people were growing still more hungry. Towards the end of the autumn, Moroni, Minister for Agriculture in the Salò government, had noted that food supplies were erratic, that potatoes were plentiful in Bologna but unfindable in Turin, that lack of transport meant that the different provinces had drifted apart, become 'economic islands' with wildly fluctuating prices. Farmers were refusing to deliver their products to the cities; there were not enough police to make sure they did so, or they were too corrupt to do so; officials and shopkeepers were keeping alive a thriving black market, and the Germans, who had spent the early months of occupation trying to curb it, were now exploiting it themselves, blaming their failings on the 'Latin mentality'. The much vaunted Italian spirit of 'arrangiarsi', making do, finding solutions, had never been more alive.

Struggling to offer some new Fascist ideology that might make him more popular, Mussolini came up with the idea of 'socializzazione', a social contract promising a shift in power from the bosses to the workers. Nowhere was the question of factory management more crucial than in the industrial triangle across the north, where Rudolf Rahn, Hitler's plenipotentiary to the Salò republic, continued to navigate a tricky line between authoritarian measures and small concessions, in an increasingly desperate attempt to keep war production turning over. A decree, on Hitler's orders, was brought in stipulating the death penalty for those who organised strikes, but then little improvements to living conditions were offered.

The Italian industrialists themselves continued to duck and weave. Many had made considerable sums of money out of the war and wanted to position themselves to make even more when the war ended and large international grants were likely to flow for reconstruction. At the same time, they could not risk totally alienating the anti-Fascists, and wished to emerge at liberation as patriots. All over the north, 'arrangements' were put in place. Factory owners supplied the German occupiers with the bare minimum to avoid reprisals, while at the same time making funds secretly available to partisan bands. That summer in Turin, a meeting of all the major industrial leaders had taken place at which it was agreed that communism had to be defeated, whatever the cost. Money was then donated to arming the strictly non-Communist partisans. News of this had reached the Allies in Rome and been greeted with approval.

No one was engaged in a subtler game, skilfully manipulating all sides, than Giovanni Agnelli, founder of FIAT, and Vittorio Valletta, its general manager. FIAT collaborated with the Germans, slipped money to the partisans – providing they were not Communists – and did its best to distance itself from all the forms of resistance taking place in its factories. When Ada visited a senior industrialist at Lancia to ask for money, she drily noted that the closer the Allies advanced, the deeper the factory owners dug into their pockets.

The strikes that year had seen 1,200 workers, many of them women, deported, but their growing contempt for the Fascists was not dented. Small acts of sabotage, undetectable until too late, were now daily events. Across the shop floors, women continued to collect money and food to send up to the partisans in the mountains. Frida and Bianca, on their rounds of the women's groups, were struck by the spirit of combativeness and intransigence. As one woman put it, there was no cult of personalities, but a great deal of 'esteem for companions who had sacrificed their lives'. Revenge was in the air.

The women's secret 'agitation committees', of Communist origin but joined by others from across the entire political spectrum, braved arrest with constant shows of strength and threats of strike action unless conditions in the factories were improved. They were offered lessons in '*socializzazione*', but largely shunned them. At FIAT, just 274 out of 29,229 workers came forward. The factory women were not in the mood for conciliation. In the late autumn, the agitation committee inside FIAT asked the partisan leadership to bring a case against Valletta for treason. A 'Purge Commission' found both Valletta and Agnelli guilty of collaboration and of having profited personally from their ties to the Germans. A trial, before a Commission of Justice, was planned and there was talk of both men having all their personal sources of income confiscated. But for the moment, this would have to wait. The Allies were still stalled behind the Gothic line, and the winter of 1944 was turning out to be exceptionally bitter.

At the heart of the partisan war lay a very simple fact: the Italian Resistance needed the Allies more than the Allies needed it. Both the British and the Americans remained deeply wary of Italy, particularly as they began to see possible parallels with events in Greece, where the Communist-led EAM/ELAS Resistance movement was controlling much of the country, reinforcing the spectre of Soviet control across Eastern Europe. The strength of the Communists within the Resistance was alarmingly confirmed when Cadorna, the Italian liaison officer parachuted into the north to guide the partisans, reported that the Communists were preparing to take control and set up a 'regime similar to the Soviet one'. The Communist threat had even acquired a name: '*il vento del Nord*', the wind from the North.

Throughout the early winter, just when the partisans were most desperate for weapons and provisions, there were virtually no Allied drops across northern Italy. 'For us,' wrote Bianco to Agosti, 'they represent our lives.' The few that arrived were directed mainly to the right-leaning Autonomi formations, leading Agosti to say that he could imagine, as a result of war-weariness and a longing for order, that the forces of his Partito d'Azione might also be obliged to slide towards the right, thereby feeding a further civil war, 'Whites against Reds'. Writing urgent letters to the Irish agent O'Regan, one commander complained bitterly: 'We no longer hope for Allied supply drops, since we have asked for them for 14 months without result.' As his men were without ammunition and warm clothes, he would have no alternative, he said, but to send all but a small number on indefinite leave. Not all the Allied agents were deaf to the partisans' pleas: one wrote to his superiors: 'They are crying out for help.' They needed boots, woollen socks, biscuits, sugar and corned beef. O'Regan reported: 'General resentment caused by lack of Allied support.' Bianco was so exhausted that he told Agosti that he was not sure he could hang on any longer. All he dreamt about were books, music, home comforts and '*della cose squisite*', exquisite things.

Some of the resentment against the Allies now expressed itself in absurd feuds over nothing. One day, Ada got a letter from the commander Marcellin, accusing her of 'buying' his men for her own Partito d'Azione formations. Her answer, though courteous, was angry. 'I can think of nothing more odious, small minded or calculating at a moment like this, when the future of our country is at stake.' She signed herself with the *nom de guerre* given to her by Bolaffi: Ulisse.

For many months now, Parri had been trying to persuade the top Allied commanders to recognise the CLNAI – the CLN for the North, or 'Alta Italia' – as the sole political authority behind the lines. Relations between the parties at its helm were kept friendly largely due to the closeness between the much loved Parri of the Partito d'Azione and the Communist Luigi Longo, representing the two largest formations. Finally, in mid November, Parri, taking with him the CLNAI president, a third man to represent the Communists, and a fourth for the Autonomi, crossed into Switzerland, from where they were transported secretly to Naples and then to Rome. Parri, described by his followers as 'a shining example in the dark years of tyranny', was disillusioned and more sceptical than ever, but what he feared most was that the Allies would prevent him from returning to the north again.

They arrived in Rome to find the new Bonomi government collapsing under feuds and bickering between monarchists and republicans, between returning exiles and those who had endured the German occupation in hiding. None could agree on the shape of a future Italy. The purge of former Fascists had ground to a halt, and tainted men were creeping back into positions of power. After boycotts and ill-tempered horse trading, a new quadripartite government was sworn in, once again with Bonomi as prime minister. The monarchists had strengthened their position, as had the Catholics under Alcide De Gasperi; the left had weakened theirs. Togliatti, determined not to be sidelined, had launched a new Communist Party, saying disingenuously that he was interested only in helping to liberate Italy and in constructing a democratic regime. When relayed to the north, the make-up of the new government found little favour; it looked like yet more compromises, horribly reminiscent of the past.

Parri and his colleagues, waiting in Rome for some kind of clarity to emerge, had brought with them a programme of their own. Along with wanting their CLNAI to be recognised as the true authority across the occupied north, they were seeking to forge close relations with the Allies and to set up proper, regular drops so that they could run a more efficient partisan war. And they needed considerable amounts of money. These sums would be added to the general occupation costs, which, as a defeated power, Italy would have to pay later.

At last, on 7 December, in Rome's Grand Hotel, an agreement was signed. Parri did not get everything he asked for, but it was not a bad deal. Under what became known as the Protocols of Rome, the Allies recognised the military arm of CLNAI as the sole fighting force, but it would have to place itself under the orders of the Allied commander-in-chief. The appointments made by the various committees of liberation would be respected. Money, food, weapons were all promised. In return, the Resistance undertook to recognise the Allied administration as the post-war governing authority in the north; to disarm the partisans as rapidly as possible after liberation; and – most important in Allied eyes – to concentrate on safeguarding factories and infrastructure as the Germans pulled out. This last was something that Allies, industrialists and partisans could all agree on – the Allies wanted to preserve Italy's resources for later use, the industrialists because they were already making deals, and the partisans to ensure future prosperity.

All in all, the visiting delegation felt, it was probably as good a '*combinazione*', a package, as could be expected, though it fell short of Parri's dreams. What had been made abundantly clear to the four emissaries was that the Allies were resolved on two things: to put in place, at whatever cost, a democracy favourable to capitalism, under leaders and politicians determined to eschew communism; and to ensure both the cooperation of the partisan leaders and, most importantly, their submission, which was much what the northern industrialists wanted. There would be no partisan mass insurrection and power would not be transferred to them. The British, wrote Parri later, more conservative, more pro-monarchy, seemed to be taking the attitude that the war against the Fascists had to be fought, not because of Fascism itself, but because Mussolini had declared war against England. The British were entitled to democracy, but second-rank countries like Italy could perfectly well make do with a '*simulfascista*', a proto-Fascist regime, as long as it was pro-British. Parri found the Americans more 'agnostic', more benevolent and not as interfering.

The second Bonomi government, no more united than the first, continued to stall over its own recognition of the CLNAI, but finally, reluctantly, conceded that it could be the 'delegate of the Italian government' and the 'sole legitimate authority' in the north. It seemed to Parri that the politicians in Rome preferred to remain ignorant about the harsh realities of the war across Piedmont, Liguria and Emilia, and he felt angry that they showed so little interest or support. He left the capital more determined than ever that the northern command would keep power in its own hands and not be subject to southern interference. Future problems were there for all to see.

Deeply relieved that the Allies had not prevented him from returning to the north, Parri dropped his usual guard. Warned by both the American and the British secret services that the Germans knew he had been in Rome and had increased their surveillance, he nonetheless insisted on hiking back into Italy from where he had been dropped in France. He crossed the mountain passes into the Val Cannobina and then took a boat over Lake Maggiore before making his way to Milan. He was in his secret lodgings in Via Monti when the Germans came for him. In the San Vittore he was treated well, the Germans sensing that he might be a valuable pawn in eventual armistice negotiations. But for the partisans, his capture was a calamity and plans were launched to rescue him.

Even after the meetings in Rome, the Allied drops and the missions remained a source of quarrels. After considerable hesitation about the Communist formations, the Allies reluctantly agreed that supplies would be dropped in direct proportion to the comparative strengths of the various bands, regardless of their political allegiances. But still the drops did not always come, and the Allies did not always keep their word. McCaffery's brusque letter to Parri perfectly encapsulated their condescension and patronage: the partisan war was an episode, a fact, even a reality, but it did not cancel out the status of Italy as a defeated enemy, under tutelage. The partisans were to be tolerated, but only up to a point. If they got out of line, they would be punished. In any case, as ever, all that was wanted from them was sabotage and information.

In November, 149 tons of supplies, in long thin cylinders weighing a hundred kilos each and full of weapons, ammunition, warm clothes and supplies, were dropped; in December 350. Bad weather, enemy action, lack of navigational aids and the non-appearance of reception committees meant that roughly one in three drops failed to reach the partisans. More tricky, however, was the question of missions. The agents parachuted into the Piedmontese valleys – some trained in sabotage, some in radio transmissions, some English, some Irish, some Italian, some American and some Italo-Americans – were all told that their job was to direct, organise and lead the partisans rather than work alongside them. For the most part they made friends among the partisan bands but, even so, their reports were unsparing, reflecting the gulf between the two sides. Bolaffi, said one, was 'four feet tall and a bore. Good administrator but hopeless in the field and as pompous as a stuffed peacock.' Frida's brother Roberto was 'politically energetic, useless in action and irritating to all other partisans of different political views'. Marcellin was deemed to be of 'peasant mentality and parochial outlook'. Others were referred to as 'superfluous elements – the apathetic, the lazy, the morally and physically exhausted'.

As for the *staffette*, they were never mentioned. The Allies clearly had no more interest in women fighters than did the Fascists. In their reports, the SOE seemed oblivious to their existence.

*

Then, in a further blow to the Resistance, Major Temple was crushed when a truck backed into him during a *rastrellamento*. Lucia went with him to hospital. As he was fading, he told her that he was sad to die because he would no longer be able to help the partisans. She was devastated. A plane was sent to take his body back to Brindisi.

The man sent to replace him was a very different animal. Lieutenant Colonel John Melchior Stevens was tall, well educated and spoke excellent Italian, '*un vero signore*' as the first partisans who met him described him. A veteran of SOE activities in both Greece and France, he was flown into the Langhe under heavy fire on the morning of 17 November as senior British mission in Piedmont, with orders to liaise with the CLNAI and to prepare to act as commanding officer for the Allied administration at the time of liberation. His friends found Stevens ambitious, enthusiastic, intelligent and, most importantly, a 'forceful character who would naturally wish to take complete charge of any situation'. This, for the Italians, was bad enough. What was worse was that he had little esteem for the partisans and intended to avoid them as much as possible, and apparently had very little interest in Italy at all; he was also deeply hostile to communism. The stories of *rastrellamenti*, of massacres, of the bodies of hostages left lying in the streets as warnings were, he said, wildly exaggerated.

Having requested Lucia as his *staffetta* – word of her prowess had reached SOE headquarters – he was chaperoned by her to the safety of a house belonging to a senior FIAT executive, whose desire to squash any kind of left-wing insurrection perfectly matched his own. Since he intended to wear his uniform at all times, Lucia got him a large black peasant cape to put over it. Even so, she despaired of his unmistakably British look.

From his hideout with the agreeably hospitable industrialists, Stevens now fired off a series of plans and orders. The partisans were instructed to work strictly under Allied orders; to prepare to put a 'provisional government' in place which would hold the fort until the arrival of the Allies, with jobs neatly allocated among the political parties, and if they behaved well, they would be rewarded. What he would not tolerate, he made clear, was another Warsaw uprising, or a Resistance which made too many demands, or an insurrection led by the Communists, or the removal, the purge, of the collaborating Fascist industrialists. The partisans were appalled. Stevens's goal, they agreed, was perfectly obvious: he intended to paralyse their movement, starve it, and particularly those movements on the political left, and in the process to weaken the CLNAI command. When the Allies arrived he intended to have everything in place, waiting for them. Meanwhile he would set about reorganising the chaotic partisans. A collision was unavoidable. The question was how soon it would come.

Duccio, the commander of the Partito d'Azione forces, had long been fearful of Allied meddling in partisan matters. Cordial relations with their agents were, he said, essential, but they must never be allowed to take command. Politically astute, self-controlled, with an almost religious belief in the anti-Fascist cause, Duccio had spent the summer and autumn of 1944 on the move, exposing himself to extreme danger, relying on his false documents to protect him at Fascist and German roadblocks, ever brazen and bold. He had been a constant supporter of the *staffette*, and he would often say that the commitment of so many women to the Resistance was the best guarantee that it was a truly popular movement.

Then, absurdly, he fell into a Fascist trap. In Turin's Via Vigone, there was a baker who acted as a letter drop for the partisans. On 2 December, Duccio went to collect a letter he knew was waiting for him. As he got there, Fascist police blocked off the road and began checking papers. Duccio was arrested with a number of other men, taken to a police station and from there to Le Nuove. Hearing of his arrest, Ada hurried to his flat, where she discovered a suitcase full of letters, reports and circulars relating to the Piedmont military command. With a young partisan friend who owned a car, she took it for safekeeping to two nearby friendly tailors.

Still unrecognised, his false papers accepted as genuine, Duccio believed himself to be, if not safe, then at least in no great danger. 'I acted only in the hope of doing good,' he wrote in a note smuggled out of the prison, 'and so I am calm, as you must be.' But in Le Nuove was a partisan acquaintance who, hoping for a mitigation of his own sentence, alerted the Germans to Duccio's real identity. Since neither they nor the Fascists wanted a public trial, he was quickly handed over to the Fascists in his native

Cuneo, who shot him in the back, ostensibly while he was trying to escape. In the process they mutilated his head and body so badly that he was no longer recognisable.

Duccio's death was a tragedy for the entire northern Resistance. Though sometimes authoritarian, maddening the other leaders with his defiantly independent ways, he was greatly loved and admired by his men and his exceptional skills as an organiser had done much to win recruits and hold the movement together. Of the five original leaders of the military command of the Partito d'Azione – Paolo Braccini, Willy Jervis, Sandro Delmastro, Duccio and Agosti – only Agosti was still alive. Bianco wrote to him, a letter full of sadness, that it was now more important than ever to see through to the end what Duccio had fought for with such courage. Ada saw the news of his murder in a newspaper. It struck her 'like a blow'. She kept remembering the journeys they had made together up into the valleys, Duccio composing little songs, his gaiety making her long for a life which was safe and serene. She had admired his strength, his vitality and the free and easy humour with which he had treated even the most serious matters. Now she wondered how they would continue without him.

From the start of the occupation, the partisan leaders had instructed the bands to avoid 'useless cruelties'. Everything, they said, should be done to limit reprisals, otherwise they would sink to the level of the enemy. But German and Fascist atrocities and their endless targeting of civilians had weakened their resolve, and even Duccio and Parri had accepted that there were occasions when the 'execution of Fascist traitors' was necessary. Duccio's murder was one of them. Orders went out to shoot 'fifty bandits of the Brigate Nere'.

With the northern partisans in mourning, the Allies stuck behind the Gothic line, and vast *rastrellamenti* sweeping through the valleys, the winter of 1944 was getting steadily grimmer. It was also the coldest anyone could remember. Deep snow closed the mountain roads and in Turin the temperature sank to −16 degrees. Ice froze the tram lines solid. The schools closed. There was enough fuel and wood only for hospitals and clinics, and the freezing Torinesi struggled out into the surrounding woods to chop down the remaining trees and drag them back into the city. The partisans shivered and starved in their mountain hideouts, while bandits, like wolves, emerged to prey on the farmers and villagers, looting what little had not already been seized by the Germans and the Fascists.

The cities had become like ghost towns. Bread rations were reduced and then reduced again. Men competed with each other over the number of new holes they had to make in their belts. Four accused of secretly butchering a cow in Rivoli were shot, and their bodies left lying in the snowy piazza. The last train carrying Jews to the camps crossed the Brenner pass on 14 December, after the Germans carried out a few final manhunts and increased rewards for information to L9,000, for 'every Jew turned in, even a child'. Agosti despaired that all forms of civilisation were breaking down and that there was nothing now but contempt for human life, property or morality. 'We all lived,' said a partisan woman later, 'in an atmosphere of bestial ferocity, and the tension sometimes seemed to us unbearable.'

No one felt easy. Not the Germans or the Fascists who, for all their jubilance over their autumn round-ups, viewed the coming liberation with fear. Not the British and the Americans who were terrified that the Resistance was moving ever closer to the Soviets. Not the partisans who now believed that the Bonomi government in Rome was firmly in the pocket of the Allies, and were therefore more determined than ever to go it alone. As they saw it, the foreign agents arriving in Piedmont were in Bolaffi's words, 'heavy on advice' and light on everything else, including their promises. The British remained in thrall to Eden's contempt for the Italians. The Americans felt unsure about future spheres of influence and were anxious about enduring isolationist feelings at home and by the age-old conflict between military and civilian power, none of which was made easier by the many channels – Vatican, exiles, anti-Fascists and Italo-Americans – through which they were operating. American reporters were filing stories about Italians dying of cold and hunger and partisans crossing the enemy lines, destitute and malnourished, only to find themselves put in prisoner-of-war cages with captured Germans and Fascists. As a journalist in Rome, Peter Tompkins, who worked for the OSS, put it, no one could possibly have believed that so much was being done to make Allied victory so inherently difficult and unlikely.

*

It went on snowing; in some places the temperature dropped to −20 degrees. But Ada and her friends were not giving up. The number of women in the GDD had grown to almost 40,000 and the organisation had finally been officially recognised by the CLNAI. All over the north, women were knitting, mending, foraging and finding warm clothes and food, both for the men up in the mountains and for those in hiding. Others had formed groups to collect the bodies of executed hostages, wash them, take them to the morgue and help their relations to identify them. No day passed without visits to places of detention. Silvia, using Ada's house in Via Fabro as her office, was producing articles for *La Nuova Realtà*.

Frida and Bianca trudged through the snow, keeping up the spirits of the factory women. What struck them was that the women were now turning their hands to everything – writing, printing, raising money, acting as couriers – and that in doing so, they were visibly changing, developing views about class and equal pay. It was as if a mass social conscience had been brought to life.

Ada organised, wrote, planned, held meetings and made expeditions into the countryside in search of provisions, returning with them under cover of night. She set up deals with wholesalers and studied the most effective way to deliver calories. Her clarity of purpose and energy, observed a partisan, 'had the physical and moral strength of 10,000 fighters'.

Women factory workers, enraged by the spectacle of sugar going to make biscuits for the Germans, staged a strike and stood outside the gates, shouting: 'We want bread for our children! We want sugar for our children!' They refused to go back until food was distributed. Ten thousand of them signed a petition to Milan's Cardinal Schuster, asking him to intervene to stop the deportation of women to Germany. As the cold grew more bitter, women working for FIAT broke down the factory gates and loaded coal from its deposits onto wheelbarrows and bore it away. There were too many to punish. Then they went on to engage in new skirmishes, challenging, protesting every move that seemed to them unfair, leaving the occupiers perplexed: how should two hundred furious women clamouring for milk be treated? Each victory was loudly heralded on posters and in news sheets.

Lisetta's flat had been discovered by the Fascists and the entire layette for her baby, put together with loving care by her fellow prisoners in the San Vittore jail and then sent to her in Turin, had been looted. She gave birth to a daughter in late December at a clinic in Turin. She called her Anna and when she and Vittorio found a new place to live, they turned a drawer into a crib and went on with their partisan activities, using the baby's pram to transport weapons, putting the baby on top of them. Later, after Anna was grown up, her parents told her that, for all its terrors and tragedies, it had been a wonderful period of their life.

On Sunday 16 December, Mussolini spoke in a theatre in Milan. Lethargic, obsessed by thoughts of Hitler's secret weapon and possible deals he might make with Churchill, he had not been seen in public for several months. The Germans had long since confiscated all transmitters and jammed the airwaves but, exceptionally, they restored them while Mussolini was speaking. Describing his plans for '*socializzazione*' and promising better food supplies, improved transport and higher taxation for the rich, he struck the diarist Chevallard, listening on his forbidden radio in Turin, as a weak parody of his fiery self, his oratory and verve gone. So little was now heard from him that what astonished many listeners was not what he said, but the fact that he was still alive, apparently healthy and on his feet. Zelmira Marazio, the fanatical young Brigate Nere auxiliary, joined thousands of other women, in their khaki breeches, black shirts and revolvers, to cheer him in the streets.

Le Nuove in Turin remained the main prison for partisans, deserters, anti-Fascists and recaptured foreign prisoners of war. The German section, which held six hundred men, was kept in almost total darkness; it was full of fleas, its detainees subject to false trials and often tortured before they were shot. The nights were punctuated by cries of pain. Eleven of the prisoners were English, in a piteous state and slowly dying of starvation before Suor Giuseppina found ways of smuggling food into their cells. They seemed to her, she wrote later, like poor ravaged and abandoned animals, shut away by some evil spirit.

Suor Giuseppina had no intention, however, of allowing Christmas to pass unobserved. She asked the prison priest, Padre Ruggero, to get permission for a Christmas tree, then sent out word to the partisans. An enormous, handsome tree arrived from the Val Chisone and with it came boxes of small presents, chocolate, cigarettes and books to hang from its branches. Siegel, the German commandant, whose humane side had not been completely crushed by the war, ordered the cell doors to be opened and the emaciated, sickly prisoners emerged into the light. Guards took the presents off the tree and handed them out to the assembled men and women. A group of Russian prisoners, through an interpreter, asked to be allowed to dance, saying that they had nothing else to offer but wanted to express their gratitude for the kindness of Suor Giuseppina and the other nuns. It brought tears to Suor Giuseppina's eyes as she watched the men, with a little orchestra improvised out of a broom, a piece of wood and a tin, weakly shuffling and twisting under the tree. Then Padre Ruggero celebrated Mass. Next morning, Siegel agreed to release a number of the sickest prisoners.

No one, however optimistic, could envisage a quick or happy ending to this war. As Bianco wrote to his wife Pinella, whom he had not seen for many weeks, both of them in hiding, changing houses repeatedly and always just one step ahead of discovery and arrest: 'Will the day really come when we can be together again, all the time? . . . If I love life, if I enjoy living, it is because there is you to give it meaning . . . But these are just dreams and who knows if and when they might become reality . . .' If they did survive, what they had gone through would not have been wasted. 'We will be better and richer (I mean spiritually), and we will have learned to live better.' There were times when he thought the war would never end and that he would never be with her again. But there were other moments, he wrote, when he was lit up by a great hope, that of 'putting their lives back together, with our love both just as it was and also profoundly new'.

Part Three

LIBERATION

15

Mothers of the Resistance

Bolaffi and the partisan leadership had been pleased with the results of Paolo and Alberto's visit to France, but they wanted closer contacts with the French Resistance and better weapons and hoped to find them both in Grenoble, where the Allied missions had their base. A second expedition from Turin was organised; this time, Ada decided to go too, taking Ettore and Paolo with her. Negotiations promised to be tricky, and Ada was seen as a reliable and sensitive envoy. Pausing only to visit Lisetta and her new baby – who was given a false name for safety – and telling no one of her plans, she left on the morning of 30 December, in a 'state of absurd, reckless delight'. This would be an adventure, her own adventure, not one lived through her husband or son. She would also take the opportunity to meet French Resistance women and find out how France was dealing with post-occupation life. Before setting out, she was told by Vittorio Foa that the Partito d'Azione wanted her to become vice mayor of Turin after it was liberated. At first, she thought he was joking, but then reflected that it would indeed be a challenge, and that making things work had always been her strong point. No woman had ever held the post.

Relations with the French had long been a matter of some uncertainty and confusion for the Italian partisans. De Gaulle did not feel forgiving towards the Italians for their attack over the Alps in 1940, and he had made it clear that there were scores that would need to be settled once the war was over. After the liberation of France in the summer of 1944, when the various different Resistance formations had been wound up and their men subsumed into the Forces Françaises de l'Interieur, de Gaulle had issued orders that all Italian partisans fleeing German attacks and crossing into

France were to be interned and given a choice: that of joining the Foreign Legion, under French orders, or accepting the status of prisoner of war, precisely in the same way as captured German soldiers. During the ferocious *rastrellamenti* of the Piedmontese valleys in the autumn, some 2,000 exhausted and hungry fighters from Marcellin's and Bolaffi's bands had fallen back into France, some bringing wives and children with them. Offered de Gaulle's choices, all but the very sick had opted to return to Italy. De Gaulle took no pains to keep secret his plans to punish the Italians further by invading the north-west once the Germans retreated, nor the fact that he had his eye on an eventual annexation of the French-speaking valleys, the '*pays français d'Italie*'.

On the other hand, the French and Italian partisans fighting the Germans since September 1943 on either side of the Alps had from early on forged friendships and exchanged helpful information. Duccio and Bianco had both negotiated pacts between their own partisans and the French maquisards, binding them to fight their common enemy. It was the Salò and Vichy governments, and not the ordinary French and Italian people, they agreed, who were to blame for the war.

The second mission to France

The new mission to France was to consist of Ada and Ettore, Alberto, Paolo, their friend Pillo, Alberto's brother Bruno, a doctor who had recently had a miraculous escape from German custody, and Virgilio and Eraldo Corallo, seasoned mountaineers who would help carry the weapons home. Eraldo was a former *carabiniere*; his brother, the blond, blue-eyed Virgilio, was just sixteen. They met at Paolo's camp at Beaulard, not far from the border, and spent the evening singing mountain hymns in the dark. A partisan arrived, took off his boots, and extracted from them secret documents from Agosti for Ada to take to France. As they began their climb, waved off by Bianca and Bruno's wife, the snow was glistening in the moonlight and the firs looked to Ada like Christmas trees. She worried that, at forty-two, she would slow the others down.

The first stage, up to a cabin recently vacated by a German patrol, was made precarious by Pillo getting his foot caught in a trap, after which he limped slowly behind them. A blizzard usefully erased their tracks but left them drenched and very cold. Ada wrapped herself up in a blanket, 'like a figure in a Goya print', and ploughed on. When they reached the summit, the boys began running about excitedly like chamois, until Pillo slipped and began sliding towards a precipice, stopping only at its very edge. Ada noticed that her hands had turned a strange yellow-brown colour and she slapped and rubbed them back to life. They pressed on.

Towards dawn, as light was creeping up over the mountains, they heard shots. They had reached the French checkpoint, with its rolls of barbed wire. They called out, were answered and soon found themselves surrounded by French maquisards with beards who gave them coffee, sardines and chocolate, while their officer phoned the nearest command post. Ada had sworn that she would embrace the first Frenchman she saw. The boy she now pressed to her turned out to be a seminarian, known to the others as '*le curé*'. There was much laughter. It was a Sunday and in Plampinet, where they were taken, all the villagers turned out to stare at their Italian visitors. In a house recently occupied by the Germans, who had written slogans on the walls, the maquisards had added words of their own. After '*Ein Reich*', they had added '*en ruines*'.

Pillo, whose foot had turned black and was now badly swollen, was taken away to hospital. The others were driven along white snowy valleys and past a frozen lake to a former grand hotel in Grenoble, for questioning. Ada was amused to see a note headed: '*Sept partisans Italiens avec leur mère*'. The French evidently found the men easier to explain but were suspicious of Ada, and she made it worse by telling them that she intended to make contact with the Frenchwomen who had fought with the Maquis. Politics of this kind, she was informed, were unacceptable. To reassure her hosts, she made a flowery speech about education and nursing the sick. In their hotel, the Italians played on an old piano and sang songs.

No one in Grenoble could remember a colder winter. Icicles hung from the balconies and when they went out, slithering along the icy streets, they were knocked over by gusts of wind coming off the mountains. Ada took to wearing a fur coat, many sweaters and five pairs of socks. Four years of German occupation had drained France and food was scarce. The party was fed first on French military rations, then on American ones. Major Hamilton, the head of the English mission in Grenoble, gave them biscuits, jam and butter. They began to relax, but then, one by one, freed from the constant tensions and fears of the previous sixteen months, they fell ill and took to their beds. Paolo came down with a high fever and pains in his joints.

They had planned to be away from Italy for ten days. But French military bureaucracy moved at a snail's pace, and Grenoble was a hotbed of rivalrous Allied secret services and soldiers. The British SOE and the French Deuxième Bureau were quarrelling with each other, and both the British and the Americans were hostile to French ambitions in Aosta. Ada, whose French and English were good, attended endless meetings, prepared maps, wrote up notes, chafing at the delays, particularly after she received the news that Parri had been arrested. Without waiting for permission, she slipped away to meet the women from the French Resistance, and came away greatly impressed by what they had already achieved and realising how similar her own aspirations were to those of the Frenchwomen. 'Politics,' she wrote in her diary, 'is not intrigue or conspiracy but an essential form of life.' It was from her new French friends that she heard for the first time about Auschwitz, another sign of how profoundly cut off the Italian partisans were from the wider war.

The weeks passed. The snow thawed, leaving a quagmire of mud in Grenoble's streets. Finally, after further interminable negotiations, it was agreed that a network of contacts would be established between the Italian partisan leadership and the French, via the Corallo brothers; and that Ada would carry back plans for a regular exchange of news and information between Turin and Grenoble. In return, they were given a generous supply of weapons to take home. Five weeks after their arrival, they finally set out for home, but they left behind them Pillo, whose foot was still very weak, and Bruno, who was to serve in a hospital in Grenoble. Ettore had mastered the Allied codes and was bringing home new radio equipment. Each of the others was given a Sten gun, cartridges, skis, fur jackets and white trousers, and military K rations for the journey. Vernon, from the Allied Psychological Warfare Branch, asked them to carry some propaganda news sheets. The British mission supplied sweets and toothbrushes. French troops were to accompany them on the first leg of the journey.

There was a last-minute change of route, when Germans were found to be patrolling the frontier, but at sundown on 18 February, the now diminished group set out with mules and an escort of French chasseurs. After two hours, the mules and the French turned back. Ada and her companions pulled their white hoods over their heads, as camouflage against the snow, and kept climbing, struggling with their heavy loads, their muscles weakened by the weeks of inactivity in Grenoble. Late that night they rested briefly in a mountain refuge, before navigating their way cautiously round a glacier. The snow was deep and at every step they fought not to slip backwards. They knew that there were German patrols not far away.

After some hours they reached a first summit, gleaming in the moonlight. They were at the very end of their strength. Even the snow seemed to look hard and hostile. Ada fainted. It was a measure of their exhaustion that none of the men came to help her. She rallied and they dragged themselves on to a second peak. All around, in the soft pink sunrise, they could see the snowy Alps, stretching away forever into the distance. They were now so tired that when they stopped they fell asleep on their feet. Paolo found the strength to mix them all some Nescafé, with snow and sugar. Because of the delays and the slowness with which they were able to move, they had been travelling for sixty-seven hours, the last twenty-seven of them on their skis.

They now decided to split up and take different routes into Italy, and Ada, Ettore and Paolo set off down one valley together. Ada felt like a sleepwalker, and began to talk to her grandmother, who had been dead for twenty-five years, about curtains. They got lost, only to be miraculously found by Alberto, who steered them towards a *grangia* belonging to the Corallos. Hoping to find food and comfort, they discovered that it had been ransacked, the weapons hidden in the woodpile stolen in what had obviously been a recent German raid. Ada, who as a woman was not in the same danger as the men, volunteered to walk down to the nearby village to see the lie of the land. She changed her mountain clothes for a dress and staggered off. The village turned out to be full of Germans, but she found the Corallos' sister and was appalled to learn that their father had been taken by the Germans and sent down to Turin, and that their cousin had had his nails pulled out in an attempt to make him say where the brothers had gone. But, the girl said, he had told them nothing. Ada was given a plate of hot soup; nothing, she said later, had ever tasted more delicious.

She pulled herself painfully back up the mountain path to the hut to find that Paolo's fever was back and his joints so agonising that he could barely stand; but it was clearly too perilous to linger. Next morning, having buried their new weapons and ammunition, they inched their way down the mountainside and found a doctor, who diagnosed Paolo with an acute attack of rheumatism. Alberto was also feverish and coughing. They were helped onto a train bound for Meana, walking the last stretch up to the house, holding each other up and pretending to be refugees from the city in search of food. They passed a group of German soldiers who watched them suspiciously: in Ada's pockets were enough incriminating documents to have them all shot.

Ada stayed just long enough to settle Paolo and Alberto in the flat in Meana and found a train still running to take her down to Turin. In Via Fabro, the canary was in its place and Espedita assured her that all was well. She sank, 'with incredible delight', into a very hot bath. Then she began to compose her reports. The mission had been an unqualified success, with excellent relations established with the French, and a pleasing amount of weapons and ammunition brought home. 'Intuitively' she wrote later, 'I felt that the end was near, and that we had to reach it'.

There had been many changes in her absence. The mood was lighter, more hopeful. After months of biting cold, the thaw had started. In the valleys, the first green shoots were appearing. Ada learned that Parri was still alive but that a bold attempt to rescue him from the SS barracks in the Hotel Regina in Milan had failed. However, negotiations with the Germans for his release were looking promising. Bianco had reluctantly taken Duccio's place as military commander and was now at the headquarters in Turin. 'I will be leaving behind my heart,' he told Agosti, adding that he now felt for his partisans all he had once felt for his books. 'They are all that is best about me.'

In their hideouts in Turin, Agosti and Giorgio Diena were locked in discussions about liberation, how to organise it, how to handle the endlessly tricky relations with the Allies, how to make certain that the men scattered throughout the north were assembled, properly armed and ready to descend to the plains. Diena was drawing up plans for a vast reform of the education system which would carry the country 'on the road to democracy'. New squads of *gappisti* and *sappisti* were forming all the time. In every office and factory, committees of liberation were deciding on their roles. A Fronte della Gioventù, a youth partisan group, had been set up with Paolo's help, with branches across the whole of Piedmont, and in the schools and universities, students were organising strikes and protests of their own. A new and livelier mood had settled over the partisans, a mixture of optimism and a desperate urgency to get to the end of their war.

Ada went to a war council and came away impressed by Bianco's seriousness and authority. She learned that at last she had formally been named Inspector of the Partito d'Azione Military Commission and Political Commissar for the 4th Alpine Division, and that her job would be to liaise, through the *staffette*, with the different commands on the day of liberation. Never had the *staffette* been more crucial: it would fall to them to carry orders and ensure coordination.

The northern cities had become eerily quiet, derelict, dirty, impoverished, with curfews every night and roadblocks on every corner. The clear skies that came with the intense cold of deep winter meant increased nightly strafing by Allied bombers. Respect among ordinary people for all Italian institutions – police, government, mayoral – had crumbled. Even the Church, which, like the industrialists, had hedged its bets, supporting both sides and leaving individual priests to navigate impossibly conflicting demands, had lost authority. With the end approaching, both Germans and Fascists were visibly more apprehensive, stepping up atrocities in a fever of denial, fearing the night, not knowing where and when an attack might come. 'In the cities is the enemy's brain,' said Giuseppe Solaro, referring to the Resistance, 'in the cities he must be struck down and destroyed.'

The Germans at least knew that they would be retreating; for the Fascists, with nowhere to go and the certainty of punishment and vendettas, the future looked grim. Having cast their lot in with the Axis powers, what would retribution look like? In Rome, when the former director of the Regina Coeli jail, Dr Caretta, was recognised in the crowd at the trial of the senior officials accused of collaborating in the massacre of the Ardeatine hostages, he was seized, lynched and his body thrown into the Tiber. A tram driver, who refused to drive over him, narrowly avoided being lynched too.

A new Fascist law specified that a list of the names and ages of all citizens was to be posted on every house; but in every attic and cellar there was someone hiding and waiting. The plains of the north, which had until recently been safe territory for the occupiers, were safe no longer: the partisans had become bolder, and young *staffette* cycled openly around the towns, noting down enemy positions to take back to their bands. Provocative anti-Fascist posters appeared, pasted all over Turin's city walls. The autostrada between Turin and Milan, which the Germans knew they needed to keep open for their eventual retreat, was patrolled by the Fascist militia, and they had built reinforced concrete pillar boxes with slit windows for their machine guns. Burnt wrecks of cars and lorries were piled up on the verges. A shift in the balance of power was palpable.

Turin had turned into a city of inventiveness. Oil was being made out of nuts, shoes out of straw, coats out of blankets, coffee out of grape pips. Those with terraces kept rabbits, chickens, reared silkworms. Bread came black and rock hard. There was no insulin for diabetics and no anaesthetic for operations. More children were dying than at any other time during the war. Restaurants were being turned into 'collective canteens', with standardised meals at set prices, and the monthly ration of butter had been reduced to 50 grams and that of meat to 150 grams. Only the Germans had salt. But even they were fighting a losing battle with the black market, while factory production shrank with every dip in electricity, air raid and act of sabotage. An SOE agent sent back to Allied headquarters a list of what the Germans had looted during 1944: 112 trucks of electric cookers and fridges, 206 trucks of sewing machines, 113 of typewriters and too many ball bearings, tools, precision instruments and insulating materials to calculate. It was said that 48 million eggs had been dispatched back to the Reich.

New restrictions and edicts reflected the growing unease of the Fascists. No civilian, it had been decreed, was to walk with his hands in his pockets, to grow a moustache or whiskers, to dress his hair in 'unusual coiffures', or to wear double-breasted jackets or heavy boots, or spectacles unless he had a medical certificate to prove that he needed them. Healthy looking men were press-ganged in the streets to work for the German Todt labour organisation, shoring up the Gothic line which, despite several breaches by the Allies, the Germans continued to hold. With all transport except trams forbidden, people walked or braved the police agents who sat perched alongside the tram drivers, inspecting the passengers. The atmosphere was one of watchfulness and suspicion. The Fascists, noted Bianco, had become 'more foxes than lions'.

In their reports on conditions in 'enemy-occupied Italy', British agents spoke of a 'feverish state of expectation among the patriots'. They also chronicled atrocities: eleven partisans caught by the enemy in Modena, one hanged from a hook, one beheaded, one disembowelled and the rest bayoneted. In Minozzo, a young man was tied to the back of a lorry and dragged at high speed along the road for ten kilometres. In

Cervarolo, a priest and his two sisters were stripped naked and the priest shot dead. To be arrested meant to disappear. Turin now had eighteen main centres of detention and countless others in barracks and police stations. Everywhere, often at random, civilians were being tortured, hanged, their bodies left lying where they fell. Pools of hostages were held against partisan attacks, becoming, as one man put it, a game of 'tragic Russian roulette'. When Fascists walked past, people were silent; disdain, mistrust, hostility was on every face.

What had also changed was the relationship between the German occupiers and the Fascists. Though the Fascists had always tried to believe otherwise, for the Germans Salò had never been anything but a subject government, seen as useful in helping run and police Italy. The myth of alliance had long since run its course. Realising bitterly that they were soon to be abandoned by their former masters, the Fascists had begun to distance themselves, dig in, make their own plans. Pavolini, the head of the Brigate Nere, had issued orders for the families of senior Fascists to join together and post people to keep watch at night. There had been changes in the hierarchy of the Fascists governing Turin, and Zerbino had been appointed by Mussolini as one of a number of 'Extraordinary Commissioners'. To break what he considered a dangerous collusion between industry and the Resistance, Zerbino ordered that all factories were to be patrolled by the Brigate Nere, to prevent thefts by the 'outlaws'. Reports were also going back to Mussolini that the industrialists – in particular FIAT's Valletta – guilty of 'corruption and excessive hoarding' were making deals on the side with Turin's leading Fascists.

The 650 men of Turin's main Fascist militia, the Ather Capelli, were angry, frustrated and demoralised, their barracks heavily fortified and surrounded by sandbags. They had developed effective networks of informers and their records included reams of information about the partisans and their whereabouts. But they were struggling. The partisans had become canny and the Fascists were stumbling around trying to track them down, despite raids by secret *'squadre della morte'*. The Casa Littorio, the Fascist headquarters, was encased in barbed wire. A *servizio informativo repressivo* (SIR) recruited thirty men as spies, to inform on everyone, including other Fascists. From its office in an abandoned palazzo on the Corso Vittorio Emanuele 11, the men from SIR ran a lucrative intelligence black market, buying and selling information. Militias, 'anti-partisans departments', special squads of killers and adventurers proliferated, their numbers growing after Salò decreed an end to the need for parental agreement to enrolling minors. Turin's streets, empty of civilians, were now full of these adolescents, strutting and menacing. Anyone sporting a flash of red on their clothing (a sign of Communist sympathy) or carrying a rolled-up umbrella (Anglophiles) risked a beating.

Early in March, on the edge of Turin, at a place called the Cisterna d'Asti, a firefight broke out between several German and Brigate Nere formations and two partisan brigades. It ended in a great victory for the partisans, three of their men dead against twenty-six of the enemy, and another forty-three wounded. In the city centre, partisans dressed as Fascist militia attacked the Treasury and made off with 30 million much needed lire. Then a list of all the Fascist Party dignitaries and senior German officers, together with their addresses, fell into the hands of the partisans. Victories and stunts like these seemed to mark a turning point, a moment when it became clear that the partisans were now an effective fighting force, even if the stakes were always higher, the reprisals harsher. They had survived the winter against terrible odds, and those still in hiding hastened to return to their bands. And, as the various embattled Fascist forces splintered and became laws unto themselves, so the power of the state, of Mussolini's Salò government, was ebbing visibly away.

By March 1945, with the Soviet Red Army advancing on Berlin, the Allies in Italy were preparing for their final great offensive: a break through the Gothic line to the plains beyond, hoping to cut off the German troops before they could retreat to the River Po. Though both sides could call on roughly the same number of troops, the Allies had infinitely superior air power. Now that liberation was no longer in doubt, Ada began to turn her thoughts to how to make sure that victory would not be in vain. Along with the new confidence that seemed to fill the air, the other great change during her absence in France had been among the women in the north. The numbers joining the GDD had leapt to some 60,000; factory workers, teachers, shop assistants, Catholics, Protestants, Waldensians, school girls and women long past retirement age were enrolling all the time. By now the groups had become so numerous that the central committee in Milan could no longer monitor all their activities.

Ada rushed from meeting to meeting, discussing the fate of political prisoners, assistance for their families, education, health, telling her listeners what she had learned in France, briefing the *staffette* on the roles they would play, returning to Oulx with documents for the Corallo brothers to take to Grenoble, visiting Milan during an air raid and finding time to scratch slogans on the city walls with the piece of chalk she always carried in her pocket. Though still not altogether convinced of the need for too much distinction between men and women, 'willingly or unwillingly', she wrote, 'I am working on women's problems'. Ada still looked very young, with her round face, her clothes chosen at random and seldom matching, her unruly black hair in pigtails. She was, noted one young partisan, 'generous with her smiles', though she herself was very conscious that she had become a point of reference for the younger fighters, calm, patient, ready to listen, exuding a kind of instinctive sympathy. She was never pompous, never lost her irreverence or sense of fun. But, like Agosti and Bianco, she was exhausted, drained, kept on her feet only by the urgency of the moment, too busy to reflect on the danger they were in.

Whenever she could, Ada joined Silvia, Bianca and Frida to design posters and leaflets and draft articles for *La Nuova Realtà* and the other women's papers circulating around Turin. They discussed, late into the night, how best to ensure that women, so long marginalised in Fascist Italy, were granted what they deserved: 'the right to be full members of society; the right to the same conditions as men; the right to work and the consequent right to rest'. Italian women, they said, had to find the courage to express their own views, and stop borrowing them from men. It was, in some sense, as Ada saw it, to be a reward for the contribution of women to the Resistance, for having fought and died and lost sons and husbands, and for their 'long, tenacious will to endure and to survive'. 'The mothers of the Resistance,' Ada declared, 'have learned that they are the builders of the future.'

By now each of the four women had somewhat different interests. Frida, as the lawyer, was drawn to the question of rights, and she contibuted regularly to the papers on questions of equal pay. Silvia, whose medical work among partisans and their families had brought her close friendships, wanted to galvanise housewives, a group that had always struck Ada as the 'most refractory to any kind of political education, and the hardest to reach'. Silvia offered to address their specific concerns and was pushing for a Fronte Femminile to challenge the historical image of submissive, cowed, Italian women. Bianca was helping to divide Turin into sectors, with a group of women in every factory. 'Because we were all so ignorant about how democracy worked,' she said later, 'we started learning about what elections involved, what trade unions could do, and those of us who knew a little taught the others.' Not one of these three young women had yet reached the age of twenty-seven.

They were not alone in trying to shape a better future for Italy's women. In October a number of women in the liberated south had set up a committee for the right to vote, and though they complained that men were still not listening to them, a law granting women the vote was finally passed unanimously at the end of January 1945 by the provisional Italian government in Rome. The first free trade union congress in twenty years, held in Rome not long before Christmas, had included items on equal pay, crèches in factories and the participation of women in running cooperatives. In February, under pressure from the Church and its concerns about the Communists, Christian Democrat women withdrew from the GDD, but they then set up their own Centro Italiano Femminile, while another women's organisation, the Unione Donne Italiane, had also formed.

And at last, though it had taken an absurdly long time, the Allies noticed the existence of women in the Resistance, and the Psychological Warfare Branch put together a report on the GDD, in tones of surprised admiration. On paper, all these things sounded promising, but Ada and her young friends were not at all confident either of Italian women's readiness for 'the serious and delicate task of reconstruction', or of the willingness of Italy's leaders – all of them men – to listen to them. As Bianca, who was emerging as the tactician of the four friends, put it, two struggles lay ahead: 'the fight for the liberty of Italy, and the fight for the liberty of women'.

None of them doubted that the fight would be bitter. When Ada, as putative vice mayor of Turin, was summoned to a meeting of the future administration, she was appalled to find them little interested in the day-to-day reconstruction of a broken society. The Communist mayor-to-be, Giovanni Roveda, was not able to attend, but her two fellow vice mayors, one a Socialist and the other a Christian Democrat, behaved, Ada wrote in her diary, 'like heirs who are finally coming into possession of an inheritance to which they were entitled and regarding whose ownership there was no longer any doubt'. One talked about new benches for Turin's broad avenues; the other about the opera. When Ada, who later admitted that she had spoken with too much 'candid fervour', mentioned the urgent tasks to be done to put the city back on its feet, she was told that she should not get so flustered. Surely, her new colleagues suggested, the point was not what they would now do, but what they had done. 'Look at what revolutionary ideas our Ada has put in her head,' said one. 'Ah! Ah! pretty, bizarre little head.'

From a meeting to discuss the purge of the Fascist educational system, Ada returned yet more discouraged. Augusto Monti, the much loved teacher of the Turin intellectuals, had been made superintendent of schools for the Partito d'Azione and emerged from hiding to attend. But though she admired him, Ada was saddened to find that he, like the others, refused to recognise that it was in the schools and the universities that a new democracy had to be launched. Ada herself wanted to close the universities completely for some months, thereby winning time to put together a truly radical and democratic programme. What worried her was letting everything revert to what it had been and 'throwing on to the market thousands of ignorant and presumptuous individuals with degrees, condemned to misery and because of this very misery to a violent hatred of the working classes'. The men in the room, she noted, were all of 'yesterday, embalmed in a correct and noble but now sterile dignity'.

She hurried away to a cheerful gathering of energetic young women. 'It is with these "new" women,' she wrote, 'that tomorrow will be built.'

16

Squashing the cockroaches

The spring was coming and the Resistance struggled on. German and Fascist *rastrellamenti* continued throughout the valleys, conducted with ever greater brutality in view of the now inevitable Allied victory. The Salò government had set up what they called RAP – Rappresaglie Anti-Partigiani – to specialise in hunting down the partisans, and when they failed to find them, they vented their anger on the villagers, hanging them from lamp posts and trees. But, like Ada and her friends, the partisan leaders were turning their thoughts firmly towards the future. As the snows melted, numbers of active fighters across the north began to rise sharply again, from around 60,000 after General Alexander's message in November, up to almost 100,000 by late January, and they continued to rise. In Piedmont alone, there were thought to be eight principal bands and over 16,000 partisans.

Some of the newcomers were farmers and peasants finally sickened by enemy brutality; some were young men escaping the repeated call-ups by Salò; some were former Fascist soldiers and members of the Brigate Nere, their eyes turning anxiously to the day of liberation, hoping that by changing sides now they would fare better later. There was much talk between Agosti, Bianco and Ada about how to use these men, how much to believe in their conversion, how far they could be depended on in the fight to come. In *Noi Donne* Silvia called on more women to join up: 'We are sisters, wives, mothers, like women everywhere . . . We are fighting today so that tomorrow we can have what *we* want . . . responsible work, a happy family and a society of free men.'

In the plains, a group of 1,500 specially trained saboteurs, the Gruppo Mobile Operativo, was conducting short, sharp and very effective attacks. Agosti and Bianco worried constantly about how to keep these mountain men, accustomed to rugged simple lives, occupied and focused on sabotage when the cities offered so may temptations. The 'patriots', they ordered repeatedly, were to show 'discipline and dignity'.

Then came the murders of Vera and Libera Arduino, the teen-aged sisters who had given their lives to the partisan cause and been executed with their father by the Fascists in Turin. There was something about the cold-bloodedness, the almost casual way in which the girls were killed, that sent waves of horror through communities by now almost inured to such violence. The presence of so many women at the funeral, the utter disregard they showed towards the Fascists who came to arrest them, and the many light-ning strikes of protest that brought the factories to a halt, were visible proof of the strength and determination of the northern partisans. Frida, a scarf pulled across her hair and face, returned to describe the event to Ada and the others. She was triumphant.

Cadorna, the man sent north by the government in Rome to act as their coordinating representative, was still agitating about his title. Having rejected a subordinate position, he finally settled on that of supreme commander, but in the febrile and confusing mix of northern men and politics, he carried little weight. In any case, unbeknown to Hitler, Karl Wolff, the supreme commander of the SS forces in Italy, had put out feelers to Allen Dulles, the top OSS man in Switzerland, with a view to possible peace terms, and been told that no negotiations could even begin until Parri, still in captivity but still alive, was released. Wolff agreed. Parri was freed and he immediately returned to shuttling up and down Italy, trying to breach the schism between the north and the gov-ernment in Rome and repeatedly saying that it was essential that the Allies avoid 'brusque, authoritarian and unilateral decisions'. Mindful of the retributions that awaited the Germans, General von Vietinghoff, who had succeeded Kesselring as commander-in-chief in Italy in March, abruptly announced a change of policy: captured partisans were henceforth to be treated as prisoners of war, under the Geneva Conventions.

A new emissary from Rome, the undersecretary for Occupied Italy, Aldobrando Medici Tornaquinci, was parachuted into the Piedmont valleys. The wily and resourceful Lucia was detailed to collect him and convey him to meetings with the Committee of National Liberation in Turin. Referred to as a person 'of absolute trust and remarkable courage', Lucia had been given a pass to move freely from one partisan area to the next.

Medici Tornaquinci had brought with him an enormous flag, stitched by women in Rome for the northern partisans to parade with on the day of liberation. Lucia wound it round and round her middle, then guided the undersecretary across the mountains. They walked for five hours, slept briefly in a hut, then walked again all next day. Medici Tornaquinci had also brought with him considerable sums of money for the northern partisans, and this Lucia transported in her stockings, bundles of notes packed around her thighs. They negotiated fourteen nerve-racking roadblocks but were not stopped. It was from Medici Tornaquinci that Lucia learned that the Rome government had finally passed the law giving Italian women the vote. Later, it fell to Lucia to get a large package of documents from the undersecretary's meetings out to the town of Chivasso. As they were too bulky to carry in bags without arousing suspicions, she again packed them round her middle and, wearing a wedding ring and passing herself off as heavily pregnant and accompanied by one of the partisan leaders, she took a series of trams and then a train, leaning on his arm.

As a future vice mayor, Ada was invited to meet Medici Tornaquinci; she came away unimpressed by his 'empty, useless' speeches. The undersecretary kept the assembled Resistance leaders waiting for several hours, then delivered an interminable speech in which he described to them their own all-too-familiar story in the Resistance. Then, hearing that the Germans had learned of his presence in Turin, he hurried away.

Regardless of Rome, the northern leadership was at last making progress towards Parri's long-held dream, that of forging a unified military command, though the process was excruciatingly slow and frustrating. Few of the Autonomi, Communist, Partito d'Azione or Matteotti bands were eager to relinquish their own independence. But Parri was adamant. Having sent word to the Allies that only with a 'strong national army' would it be possible for Italy to 'rehabilitate herself morally by avenging her good name stained by Fascism', he forced through agreement of a sort. A fusion of the bands was announced: all political distinctions were to be set to one side until Italy was liberated; the Corpo Volontari della Libertà would provide a single united command, with divisions and brigades fighting under the names of dead heroes; and the partisans would all wear a similar uniform of long trousers and a waistcoat. Their new emblem was to be a tricolour flag and a five-pointed star. There would be no grades, only duties. However precarious, this pact was a major achievement.

Politics were indeed shelved, but not for long. As was all too clear, unity in the new Italy promised to be a chimera. The conservatives and the industrialists feared damage to their interests and had little desire for an uprising of the masses; they favoured doing nothing and waiting for the Allies to liberate them. The left believed passionately that only with a wholehearted uprising could Italians hold their heads high. The Church continued to be haunted by the spectre of communism. As one Resistance leader noted, what was being played out was not a war between states but a war 'waged on behalf of civilisation'. There was much grumbling, but Parri pressed on.

There was, however, more agreement when it came to strategy, with the northern Resistance pledging to slow down the German retreat, to get information to the Allies about targets for them to bomb, and to consider the protecting of industry more important than the killing of Germans. Circulars, orders, drafts and memoranda flooded out of the secret headquarters in Milan and Turin, urgent, exhortatory, carried by *staffette* to the bands, to the women's groups, to factories, offices and businesses. New songs were composed about victory and freedom. The tone of the clandestine broadsheets was excited, urgent. 'The decisive moment is about to come, when the world will be delivered from the incubus of an oppressor that has no equal in history.' Fighters were to understand that they were soldiers in a 'new revolutionary army' and that they were to be prepared to sacrifice everything, including their lives, for the triumph of 'justice and liberty'. When the call finally went out, they were to rise up and go to war, do what the Florentines had done, descend from the mountains into the city and fight.

As to the fate of the Fascists, all were adamant: there was to be no mercy towards the Italian SS, the Brigate Nere or the many Fascist militias. These people were to be regarded as war criminals and 'eliminated', along with all spies and informers. Partisan police units were formed to take charge of the collaborators the

Resistance intended to hunt down; tribunals were appointed to judge war crimes. Though 'Jacobin violence' was to be eschewed, the purging of the Fascists from the fabric of Italian society was to be 'radical and pitiless'. These two last words were heavily underlined. The only exceptions were to be the young Salò conscripts who, providing that they surrendered to the partisans immediately, could still save themselves. 'Tomorrow may already be too late. After that, it will certainly be too late.' If they did cross over to the Resistance, they should carry a white flag and they would be treated 'justly and humanely'; but if they failed to do so, there would be 'no compromise, no indulgence, no pity'.

A circular issued to the bands phrased it more bluntly. Under the heading 'The Dead for the Dead' it said: 'The cockroaches will be squashed! Partisans will crush them without mercy! Every last corner of Italy must be cleansed of the Fascist putrefaction!'

Orders from the CLNAI leadership now went out for the partisans to go on the offensive and make the enemy feel constantly observed, harried, menaced. Posters with the words *'arrendersi o perire'*, surrender or perish, appeared on the walls of every town and city. All over the north, the partisans were finalising their plans for the day of liberation.

The Allies, however, were fed contradictory information by all sides about the future intentions of the Italian Resistance, and continued to vacillate. Even Cadorna warned that the Communist Party would rebel 'rather than submit to the orders of the Western Allies'. Torn between fears of a Communist takeover, and that food shortages and mass unemployment might prove 'fertile ground for some extreme' uprising, and the need for sustained help from the partisans in their final push to the north, the messages the Allies gave out were ambivalent.

On the one hand, finally convinced of the numerical strength of the Resistance, the Allies at last began making more substantial drops of weapons and supplies; but on the other, what they dropped seldom contained what they knew the partisans needed most – small arms, rifles, ammunition – and they continued to supply the bands on the political centre and right less grudgingly than those on the left, thereby feeding further jealousy among the fighters. And they made mistakes, fuelling suspicion among the Italians: an air raid on Turin, which hit a maternity hospital and left many casualties 'considerably helped the Fascists', as one agent reported. In March 1945 alone, Allied air raids caused more civilian damage than in the entire preceding three years. The Allies themselves were also finding it hard to find their way through the labyrinth of conflicting parties, bands, groups, allegiancies and rivalries. As a desperate note attached to a long report put it: 'This is as clear as mud.'

The confusion was not helped by enduring disagreements between the Americans and the British. The British continued to be swayed by the curmudgeonly Foreign Office. Churchill's words, that he foresaw disaster when 'violent and vehement' politicians were thrown 'hungry upon the fragile government in Rome', and that Britain needed 'Italy no more than we need Spain', were not lost on the Italians. Macmillan was now head of the Allied Commission and railed against Whitehall's 'childish animosity', later famously remarking: 'It was hard to know which process [being occupied by the Germans or liberated by the Allies] was the more painful or devastating.' But even he could sound condescending about the Italian leaders. Bonomi he described as 'wet as the ocean', while Luigi Longo of the Northern Alliance was 'fat, genial, good tempered . . . sensible and patriotic . . . almost (but of course not quite) like an Englishman'. The Americans were more detached, and less niggardly. As for the Soviets, they wanted the British and the Americans to stop demanding that they loosen their hold on Eastern Europe, in return for loosening their own on Italy.

Matters were not improved by the choice of some of the British agents dropped into the north. Lt Col. Stevens, officially in charge of Allied missions in the region, would later be judged harshly by much of the Italian Resistance, but even at the time the northern leadership found him difficult and maddening. Having drawn up his own detailed plans for the day of liberation, he refused to visit Turin 'for reasons of caution', and when General Trabucchi, military commander in the north, went to meet him at his safe house in the Langhe, travelling part of the way on foot in 'Siberian conditions', he failed to turn up for their encounter.

Stevens announced that he personally intended to oversee the Piedmont Resistance, and would keep the right to appoint and dismiss its leaders if he felt that his own agents could do the job better. He also let it be known that he was to be the sole channel between the partisans and the Allies, bypassing the northern CLN altogether. His report to headquarters was characteristically scathing. 'The whole movement is unsound . . . The partisans are not brave and have a flair for muddle . . . Like all Italians, they are moody and unreliable . . . There are too many comfortable partisans who dislike walking and sleeping out, and, incidentally, fighting.' In the struggle to come they would be incapable of tackling even small enemy units, not because they lacked weapons, 'but because they are afraid'.

On liberation, he decided, only the Liberals, the Christian Democrats and the Partito d'Azione would be allowed to control public order; the Communists were to be excluded altogether from the various committees and commands. There was to be no question of a 'duplicate' government in the north, no challenge of any kind either to the Allied military government or to the existing Bonomi government-in-waiting in Rome. It is perhaps not surprising that, increasingly, the northern command chose not to listen. Nor that the partisans, observing that the purpose of the Allied agents dropped into the north was to make certain that the Resistance did not turn into a revolutionary movement, became very wary of their foreign overlords. Fear of a Communist Italy continued to obsess many of the Allied leaders, who made no effort to understand what, in the context of Italian politics, communism actually stood for.

After Captain O'Regan decided to parcel out a drop of weapons according to a clearly political criterion, one partisan commander banned him from his area, while others refused to offer hospitality to the missions. On another occasion, O'Regan called in a drop too early and four hundred cases of weapons and supplies fell into German hands. There was talk of him being a 'British spy', and of the Allies' intention to 'reinstate Fascism under another name'. Though the breach was mended, it was symptomatic of the growing estrangement between the Allies and the Resistance; what one man called the 'wall of diffidence' between them grew taller. There was, noted the northern Resistance irritably, 'a pullulation of missions all acting independently'.

Matters improved slightly when a more emollient figure was dropped into the north. Max Salvadori was an Italian who had spent some time as an exile among the anti-Fascists in the United

States. He was shrewd, urbane, bilingual, a friend of the pre-war Turin intellectuals, and his dealings with the Resistance came in the form of consultations and suggestions rather than orders. The reports he sent back to his superiors praised the Piedmontese leadership as the best organised, politically and militarily, in the whole of the north and repeated that the Communists, knowing full well that they could not manage without help from the Allies, were willing to compromise at every level and had no intention of challenging the legality of any future government.

Privately, Salvadori considered the Communist partisans the 'real thing', disciplined and extremely efficient, and he insisted that there would be no disturbances in the big northern cities. He added that Stevens had made a fundamental error in portraying himself as the military commander. General Trabucchi, who disliked Stevens intensely, went further: he was a man 'of colonial stamp, believing that the British were born to command and all others to obey'. For his part, Raimondo Craveri dismissed the British missions generally as 'myopic and incomprehensible'. But Salvadori's reassurances came too late to influence Allied policy, which now seemed firmly intent on moving towards liberation with a resolve to limit and control the northern Resistance.

The Allies were also aware that, given the speed of their planned advance, there were bound to be several days between the German retreat and their own arrival in the north. With great reluctance, they conceded that the Resistance would be allowed to use this period to restore order, and carry out their own punishments of the Fascist collaborators, which they recognised might be extremely brutal. This was 'Rankin B' in the Allied plans for liberation.

Once the Allies arrived, however, the administration of Italy was to be handed over immediately and the partisans disarmed, in 'patriot separation centres' with showy 'stand down parades' complete with flags, bands and fulsome speeches. A very small number of those 'who had given most to the cause of liberation' would be offered advisory roles on a consultative committee. As a memorandum drafted by the Psychological Warfare Branch rather chillingly noted: 'Whether we hate the Italians or not is of no importance, the important thing is that we must obtain from Italy everything possible for our war effort . . . We must pretend the greatest friendship possible and act without mercy when it is no longer necessary to hide our real sentiments.' Meanwhile, the Italians were to be treated 'firmly and with sympathy'. A patronising tone runs through almost every report sent back to Allied headquarters: the Italians were unruly, needy, venal, guileless, useful children who had to be coaxed into line and spoken to sharply when they strayed.

The northern leadership had little choice but to accept. As Medici Tornaquinci phrased it: 'We must remember that we are a nation liberated by them, not an ally.' Even a report that, in just three months, the partisans had killed or captured 2,670 Germans, derailed 19 of their trains, blown up 75 bridges, destroyed 41 engines and 5 factories making explosives, along with many miles of telephone and high-tension cables, did little to improve their position. At the Yalta conference held in February to discuss Europe's post-war reorganisation, Roosevelt, Stalin and Churchill had not granted Italy a seat at the coming San Francisco Conference to frame the new United Nations Charter. What had at last become unmistakably clear to the Italians was that the Allies, for all their promises, were unlikely to be generous either at the peace table or afterwards, though they continued to hope that the more forgiving Americans might perhaps allow Italy to escape what the British continued to insist should be her 'just retribution'.

Less rancorous were the exchanges over the gathering of information. By the early spring of 1945, the northern command had put in place their own military intelligence, and this was soon acknowledged by the Allies to be their most reliable source of information. Some of it, at least, was due to the people involved and their old relationships of trust and friendship, and here Ada's long ties to Croce's family came in useful.

What no one, not even the Allies, could fail to acknowledge was that, far from making the Resistance in the north fade away, the long, cold, brutal winter had strengthened and toughened it. It had become a true movement, with hardy and united fighters and a clear mission of its own, no longer prepared to pay any heed to the 'attendisti', those industrialists and conservatives who kept urging that nothing should be done before the arrival of the Allied forces. The CLN which now existed in every town and city and often village across the north, had acquired stature and authority.

The Northern Italians had cut their teeth on the free republics, where partisans had held power, which however short-lived had given people a taste for, and practice in, the processes of democracy long denied them under Fascism. However frowned on by Rome and the Allies, the city administrations they appointed were working well. Italy was full of new men and women, with new ideas and aspirations; with victory in sight, they were preparing to prove themselves. And what they had in mind was not a liberation, but an uprising.

Staffette as armed fighters

In Turin and the valleys of Piedmont it had become a race against time. As the Fascists saw defeat looming, so they intensified their search for hostages, useful as barter for their own safety or simply as victims on whom to visit their fear and anger. What they dreaded most was the thought of the hiatus between the departure of the Germans and the arrival of the Allies. Agosti, Bianco and Pinella, Foa and Lisetta, and Ada and her family lived on the very edge, mindful of every strange noise, every unexpected encounter. All of them were known, to a greater or lesser degree, to the

Fascists and the German occupiers; what was extraordinary was that they had survived for so long.

Very early one March morning in Turin, while it was still dark, loud bangs were heard on the courtyard door to Ada's building in Via Fabro, followed by shouts of 'Police! Open the door!' Paolo, still in bed with a fever, remained asleep. Ettore and Ada leapt up, rushed about, wondered what to do. Should they wake him and try to get him out over the roof to the next-door house? Then they heard footsteps coming down the outside stairs from the floor above. It was their neighbour, a doctor, and he was being called out on police duty.

Not long after this, Ada was returning to Turin from Milan with a large envelope of secret documents to give to Bianco, when her car was stopped at a checkpoint. She was told to get out. The car was then minutely searched by the patrol, while Ada stood mutely by, the envelope in a briefcase under her arm. Fearing that it contained essential orders for the day of liberation, she considered throwing herself down a nearby escarpment and running away. In the event, she did nothing.

In due course the soldiers turned their attention to the car's occupants. One by one, their papers were scrutinised. Then the officer in charge asked Ada what was in her bag. 'A sweater,' she replied. He took the briefcase, opened it, took out the sweater, saw the envelope and said: 'And what is this?' She could barely speak. 'Letters.' 'Ah,' he said. He put the envelope back, then the sweater, and handed the briefcase back to her, before waving the car on. 'I felt,' Ada wrote later, 'like I no longer had a drop of blood in my veins.'

Up in Meana, she had a third near miss. Trying to board a train without the necessary new German pass, she was arrested and told that she would be taken to Susa for questioning. When the German officer was called away and turned his back, she slipped into the men's lavatory, from where she tore 'like a thunderbolt' to the train as it was leaving, while the officer ran along the platform shouting, 'Signora, signora, do not leave.' Afterwards, she and Ettore laughed. There were too many people to see, too many decisions to make, too many things to do, to waste time on fear.

But she was lucky. As was Cesare, Ada and Paolo's young friend, picked up in a restaurant in Turin. Hearing that he had been taken to the SS headquarters, Ada wrote in her diary: 'I am exhausted and furious with everyone. I want to go to sleep and never wake up.' But Cesare played the fool, pleaded innocence, pretended he was a medical student and was eventually released, after turning down an invitation to join a Fascist brigade. He left the barracks, went straight to the station and caught a train up into the mountains, where he hid. Agosti too was lucky. In early March, two of his three hiding places were discovered along with many of his false documents and aliases. He changed house every night. One day, the Fascists closed in. He was not at home, but his father was there and they took him instead. In one of those rare moments of good fortune, Signor Agosti was unexpectedly released. His son remained free.

For Ada, life had become an incessant round of meetings. Bianca, Frida and Silvia flitted in and out of her days, helping to draft papers and draw up schedules for the day of liberation. Whenever she had a moment, she used it to study documents that might help her in her coming job as vice mayor. Haste was making her careless. One day, having overstuffed a bag with documents and flyers in Agosti's office, she reached the street only to have it burst open, scattering incriminating papers all over the pavement. The street was full of passers-by. In silence, not looking at her, they hurried forward, gathered up the papers and flyers and handed them back to her, before walking away. As she left, one woman whispered to Ada: 'I'll keep one. I know just who to give it to. Good luck.'

All the leadership lived in fear of spies. They had good reason, though it only became clear after the war, when documents became available, just how many informers there had been and how much they had known. A useful *staffetta*, known to all of them, was a man they called 'Bernardo'. Sometime in the late summer of 1944, Bernardo had approached Bianco, saying that he was making a bit of money from the black market, and if the partisans could give him a hand he would happily act as courier for them. Bianco liked him, though he sometimes complained that Bernardo was a *'chiacchierone'*, a chatterbox.

Bernardo spent the autumn going up and down the valleys carrying papers and messages along with his black-market goods. Soon, he knew the names and pseudonyms of all the principal partisans. After Duccio's arrest, all the other couriers were suspended; Bernardo was kept on.

Then, in January 1945, Bernardo went quiet. On 5 February, it was learned that he had been arrested by the Fascist militia Decima Mas. Agosti sent out orders that passwords and pseudonyms were to be changed, along with safe houses and stores of weapons. After negotiations by the ecclesiastical authorities, Bernardo was released and went back to work. What Ada and Agosti did not know was that, in return for money and the promise of safety, he had made a deal with the Fascists. For a while, he was paid by both the Fascists and the partisans. Then one day he led a Fascist patrol to the house of a '*pesce piccolo*', a small-fry partisan organiser. This man was able to hide under the bed where he remained unseen. But he had the presence of mind to take a close look at the informer's shoes and to listen carefully to his voice, so that later he was able to identify him. As Bernardo was led out to execution by the partisans, at dusk on 10 April, having sworn that he had never given away the leaders, but only a few '*pesci piccoli*', he addressed the crowd assembled to watch him die. 'Young people! Never let yourselves be seduced by money! I made a mistake, don't do what I did. It's fair: I deserve to be shot.' Bernardo's wife Carmelita was taken prisoner by the partisans, to be detained until liberation, in case she too gave names away.

By early April it was clear that the liberation of Piedmont was imminent. In Germany the Americans had reached the Rhine and were moving towards the Ruhr. Berlin had now been bombed for thirty-six consecutive nights. On 10 April, the Allies finally broke through the Gothic line and began to advance across the plain of Lombardy towards Bologna, Turin, Milan and Venice. British soldiers reported that in the villages and towns they liberated, the squares, barns and houses were full of bodies.

The Resistance, determinedly pursuing its own path, had planned a dry run for the day of liberation, a 'pre-insurrection', organised largely by Ada, Bianca, Frida, Silvia and the women's groups. It was to take the form of a general strike in and around Turin. In the days leading up to it, the women's papers carried instructions and orders. Copies of the Christian Democrat bulletin, *In Marcia*, printed in a room behind the church of Nostra Signora della Salute, were given to the mother of the royal chaplain, who hid them in her apartments in the royal palace. From here they travelled, concealed in baskets under shopping, to be distributed by other women in parishes all over the city.

It was Bianca's job to make certain that the factory women working in the outlying industrial suburbs knew exactly what they were to do, and she briefed them on how to take stock of the deposits of food and weapons held on the premises and how to organise themselves into teams of messengers, nurses and cooks. Others were shown how to prevent the escape of the Fascist bosses and how to occupy the premises of the female Fascist auxiliaries. In the factories, the women *sappiste* called themselves 'football teams' to disguise their real activities. Bianca gave them tricolour ribbons to wear on the day. 'The great moment has arrived!' the northern leadership announced. 'The moment we have so long desired.'

Getting wind of what was happening, the Fascists posted men all over the city, outside hotels, offices, restaurants. Trams were given escorts to ensure that they kept running. Soldiers were planted in every factory, and told that if workers went on strike, they were to be given ten minutes to return to their posts. If they failed to do so, guns were to be fired into the air. If they still disobeyed, they would be shot. Anyone who was arrested would be taken to Le Nuove.

At nine o'clock on the morning of 18 April, women poured out of the factories to join the thousands who were emerging from their houses, offices, schools and shops. It was a cold, blue, still morning and the distant mountains shone in the spring light. The young *staffette* had been carrying messages around the city since long before dawn. Outside one textile factory, which the workers had decided to occupy, a group of women stood and shouted out to passers-by: 'Stand with us, Torinesi!' A car full of Germans drove up, followed by tanks. The women stood firm and continued to call out: 'Come with us, we're all brothers.' The Germans held their fire. The women set out to walk to a nearby factory.

The tram on which Bianca was travelling stopped and the driver turned to address the passengers: 'Ladies and gentlemen, alight now. The hour has come.' The shops lowered their shutters, the civil servants left their desks, the lawyers and magistrates abandoned the law courts. Nothing moved, nothing opened, nothing was bought or sold. A city of 800,000 people appeared to be paralysed. On the corner of one street, a tram had been pushed over by the crowd. Women, waving red flags, clambered on top of it. Another tram crashed, leaving four people dead and many injured, and the Fascist tram driver narrowly escaped being lynched. Just outside Turin, the town of Chieri was taken over by partisans, and a female Fascist auxiliary who had found shelter in a convent was also nearly lynched. *Staffette* cycled furiously around, distributing leaflets about the coming insurrection, pausing every now and again to address the crowds. By the end of the day, the women had settled on their battlecry: 'We have conquered the piazze, now we must not lose them!'

It had been, noted Ada, a most promising dress rehearsal for the day of liberation and she took particular delight in the presence of so many people 'traditionally devoid of courage, such as employees and store owners'. After the first hour, the Fascists were nowhere to be seen. The few Germans on the streets had the 'appearance of beaten dogs'. For the partisans, the strike had exceeded their wildest hopes and promised great things for the day of liberation itself. For the Fascists, it spelt a future even grimmer than the one they had feared. But they took their revenge. That night, several hundred women were taken from their houses. Thirty-six were shot.

The Allies were on the move. On 21 April Bologna fell to them, and Modena followed two days later, and in both cities they arrived to find the partisans already installed and keeping order. In Bologna the partisans captured 1,300 Germans and saved the city's waterworks and gas and electricity supplies. The Piedmont partisans were also on the move, freeing first Val Pellice, then Alba and Pinerolo. From the Tyrrhenian sea to the Adriatic, across the rugged backbone of the Appenines, twenty-five German divisions – perhaps the best fighting force left in the German army – supported by five Fascist divisions were facing twenty-one Allied divisions and a number of Italian combat troops, armoured brigades and infantry. Then there were the partisans, their numbers of active fighters put at somewhere between 250,000 and 300,000 – Italians from all over the peninsula, Russians, Czechs, French, Mongols and Allied prisoners of war – finally, at the very last hour, united into Parri's single fighting force. Three-quarters of the fighting partisans were under the age of twenty-five; a few were no more than fourteen. Thirty-five thousand of them were women.

The outcome was not in doubt. The Allies had more planes, more artillery and more tanks than the enemy. The final push had been planned as a series of giant forward lunges, accompanied by full-scale aerial attacks against the retreating enemy lines, while the partisans were to stand guard over the industrial centres, the roads, railways and electricity pylons. They were also to harry the Germans who, in spite of the fact that the war was clearly ending, had been ordered by Hitler to resist. The question was only at what price victory would come. As the Germans retreated, they left behind them devastation: mines, ruined houses, hunger, people living in ditches or on the streets. Italy was awash with the fugitives of war, British and American POWs trying to reach the Allied lines, militiamen and Fascists seeking new identities, refugees driven from their homes, collaborators heading for the border. Everyone was working out how to survive.

Through Cardinal Schuster, who had become the northern mediator, some of the senior Germans had made overtures to the Resistance and to the Allies, saying that they would leave the factories intact if they were allowed to pull back unmolested. Though Hitler continued to refuse all talk of capitulation, General Wolff was secretly negotiating for a deal that would save his own skin. To all of them, the answer was the same: only unconditional surrender would be accepted. Talks continued. News had just reached Turin of the conditions found in liberated Bergen-Belsen, adding to the disgust and hostility felt towards the occupiers.

For their part, the Fascist forces were in disarray. Despite threats by their officers – often carried out – that their families would be held as hostages or executed, the numbers of men deserting to the Resistance multiplied, day by day. The crack San Marco Division, one of Mussolini's flagship regiments trained in Germany, had already lost a quarter of its men, either now in hiding or having slipped across the lines to join the partisans.

Pavolini, the head of the Brigate Nere, had assured Mussolini that there were still 50,000 followers ready to join him in a last-ditch stand, possibly at the Valtellina in the central Alps, between the plains of Lombardy and Switzerland. The idea was first to try to broker a peace deal with the partisans, using Cardinal Schuster as go-between, then, if that failed, to retreat, carrying with them Dante's ashes as a symbol of Mussolini's much vaunted '*italianità*'. But many of the old Fascist *gerarchi* were slipping away or sending secret messages of their own to the northern command, suing for peace.

In Turin, in a last frenzy of violence, the nocturnal killings continued, but now some of the bodies were those of Fascists and collaborators, hunted down ahead of liberation. To raise morale, the Fascist Party secretary, Solaro, called a meeting of the 5,000 or so declared Fascists in the city, and many came to parade in front of the Casa Littorio and to sing battle hymns to the patria. On the city walls was scrawled a bold new message: the letters PFR, no longer to stand for Partita Fascista Repubblicana, but for Pocchi Fessi Rimasti – not many arseholes left. What worried the Fascists most was the fact that the Germans, busy preparing their own retreat, code-named *Herbstnebel*, Autumn Mist, were totally indifferent to their plight. Solaro set about burning incriminating papers. Those Fascists who could do so joined others already in hiding; others made plans to join the columns of retreating Germans.

The Piedmont partisan leadership, the Commando Piazza, was busy finalising its battle plans. Orders and decrees, carried by the speeding *staffette*, went out to the leaders of the various formations. Special passes and identifying badges were prepared; lists of installations to be protected drawn up; a strategy for dealing with collaborators agreed on. Trenches were dug in courtyards and machine guns placed on roofs. In every sector of the city, groups of women set up first-aid centres: there was one in the crypt of a church, another in a florist's shop. Agosti was put in charge of the police and restoring order. Bolaffi and his 500-strong Stellina Brigade were to defend the infrastructure of the high valleys, police the area and round up local Fascists.

Bianco, from his headquarters in Turin, dispatched a message to the men of the Partito d'Azione brigades. 'Prepare yourselves to advance on Turin. One thing I must insist on since it will be crucial in how the Allies judge us is: keep order and discipline with an iron fist and crush, without mercy, anyone who fails to obey.' The disobedient were to be shot immediately, even if they were partisans. The *staffette*, a 'swarm of girls with bicycles' that included Bianca, Frida, Lisetta and all the young girls who had rallied to Ada's side, were everywhere. 'Every one of my women,' Ada wrote, 'knows where they must go, whom to contact and what to do.' Silvia was to look after the wounded and check on casualties.

It fell to Bianca to be one of a pair of *staffette* sent to issue final instructions to the Bergman rubber factory in the Borgo Vittorio. They took the tram, accompanied by two armed men. The workers had assembled in the refectory, and a table had been placed for Bianca to stand on. She had been told to start her speech with the words 'Citizens, workers, employees' but in the flurry of the moment came out with 'Companions'. 'The Allies are advancing!' she shouted. 'The glorious Russian army is at the gates of Berlin!' There was a roar of applause. The women before her began to cry. Seeing them, Bianca burst into tears too. 'Go on, Nerina, go on,' urged her partisan friend. But by now Bianca was crying so much that she could not speak. Her friend took her place and shouted: 'Let us prepare for insurrection!' Later, with some other members of the CLN, Bianca went to FIAT to inform Valletta that the workers would soon be taking over the factory. Wisely, he said nothing and went home.

On 23 April came the news that the Allies had crossed the Po south of Mantua. It was, in the words of General Sir William Jackson, 'like the bursting of a giant cascade of fireworks'. At a conference of war held in Bianca's house the Turin leadership decided that the moment to rise up had finally come. Stevens continued to declare that no one was to proceed without his express orders, and that if they moved too soon they would have to take responsibility for a massacre. 'I am in charge here,' he told them, 'you are working for us.' They ignored him. They had accepted, with some bitterness, that they would effectively be denied all real power once the Allies arrived, but they did not intend to be deprived of liberating Piedmont for themselves.

The code for insurrection was to be 'Aldo says 26 x 1': one o'clock on the morning of 26 April. According to long-agreed plans, the workers were immediately to take possession of the factories; the *gappisti* and *sappisti* urban partisans were to begin coralling the Germans and the Fascists in the city centre, while the partisan formations, ready and waiting at the gates of Turin, were to march on the city. Two hundred and fifty committees of liberation all over Piedmont stood prepared to take power as the enemy retreated, in the hopes that when the Allies arrived and saw the efficiency with which they had re-established order, they would not replace them. Together with the code, a brief message went out. 'Enemy in final crisis . . . Stop all vehicles and rigorously check passengers, detaining suspects.' There would be very little mercy either for Mussolini or for his followers. 'Be clear: all who do not surrender will be exterminated.'

To confuse Stevens, the CLN decided to downplay the number of men to be included in the first assault. They spoke vaguely of 3,000. In fact 8,000 Autonomi, Garibaldini, men of the Partito d'Azione and the Matteotti were standing ready to march. Bianca asked her sister to make her a Red Cross armband and to hang a red flag from the window of their house. When Ada paid a brief visit to Via Fabro, she found Ettore and Espedita busy dyeng sheets red, with which they planned to make flags. Seeing them hanging from the line, Ada found herself in tears. An enormous package was delivered, with English, American and French flags and pennants. Ada quickly wrote a speech to go out over the radio: 'Women of Piedmont! Today every woman faces a struggle in her heart. May this not be in vain. Do not abandon yourselves to sterile acts of violence, do not retreat, exhausted, into indifference . . . The true battle begins today.'

Now that the hour had come, Bianco felt sad not to be with his men at the gates of the city; his fear was that the 'golden age of the revolutionary partisan war' was about to end, and that much bitterness would surely follow. In his last message to the men of the Partito d'Azione, he wrote: 'But at least when we greet each other again it will be as free men. Think only of the importance of what we are doing today.'

In her diary, Ada just found time to write: 'It is strange, but I do not feel excited in the least: neither anxiety nor worry nor exaltation. I am extraordinarily lucid and serene. But it is this very serenity, which is almost reckless, that is the symptom that signals for me the advent of the gravest of times.'

17

Insurrection

The liberation of Turin and Piedmont was rapid and murderous. As Chevallard noted, it was almost impossible to believe that twenty years of Fascist dictatorship and twenty months of German occupation were shed in a little over two days. Spring had come to the valleys, bringing squalls of rain and sudden flashes of sunshine. Something of the very blue sky, the soft air and the snow sparkling on the high mountains played into the general mood of euphoria as, street by street, village by village, city by city, the Italians liberated themselves. Turin, the most '*vistosa*', the most conspicuous, heart of Fascism in the north had seen the most systematic brutality; here the Fascists knew they could expect no mercy. The hunters became the hunted.

Partisans taking Fascist prisoners

From the late afternoon of 25 April, the first tricolour flags appeared on buildings and factories on the outskirts of the city as, one by one, they were occupied by the workers, who had agreed to barricade themselves in, ready to defend them from destruction by the Germans. The women inside had stockpiled provisions of food, knowing that they might well be there for some time and that the arriving partisans would also need feeding. Those with young children had been sent home.

While it was still dark, very early on the 26th, the leading brigades of *sappisti* and *gappisti* took over FIAT Montefiore, Incet, FIAT Grandi Motori, Lancia and a number of foundries and plane manufacturers. They had been planning their campaign for weeks. In one factory, workers hastily put together a radio transmitter, invaluable to the partisans in the hours to come. Supported by small numbers of partisans arriving from the valleys, the *sappisti* and *gappisti* began to push the German and Fascist forces towards the city centre.

They would have moved faster had there not been a strange intervention by Stevens. At nine o'clock on the evening of the 25th, the 6,000 men of a Garibaldi formation, preparing for their descent from the hills into the city, received a message, apparently from the partisan leadership. Written on official paper but carrying an indecipherable signature, it countermanded the earlier order to advance, replacing it with instructions to do nothing until further orders. Word went out to the various nearby formations to suspend the attack. It was not until late on the morning of the 26th, by which time the initial forces inside Turin were desperate for reinforcements, that the partisan leaders realised that the order had been a false one, put out by Stevens in a last-minute attempt to hold the partisans back. Whether he did so, as he later maintained, in order to save the partisans from being massacred by the two nearby German divisions before the arrival of the Allies, or because the men to whom his false order was addressed were Communists and he feared their takeover of the north, was never established. The Communists were duly furious, orders went out to advance immediately 'with boldness and decision' and to arrest anyone trying to interfere with these orders. There was angry talk of Stevens sabotaging the insurrection. Whatever the true story, what remained certain was that for much of the 26th the urban fighters of the first wave were largely on their own.

Most of that day was spent trying to corral the enemy forces, who were busy barricading themselves into barracks and strongholds, while armoured German and Fascists vehicles raced up and down the avenues firing machine guns. The fighting was fierce, with high casualties on both sides. The first woman partisan to die was Virginia Ruffino, a 33-year-old glove-maker serving with the 47th Garibaldi Brigade, who was shot on her balcony. Her older sister Felicita, with the same brigade, was shot at the same time and died soon after of her wounds. Any Fascist caught in the streets was immediately shot. In their barracks in Via Asti, the Leonessa Fascist militia tied prisoners to the bars of the windows to deflect attack. Offered the chance to surrender, they refused, knowing full well what their fate would be. Solaro, recently promoted to Inspector of the Brigate Nere for Piedmont, tried to negotiate peace terms with the Resistance, using Monsignor Garneri as go-between. The partisan leadership refused. On the morning of the 26th, Solaro held a meeting with his Fascist colleagues to discuss EsigenzaZ2, a plan drafted earlier for escape. Fearing above all things falling into partisan hands, no one could decide what to do. Solaro and the men from the Decima Mas favoured a last-ditch stand in the city; others wanted to leave at once.

Needing money to buy new identities, twenty-six *brigatisti* were dispatched to the head office of the Banca d'Italia, to empty the reserves. The director had barricaded himself behind an immense wooden door and refused to let them in, but a deputy treasurer was coerced into releasing 17.5 million lire in bonds. At a nearby branch, Fascists threw explosives at the entrance but failed to break it down, so they made off with the director's wife's jewellery instead. Anna Maria Bardia, head of the local Fascist women auxiliaries, turned up disguised with dark glasses and a capacious hooded jacket to demand money for herself and her women. There were squabbles, altercations over vehicles, many of which in any case lacked fuel.

The Germans stationed in the city were no better prepared. Having failed to organise the destruction of the factories, they had now lost all interest in their former Fascist collaborators and were intent on negotiating their own safe withdrawal. Again using Monsignor Garneri as a go-between, they proposed to the Resistance that Turin be declared an open city, thus sparing all fighting, in return for safe conduct for themselves, and an equally safe passage for the 35,000 German soldiers, in two divisions, retreating from the West and wishing to cross the city. This too the partisan leadership refused: it was to be unconditional surrender or nothing. News came that Milan had fallen to the partisans, and that a deal had been struck between General Wolff and Cadorna. Almost every city in Lombardy was now free. The Germans were threatening to blow up a train packed with explosives in the Porta Nuova station which, they warned, would destroy at least a quarter of Turin. The partisans paid no attention. The German demands grew smaller: soon, all they were asking for was a couple of hours' grace in which to withdraw in safety. Again, the Resistance refused.

In the valleys, meanwhile, Bolaffi and his fighters had been standing ready to protect bridges, railway lines, hydroelectric plants and dykes, as well as factories. They intercepted a German message to their own saboteurs, men planning to wreak destruction in the event of defeat by the Allies. The partisans prepared themselves. Susa remained full of Germans, milling around, looking for hostages. Bolaffi heard one say: '*In zwei minuten Susa kaput.*' He wrote in his diary: 'Susa is in a state of terror. Nothing moves.' The German garrison in Torre Pellice was reinforced by men from Pinerolo.

Before the Germans had time to act, however, the partisans did. Obedient to the Aldo code to rise up, they had spent the previous evening in their bases waiting; at one o'clock on the pitch-black morning of the 26th they set forth. Orders went out: 'Attack the enemy everywhere without mercy.' The local German commanders proposed a deal: safe passage and the infrastructure untouched, or total destruction. As in Turin, Bolaffi and his fellow commanders refused.

The German and Fascist retreat towards the plains was marked by ferocious battles, particularly in the town of Exilles, where the SS had positioned a machine gun in a belfry, turned schools into fortified garrisons and taken hostages. But the Germans were outnumbered. Encircled and harried, they suffered many casualties, but caused deaths as they fell back. The retreat from the valleys left 128 civilians, 113 partisans and 63 *sappisti* dead; 11 of the casualties were in Susa, 5 in Torre Pellice. The last woman to die there was a *staffetta* called Jenny Peyronel Cardon. A 32-year-old worker in a sweet factory, not long married, Jenny had been on her way to take a message to a partisan band when she was surprised by a group of retreating Germans. They forced her to remove her dark coat, keeping on a brightly coloured striped sweater, visible from afar, and positioned her in the middle of their column as a human shield. Jenny died, along with seven men from the Wehrmacht, when the partisans attacked. She left a two-year-old daughter.

Apart from a few small bridges, the Germans had done little to set off their explosives; one by one the hydroelectric plants and railway lines were de-mined. As they fled, trying to hide in the vineyards and the forests, the villagers rounded them up and locked them in pigsties. Leaving civilians to mop up the remaining pockets of Fascists and Germans, the men of the Unified 41 Division now hastened down towards Turin, to join in the last struggle for liberation. In Susa, Bolaffi spoke from a balcony to the crowd assembled below, then he led a procession to the cemetery to lay wreaths for the dead. In every village and town, women emerged to join mourners walking to the places where executions had taken place. The mountains sounded to the ringing of church bells, the peals carrying from one village to the next, across the valleys.

Because of her importance to the future of Turin, Ada had been instructed by the Resistance leadership to set up her base in Maria Daviso's villa in Borello, far from the expected heavy fighting in the centre. From here she could run her *staffette*, the youngest and strongest to act as messengers, the housewives to gather food and medicines, the trained nurses to stand by to help the injured. She was deeply irritated at being kept from the action. *Staffette* came and went, bringing news of victories and casualties, of partisan attacks on the German roadblocks in the surrounding hills, of factories turned into fortresses by the partisans, of areas of the city taken, then lost, then retaken. In the afternoon, Ada slipped home on her bicycle, but finding neither Ettore nor Paolo in the house, she returned to Borello, having first sewn a partisan badge into her jacket in case she were stopped by the fighters. Silvia appeared, in her uniform of a partisan doctor, and reported that the Germans were fighting hard in Via Cernaia.

As night fell, the dozen women gathered at Borello decided that it was safer to spend the night where they were. Bianco's wife Pinella, who had been going around the city looking after the wounded, cooked dinner. Ada noticed that Esther, the fiancée of Sandro Delmastro, killed by the Fascists, had gone into a shadowy corner and was crying. 'Our dead, those of today, those of tomorrow, those of yesterday, were with us,' she wrote in her diary. Over Radio London, they heard that half of Berlin was in Soviet hands. Later, the women lit a fire and began to sing the partisan songs they all knew by heart. Ada felt a sense of warmth, safety, pleasure in what they were sharing, 'almost of joy, to which, more or less unconsciously, we abandoned ourselves'. Pinella made up a bed for her by the fire, but she slept fitfully. Whenever the dog barked, she took her gun and went outside to check all was well. It was raining, but in between the cloudbursts the moon shone brightly.

Throughout the city, the *staffette* had been hard at work. Matilde de Pietrantonio, the young woman who had specialised in kidnapping German officers to use in prisoner exchanges, was in command of her group of fighters and opened fire against a tank and four armoured cars of the Fascist Leonessa Division. Finding themselves under attack from militiamen stationed on a balcony, she ordered the others to cover her, then crept up the nearby stairs, taking with her a companion. At the top, she discovered seven young Alpini, who immediately put up their hands. Her companion lifted his sub-machine gun to shoot them. Matilde told him to put it down. 'No. The war is over. You are not going to kill anyone in cold blood.' The seven militiamen crept out, trembling. 'Go home,' she told them. 'Go. Run.'

Lucia Boetta, freed from her duties as *staffetta* to visiting dignitaries, had spent the night with her partisan formation up in the hills. She was asleep when orders came to move. She woke to find that the men had left without her, evidently deciding that the assault on the city was not suitable for a woman. She was outraged. Had she not served among them, fought as hard as they had, lived in acute danger for the same period?

Marisa Diena, ordered at first to serve with her unit in the mountains, came to the Garibaldi headquarters in Via Arsenale and began to write the obituaries of those killed in the fighting.

Silvia worked on a special edition of *La Nuova Realtà*. Under the headline 'Justice and Not Vendetta', she wrote that the role of women was to moderate the harsh reprisals against collaborators. And above all to 'never forget'.

Fifty special passes had been issued to the most experienced *staffette*, in order to allow them to move freely around the city, carrying messages between the central partisan command, the arriving partisan formations, and Ada at Borello. One of these had gone to the fearless Frida, who raced off on her bicycle, her German and Fascist false papers in one pocket, her partisan laissez-passer in the other. One of her ports of call was to the Lancia factory, now sealed off by German soldiers. Her pass got her through, and she found the women, frightened but determined, busy preparing food. They had cut the phones, told the managers to leave and had tied red handkerchiefs around their necks.

Lisetta too was carrying messages. She left Borello at seven o'clock on the morning of the 26th, bound for Agosti's office in the centre, where she was to pick up orders. Later she made notes about her day. Having been blocked from reaching Agosti, she joined up with another woman and sequestered some weapons, a man's bicycle and fifteen litres of petrol, and delivered them to a partisan command post. She then carried a message to an outlying factory, returning to search for a Garibaldi brigade for whom she had orders. Nothing was written down; everything was memorised. By the time she returned to Borello that night she had delivered five different sets of messages between central command and outlying partisan positions. Where she left her baby she did not say.

At a certain moment word came that the dead were not being buried and there were fears of epidemics. Two young girls calmly left and went to see what could be done. Another woman, a partisan from the valleys not known to the others, had got hold of a bazooka and was using it against the retreating forces.

Liberation day in Turin

Early on the 27th, with the Fascist soldiers still holding the bridges as well as strategic roads leading out of the city, thousands more partisans began to flow into the city, released from Stevens's false order. They came in lorries, on bicycles, on horseback, on their feet, in orderly lines, formation by formation. Women telephone operators, listening in on German and Fascist calls, set up a system of warnings from switchboard to switchboard, so that the partisans could follow their movements.

Solaro summoned all remaining Fascists in the city to his office. Most were terrified. The atmosphere was one of a 'shipwreck'. Solaro told them that he was releasing them from their oath to Mussolini and the Salò government. 'Today,' he said, 'it is dead.' He offered them the choice of either joining a cortège of Fascist forces which would leave the city after nightfall with the hopes of reaching Valtellina, or making their own escape. In ones and twos, taking the children with them, many chose to leave. Solaro decided that he would stay and face the coming 'hurricane'.

At Borello, Ada was coordinating a 'whirlwind of needs, all urgent and all different'. Calls had gone out for more women to help and hundreds had come forward. Young girls were dispatched to remove or switch around German signs, to scatter nails on the roads by which they were trying to retreat, and to get wounded partisans to safety before the Germans could finish them off. News came that the factories had been surrounded by German tanks and that the women barricaded inside were throwing Molotov cocktails from the windows. Those inside one of the FIAT factories, unable to leave the building, were eating spicy sardines and stale biscuits from the canteen. A *staffetta* arrived to ask for a partisan flag for the Lancia factory and disappeared again with it on her bicycle. Later Ada heard that the flag had been smuggled in and was flying from the roof.

At eleven o'clock that morning came a rumour that the Germans had left the city and that the partisans were in control; but then came another to say that the Germans were fighting hard and that the Fascists, having lost the city hall, had now retaken it. 'The most absurd, strange and terrible pieces of news,' Ada wrote, followed fast one upon another. A wagon full of bodies had been spotted near the Porta Nuova, a woman walking in front brandishing a white flag on which a red cross had been traced in blood. Casualties on both sides were mounting, and among the dead were many friends. Mourning them, Ada thought, would have to wait. Then came news that the partisan prisoners held by the Germans and the Fascists in jails around the city were being massacred.

But Ada had not reckoned with Suor Giuseppina in Le Nuove prison. When word had come that the insurrection was only hours away, Cardinal Fossati had visited the jail, which held some 250 partisans, most of them awaiting imminent execution. The men were forbidden to leave their cells, but the cardinal recited Mass, which was relayed throughout the ancient fortress over loudspeakers. At the end, he released the prisoners from the need for confession and pronounced absolution. The men stood in their cells, filthy, hungry, fearful of what was to come; total silence reigned.

Later in the evening, Suor Giuseppina, Pilado Garella and his son Giuseppe, both members of a lay order which looked after donations to the prison, approached the German commandant, Siegel, with a proposition. They would protect him, save his life, if he agreed to open the prison gates and release the partisan prisoners. Siegel agreed. The time was set for 10.30 that night. But shortly before the agreed moment, SS soldiers arrived to reinforce the contingent of Brigate Nere guarding the prison. The gates remained locked. Next morning, shots could be heard from all sides. Word came that fifty of the most important partisan leaders were to be taken away by the SS and held as hostages for all German casualties. Suor Giuseppina feared a bloodbath. She passed the 26th in despair.

Early on the 27th, partisans occupied the headquarters of Westinghouse, just across the street from Le Nuove and opened fire. In the confusion, some of the political prisoners were able to break out of their cells and occupy the central wing. The SS and the Brigate Nere retreated to the ramparts and the outer perimeter and returned the partisan fire. The telephones were now down. Suor Giuseppina believed it was only a matter of time before enemy reinforcements arrived to take back the prison and slaughter the inmates. Siegel was nowhere to be seen.

During the afternoon, she and the Garellas hatched a new plan. They would drive to the Fascist prefecture and try to make a deal with Solaro and the Germans to spare her prisoners. 'And so,' she wrote later, 'putting ourselves in the hands of the Madonna and reciting the sainted rosary,' they set out. Pilado walked ahead, with a Red Cross flag. Giuseppe was at the wheel. Suor Giuseppina hitched up her habit and perched on the boot, also waving a Red Cross flag. Moving very slowly through Turin's deserted streets, they reached the prefecture. As they passed, both the German and partisan snipers suspended their fire. 'An invisible divine Hand,' wrote Suor Giuseppina in a letter to the cardinal, protected them.

Once in the prefecture, she had little difficulty in persuading Solaro that he had nothing to lose, and might even have something to gain, if he let the partisan prisoners go. The German command was harder to convince, but Suor Giuseppina's mixture of charm and steeliness persuaded them. She and the Garellas returned to Le Nuove the way they had come, this time following Contessa Irene Provana di Collegno Rignon in a nurse's uniform, brandishing a Maltese cross; they were 'miraculously untouched', the fighters once again holding their fire. At Le Nuove they received a rapturous reception. Alberto Salmoni was now sent from the Resistance headquarters to take the prison. After a brief firefight the Fascists were beaten back, the gates were opened and the men, preceded by twenty-seven women whom Suor Giuseppina insisted on leaving Le Nuove first, poured out. Among them was Don Marabotto, held under sentence of death since October 1944. Hours later, Le Nuove began to fill with captured Fascists and

Germans. Suor Giuseppina hastily put them into civilian clothes, hoping thereby to avoid more killing.

Late on the night of the 27th, a long line of Fascists, preceded and followed by armoured cars, with women and children in the middle, left the prefecture and began to make their escape, hugging the walls, hoping to leave unnoticed. It was raining hard. Some rode bicycles. A few had carts pulled by oxen, but they soon had to be abandoned. Solaro, realising no last-ditch stand was possible, slipped away with a small group of senior Fascists, exchanged his uniform for civilian clothes and collected the false identity papers he had thought to prepare in advance. The men left their guns behind. Someone suggested hiding in the basement of a nearby agricultural consortium. The little group hurried through the deserted streets, entered the building and descended into the cellars. Here they sat silently, in total darkness, drinking cognac and praying for the Allies to arrive quickly.

There were still pockets of Fascists scattered around the city, holed up in their barracks and offices, blockading the factories and fighting on the hills, but they too were preparing to leave. That night, a final contingent of Salò's soldiers pulled out of their infamous barracks in Via Asti, where so many partisans had been tortured and killed. They covered their armoured vehicles with mattresses, for greater protection; inside were weapons, food, money and precious objects looted from Turin's Jewish families. Soon after they left, partisans entered the building and freed the surviving prisoners, though at the last moment the Fascists had found time to hang and shoot a number of them. Another group of Salò men wound red handkerchiefs around their necks and, flying red partisan flags, sped off down the street. When they encountered civilians, they shot them. Two of the dead were nine-year-old children. Where people fell, the puddles of water left by heavy rain showers turned red.

The last Germans too were preparing to escape. Pretending to be considering unconditional surrender, they had used the time to organise their getaway. Very late that same night, the several thousand remaining Germans, who had been trapped by the partisans into an area between the River Po and the Dora station, formed into an armoured column in the royal gardens and began to fall back towards the motorway leading to Milan. They took with them, as one Allied officer reported, 'a bevy of the best-looking girls, Poles,

Czechs, French etc, which any could wish to see'. When partisans began to shoot, the Germans responded by forcing hostages, many of them children, to walk in front. General Schlemmer, having been refused permission to cross the city with his two divisions, the 34th Armoured and the 5th Alpenjäger, and faced with the imminent arrival of yet more partisans from the mountains, was now sending his men around the periphery, to the north. Stevens had wanted the partisans to blow up the bridges over the Po, but this, too, by good fortune, they had refused to do. That night, the Allies helpfully dropped more weapons and ammunition.

Ada and her *staffette* again spent the night at Borello. Silvia, in her doctor's coat and with a Red Cross armband, arrived with news of pockets of heavy fighting near Via Fabro. Bianca, who had been with her, later described Silvia as fearless and decisive, never hesitating and quick to see what needed doing. Ada reflected that whereas once she would have been consumed with anxiety for Ettore and Paolo, now all she could think was that the fate of the partisans felt more important. Personal matters would have to wait. What concerned her was preparing an immediate edition of *La Nuova Realtà*, along with flyers addressed to the women of the GDD, and the speech she would have to make to liberated Turin over the radio. On Radio London, they heard that the American army had reached Vienna and that Genoa had fallen to the partisans, who had taken 7,000 Germans prisoner.

Pinella lit a fire. The women gathered round but no one felt like singing. They sat in silence, listening to the distant gunfire, thinking about what awaited them in the morning. Three very young *staffette*, who had cycled several hundred kilometres in the past two days, fell asleep on their chairs. Silvia, with her usual impetuous fluency, began to write; within a couple of hours she had produced four pages for the paper. Ada had trouble finding the words she needed for her speech. She kept thinking about what they had all gone through and survived, about the boy she had found hanging in Meana, about her journey to France and all the friends she had lost: Braccini, Sandro Delmastro, Paolo Diena, Duccio. She pulled herself together and, to the sound of Silvia's rapidly scratching pen, began to assemble her thoughts. 'Piedmontese women,' she wrote, 'today, all women who have grief in their hearts . . . May this grief not have been in vain . . .' She could think of nothing else to say.

At first light, she set off on her bicycle for Via Fabro. The city was eerily still and silent. Catching sight of a group of men standing on a street corner, she called out: 'Well?' The men called back: 'They went away!'

It was true. The Germans and Fascists had gone. Nearing home, Ada was alarmed to see signs of recent heavy fighting. But Ettore was there, and Espedita and Paolo soon turned up; neighbours crept out of the surrounding flats, confused, questioning. The house was in a state of complete disorder, having been taken over the previous evening by a brigade of Garibaldini who had been attacking the retreating German column. A trailer full of munitions had been hit and it had exploded, causing considerable damage. But everyone was alive.

Ada was exhausted. She had not slept for forty-eight hours and suddenly it was all over. The war had ended and she had not lost her son. Ettore discovered a few grains of real coffee hidden away and she drank a cup and felt better. Then the doorbell began to ring. Friends, neighbours, colleagues, partisans poured in. The excitement felt like an explosion.

Right up until the middle of April 1945, Mussolini continued to think that he might still make some kind of deal, if not with the Resistance or the British, then with the Americans, and thereby save his own life. Visitors reported that he had lost touch with reality and seemed to be living in a world of memories and prophecies. A journalist noted that he looked like a convict, his black eyes lacklustre, his face very white under his shaven head.

But then events had moved very fast. Having travelled down to Milan and installed himself in a room at the prefecture, Mussolini received a string of visitors, many of them urging him to escape, to Spain, to Switzerland, to Argentina. On 25 April, as news poured in that one northern town after another was falling to the partisans, he told Cardinal Schuster that he planned to retreat north of Bergamo, with 3,000 faithful Brigate Nere under their commander, Pavolini. Informed by Cadorna and two other leading members of the Resistance that no further negotiations were possible, but that the Fascists would be treated correctly under the Geneva Conventions if they surrendered, the Duce asked for time to talk to the senior German officers still in Milan. Then he learned that they were negotiating for their own safety. He declared that he had been 'betrayed'. 'I have gambled right up to the end,' he told a friend, 'and I have been beaten . . . No more illusions. Addio.'

Protected by a squad of Brigate Nere, Mussolini set out for Como in a convoy of thirty cars and lorries, containing many of his ministers, with his secretary, Luigi Galli, perched on the bonnet of his car with a machine gun. Rachele and his children were not with him. Claretta and her brother Marcello were in another car; two lorries with SS soldiers brought up the rear. In Como, Mussolini hoped to find Pavolini and his 3,000 men and perhaps retreat with them to join up with the Nazis in Bavaria. In his car, he had two briefcases, later said to contain documents – including incriminating letters from Churchill – which he intended to use in his defence, and gold bars, jewellery and money. There was no sign of Pavolini in Como and the convoy moved on, apparently having failed to persuade Swiss frontier guards to let them across. In the small village of Grandola, the party spent an agitated night, the phone ringing constantly with news of further partisan victories. During the night Pavolini arrived to say that the Brigate Nere had surrendered. All thoughts of a possible heroic last stand were abandoned.

Mussolini and his small group of remaining followers now joined a Luftwaffe anti-aircraft convoy retreating towards Innsbruck. For a while, he drove himself, in his Alfa Romeo, but soon moved for greater safety to an armoured car. Claretta wore a mink coat and a hat shaped like a turban. At 7 a.m on the 26th, the convoy was stopped by partisans, who had cut down a tree and blocked the road. After long negotiations, it was decided that the Germans would be allowed to leave, but not the Fascists. At this stage, Mussolini had not yet been identified, having put on a Luftwaffe greatcoat; he was slumped, apparently drunk, in one of the lorries. But at Dongo, where the captives were taken, he was recognised. Later, ten different people would claim the honour of being the one who had identified him. Mussolini looked old, weak and ill; he gave up his gun but tried to hold on to his briefcases. His captors took him to the mayor's office and told him that he would not be harmed. The German convoy left and a message was sent to the local CLN asking for instructions. It was very cold and raining hard.

The partisan commander of the 52nd Garibaldi Brigade in Dongo was 25-year-old Count Pier Luigi Bellini delle Stelle. To prevent a possible rescue attempt, he moved his prisoners up the mountain to the barracks of the frontier guards at Germasino. Claretta begged to be allowed to be with Mussolini; Bellini acquiesced. Fearing these barracks to be insecure, he moved the couple again, this time to a remote peasant house. The storm continued to rage. Exactly what happened next, who decided what and where, whether it was Togliatti and the Communists who influenced the others not to hand Mussolini over to the Allies, has been the subject of intense debate. The sequence of events that followed, however, is clear. The leaders of the Resistance in Milan talked all night, and in the morning sent word, via a Communist partisan, a veteran of the Spanish civil war called Walter Audisio, that Mussolini was to be executed immediately, before he fell into Allied hands and stood trial.

Audisio and a dozen partisans, armed with machine guns, reached Dongo on the afternoon of the 28th. Bellini, who was vehemently opposed to a summary execution, was still thinking of moving Mussolini and his mistress into hiding elsewhere. But it was too late. Audisio found the peasant house, ordered Mussolini and Claretta to follow him down the steep hill, Claretta tottering in her high heels, and drove them to a villa. Earlier, Claretta had told her captors: 'To become the Duce's lover was the secret or avowed ambition of almost every woman in high society.' Whether it was or was not Audisio who fired the killing shot – another matter of much debate – it is accepted that Claretta, who was standing in front of Mussolini, died first and that Mussolini was only injured and had to be finished off with a bullet to his chest. While the two bodies were loaded into a car, Audisio went off to execute the seventeen senior Fascists captured with them.

What no one disagrees about is Mussolini's grisly finale. Very early on the morning of 29 April, the corpses were tipped out into the dirt, to lie like a pile of rubbish in front of a garage in Milan's Piazzale Loreto, not far from the central station. With Mussolini and Claretta were the bodies of the other dead Fascists. The spot had been chosen with care, as the place where the Germans had killed fifteen hostages not long before and left them exposed. Mussolini lay with his head across Claretta's breast. As word spread, crowds descended on the square, furious, frantic, relieved people running along the streets in order not to miss out on the spectacle. Two young men began kicking Mussolini's face until it was disfigured; others spat. A woman, who had lost five sons to the Fascists, pulled out a gun and shot bullets into his body. Another tried to stuff a dead mouse into his mouth. The partisans had to use hoses to try to keep the people back.

Ropes were found and Mussolini, in the uniform of a Fascist militiaman, was pulled up to hang upside down – to symbolise the overthrow of his long rule – from girders in the garage roof. Then Claretta, the only woman, was hauled up. Her skirt fell down over her face, leaving her thighs and hips bare. A partisan clambered up onto a box and tethered the skirt with the rope. The bodies were prodded with sticks, to make them swing, the arms outstretched. There were shouts, jeers, tears.

The next day, photographs of the dangling corpses of the Duce and Claretta were on sale on street corners. Later, both Allied leaders and the Resistance expressed disgust at the spectacle. Parri called it a '*macelleria Messicana*', a Mexican-style butchery. But to many at the time, his swinging body seemed like a necessary gesture of reckoning, the longed-for moment when at last Fascism in Italy, with its twenty-two years of brutality and despotism, could be said to have ended.

Most of the northern towns had been liberated with a surprising lack of bloodshed. The same was not true of Turin. The city was officially considered free by midday on 28 April, but, having fought their way out street by street, the departing Fascists left behind them some fifty to sixty snipers, positioned at vantage points. Some of them were women. They had prepared for this moment carefully, having got the idea from a similar band of Fascist militia left behind during the battle for Florence. Among them were people so imbued in the Fascist culture of obedience and violence that they preferred to go to '*la bella morte*' in a blaze of glory. It would take several days, and many deaths, before they were silenced. When caught and led to execution, several of these snipers died giving the Fascist salute. One, having fired his last rounds from a tower, threw himself out. The last sniper to die was an eighteen-year-old boy, firing from a ruined house.

Nor had the Germans finished with the killings. As they pulled out of Turin, heading for the motorway to Milan, they carried out a last, devastating massacre. The two adjoining communes of Grugliasco and Collegno, at the gates of Turin, were already in a festive mood celebrating the end of Fascism, when a 'torrent' of troops from the 34th Armoured Division began to flow through the area. These soldiers were exhausted, frightened, and many of them were drunk. They began looting, piling everything they could find in people's houses – bread, flour, clothes, clocks, linen, wine and even bicycles – onto their vehicles. From the sidelines, groups of young *sappisti* harried their retreat. Then, three German soldiers were shot dead. The skirmishes turned deadly.

The Germans embarked on a final, bloody *rastrellamento*: local inhabitants and any partisan they could catch were taken as hostages. Next morning, sixty-eight people, among them a priest, were lined up and shot. Over half were under twenty. The youngest and last to die was Romano Dellera. He was thirteen. Later, a witness described the scene. 'I saw blood, blood, blood everywhere, a scene of carnage.'

It was perhaps because the twenty months of German occupation and Fascist collaboration in Turin had been so particularly vicious, with so much killing and so much torture, that the city needed its own gruesome sacrifice. They found it in Giuseppe Solaro, the youngest Fascist Party secretary in Italy, who had once written that, as a Fascist, he had fought to save Italy's honour 'against an old world of egotists, the privileged, Conservatives, the oppressive capitalists'. Solaro, like Mussolini, had dreamt of making a last heroic stand.

As the city was being cleared of the snipers, it was reported that a group of men had been seen the night before going down into the cellars of the agricultural consortium. Garibaldini partisans went to investigate, found Solaro and his companions, and took them to their headquarters. At first, in the chaos of the moment, Solaro was not recognised. But then he told them himself who he was. Like Mussolini, he had documents which he believed would prove that he had in fact been a protector of the partisans. Interrogated by the Resistance leadership, he laid the blame for most of the violence on his deputy, Pavia; he also told them exactly where the snipers had been placed. It was not enough to save him. A quickly convened tribunal sentenced him to hang. Monsignor Garneri tried and failed to allow him to be shot instead, but the partisans remembered all too clearly Solaro's earlier instructions: 'For the partisans, a bit of rope is enough.'

Solaro was then driven slowly in an open lorry through the streets, between rows of jeering onlookers, to the corner of the Corso Vinzaglio, where nine months earlier four partisans had been publicly hanged. Garneri sat by him, holding his hand. As Solaro was being strung up from the branch of a tree, the rope snapped and he fell to the ground. The angry crowd, which had gathered to watch, surged forward. Solaro would have been lynched had the partisans not fired into the air and quickly pulled him up again. The crowd, at first jubilant and excited, fell silent, before breaking out into shouts and cheers.

Giuseppe Solaro on his way to execution

Solaro's body, a cigarette stuck between his lips, was then hitched up, in a hideous spectacle of death, to a bar at the back of a lorry and driven, once again very slowly, to the banks of the Po, where it was thrown into the water. Boys used it as target practice until it sank out of sight. With Solaro's death, Turin marked its own end to Fascism. As one man put it, 'We all wanted to kill someone.'

Time was running out. Turin was free but the Allies were approaching, their advance slowed down only by a shortage of fuel. The Resistance had achieved exactly what it had set out to do: it had put together a united force, in which even the Monarchists had agreed to put aside their differences, and liberated Piedmont and the north from the Fascists and the Germans on its own, without Allied interference. The factories were safe; the infrastructure was standing. But now it had to clean up, impose discipline, appoint bureaucrats and police, so that when the British and the Americans arrived they would find peace and order.

Ada returned to Borello on her bicycle along avenues in which the first buds were sprouting on the remaining trees, past buildings which were to a greater or lesser extent in ruins. The rain had stopped and a pale spring sun shone. Bells were ringing from every church and in the streets strangers were laughing and crying and hugging each other. Songs were played over loudspeakers. Flags were flying, the red flags of the Resistance, the tricolour of Italy. In the Hotel Svizzera, the partisans danced, their stick grenades and pistols stuck into their belts. It was as if a long grey pall of silence had lifted. 'We began to move,' wrote Italo Calvino, 'in a multicoloured universe of our stories.'

Vittorio Foa and Anna

Most of the young *staffette* had gone home to find out how their families had weathered the uprising. Lisetta had returned to her baby and to Vittorio; Silvia and Giorgio Diena were preparing to go up to Torre Pellice to retrieve their son. Ada found Pinella waiting for her. The two women discussed the urgent need to find somewhere for the released political prisoners who did not have homes in the north to gather, and agreed that a hotel should be requisitioned. Then there were the women's GDD to press into service. Both Ada and Pinella were drained, a little melancholy. The wonderful closeness of the last few days, of working harmoniously together as a group, was over. They had to become individuals again, separate people, each with their own ideas and ambitions. It was, Ada wrote later, 'sad, but it was reality, and we had to confront it with courage'.

A messenger arrived to tell Ada that the time had come for her to report to the town hall and take up her new job as vice mayor. Despite Pinella's protests, she insisted on travelling there on the ancient bicycle she had spent the last twenty months riding up and down the valleys; as she left through the villa's gates, the people in the street cheered her. She had not gone far when the car sent to collect her tracked her down and drove her to the cortège taking the new city administrators to their offices in the centre of the city, vacated only hours before by the Fascists. Switching cars, Ada found herself with the new mayor, Giovanni Roveda; she liked him at once. A lorry full of partisans led the way, and another with more armed men made up the rear. They travelled to the sounds of cheers and gunshots. More and more people were emerging into the streets, women running with small children in their arms, or clutching each other in disbelief. From every window, flags appeared.

Sniper fire was still intense, preventing the party from reaching the town hall, and so they headed instead for the prefecture. As they got out, a sniper opened fire and their escort shouted at them to take cover. 'On foot, smiling,' wrote Ada later, 'we did not even think of it . . . We filled our lungs with the air of freedom. To us, the shots seemed like fireworks of joy.'

The new prefect, Pier Luigi Passoni, was waiting to greet them. Agosti, who had been appointed police commissioner, had also just arrived. He found the Palazzo della Questura deserted and semi-derelict, the Fascists having wrecked the offices as they pulled out, leaving intact only the *questore*'s private apartments, which were strewn with bottles of grappa, and full of works of art and furniture looted from Jewish families. Since many pieces still had the labels of their owners stuck to them, Agosti made a note to return them as soon as he could find time. The Fascist *questore* himself, Emanuele Protani, who had given orders for soldiers to fire on the women leading the 18 April strike, was caught and executed.

Agosti would say later that he had no idea what the job of *questore* – a role in Italy somewhere between chief constable and police commissioner – actually entailed, and was saved from embarrassment only by finding an old and trusted colleague to teach him. Since his first task was to restore order, he quickly disbanded all police bodies who had served in any way with the Fascists. Then he summoned up a partisan group belonging to his own party, the Partito d'Azione, and appointed them as policemen along with some three hundred *carabinieri* sacked during the months of occupation and three hundred men from the Guardia della Finanza, not normally used for public order. In the drawers of a desk he found a list of 16,000 names of Turin's Fascist members. Those he considered merited immediate arrest –'*persone da epurare*'– he had broadcast over the radio; among them was Agnelli, owner of FIAT. Then he drafted a statement of his own aims. He would re-establish democracy, he said, restore the impartiality of the judiciary, and he would be direct, honest and clear in all his dealings with the public. He ordered the trams to start running again and the shopkeepers to open their premises.

Ada's first move was to organise the hotel for the former prisoners and arrange for the women from the GDD to make up rooms and bring in food. After a first formal meeting of the Giunta Popolare, the new city administration, she was taken to the town hall to choose an office. As she climbed the stairs, the clerks cheered. An official said to her: 'We have dreamt of this moment so much, when people worthy of their position had their turn to serve.' From a rooftop opposite, a sniper kept firing, shattering the windows in the town Hall. Then Ada set off for Le Nuove to oversee the transfer of the remaining political prisoners. To her annoyance, the young partisan guarding the jail stopped her: 'What? A woman as vice mayor?' She spoke sharply and he hastened sheepishly away to call the new director. Later, disregarding the warnings of the partisans that there were still snipers on the roofs, she insisted on walking alone up the long Via Garibaldi. A bullet whirred past her head, missing her by a few centimetres. She felt chastened and angry with herself. Given the responsibilities she had assumed, such 'reckless bravado' was unacceptable.

What she faced – what awaited Agosti, Bianco, Foa and all the other fighters now entering politics in order to create and administer a new Italy – was indeed daunting. The country was bankrupt, its infrastructure largely destroyed, its health system in ruins, its offices deserted, its former Fascist civil servants in hiding. Pockets of Germans and Fascists were still fighting, barricaded into attics and on the hills overlooking the city. Turin looked like a war zone, the skeletons of houses crumbling into the avenues where only the stubs of tree trunks remained, its factories damaged, its roads full of potholes, sandbags and barbed wire, with the bodies of Germans and Fascists lying around the streets, and passers-by standing and staring at them. Twenty months of plunder meant that there was very little electricity, transport or food. The telephones were not working. People were homeless, malnourished, tired and ill. Crops had not been planted, and the fields surrounding Turin were strewn with unexploded mines. The lira had fallen to just 3.5% of its pre-war buying power. But on people's faces could be seen relief and hope.

On 1 May, when the citizens of Turin were summoned to a ceremony to mourn those who had died to liberate their city, over 100,000 people walked in silence from the Royal Gardens to the main cemetery. In Piazza San Carlo, the 'Internazionale' was sung, then 'Va, Pensiero', the chorus of the Hebrew slaves from Verdi's *Nabucco*. 'We sang and sang and sang,' one woman said later, 'until we no longer could.' That night, lights were again lit in the streets after many months of darkness. For Chevallard, it was the moment when he understood that the war was really over.

Ada was under no illusions about what lay ahead. It would be a question of clinging on to and keeping alive the great ideals about 'a universal and fraternal humanity', about equality and parity and social justice, a flame that had burst into life twenty months earlier, and must not now be allowed to go out. She knew that another battle, '*la vera battaglia*', was about to begin. It would no longer be a matter of fighting arrogance, violence and cruelty, all things ultimately clear and easy to detect, but of struggling against 'interests that would try to rekindle themselves treacherously, against habits that would soon reaffirm themselves, against prejudices that did not want to die'. This battle, she thought, would be less bloody, but it would be harder, longer and much more lonely. She wondered whether she had the heart for it.

18

Bloodletting

Even the haughty Lt Col. Stevens was forced to admit that the liberation of Piedmont had been carried out efficiently, rapidly and without excessive bloodshed; but he was not able to refrain from lecturing the northern leadership, in his 'picturesque but perfectly comprehensible Italian', on the need to bring the partisans firmly into line, obedient to the Allies and under their military control. When the first Allied soldiers, a small group of Americans in jeeps, entered Turin on 30 April, they found the traffic lights working, the shops open, the trams running, the streets swept and the people walking calmly about. Many of them sported red handkerchiefs, as if, noted an onlooker somewhat sourly, 'they had all fought with the partisans'. Bunches of flowers with names and sometimes photographs were lying where partisans had died.

Apart from marvelling that many of the American tanks had women's names – Barbara, Bella and Madge – and resenting the fact that the Allies took the Palazzo Reale as their headquarters, the Torinesi did not seem to be greatly interested in their new wave of foreign occupiers. They clapped briefly when they first encountered them, admired the neatness of their appearance, then went about their business. Most of the Turin newspapers, rushed out under new post-Fascist management, did not even bother to cover their arrival. The sense of exultation in this *'primavera rossa'* was a very Italian affair, a matter of pride and exhausted relief. It was, wrote one man, 'a longing to live, to enjoy simple pleasures and a great weariness with struggle, suffering, privations'. The battle for the liberation of Turin had cost the lives of about a thousand people; 320 of them were partisans, many still teenagers, and twenty-nine were women. But after twenty months of merciless occupation, the city was finally free. 'We share,' wrote Chevallard on the last page of his diary, 'a hope that those who come after us will never again experience the horrors through which we have lived.'

Separate surrender deals had been negotiated in various places. On 29 April, in Caserta, representatives of the German army and of the Repubblica Sociale Italiana signed a document of surrender agreeing to a ceasefire of all forces at two o'clock on the afternoon of 2 May. On 30 April, Hitler committed suicide in his bunker in Berlin, together with Eva Braun, whom he had married three days earlier. In Bolzano, where he was still hoping for a deal, General Wolff was arrested. In the north, some 61,000 German soldiers, and 12,000 Fascists – most of the rest having slipped away, hoping to escape capture by the partisans – laid down their weapons and were taken into custody, leaving the countryside through which they had passed littered with abandoned vehicles, spent ammunition, discarded loot and burnt-out lorries. Allied bombers ceased to attack the German retreat. How the captured Fascists were treated, after interrogation, depended on what they had done. Money seized from German and Fascist funds began to be distributed to families who had lost men in the fighting. Eminent hostages who had been held as possibly useful barter were freed from captivity. Two Dakotas landed in Milan bringing medicines, and especially insulin, desperately needed in the north.

The calm, however, was deceptive. The twenty months of civil war had been too brutal, with death made a spectacle to be relished, and the long years of Fascism with its punishing wars in Ethiopia, Spain and the Balkans had schooled the Italians in violence. Many people now realised that unless they took matters into their own hands, the Fascists would go unpunished. The reprisals were ferocious. The Resistance knew they did not have long. As Giorgio Amendola, who had witnessed Solaro's botched hanging, wrote in L'Unità, 'a rapid and radical cleansing' was essential. 'Our dead must be avenged, all of them. Criminals must be eliminated. The Fascist plague must be annihilated. Only this way can we march forward . . . This is not the moment for leniency, which would only betray the cause for which we have fought . . . With Jacobin resolve, the knife must be plunged into the wound, and everything rotten cut out.' Areas of the industrial north acquired a new name: '*il triangolo della morte*', the triangle of death.

Even as the fighting was ending, the hunt for the senior Fascists rapidly yielded the Salò *gerarchi*, many of whom met ugly ends. Buffarini Guidi, the Minster for the Interior, who had presided over the deportation of the Jews, was dragged into a square in Milan, half dead after taking a bottle of barbiturates, and shot. The Fascist mayor of Cumiano was seized, pulled around the city for all to see, then shot in the market square. Within days, 111 of the leaders of the infamous militias had been caught and executed. On 29 April, Osvaldo Valenti and Luisa Ferida, who had tormented Koch's victims in the Villa Triste with her strip-teases, were caught and shot. Koch himself evaded capture until the end of June, when he was tracked down to a hotel in Florence, tried and sentenced to death. Five of his seventy henchmen were executed after trials; a further eight were summarily killed during the liberation. Often, the question of who lived and who died came down to a simple matter of chance.

Nowhere was the spirit of revenge more visible nor the number of reprisals higher than in Turin, long regarded as the epicentre of Fascist and German sadism but also of the northern Resistance. Here, as Max Salvadori observed, there were many 'would-be imitators of Marat and Robespierre'. Even Agosti, not a vindictive man, had the five policemen in the prefecture who were guilty of a spate of recent brutal killings immediately taken out into the courtyard and shot, later saying that a court would certainly have upheld his decision. All over the city, spies, informers and collaborators were hunted down, flushed out of their houses and hiding places, often having been identified by women. Some were quickly executed; others were lynched by mobs as they tried to run away, partisans trying and failing to calm the crowds by firing shots above their heads.

Members of the hated Brigate Nere and the Italian SS were punished hardest, often spat at and beaten up before being executed on the exact spots where partisans had been killed. For several days, bodies kept on turning up – of people who had translated for the Germans, or who had worked by their side in factories, or who had been the wives or mothers of violent Salò militiamen. When cemeteries overflowed, the corpses were dumped into the Po or burnt. 'Violence and death,' wrote one observer, 'entered the daily life of Italians . . . we heard shots, we saw houses set on fire, we saw bodies left hanging.' There were, inevitably, errors, cases of mistaken identity. It was barbaric; but it was not anarchy.

There were also unedifying instances when parents, terrified that the actions of their Fascist children would rebound on them, offered them up to partisan justice. Anna Orlandi went to the police and told them that her daughter Luciana had worked for the Folgore militia. 'I declare,' she wrote in her statement, 'that I regret that she was not eliminated sooner.' Luciana vanished from her home and was not seen again.

It was in fact against the women, the *'puttane dei nazisti'*, the Germans' whores, that some of the most extreme violence was levelled. In Turin, sixteen-year-old Marilena Grill, who had shortly before joined the Fascist women auxiliaries, was dragged from her house and shot. In the days after liberation, the bodies of thirty women, some of them no more than girls, were pulled out of the Po, one of them showing severe 'injuries to her head, abdomen and chest'. Of the 6,000 women who had volunteered for the Salò auxiliary force, three hundred were killed, often having been repeatedly raped first; others had their heads shaved and were paraded naked to their executions, a swastika painted on their foreheads. The reprisals, though horrible, were to some degree understandable, a reflection on the atrocities carried out by Fascists and Germans alike for the long twenty months of civil war.

Contessa Piera Gatteschi Fondelli, founder of the SAF volunteers, escaped and spent the next two years hiding in convents, churches and even a mortuary, before emerging to discover that everyone had forgotten all about her. Many years later she wrote her memoirs in which she declared plaintively that, like most of her female companions, she had believed that what she was doing by fighting with the Fascists was saving her 'betrayed' homeland. As the Fascists pulled out of Turin, they forced a group of SAF women off a lorry, in order to give their places to their male colleagues, along with their families and their luggage.

One of the more painful incidents was recounted by a priest called Don Raimondo Viale. Called to hear the confession of a middle-aged woman condemned to death for having spied for the

Fascists, he found her distraught. When she was led off to her execution, she clung to him, begged him not to leave her and kept whimpering, 'Father, stay by me, help me.' Night was falling and on all sides, in the liberated streets of the city, he could hear sounds of merriment and celebration. 'I wept,' wrote Don Raimondo later. 'I wept the whole way home. I am weeping still.'

Though at its most dramatic in Turin, Piedmont's reprisals were not limited to the cities. Wherever the Germans and the Fascists had been most brutal, the bloodletting that followed their departure was implacable. Up and down the valleys, in the villages and little towns, former Fascists were hauled out of their houses and punished. Along with thirty-two-year-old Jenny Cardon, four other civilians in Torre Pellice had lost their lives in the last days of fighting. One was an 84-year-old man.

The day that followed liberation in Torre Pellice, as Micki Cesan remembers, four girls who had been friendly with the Germans and the Fascist soldiers were taken to the Piazza della Libertà and had their heads shaved. One, she says, was a *'puttana cattiva'*, an evil whore who slept with everyone. Three brothers, Ludovico, Carlo and Olivero Merlo, were also picked up, along with a local *squadrista* who had organised a massacre, and a woman who had slept with some Germans. Of the three Merlo brothers, one was indeed a Fascist who had taken part in criminal acts, but the other two had had nothing to do with politics. All three were executed, together with the *squadrista* and the woman, who, having escaped to a hospital, was dragged out of her bed and shot. Later, the partisans would say that it had been a mistake to execute them then and there. They should, they said, have been taken elsewhere and tried.

The reaction of the northern partisan leadership to the violence was not entirely consistent. While on the one hand advocating the rapid 'extermination' of all who had belonged to Fascist militias – to be carried out during the 'parenthesis of blood', the days of partisan justice agreed with the Allies – they also ordered the immediate establishment of partisan and people's tribunals to hear the cases of those accused of 'grave crimes against the partisans'. The first of these was already up and running in one of Turin's factories, the FIAT Mirafiore, even before the fighting was over.

By midnight on 2 May, when the unconditional surrender of the German forces was announced, along with the end of the state of emergency, people had in any case grown weary of vendettas and were turning to the law. A process of cleansing had taken place, horrible but necessary, with a tacit recognition that there are some kinds of brutality for which no kind of legal redress can ever be sufficient. But the bloodletting was now for the most part over, and the Allies accepted that it could not have been avoided; any killings that continued took place only at night, in secret. Figures for the dead during the '*resa dei conti*', the settling of scores, would later be widely disputed. The neo-Fascists claimed that 300,000 people across Italy had died during these few days; the Ministry for the Interior put the figure at just 1,732. Most reliable historians came to accept that the true number probably lay around 10,000, with Turin, at 1,138, the highest proportion, and Piedmont as a whole 2,523.

From right: Bolaffi and Ada at the liberation of Turin

At nine o'clock on the morning of Sunday 6 May, under a blue sky and a bright sun, the Piedmontese partisan formations began to converge on Turin's immense Piazza Vittorio Emanuele for their standing-down parade. Those who had fought in the Valli di Lanzo advanced along the Via Po; those from the Langhe down the Via Napione; the men from the first sector of Turin took the Via Garibaldi. Bolaffi, proudly leading his Stellina formation down from Susa, made a detour via the Via Fabro, where they solemnly and ceremoniously saluted Ada, before marching on, a trumpeter leading the way, flags flying, towards the centre.

By 9.30, the Piazza Vittorio Emanuele was crammed with fighters in their distinctive coloured uniforms, the Autonomi with their blue neckerchiefs, the Garibaldi with their red stars, the Partito d'Azione fighters with their red flames. Here and there in the crowds were Allied soldiers, Americans, British, French, a few Poles, some South Africans. They carried flags and their commanding officers watched from the sidelines. Several of the partisans remarked on the sheer number of their comrades, never having quite realised that there had been so many of them. It filled them with pride. The mood was festive. Onlookers put their children on their shoulders so that they could see across the crowds.

There were, however, very few women among the marchers. The Communist Garibaldi brigades had been the first to maintain that 'normalisation', the word on everyone's lips, did not include the idea of women as fighters. Their *staffette*, who had fought, carried messages and weapons, provided safe houses, laid mines and taken prisoners, were forbidden to parade with their comrades. Other formations, such as those of the Partito d'Azione, who had reluctantly allowed their women to take part, placed them towards the back. And as these women filed defiantly between the dense rows of spectators, they heard murmers of disapproval: 'Look at them! Whores!' Even at the time, it seemed a bitter taste of what was to come.

Two days before the parade, Prince Umberto had arrived unexpectedly in Milan, saying that he wanted to review the northern fighters. To his discomfiture, the leadership refused. It was not the moment, he was told, for a show of royalty. Umberto slunk back to Rome.

A rare group of parading *staffette*

At ten o'clock General Trabucchi, as the partisans' commander, stood on a raised platform in the square with other dignitaries. Then General Perotti's widow presented one of the foremost partisan leaders with the flag of the Corpo Volontari della Libertà; other flags were produced and flown, among them the one that Lucia had so laboriously carried over the mountains wound round her waist. The 'Song of the Piave', one of the best-known partisan hymns, was sung, to a fanfare of trumpets. All stood to attention. The first to speak was Franco Antonicelli, made president of the Piedmontese CLN on the eve of insurrection. 'Oh patriots,' he shouted out to the assembled men, straining to make himself heard in the vast piazza, 'it was your blood that brought us victory . . . Now we need your strength to build, stone upon stone, the vast edifice of a new Italy.' Those who spoke after him repeated the same message: the partisans had won the war, but now the hard work had to begin.

With the first Allied troops reaching the north had come an American colonel called Marshall, whose job it would be to run the Allied military government in Piedmont. Standing on the podium, he remarked quietly to General Trabucchi, in French, '*C'est beau et émouvant*'. But under his breath he was heard to add, in English, 'It is also fearsome.' This, too, did not bode well.

There is no record of Bianca, Lisetta, Frida, Silvia, Pinella or indeed Ada being present at this great closing ceremony of the war, though it is likely that Ada was somewhere nearby, not in her capacity as partisan and organiser of the *staffette*, but in her less threatening role as vice mayor of Turin. She does not appear to have been called on to speak. Later, one of the women in the Piazza Vittorio Emanuele that bright May morning would remember thinking: 'It was the end, for us girls and women, of our transgressions.' She already felt nostalgic for what they had been through, the dangers and excitement and the camaraderie. 'We knew,' she wrote, 'that our lives would never be that exciting again.'

All Italy was now free and VE Day, the end of the war in Europe, was celebrated across the Allied nations. But the show of unity between them was beginning to fracture. On 12 May, Churchill referred to an 'iron curtain' coming down on the Russian front, adding 'we do not know what is going on behind it'. The Cold War was beginning; and in any case the Second World War itself was not quite over: the Japanese still had to be defeated.

For many months now, the Allies in Italy had made it clear that they expected the partisans to hand over all the weapons that had been dropped to them as soon as the north was liberated. Tacitly, it was understood that this would cause food and medical aid to flow. What one Allied officer described as the 'bad behaviour', the reprisals in Turin, made the matter more urgent, and there were fears that if they left it too long partisan 'disillusionment' would turn into 'apathy and then bitterness'. And on one subject the British and the Americans were absolutely united: there was to be no Communist takeover and no weapons with which to do it. On 9 May, the process of disarming the partisans began. Fighters were invited to turn up at special centres, hand over their guns and ammunition and in return receive a bolt of cloth and L7,000 with which to turn it into civilian dress. This, noted one Allied report, should 'sugar the pill'.

It was, however, tricky. Though the Allies staged the handover with some degree of ceremony, with flags and bands and speeches, they did not seem to understand that the men they were dealing with were not 'eager, self-respecting and docile' but seasoned, war-weary veterans, intoxicated by what they has just been through. The Allies were quickly perceived by the Italians to be inept and peremptory, and even more so when, within a week, orders went out that all radio transmitters, carrier pigeons, cameras, telescopes and binoculars were to be registered by the military authorities. All newspapers were to be subject to Allied censorship and all public meetings authorised. Two government ministers come north from Rome who ignored this rule were threatened with arrest.

Not surprising, then, that the partisans did not wholly trust this new set of occupiers and did not like the way they were treated. Those who were uncertain about what to do next, or who had lost much in the fighting, saw in their guns a small measure of worth and safety. Even Agosti, a man attuned to practical realities, spoke of the need to 'keep souls and men and weapons in readiness'. As he wrote to Bianco, they had earned their weapons and should not now allow them to be taken away, either by the right or by the left. It was, he said, a question of recognising the will of the people, 'born during the partisan war'.

As the weapons were being handed over, the Allies noticed that they consisted mostly of larger items, with very few of the revolvers which had been so much in evidence on the belt of every fighter in the days leading up to liberation. Borne away into the valleys, concealed in attics and cellars, and even buried in pits in the garden, and sometimes put aside simply to settle scores, pistols, radio transmitters, grenades and a few machine guns were carefully stored away for later use. Later, the Allies, who made fifty raids across Piedmont in search of the hidden weapons, would say that less than 60 per cent of what had been dropped was actually returned.

The reluctance to do the Allies' bidding was made more complicated by a growing resentment that the German prisoners of war were being too well treated and too well fed while the Italians were starving. Returning to their homes without jobs, to houses damaged in the fighting, and animals and crops lost, the partisans were forced to witness generous supplies of scarce food going to the prison camps. Their anger grew when they learned the extent of the damage inflicted by Allied air raids on Italian cities and Italian art. On 1 June, the Allied military government was officially installed in the north, thereby effectively depriving the CLN of any proper role. From now on it was the Allies and not the Italians who were in charge.

And, for a while at least, the Italians had the pretext that they needed their weapons to mop up enemies still at large. It was Bolaffi, the neat, independent, awkward commander of the Stellina Brigade, who was at the centre of one of the more unexpected episodes of the end of the Piedmontese war. Some 2,500 partisans had managed to free the Val d'Aosta ahead of the arriving French troops, but the French had long had their eye on the hydroelectric plants and through them on the economy of Turin, whose electricity they supplied. Furthermore, they continued to feel contemptuous towards 'les sales Italiens fascistes' and intended to make them pay for their earlier treachery. Their plan was to annex the area. Soon, posters went up urging the local population to opt for union with France. People were given voting slips, accompanied by veiled threats that the French would not be leaving.

No sooner had the Germans surrendered than a French infantry division appeared just above the town of Exilles. Bolaffi was dismayed to find them high-handed and hostile. The French soldiers removed the Italian flags and replaced them with French ones. They occupied Bardonecchia, on the border, moved down towards Susa and announced that they intended to deny all access to Mont Cenis to Italians. The local inhabitants, at first welcoming, and even seduced, were soon annoyed by the arrogance of the French, particularly after they started helping themselves to anything that the Germans had not already looted – mirrors, radiators, even washbasins. New posters went up, this time put there by the villagers: 'French, go away . . . We liberated our valleys ourselves and will keep them liberated.' Bolaffi and his men tried frantically to reach some kind of accommodation with the invaders.

Then came an evening when two French soldiers, playing cards in the Albergo del Sole in Susa, which they had commandeered as their mess, were killed in an explosion. It was an accident but the French garrison ran into the streets and accused the people outside of trying to murder their men; they then imposed a curfew and began to make sweeping arrests. Two Italian men were punched; others were roughly interrogated.

Alerted to this growing altercation, the American command in Turin contacted de Gaulle, who at first seemed disinclined to step in, instead ordering his men to occupy the whole of the Val d'Aosta and the Piedmontese mountains. President Truman was called in to intervene. De Gaulle was reminded that a French occupation of Italy was in breach of Allied policy. He did nothing. Truman now sent an ultimatum, threatening to block all military supplies to France unless the French withdrew. To Bolaffi's immense relief, de Gaulle gave in, the French left, and the Allied military government sent troops to take charge of the frontier, from which the French were excluded for twenty kilometres. Cesare Alvazzi, who was attached to them, entered Susa to find that his particular group of men, before disbanding, wanted him to review them formally, as their commanding officer.

Bolaffi had been longing for the war to end. He took off his smart uniform and was reunited with his two children, whom he had not seen for fourteen months, and with his remaining stamp collection, impeccably guarded by his Aryan colleague. He would spend the next few months trying to find jobs for his disbanded Stellina fighters. Bolaffi had been difficult and averse to obeying orders, accusing the political commissars of 'therapeutic chattering' – he was, as Ada put it, *'particolare'*, an odd character – but his care of his men had been remarkable. Ada, in Bolaffi's eyes, had always been an exceptional figure and to the very end he signed his letters to her *'i miei deferenti ossequi'*, my deferential homage. When, in May, the partisans were awarded retrospective military ranks, Bolaffi was made a major.

It was not only the French who could not forgive the Italians their misdeeds. The British and the Americans remained ambivalent. Even if the dire conditions predicted by Macmillan in his diary not long before – the factories destroyed, the raw materials gone, a threat of 'total collapse to anarchy, revolution and despair' – had singularly failed to come to pass, the Allied political leaders were slow in praising the Resistance for its part in the war. There was talk of the Resistance having been a badly trained, disorganised 'Dad's army'. It would be some weeks before an official report prepared by the Special Forces acknowledged that the partisans had effectively 'broken the strength and morale of an enemy of greatly superior strength . . . Without their successes, the Allied victory in Italy would not have been as rapid, as crushing or as little costly.' Another report spoke of the Resistance as having 'in a display of swiftness, energy and discipline which astonished the whole world', risen up 'like a wave and rolled through the length and breadth of Italy'.

Kesselring later said as much. In his memoirs, he wrote that the partisans had indeed presented the Germans with a real danger and that their elimination had been of 'capital importance'. Even Churchill and Alexander were eventually forced to concede that Italian partisans had tied down six out of twenty-five German divisions and that Italy had effectively 'worked her passage back'. Not that the Allies themselves had always performed well. As one officer later put it, the twenty months of the Italian campaign had often been marked by 'ponderous, overlapping and mutually untrusting alien military bureaucracies'.

And it was widely conceded that the help given by the partisans and civilians alike to the escaped Allied prisoners of war had been critical.* In the months that followed, an Allied Screening Commission paid ninety visits to Piedmont to identify and indemnify some 5,000 individual Italians whose generosity had been exceptional. But the British, unlike the Americans, declined to give out the 443 proposed decorations, on the grounds that some might go to Communists, and that the medals might in any case give offence to British families 'bereaved at Italian hands'.

What all agreed was that the information gathered by the Italian Resistance in the closing months of the war had been crucial, allowing a 'periscope' onto German movements. Raimondo Craveri, the man who perhaps more than any other had been influential in making the secret networks run, had been separated from his wife Elena and two young children for almost two years. He took a jeep and reached home in May. His son Piero, a little boy when he left, recognised him; but he had last seen Benedetta when she was just eleven months old. He was a stranger to her.

---

* The final figures were that 53,372 were deported to Germany; 11,776 crossed the lines; 4,852 escaped to Switzerland.

By the time of the Potsdam Conference on 2 August, the Allied tone towards the Italians had become considerably more affable. Italy, said a communiqué, had undoubtedly made a 'decisive contribution to Germany's defeat'. She had liberated herself from the Fascist regime and 'is making good progress towards the re-establishment of a government and democratic institutions'. Even when giving praise the Allies seemed to find it hard to avoid sounding patronising. The thoughtful, strategic, wise Ferruccio Parri phrased it rather more gracefully. The Italians should now be able, he said, to negotiate with the Allies on an equal footing, but only because they had shown that Italy had known 'how to pay with its blood for the lost liberty and independence'.

The final peace treaty, signed in Paris in 1946, did not reflect his optimism. Italy was forced to pay heavy reparations, dissolve parts of its army and give up its empire, along with Istria and Dalmatia which it had won in 1918. De Gaulle had succeeded in putting a gloss on France's *années noires*, the years of collaboration, turning them into a national trauma in which all but a very few French people were somehow guiltless. The Italians could not quite escape the widespread contempt felt for the way they had apparently so willingly tolerated twenty years of Fascist greed, corruption and incompetence. Nor the fact that the war, which all had hoped would be short and victorious, had turned out to be prolonged and terrible, and that the Armistice and the botched changing of sides had opened Italy up to invasion, occupation, destruction, the collapse of the army and the end of a discredited monarchy.

Mussolini's body, meanwhile, having first been buried in an unmarked grave outside Milan, was kidnapped by a group of neo-Fascists, who managed to lose two fingers of the disintegrating corpse, and taken to the Valtellina, where he had hoped to make his last stand, accompanied by two priests. It took the police a hundred days to track down the body, after which it was reburied in a Christian ceremony in the Capuchin chapel of Cerro Maggiore outside Milan, before being moved again, to the family crypt in Predappio, the family town where Rachele returned to live. Predappio became and has remained a place of pilgrimage.

And as for the briefcases with the important papers and what became known as the Dongo Treasure – 1.6 million lire in cheques and a considerable amount of gold bars, jewels and cash – in Mussolini's Alfa Romeo, their fate has never been solved. The Germans, too, had five suitcases belonging to the Duce, full of ingots and cash. Some of this wound up in Lake Garda. But some was retrieved and taken to the Resistance headquarters in Milan, where it was used to pay urgent bills. The rest vanished.

By early summer a degree of calm had settled over Turin and the valleys of Piedmont. When figures were collected, it was estimated that Italy had lost a little under half a million of its people in the course of the war, 40,000 of them civilians killed in air raids. There were very few of Piedmont's communes that had not been attacked and over 5,000 of its houses and schools had been destroyed or sacked. The Fascists and Germans between them had shot 1,776 partisans, and hanged 42, and they had executed 527 civilians in reprisals. These figures did not include the fighters killed in action. Of Italy's 200,000 active members of the Resistance, and about the same number of helpers, a fifth were dead. In Piedmont alone, 98 *staffette* had died, eight of them in the liberation of Turin. The two youngest were fourteen-year-old Maria Albarelli, who had served with the urban partisans and fifteen-year-old Elsa Falerno, a sublieutenant in charge of a brigade of 106 men.

Whether what took place, during the twenty months of occupation, was or was not a civil war continues to exercise people to this day. Claudio Pavone, one of Italy's most respected historians, was the first to suggest that there were three wars going on simultaneously: a civil war between Italians – or perhaps a war of 'civilisation' against the forces of evil; a class war against powerful vested interests; and a war of national liberation against the enemy. Most partisans saw themselves as fighting several at the same time. The Church, because of its own ambivalence over the Communist partisans, disliked the idea that it had been a civil war, as did many partisans, who protested that it legitimised the Fascists and gave Salò the dignity of a sovereign state.

The legacy of the war left more questions than answers: was a *padrone*, an employer, who was also a Fascist and a collaborator, not a real Italian? How totalitarian had Fascism been? Was a single man, Mussolini, to blame? Should the Resistance be seen as a second Risorgimento, in the sense that in the first there had also been 'reactionary Italians' allying themselves with the occupying Austrians? Had Fascism, as Benedetto Croce maintained, been nothing more than a 'parenthesis' in history, a transient moment of despotism and immorality, quickly forgotten? One thing was clear though: the twenty months of occupation had changed every Italian. The conflict had been too brutal, too destructive, too divisive to imagine going back to Italy as it had once been, even for all the 'attendisti', those who had sat on the sidelines in Levi's grey zone, between the territory of good and the territory of evil.

As the prisoners of war and those deported by the Germans came home, the full extent of Italy's losses became clearer. Of the 600,000 Italian soldiers captured by the Germans and sent to Germany after the armistice, some 40–50,000 had died. Many more succumbed to cold, sickness and their injuries on the Eastern Front, but it took months to establish what had become of the others. From those captured, Italy put together 85,000 names of the missing men and kept pressing for news, but it was not until August 1945 that the Soviets liberated the remaining prisoners. Over the next year, 21,193 men struggled home, most of them emaciated, sickly and angry, with long beards and shreds of clothing. It was years before grieving families stopped believing that it was just possible that husbands and sons, lost in Russia's great wilderness, would appear. Jacopo Lombardini, who had witnessed Artom's torture, did not survive Mauthausen, where he was sent soon after his last visit from Frida. On the eve of Turin's uprising, he was sent to the gas chambers.

And as the concentration and extermination camps across occupied Europe were liberated, and the surviving Italian Jews came home, so a tally of these losses too was made. Before the war, Italy's Jewish population stood at around 46,000. Nine thousand had managed to emigrate. But of the 6,806 who were deported on forty-eight transports, just 836 lived to see the end of the war. Of the three Turin friends deported together from Fossoli to Auschwitz – Levi, Luciana Nissim and Vanda Maestra – only Luciana and Levi were still alive. Vanda, who had grown steadily thinner, her eyes duller, her mood more subdued, her legs hugely swollen, had been sent to the gas chamber on 31 October 1944, shortly after Luciana had been transferred as doctor to a sub-camp at Birkenau. Escaping from a death march, Luciana was liberated by the Americans on 24 April 1945. In 1946 Luciana married Franco Momigliano, who had so narrowly escaped death in Milan's San Vittore prison; they called their first child Vanda.

In June 1945, from Katowice, the holding camp that was a stage in his long odyssey home, Levi wrote to Bianca: 'I am dressed in rags, will probably arrive home without shoes, but in exchange I have learned German, a little Russian and Polish and furthermore have learned how to extricate myself from many situations, how not to lose courage and how to withstand moral and physical sufferings.' He was now able, he told her, to make cabbage and turnip soup, cook potatoes in several different ways, and lay, light and clean stoves. I have, he added, 'done an incredible number of jobs: assistant builder, navvy, sweeper, porter, interpreter, cyclist, tailor, thief, nurse, receiver of stolen goods, stone breaker: even that of chemist!'

Levi reached his home in Turin on 19 October 1945 and immediately telephoned Bianca. She hastened to see him. He had been away almost two years. That first night he said nothing about the camps. But later, on the many walks he and Bianca took together, he told her, in great detail, about everything he had endured and seen, analysing every incident, trying to understand and make sense of what had happened.

Jewish partisans contributed a disproportionately high number of fighters to the Resistance and they had paid for it dearly. Well over 2,000 had joined bands, and close to half were arrested, executed or deported. Seven years after the war ended, the *corte d'assise* in Turin tried two members of the Italian SS and one Salò militiaman for the deaths of Emanuele Artom and Willy Jervis. One man received a life sentence, commuted to thirty years. The other two were released for lack of evidence. Though Italy's Jews had their full rights restored in June 1944 after the liberation of Rome, the actual restoration of what had been looted and taken moved slowly and reluctantly. A street and a park in Turin were eventually named after Emanuele Artom, and he was awarded a posthumous silver medal.

In 1980, while he was writing *The Drowned and the Saved*, Levi sent Bianca his chapter on the 'grey zone' for her to comment on. He was not, he told her, primarily a writer; and she agreed. For her, Levi remained a scientist, a man who analysed everything meticulously under a microscope and then felt the need to communicate what he had discovered to the world, without embellishments. Before it was published, he sent her a poem called 'Thaw' about the past and their walks together:

'*Quando la neve sarà tutta sciolta*
Andremo in cerca del vecchio sentiero,
Quello che si sta coprendo di rovi
Dietro il muro del monastero;
Tutto sarà come una volta.'

When all the snow has melted
We'll go to look for the old path,
The one with brambles growing over it
Behind the monastery wall;
Everything will be the way it used to be.

Bianca always refused to believe that Levi's death in 1987 was suicide. 'A mild, just, coherent man,' she wrote in her memoirs. 'A friend.'

19

A love of forgetting

Ada was not the only partisan to have fears for what a liberated Italy would look like. But what neither she nor the other northern leaders knew was quite how frustrating and unpredictable the months following liberation would be. The close relations between Parri of the Partito d'Azione and the Communist Luigi Longo had papered over the very real differences between their parties, while the brief spell of military unity leading up to the insurrection had only been tacitly supported by the other groupings. When the fighting ended, these conflicting views flared into life. As did the fundamental schism between north and south, the northern Committee of National Liberation and the Badoglio government in Rome, with which it had had virtually no communication for twenty months. As Parri said, the real war had been fought in the north, between the Fascists and the Resistance, and not between the government in the south and Salò. All Italy had known the misery of conflict, but only a few 'the moral jolt of insurrection'; and the south, after all, had not liberated itself. Il 'vento del nord', the wind of revolution and change, was soon becalmed in a sea of disagreement.

Fascism had not destroyed democracy: the Liberal Italy of the early twentieth century was very doubtfully either politically or socially democratic. The newly united nation had endured by imposing itself on every aspect of life, by suppressing parliament, the press and the unions, by corrupting the law and by diminishing women. It was now a question of reconciling a vast array of divided hopes, aspirations and demands in a country whose only proper experience of democracy had come from the short-lived free republics in the autumn of 1944, quickly marginalised and taken over as the war ended. Who was there to lead a country which had seen three-quarters of its agriculture collapse, many of its vehicles, train stock and roads destroyed, and whose national revenues were half those of 1939? In Livorno alone, seven out of every ten buildings were no longer habitable.

For Ada and her friends, the twenty months had been a period of intense activity and camaraderie, a time of heady equality, when differences in age, class and background were dissolved and a new kind of mutual respect was born. And pride: Ada felt, as they did, that the Italian partisans had proved themselves to be one of the most effective Resistance movements in Nazi-occupied Europe. Though exhausted, they plunged, full of optimism, into creating the kind of Italy they had fought for. One of the first things that Ada did in her magnificent offices, in her role as vice mayor of Turin, was to marry Bianca and Alberto. Not long afterwards came the wedding of Gigliola Spinelli and Franco Venturi, and that of Lucia Boetta and Renato Testori, for which, somewhat surprisingly given his role in the insurrection, Lt Col. Stevens was a witness. Marrying her friends was one of Ada's pleasures. Most of her life was now consumed by the Herculean task of putting Turin back on its feet. Public works, education, staffing, help for the elderly and the sick, the restoration of museums and galleries – all fell to her. She had little time to observe the fragility of Italy's wider struggles.

True liberals and radicals, it quickly turned out, were in a small minority. Most Italians had little faith in their new liberty, and were terrified of leaping into the dark. As Vittorio Foa said, they had no precise contours for how they saw the future, beyond the fact that everything – free speech, social justice, the distribution of wealth – had to be thought out anew. 'The world about us,' he wrote, 'seemed open and limitless . . . and our only fear was of going back.' The radicals were full of honesty and sincerity but lacked political acumen and were unwilling to make compromises. The six parties within the CLN were now disputing their claim to the leadership of the new Italy, as were a further twenty other small parties outside it. The Socialist Party, meanwhile, decided to abandon the extremism of its war years and champion instead a bridge between left and right, but this effort was soon blocked by the Liberal Party. Only the Church and the Communist

Party seemed to offer certainties. It was true that the Church had shown itself willing to serve Fascism, but then so had most Italians. As for the 1.7 million Communists still believing that Togliatti's support for the centre had been no more than a holding operation, and that the end of the war would see a totally new deal, they were forced to recognise that the Italian Communist Party had abandoned revolution, made its peace with capitalism and was in favour of a parliamentary road to socialism.

In these shifting, perilous quicksands, before power slipped from the CLN's grasp and the Allies effectively took over, Ferruccio Parri was appointed the new president of Italy. But this deeply moral, gentle and straightforward man was no match for the intrigues and ambitions of Roman politics. There was something inherently tragic about him, with his modesty and his high-mindedness. He was neither prepared for nor did he want the presidency, but felt it was right that the first post-war president should remain faithful to the shadow cast by those who had fallen in the civil war. 'Zio Maurizio', as he continued to be called by his followers, disliked the trappings of power, insisted on sleeping on a camp bed in his office, and resisted being called '*Eccellenza*'. In his probity and dignity, he reminded his friends of Abraham Lincoln.

Parri took office on 20 June 1945. But he was soon struggling with the turmoil of continuing Communist violence in the rural areas, sporadic strikes, widespread discontent, the black market, separatist agitation in Sicily where the Mafia was lurking, famine in the south and economic paralysis, along with the plotting and scheming of the Allies, especially the British, who remained determined to thwart all moves to the left. Stevens, as part of the Allied mission, had moved into rooms in the Giunta's Palazzo della Cisterna so that he could attend meetings. Two hundred and fifty thousand hectares of Italy were covered in unexploded mines and hand grenades. Renegade bands, of both Fascists and partisans, roamed the countryside seeking vengeance, and there were clashes between landless labourers and landlords. Italians were exhausted, sick of the violence, appalled by the chaos.

Parri was further weakened by an unequivocal message delivered by the Communist leader Togliatti that his party would not be challenging the Catholics for power. And his life was made harder by the emergence in the south of an anti-party, L'Uomo Qualunque, the Common Man, under a noisy, strident, sometime comedian and playwright called Guglielmo Giannini. He drew support both from the many disaffected people across Italy and from former Fascists, though the new party would soon lose its way, made irrelevant by the rise of a neo-Fascist Movimento Sociale Italiano, under a virulent nationalist called Giorgio Almirante and some of the fanatics who had backed the Salò government.

In November, Parri resigned. It had taken just five months to show that the very thing that he and Agosti, Ada, Giorgio Diena, Vittorio Foa and their friends had believed in and fought for, the idea of a true democracy founded on new grass-roots organisations uncontaminated by the past, could not compete with the political realities of peacetime. Parri's place was taken by the astute Alcide de Gasperi, a former Vatican librarian and translator and a Catholic superbly attuned to the serpentine world of Roman politics. De Gasperi was backed by the Church, by a well-organised Catholic bureaucracy and by the Allies. The rebirth of Italy, noted Don Luigi Sturzo, the former leader of a popular left-wing group, would have been hard whatever happened, but it was made considerably harder by 'the incomprehension of the Allies and their uncertain and incoherent policy'. Togliatti was made Minister for Justice. The long reign of the Christian Democratic Party had begun. The Partito d'Azione, which had always been a party of many colours, a 'club of intellectuals, moralists, philosophers' did not long survive Parri's fall and soon shrivelled and died.

The partisans, who had come home believing that Italian society would now be like the one they had forged in the mountains, felt betrayed; they were strangers in a country they had helped to transform but were no longer part of. As Agosti observed not long after liberation, with considerable bitterness: 'We must all take a large share of responsibility for returning to our own private interests too quickly and for failing to understand that the battle was not over . . . Out of laziness, egotism, impatience with necessary compromises, we allowed the legacy of our fallen patriots to trickle away.'

More important, perhaps, was the fact that the Italian state was still in the hands of the old leading class, which was not willing to forgo its allegiance to private and state capitalism, those who, 'blind and deaf', had preferred to wear the 'Fascist livery' and refused to 'hear the volcano erupting under their feet'. Twenty months of civil war had not been long enough to change deeply ingrained habits and ways of thinking, though a Constituent Assembly did duly draw up a new constitution, with women voting for the first time. In June 1946, by 12.7 million votes to 10.7 million, Italy decided to eject the monarchy and become a republic. Umberto left for exile. He had been King for barely a month.

But Italy did not have its Nuremberg trials. Field Marshal Kesselring was initially sentenced to death in Venice for the shooting of 335 Italians in the Ardeatine massacre and for inciting his troops to kill civilians. But the sentence provoked loud protests in Britain, with General Alexander arguing that Kesselring had fought a 'hard but clean war', and was in any case commuted when the new Italian government abolished the death penalty, saying that it was a relic of the Fascist regime. Many of the Germans captured in Italy, including General Wolff, were let off very lightly. What the Allies wanted, and were determined to achieve, was for Italy to become a functioning country as rapidly as possible, with as few Communists as possible in positions of power and workers coerced and cajoled into falling into line. American bankers arrived to stress the need for economic order. Rumours began to circulate that most of the major crimes of violence had been committed by Communists. What mattered was not justice, but reconstruction. Later it would be said that Operation Sunrise, the German surrender in Italy, was simply a pause, a moment between the end of the Second World War and the Cold War, when the perceived enemy of the British and the Americans ceased to be Germany and became the Soviet Union.

Even before the insurrection, Vittorio Valletta and Giovanni Agnelli of FIAT had been found guilty of having, among other things, profited financially from Fascism. Valletta was arrested, held briefly, then returned to FIAT Mirafiore, but on 25 April, as the partisans closed in on the factories, he went into hiding, fearing that he might be shot. In May, he produced a 23-page refutation of all the crimes he was accused of. Pleading '*dissimulazione onesta*,' feigning to help the Fascists while really supporting the partisans, he called witnesses to show how FIAT had delivered

radio transmitters, vehicles and large sums of money to the Resistance, while facilitating acts of sabotage against German production
in his factories. But as his fate was being discussed, Valletta, after
pressure from the Christian Democrats and the Allies, was made
the Italian government's delegate for trade with England. Agnelli
died before sentencing took place. And as production at FIAT
appeared to falter, many of its senior managers having initially
been sacked for collaboration, so Valletta was brought back as
managing director. In this spirit of wilful forgetting, the army, the
police, the civil servants and the businessmen were all recast as
resisters, and the horrors of the civil war blamed on a few renegade Fascists.

What took place at FIAT was mirrored across the northern
industrial triangle. Efforts to jail other factory owners and senior
executives, who had openly made fortunes out of collaboration,
failed, as these men too produced evidence, some of it fabricated,
to prove they had also been playing double games. With Parri's
departure, investigations against industrialists, senior bureaucrats
and financiers effectively ground to a halt. The solidarity and sense
of equality, 'with no exploited and no exploiters', that the workers
had imagined would translate into better deals, evaporated, like
the 'vento del nord' that had blown them into existence.

Perhaps the greatest failure of the purifying wind, however, was
its inability to cleanse Italy of its tainted politicians and civil
servants. As the author of a report for the Allied Psychological
Warfare Branch shrewdly put it, 'The people are not sure that
they believe in democracy, nor are they always sure what a Fascist
is.' Long before the north was freed, a pattern had been established. With the liberation of Rome in the summer of 1944 had
come a High Commission for Sanctions against Fascism, given
the task of 'de-Fascistising' the state and sending to prison those
who had 'compromised the Nation'. These were to include men
and women accused of violent attacks, the organisers of the
original March on Rome in 1922, the authors of the coup which
had brought in the Fascist dictatorship in 1925, and the Fascist
gerarchi and collaborators.

One immediate problem was the sheer number of people
involved: not only every person who had run a hospital, a museum,

an academy, a public utility or a school, but also the many thousands who had joined the obligatory Fascist organisations and then gone along with the German invaders. Soon after liberation, the people's tribunals were replaced by *corti d'assise*, set up in eleven cities across the north and anxious to demonstrate to the Allies their competence and impartiality. The crowds of spectators were such that loudspeakers relayed the proceedings to the streets outside. Within a year, some 40,000 former Fascists were in jail, the majority still awaiting trial; there had been a small number of executions of the most egregious torturers. But fearing that many would escape justice, some of the prisons were attacked by bands of former partisans, and their inmates kidnapped and executed; and when the jails were reinforced, the partisans became more wily, dressing themselves up as guards and stopping the vans transporting the Fascist prisoners.

The gesture, though bold, was futile. For Italy's judiciary had not been purged. Most of Italy's lawyers, magistrates, judges and court officials had made their careers under Fascism, when the Minister for Justice and other political leaders exercised control over the courts, thereby denying them independence. Virtually all 135 local police chiefs had begun their working lives under Mussolini. Few of these men had any taste for cleansing their own and no one was keener to muddy the waters than those who had most to hide. In police stations and lawyers' offices across the country, thousands of files went missing. In Rome, parliament preferred to drag its heels and pass '*leggine*', little laws, rather than to issue firm guidance. Decree after decree watered down the penalties for collaboration and by November 1945, all but 495 out of 28,399 cases had been dismissed. The Police Code put in place under Mussolini in 1931 was not rescinded. The High Commission for Sanctions, which saw four commissioners in a single year, was dissolved, and in June 1946, Togliatti, in his capacity as Minister for Justice, announced a widespread amnesty for most of those in jail. Spies, informers, those who had turned Jews over to the Germans, those who had sent partisans to their deaths and executed civilians in reprisals, all emerged from the prisons.

The women of Turin, whose husbands and sons had been tortured to death in the infamous barracks in Via Asti turned out for the trials of those responsible. Sixty death sentences were passed. Not one was carried out. Those who received life sentences were quickly amnestied.

To make things worse, what was described as 'ordinary torture' was decriminalised, while 'tortures of a particular atrocious nature' remained on the books. Due to the bias in the judiciary, much of the Fascist violence was deemed to have been 'ordinary'. Seven Fascists accused of raping, knifing and impaling a woman partisan were exonerated, their crimes not judged as 'atrocious'. Those who had denounced Jews were often identified, but very little was done to bring them to justice; the few cases that reached the courts trickled away in inertia and statutes of limitation. As Bianco put it, Togliatti's amnesty was a 'questionable compromise with a still menacing past'. The 'bacillus' of Fascism remained.

By late 1946 the number of Fascists still in prison dropped to 4,000; and many of these too soon saw their sentences annulled. One of them was Gino Boccante, Italy's best-known artist and designer. Boccante had worn the uniform of the German SS, strutted about Milan and drawn posters portraying partisans as traitors. Captured at the time Milan was liberated, he quickly began designing pictures of scruffy partisans transformed into smart, helmeted promoters of public safety. Boccante was soon released. In Piedmont, 204 of the most violent Fascists were sentenced to death; but just eighteen were executed.

Then came a very bitter twist. Togliatti's amnesty covered crimes of violence committed by Fascists and partisans alike up to the day of liberation, but no further. Any reprisal or summary killing that took place after 25 April 1945 was declared to be an indictable crime. To this end, the partisan execution of spies and collaborators that took place during the 'days of blood' before the Allies arrived, and which had been agreed by them, were now made cases of premeditated murder. And robbery was excluded from the amnesty, so that the commandeering of vehicles or food by the Resistance became a retrospective crime.

Arrests of partisans began, particularly of the *gappisti* and the *sappisti*, the urban fighters who had been told that they were the avant garde troops and executioners of the Resistance and that they should never weaken, and who were now accused of having been terrorists who had provoked reprisals by their assassinations. In Piedmont alone, 1,486 former partisans were rounded up and brought to trial. Five hundred others, who had fought with the Garibaldi brigades, took refuge in Eastern Europe. Over the next few years, tens of thousands of men and women all over Italy who had fought in the Resistance were arrested and went before the courts on charges of murder, the possession of weapons, robbery and sabotage. Even though, in the event, of the 90–95,000 partisans arrested, only 19,000 were actually prosecuted and just 7,000 pronounced guilty, many spent years in preventative detention before being released. As one woman partisan, who had fought bravely for the entire twenty months, put it, it was 'as if they cut off our wings'.

After this came yet a further blow. The Fascist military, the soldiers of Salò, petitioned for and were awarded 'belligerent' status, while the partisans were declared to have been 'irregulars' and 'rebels' and were denied it. This opened the way for people to bring civil suits against them. The families of the hostages murdered by the Germans in the Ardeatine caves in reprisal for the attack on the German patrol brought cases against the young *gappisti* who had carried it out. Their murdered relatives, they said, had been 'sacrificial lambs' in an illegal war. At much the same time, those senior Fascists who had received prison sentences were released or acquitted on appeal. Julio Valerio Borghese, commander of the infamous Decima Mas which was widely accepted as having carried out more than eight hundred murders, was released 'due to extenuating circumstances'.

The judicial harassment of the Resistance continued, with the Christian Democrats, now dominating the government, accusing the partisans of 'brutality'. In the right-wing press, a campaign of denigration and vitriol was launched. There was even talk of Parri having been the 'highest expression' of an 'Italy of massacres, killings and robberies'. Fascism and anti-Fascism were recast as two sides of the same coin, neither one of them better than the other. Not surprising, then, that the Resistance came to view their twenty months of combat with anger and resentment, nor that Italy remained a place of unrest, strikes and clashes, particularly in the northern industrial belt. Graft and corruption returned to haunt Italian politics; ambiguity, entitlement and suspicion, all hallmarks of the Fascist years, once again settled over the country, while the 'trials of the Resistance' soon made life as difficult as possible for anyone supporting the left. As Bianco wrote to Agosti, politics had become very 'grubby'. It was all that he, Agosti and Ada had most dreaded: Italy had become 'feeble, slack and full of fear'. As they saw it, the twenty months had been a fight between two conceptions of life: on one side compromise, obsequiousness, conformity; on the other, liberty, openness, a new kind of Italy. And their side had lost.

In July 1948, Togliatti was shot by a lone fanatical student as he left parliament. He survived, but strikes were called, factories were occupied and workers clashed violently with the police. The weapons used in these clashes, those that had been hidden away from Allied requisitions at the end of the war, were tracked down and confiscated; more former partisans went to prison; others lost their jobs, the Christian Democrats artfully pointing to the hidden weapons to prove that the anti-Fascists still represented a threat to Italian society. For a while, there were fears of further civil war. In 1947, the Communists and the Socialists had been eased out of government and in the elections of April 1948 the Christian Democrats won an overwhelming majority. Though in theory the judiciary would now be completely independent, in practice political interference continued. One by one, each of the Resistance's hopes and ambitions, along with the sense of morality that it believed defined it, crumbled away. An uncleansed former Fascist state was able to slow down the advent of democracy and put an end to the process of coming to terms with the past. As a correspondent for *Avanti!* put it: Italians had 'a love of country and a love of forgetting'.

In May 1945, as peace returned to the streets of Turin and the mountain valleys, the role of the women partisans in the war was spoken of with pride and admiration. Women, declared Parri, 'were the Resistance'. Even Togliatti, leader of the party that refused to let its women fighters march in the victory parades, told a large gathering of voters that women 'fought valiantly for emancipation' and were now entitled to it. The first figures collected showed that 4,633 Italian women had been arrested, tortured and imprisoned during the twenty months of civil war, and that 2,750 others had been deported to the Nazi concentration camps. The number of dead was 620 – some half of them in Piedmont – having been executed or died fighting. Unlike the men, who had to make a choice to join one side or the other, the women partisans could take pride in having truly been volunteers, for they could have stayed at home and done nothing. And, as they told each other, there had been more women partisans in the Italian Resistance than in any similar movement in occupied Europe. 'We were conscious,' said one, 'that for the first time we had been players in history.' They had much to be proud of.

On paper, their future looked good. Article 3 of the new constitution spoke of women as 'equal before the law, without distinction of sex, race, language, religion, politics, personal and social circumstances'. There were provisions on equal pay, the right to work and suffrage. Even as the north was liberated, women's organisations – Catholic, lay, Communist – burst into life, their members meeting to discuss shorter working hours, housework, access to education. The 70,000 members of the GDD, still busy handing out clothes, food, blankets and shoes to prisoners returning from the camps in Germany, officially merged with the Union of Italian Women at a national congress held in Florence in October 1945. Of the first women elected to parliament, half were partisans.

In Turin, the four friends kept meeting to keep alive their own ideals. On platforms, in schools, at union meetings and in the newspapers, Ada, Silvia, Frida and Bianca spoke out, urging unity and above all equality. What they, and countless other women across Italy, said was that they now felt different. The war had made them curious, hungry for knowledge and responsibility, and they were full of optimism. They wanted things they had never thought to want before. Those who had gone into the war unable to distinguish one political party from another now spoke with confidence about the different agendas. For the first time, as one woman put it, they had become people, individuals, not mothers, daughters or wives. Five hundred and twelve had been commissars in the Resistance, instructing the bands on history, economics and politics. One woman, asked what she felt, replied simply: 'Happy, happy, happy'.

As it turned out, the optimism, hope and happiness were all misplaced. The exclusion of women from the victory parades was a sign of a far deeper discord. No one wanted to reflect on the embarrassing and distasteful fact that for twenty months, young men and women had lived side by side as equals. The Communist Party turned out to be more Catholic than the Catholics in urging women to moderate their tone, accept the fact that the family still was, as it had always been, the cornerstone of Italian life. The right to work came with a proviso: that a woman's 'essential family function' was paramount. The cooperation between the women's groups began to splinter under the weight of political disagreements and did not long outlive the war. All the old prejudices, enshrined in twenty years of Fascist rule, resurfaced: women were again viewed as intrinsically weak and politically ignorant. The Catholic Church saw to it that decisions regarding children and property would continue to be taken by men, and that the old laws on birth control, divorce and adultery would not be altered. When women went electioneering, local priests would often ring the church bells to drown out their speeches. And within families, who had united to fight the Germans and the Fascists, relations soured as the young blamed their parents for the long years of Fascist rule.

In the rush for economic regeneration, women were simply shunted aside. On paper, those who had acquired voices made their points, but they were not strong enough to push them through. It was not until 1963 that a law was passed giving women access to all professions. The 4,000 women who had taken the place of men on the railways were quickly dismissed. We were, one woman wrote, 'sent home like chickens to the coop to lay our eggs in solitude and silence'. Many felt that they had no alternative but to marry, '*per desiderio di normalità*', in order to be normal: in 1939, there had been 315,000 marriages; in 1946 there were 415,000. The following year, a million babies were born. The boyish look favoured by the partisans – cropped hair, shorts, heavy boots, berets – gave way to ample long skirts down to the ankle, to accentuate the figure.

There were, however, flickers of rebellion. When it became clear that equal pay for women in factories was not forthcoming, Bianca led a strike in Turin. Ten thousand women from across the motor car, textile and chemical industries came out to parade through the streets of the city, singing the Resistance hymns and waving banners. For a moment, it bore fruit. In Piedmont at least, women were grudgingly accorded equal wages. But not for long. There were other strikes, but they achieved very little. 'It was sad,' as Ada said, 'but this is the reality.'

The fate of the partisans remained confusing and contradictory. While some went to jail, others were honoured. When General Trabucchi was appointed to lead a commission to decide on the recognition of the partisans' contribution to the war, 88,902 names were put forward. The highest rank, that of '*partigiano combattente*', was awarded to those who had served for at least three months with an armed formation recognised by the Resistance leadership, and to have taken part in at least three actions 'of war or sabotage'. Below this came the 'patriots' and the 'deserving', according to the degree of help they had provided. Some half of those on the list received the top ranking, among them Ada, Frida, Silvia and Bianca. They were four out of just 1,304 women. When retrospective military ranks were assigned, Ada found that she had been made a major, along with Lucia; the others became captains. The seventeen gold medals that went to women, thirteen of them posthumously, spoke of 'devotion, tenderness, sacrifice' and a 'virile' courage. Lucia was too disgusted to collect hers. Before the war, she had never expected to do anything with her life other than marry. Now, having achieved so much, she felt abandoned, forgotten, unwanted.

In the huge spate of novels and memoirs, exalting and mythologising the Resistance, that were rushed out after liberation – 4,500 in 1945, 6,500 in 1946 – there were almost none written by a woman. In the many thousands of histories written by men about the twenty months of occupation, many of them nostalgic essays on the 'betrayed Resistance', feeding on myths and counter-myths, women are very seldom mentioned, and when they are, they are rarely given names. Eulogies are reserved for men. That the armed Resistance could not have survived without the *staffette*, the young women who risked their lives every day, is glossed over. It is as if they had never existed. After the trials of the torturers in Via Asti, one woman remarked bitterly: 'I sacrificed a father, I sacrificed a husband, I very nearly sacrificed myself. And for what?'

In the year after the end of the war, Italy staged eight major exhibitions on the Resistance. Women flitted across them like shadows. They neither wrote their own memoirs nor were invited to do so, and they did not attend anniversary celebrations. 'It is an injustice,' wrote a correspondent to *Noi Donne* in 1947, 'no one at all remembers us.' It was, said another, to be doubly betrayed, first by the politicians and the voters, then by their own colleagues in the Resistance. 'We thought we would find a new world. We didn't.'

It would take twenty years and the arrival of the feminist movement before Italian women partisans – along with Jews and the clergy who had fought and died with them – received their due. And even then, very few of the women who took up their pens chose to write about the rape and the violence to which they had been subjected by the Germans and the Fascists, or to the many rapes carried out by France's Moroccan Goumiers in the weeks after liberation, about whom the Algerian president Ben Bella would later say that their French officers had given them *'carte blanche'* to do as they wished with the perfidious Italians. It was only in the 1970s that women academics and historians began suggesting that it had been wrong to see women's contribution as *'resistenza passiva'*, with all its soft undertones. What the female partisans had done, they argued, needed to be recast as *'resistenza civile'*, often not with weapons, but with moral courage, inventiveness, flexibility, the ability to follow orders and forge relationships; and it had been no less dangerous.

In the months after liberation, in the northern cities and the mountain villages of Piedmont, plaques went up to mark the places where the partisans had fallen. Cemeteries created special areas where the partisans could lie together, the photographs on the graves showing faces that look little older than children. In the graveyard at Torre Pellice, few of those who lie buried there had reached their twenties. One boy had only just turned seventeen. In Villar, a few kilometres further up the valley, there is a plaque to Willy Jervis and the two young men shot with him. On it are the words he wrote to his wife Lucilla shortly before his death: 'Do not pity me or call me "poor" . . . I am dying for having fought for what I believed in.'

And when Turin's small close-knit intellectual community took shape again, its members returning from the mountains, from the German concentration camps, from exile, the gaps left by the dead became more painfully apparent. Natalia Ginzburg came back with her children, but Leone, the man who had been the moral centre for them all, did not. Nor did Willy Jervis, Sandro Delmastro, Emanuele Artom and his brother Paolo, Jacopo Lombardini, Vanda Maestra and many others who had climbed together and talked with such passion during the long years of Fascism. The group of friends was much reduced.

Things did not turn out as Ada, Silvia, Bianca and Frida dreamt they might. The new Italy looked very like the old one. But what no one could take away from them was one very simple fact: that an impressive number of ordinary Italians had risen up to challenge both the Germans and the Fascists, whose long reign had seemed as if it might last forever, proving what resolve, tenacity and above all exceptional courage could achieve. For the survivors, Natalia Ginzburg wrote, the twenty months of the Resistance had given them the feeling of being both different and better; and that feeling of extraordinary well-being never quite left them.

Afterword

Ada, Bianca, Frida and Silvia fought on, each in her own way, talking, writing and championing the causes they felt most passionate about. Ada, made president of one of Piedmont's main women's organisations, took part in many meetings and conferences, travelling to Paris in the autumn of 1945 to join 860 women delegates from all over the world for the first International Democratic Federation of Women. When the Partito d'Azione fell from power, she lost her job as Turin's vice mayor and, turning down an offer by the Ministry for Foreign Affairs to continue as a representative on international women's affairs, returned to her teaching and literary work, translating Boswell's *Life of Johnson*, but remaining close to women's issues. As she told Benedetto Croce, she was not at heart a political animal, and learning to live again was a 'little like recovering from an illness or better still an obsession: it takes a lot to readapt one's vision to normal dimensions'.

During a visit to London in 1947, she was hit by a car and taken for dead, until a nurse in the mortuary overheard her reciting some lines from Shakespeare. She was flown back to Italy in a plane sent by FIAT and she recovered, but slowly, and the accident left her with vertigo. Not long after the war, she joined the Communist Party, saying that it was the 'cleanest' party in Italy. As she grew older, she came to see the months of Resistance as a 'Utopia of absolute liberty'. Her son Paolo became a filmmaker and critic.

Renewing her long, loving, respectful friendship with Croce, she answered his request to tell him what her war in the Resistance had been like and turned her diaries, with their scribbles, hieroglyphics and patches of English, into what became one of the defining books on the Italian Resistance. *Diario Partigiano* was published in 1956 and has seldom been out of print since. When the novelist Italo Calvino read it, he wrote to her: 'Mamma mia, what fun you had!' Ada died in 1968. Not long before, she wrote that she did not mind the thought of death, because she felt that she had done her duty. She never lost the 'affectionate exuberance' for which her young husband Piero had loved her.

Bianca used her legal training to champion the cause of equal pay, to work with the unions and to become involved in the trials of the Red Brigades and the student protests of the late sixties. She campaigned for a republic in the referendum over the monarchy, and raised her son Fabrizio, adopted with Ada's help after the war. Their 'immense and uninterrupted friendship' shone throughout their lives. Bianca was, Fabrizio says, a serious, conscientious mother, in the long tradition of Piedmontese women. In the 1970s, she put together a two-volume collection of testimonies, *Compagne*, from women who had fought in the Resistance. Bianca left the Communist Party after the Hungarian revolution in 1956, and died, after a long and distinguished legal career, in 2014, at the age of ninety-five. But she remained always on the left and was known affectionately to her friends as Bianca la Rossa.

The voluble, boundlessly curious Frida went into local government, becoming the first woman *assessore*, the councillor who sits on the Italian criminal court and advises the municipality. She tried, but failed, to win a seat in parliament. She never married, saying that she preferred to devote her considerable energy to politics and teaching. She died, still beautiful, still endlessly talkative and full of curiosity, with her white hair piled high on her head, in 2002. She was eighty-five.

Suor Giuseppina, who had watched over so many desperate women in Le Nuove, stayed on in the prison, refusing to remove her wimple even after her order decided that it was no longer necessary. Soon after her sixty-third birthday she had a stroke. She asked to be taken back from hospital to Le Nuove to die. Her nuns sat by her day and night. When she died, Archbishop Fossati came to kneel by her coffin.

Silvia returned to her medical career, to Giorgio and their son Vittorio, writing and campaigning furiously on behalf of working-class women, but her restless, dissatisfied nature drove her into addiction. She became a familiar, battered figure, haunting Turin's chemists in search of morphine, her sharp intelligence fading, as if she had lost the will to live. She was fined for falsifying prescriptions and begged her friends to lend her money. Weakened by anorexia and depression, heartbroken after a failed love affair, soured by the political climate, she died in 1958, at the age of thirty-nine. Matilde di Pietrantonio, who saw her body in the mortuary, said that her face was a tragic Greek mask of pain. Giorgio, whose brilliant mind had helped shape the Partito d'Azione, developed schizophrenia and persecution mania. He survived her by barely a year.

It was Silvia, the quickest, the most perceptive, but also the most fragile of the four friends, who best expressed the profound sense of disillusionment and anger they all shared as they watched, bit by bit, everything they had fought for shrivel away in the bright glare of peace. In a poem addressed to 'My Companions', she wrote:

Free to cry and to suffer:
For us the revolution came too late,
And is now undone and rotten.

Among her papers, is another verse, never published:

And so begins our new slavery,
Free to cry and to die,
Our blood was red
Just as yours was . . .

But it was Ada, organised, calm, patient, meticulous and irreverent, who had held them all together, who had watched over them, worried about them, listened to their stories. In due course she set up an centre for the study of the Resistance in memory of her husband Piero and started a paper, the *Giornale dei Genitori*, about children and their development, which she wrote with friends at her kitchen table, on Sundays, her day off. After the war, with money from her car accident, she bought a house with Ettore and Paolo at Reaglie in the hills above Turin. Here, on 25 April every year, friends gathered to walk in the mountains and remember the liberation. When Bianco was killed in a climbing accident in 1953, Parri picked three red carnations that had been growing on Duccio's grave and placed them on his coffin.

The war, Ada said, had taught them about friendship, about how much women have in common with each other, and what they can achieve when they work together. They told each other that they missed the intensity of the wartime comradeship, and their hikes into the mountains carrying messages, looking up at the snow on the peaks, and the clarity of the skies and the changing colours of the trees. Ada dedicated her *Diario Partigiano* to her friends, saying that it was this link of solidarity, founded not on 'shared inheritance, nor on Patria, nor on their intellectual tradition', but on a simple human rapport, each feeling herself to be one of many, that had been the most significant thing about '*la nostra battaglia*'. It had been, as Lisetta Foa said, for all its terrors and losses, a magical moment in their lives, and no one who had taken part in it ever regretted it.

Acknowledgements

First and foremost, I am very grateful to the descendants and friends of my main characters – Aldo Agosti, Anna and Lisabetta Foa, Andrea Gobetti, Fabrizio Salmoni, Vittorio Diena – for their time and help. The book could not have been written without them.

I would also like warmly to thank Cesare Alvazzi de Frate, Eldina Bellion, Bruna Bertolo, Marta Bonsanti, Richard Bosworth, Piera Egidi Bouchard, Micki Cesan, Graziella Codola, Philip Cooke, Benedetta and Piero Craveri, Maria Rosa Fabbrini, Mimmo Franzinelli, Yvetta Fuhrmann, Donatella Gay Rochat, Michael Howard, Christian Jennings, Fabio Levi, Marilda Musacchio, Ersilia and Gianni Perona, Guri Schwarz, Marcello Sorgi, Felice Taglienti, Mark Thomson, Emanuela Tomassone.

Much of my research was done in Turin, in the archive and library of ISTORETO – Istituto Piemontese per la Storia della Resistenza e della Società Contemporanea 'Giorgio Agosti' – and I thank its director, Luciano Boccalatte, as well as Andrea d'Arrigo, Chiara Colombini and its extremely helpful staff for their assistance and the many weeks I spent in their archives. I also worked in the Centro Studi Gobetti, and there I would like to thank the director and staff, and in particular Angela Alceri and Francesco Campobello.

For research in Torre Pellice, I am most grateful to Alessandra Quaglia and Sergio Benecchio in the Biblioteca Carlo Levi; in Pieve San Stefano to the archivist and staff of the Archivio Diaristico; in London to the staff of the British Library and the National Archives in Kew.

David Ellwood and Anne Chisholm kindly read my manuscript and I am very grateful to them. All errors are naturally my own.

And my thanks go to my travelling companions: Annie Blaber, Virginia Duigan, Kate Trevelyan and Guy Slater.

Most of the English translations of Ada Gobetti's diaries come from *Partisan Diary: A Woman's Life in the Italian Resistance*, translated and edited by Jomarie Alano, OUP, 2014. All other translations are my own.

As ever, my warmest thanks go to my editors, Poppy Hampson, Jennifer Barth and Pamela Murray, to Greg Clowes and Katherine Fry, and to my wonderful agent, Clare Alexander, and her assistant Geffen Semach.

List of Illustrations

p. xx Vera and Libera Arduino (courtesy of Bruna Bertolo)

p. xxiii Ada Gobetti (courtesy of Centro Studi Piero Gobetti)

p. xxiii Bianca Guidetti Serra (courtesy of Centro Studi Piero Gobetti)

p. xxiv Frida Malan (courtesy of Istituto piemontese per la Storia della Resistenza e della Società Contemporanea 'Giorgio Agosti' Torino, ISTORETO)

p. xxv Silvia Pons (courtesy of Vittorio Diena)

p. 9 The Sons of the Wolf (courtesy of the Bruni Archive / Alinari Archives Management, Florence / TopFoto)

p. 15 Benedetta Croce with Ada and Paolo Gobetti (courtesy of Centro Studi Piero Gobetti)

p. 19 Frida, Roberto and Gustavo Malan with their parents (courtesy of Biblioteca Resistenza Torre Pellice)

p. 20 Leone and Natalia Ginzburg

p. 25 Victor Emmanuel III and Field Marshal Badoglio (courtesy of TopFoto)

p. 36 Ada and Paolo Gobetti (courtesy of Centro Studi Piero Gobetti)

p. 45 Emanuele Artom (courtesy of ISTORETO)

p. 48 Giorgio Diena and Silvia Pons (courtesy of Vittorio Diena)

p. 58 Mussolini and Hitler (MNR1GN: Vintage Corner / Alamy Stock Photo)

p. 69 Lucia Boetta (courtesy of Bruna Bertolo)

p. 73 Roberto and Frida Malan (courtesy of Biblioteca Resistenza Torre Pellice)

p. 75 Willy Jervis with Giovanni and Paolo (courtesy of the Jervis family archive)

p. 76 Willy and Lucilla Jervis (courtesy of the Jervis family archive)

p. 77 A young volunteer

p. 79 *Staffette* (courtesy of ISTORETO)

p. 92 Primo Levi, Bianca, Alberto Salmoni and two friends (courtesy of Centro Studi Piero Gobetti)

p. 109   Luciana Nissim and Vanda Maestra (courtesy of ISTORETO)

p. 113   *Staffette* discovering new skills

p. 115   Oriana Fallaci

p. 117   A young partisan braving a checkpoint (courtesy of ISTORETO)

p. 122   Suor Giuseppina (courtesy of Bruna Bertolo)

p. 148   Sabotage (courtesy of ISTORETO)

p. 150   Reprisals (courtesy of ISTORETO)

p. 153   Jacopo Lombardini (courtesy of ISTORETO, Comune di Cinisello Balsamo)

p. 160   Leone Ginzburg (KEA2A6: Historic Collection / Alamy Stock Photo)

p. 163   Maria Gorlier and Don Marabotto (courtesy of Bruna Bertolo)

p. 171   Consorting with Fascists (courtesy of ISTORETO)

p. 176   Dr Bersano Begey's hospital in the mountains (courtesy of Bruna Bertolo)

p. 186   A Fascist massacre (courtesy of ISTORETO)

p. 188   Cleonice Tomassetti leading partisans to their execution (courtesy of Bruna Bertolo)

p. 211   A patrol of partisan skiers (courtesy of ISTORETO)

p. 217   Lucia Boetta

p. 250   Lisetta and her daughter Anna (courtesy of Anna and Lisabetta Foa)

p. 256   The second mission to France (courtesy of Centro Studi Piero Gobetti)

p. 279   *Staffette* as armed fighters (courtesy of ISTORETO)

p. 289   Arresting Fascists (Courtesy of ISTORETO)

p. 296   Liberation in Turin (courtesy of Bruna Bertolo)

p. 301   Liberation (courtesy of Bruna Bertolo)

p. 306   Giuseppe Solaro on his way to execution

p. 307   Vittorio Foa and Anna (courtesy of Anna and Lisabetta Foa)

p. 317   Ada Gobetti and Bolaffi (courtesy of Centro Studi Piero Gobetti)

p. 319   Liberation parade (courtesy of Bruna Bertolo)

Every effort has been made by the publishers to trace the holders of copyright. Any inadvertent omissions of acknowledgement or permission can be rectified in future editions.

Bibliography

Abertoni, Ettore A., Ezio Antonini & Renato Palmieri (eds), *La generazione degli anni difficili*, Bari, 1962.

Absalom, Roger, *A Strange Alliance: Aspects of escape and survival in Italy 1943–45*, Florence, 1991.

Absalom, Roger, 'Allied escapers and the contadini in occupied Italy (1943–5)', *Journal of Modern Italian Studies* 10, 2005.

Addis Saba, Marina, *Gioventù Italiana del Littorio*, Milan, 1973.

Addis Saba, Marina (ed), *La corporazione delle donne*, Florence, 1988.

Addis Saba, Marina, *Partigiane: Le Donne della resistenza,* Milan, 1998.

Addis Saba, Marina, *La Scelta: Ragazze partigiane, ragazze di Salò*, Rome, 2005.

Adduci, Nicola (ed), *Che il silenzio non sia silenzio*, Turin, 2003.

Adduci, Nicola, *Gli altri: Fascismo repubblicano e comunità nel Torinese 1943–45*,Turin, 2014

Adler, Franklin Hugh, 'Why Mussolini turned on the Jews', *Patterns of Prejudice*, Vol. 39, 2005.

Aga-Rossi, Elena, *L'Italia nella sconfitta*, Naples, 1985.

Aga-Rossi, Elena, *A nation collapses: The Italian surrender of September 1943*, Cambridge University Press, 2000.

Aga-Rossi, Elena, & Bradley F. Smith, *Operation Sunrise: La resa tedesca in Italia 2 maggio 1945*, Milan, 2005.

Agosti, Giorgio, & Dante Livio Bianco, *Un'amicizia partigiana: Lettere 1943–45*, Turin, 2007.

Alano, Jomarie, *A Life of Resistance: Ada Prospero Marchesini Gobetti (1902–1968)*, Rochester, 2016.

Alessandrini, Luca, & Matteo Pasetti, *1943: guerra e società*, Viella, 2015.

Allason, Barbara, *Memorie di un'antifascista 1919–1940.* Turin, 2005.

Alloisio, Mirella, et al., *Mille volte no. Voci di donne contro l'oppressione 8 Settembre 1943–25 Aprile 1945*, Rome, 1965.

Alloisio, Mirella, & Marta Ajo, *La donna nel socialismo Italiano. Fra cronica e storia*, Cosenza, 1978.

Alloisio, Mirella, & Giuliana Beltrami, *Volontarie della libertà*, Milan, 1981.

Amsallem, Daniela (ed), *Primo Levi: Actes du colloque international, Chambéry, Université Savoie Mont Blanc, 25–26 March 2015*, Chambéry, 2015.

Andrae, Friederich, *La Wehrmacht in Italia*, Munich, 1995.

Angier, Carole, *The Double Bond: Primo Levi, a Biography*, London, 2002.

Arbib, Gloria, & Giorgio Secchi, *Italiani insieme agli altri: Ebrei nella resistenza in Piemonte*, Turin, 2011.

Aspetti dell'attivitá femminile in Piemonte negli ultimi cento anni 1861–1961, Turin, 1962.

Aspetti della resistenza in Piemonte, Turin, 1977.

Augusto Monti nel centenario della nascita, Atti di convegno di studio, Turin, 9–10 May 1981, Turin, 1982.

Banfo, Emmanuela, & Piera Egidi Bouchard, *Ada Gobetti e i suoi cinque talenti*, Turin, 2014.

Bartoli, Domenico, *L'Italia si arrende: 8 Settembre 1943*, Milan, 1983.

Battaglia, Achille, *I giudici e la politica*, Bari, 1962.

Battaglia, Roberto, *The Story of the Italian Resistance*, Turin, 1957.

Battaglia, Roberto, *Un'uomo, un partigiano*, Turin, 1965.

Bedeschi, Giulio (ed.), *Fronte Italiano: c'ero anch'io*, Milan, 1987.

Behan, Tom, *The Italian Resistance: Fascists, guerrillas and the Allies*, London, 2009.

Benfante, Filippo, 'Carlo Levi: Direttore della Nazione del Popolo', *Mezzasecolo* 14, Turin, 2001–2002.

Berga, Ugo, *Diario partigiano*, Turin, 2003.

Bersano Begey, A., *Il servizio sanitario partigiano in Piemonte 1943–1945*, Turin, 1970.

Bertoldi, Silvio, *L'ultimo re, l'ultimo regina*, Milan, 2001.

Bertolo, Bruna, *Storia della valle di Susa*, Turin, 2009.

Bertolo, Bruna, *Donne nella resistenza in Piemonte*, Turin, 2014.

Bertolo, G., et al., *Operai e contadini nella crisi Italiana del 1943–44*, Milan, 1974.

Bessone, Vera, & Massimo Roccaforte, *Partigiane della libertà*, Rimini, 2015.

Bianco, Dante Livio, *Guerra partigiana*, Turin, 1954.

Boca, Federico del, *Il freddo, la paura e la fame*, Milan, 1966.

Boccalatte, Luciano (ed), *Un filo tenace: Lettere e memorie 1944–69: Willy Jervis, Lucilla Jervis Rochat, Giorgio Agosti*, Florence, 1998.

Boccalatte, Luciano, Giovanni de Luna & Bruno Maida (eds), *Torino in guerra 1940–45*, Turin, 1995.

Boccalatte, Luciano, Andrea d'Arrigo & Bruno Maida (eds), *Guida ai luoghi della guerra e della resistenza nella provincia di Torino*, Turin, 2006.

Bolaffi, Giulio, *Partigiani in Val di Susa: I nove diari di Aldo Laghi*, (ed. Chiara Colombini), Milan, 2014.

Bolaffi Benuzzi, Stella, *Un partigiano 'ribelle'*, Susa, 2010.

Bonacina, Giorgio, *Obiettivo: Italia: I bombardimenti aerei delle città italiane del 1940 al 1945*, Milan, 1970.

Bonomini, Luigi, et al. (eds), *Riservato a Mussolini: Notiziari giornalieri della Guardia Nazionale Repubblicana Novembre 1943–Giugno 1944*, Milan, 1974.

Bonsanti, Marta, *Giorgio e Silvia: Due vite a Torino tra antifascismo e resistenza*, Milan, 2004.

Borgis, Maria Elisa, *Resistenza nella valle di Susa*, Bussoleno (n.d.).

Bosworth, R. J. B., *Claretta: Mussolini's Last Lover*, London, 2017.

Bosworth, R. J. B., *Mussolini*, London, 2002.

Bosworth, R. J. B., *Mussolini's Italy: Life under the Fascist Dictatorship*, London, 2005.

Bouchard, Piera Egidi, *Frida e i suoi fratelli*, Turin, 2003.

Bouchard, Piera Egidi, *Eppur bisogna andar . . .*, Turin, 2005.

Bravo, Anna, & Daniele Jalla, *La vita offesa*, Milan, 1986.

Bravo, Anna, 'Armed and Unarmed: Struggles without weapons in Europe and Italy,' *Journal of Modern Italian Studies* 10, 2005.

Bruzzone, Anna Maria, & Rachele Farina, *La resistenza tacuita: Dodici vite di partigiane piemontesi*, Milan, 1976.

Bussoni, Maria, *1943: I giorni più cupi*, Parma, 2013.

Calamandrei, Piero, *Uomini e città della resistenza*, Rome, 1955.

Calamandrei, Piero, *Diario Vol. 1 e 2, 1935–1945*, Rome, 2015.

Cappellano, Filippo, & Salvatore Orlando, *L'esercito italiano dall'armistizio alla guerra di liberazione: 8 Settembre 1943–25 Aprile 1945*, Rome, 2005.

Carcano, Giancarlo, *Torino antifascista*, Turin, 1993.

Carlotti, Anna Lisa, *Italia 1939–1945: Storia e memoria*, Milan, 1996.

Carmagnola, Piero, *Vecchi partigiani miei*, Milan, 2005.

Caruso, Tiziana, *L'occupazione tedesca a Torino attraverso i rapporti della Militärkommandantur Ottobre 1943–Settembre 1944*, Thesis, Turin, 2004.

Casadio, Quinto, *Una resistenza rimasta nell'ombra: L'8 settembre 1943 e gli internati militari Italiani in Germania*, Imolo, 2004.

Cavaglion, Alberto, *La scuola ebraica a Torino 1938–1943*, Turin, 1993.

Cavaglion, Alberto (ed.), *La moralità armata: Studi su Emanuele Artom*, Milan, 1993.

Cavaglion, Alberto, 'Torino ebraico', in B. Ganglio & Riccardo Marchio (eds), *Cattolici, ebrei e evangelici nella guerra*, Milan, 1994.

Cavaglion, Alberto, 'Foreign Jews in the Western Alps 1938–1943', *Journal of Modern Italian Studies* 10, 2005.

Cavarra, Maria Lea, *Quando si dice staffetta . . .*, Modena, 1982.

Cerchia, Giovanni, & Giuseppe Pandini, *Italia spezzata: guerra elinea Gustav in Molise*, Naples, 2008.

Ceva, Bianca, *Cinque anni di storia italiana 1940–1945*, Milan, 1964.

Chevallard, Carlo, *Cronache del tempo di guerra: Diario 1942–45*, Turin, 2005.

Chiappano, Alessandra, *Voci della resistenza ebraica Italiana*, Aosta, 2011.

Chiavi, E. C., *Condemned Pasts: A topography of memory from the Le Nuove Prison*, Turin, Thesis, London, 2006.

Chirico, Paolo, 'Il contributo della polizia alla guerra di liberazione in Piemonte', *Mezzosecolo* 14, 2001–2.

Cocco, Mara, 'Donne e esercito: le 'volontarie' di Mussolini nella Republica Sociale', *Mezzosecolo* 12, 1978.

Collotti, Enzo, *L'amministrazione tedesca dell'Italia occupata*, Milan, 1963.

Collotti, Enzo, Renato Sandri & Frediano Seni (eds), *Dizionario della resistenza*, Turin, 2000.

Contadini e Partigiani. Atti del Convegno storico Asti 14–16 Dicembre 1984, Alessandria, 1986.

Cooke, Philip (ed.) *The Italian Resistance: An Anthology*, Manchester, 1997.

Cooke, Philip, *The Legacy of the Italian Resistance*, New York, 2011.

Corner, Paul, *The Fascist Party and Popular Opinion in Mussolini's Italy*, Oxford, 2012.

Crain Metz, Naomi, *L'illusione della parità*, Turin, 2013.

Craveri, Raimondo, *La campagna d'Italia e i servizi secreti: La storia dell'ORI 1943–45* Milan, 1980.

Creonti, Fernando, *Memorie di vita clandestina*, Turin, 1973.

Crippa, Arianna Rachele, *Pavese editore*, Milan, 2014.

Davidson, Alastair, & Steve Wright, '*Never Give In': The Italian Resistance and Politics*, New York, 1998.

Deakin, F. W., *The brutal friendship: Mussolini, Hitler and the Fall of Italian Fascism*, London, 1962.

Delzell, Charles F., *Mussolini's Enemies: The Italian Anti-Fascist Resistance*, Princeton, 1961.

Diena, Marisa, *Un intenso impegno civile*, Turin (n.d.).

Dondi, Mirco, 'Azione di guerra e potere partigiano nel dopo liberazione', *Italia Contemporanea*, September 1992.

Donne Piemontesi nella lotta di liberazione, Turin (n.d.).

D'Orsi, Angelo, *La cultura a Torino tra le due guerre*, Turin, 2000.

Duggan, Christopher, *Fascist voices: An Intimate History of Mussolini's Italy*, London, 2012.

Dunnage, Jonathan (ed.), *After the war: Violence, Justice, Continuity and Renewal in Italian Society*, Hull, 1999.

Einaudi, Giulio, *Frammenti di memoria*, Milan, 1988.

Ellwood, David, *Italy 1943–45*, Leicester, 1985.

Etnasi, Ferdinando (ed.), *Donne italiane nella resistenza*, Turin, 1966.

Fabbrini, Maria Rosa, *Bonsoir Madame la Lune: La vita incompiuta di Silvia Pons*, Turin, 2012.

Fabbrini, Maria Rosa, *Mille famiglie a Torre Pellice*, Saluzzo, 2017.

Falaschi, Giovanni, *La resistenza armata nella narrativa Italiana*, Turin, 1976.

Farrell, Nicholas, *Mussolini: A New Life*, London, 2003.

Favelle, Brigitte, *Natalia Ginzburg: Temoin de son temps et temoin d'elle même*, Thesis, Aix-Marseille, 1995.

Favvetto, Sergio, *Una trama sottile: FIAT fabbrica, missioni alleati e resistenza*, Turin, 2017.

Floria, Michele, *Resistenza e liberazione nella provincia di Torino 1943–45*, Turin, 1995.

Foa, Vittorio, *Il cavallo e la torre*, Turin, 1991.

Foa, Vittorio, *Lavori in corso 1943–1946*, Turin, 1999.

Foot, M. R. D., *SOE: An outline history of the Special Operations Executive 1940–1946*, London, 1999.

Le formazioni G&L nella resistenza. Atti del convegno Milano 5–6 Maggio 1995, Rome, 1995.

Fraddosio, Maria, La donna e la guerra, *Storia Contemporanea Anno XX*, 1989.

Fraddosio, Maria, Le donne e il fascismo: Ricerche e problemi di interpretazione, *Storia Contemporanea Anno XX*, 1989.

Fraddosio, Maria, La mobililitazione femminile: I gruppi fascisti repubblicani femminili e il SAF, in *Annali della Fondazione Luigi Micheletti*, 2, Brescia, 1996.

Franzinelli, Mimmo, *Delatori: Spie e confidenti anonimi: l'arma secreta del regime fascista*, Milan, 2001.

Franzinelli, Mimmo, *La Repubblica del Duce 1943–45*, Milan, 2007.

Franzinelli, Mimmo, *Disertori, Una storia mal raccontata della seconda guerra mondiale*, Milan, 2016.

Fucci, Franco, *Spie per la libertà*, Milan, 1983.

Fusi, Valdo, *Fiori rossi a Martinetto: Il processo di Torino Aprile 1944*, Turin, 1996.

Gamba, Aldo, Cenni sui servizi military e politici di spionaggio e di informazione, *Annali della Fondazione Luigi Micheletti*, 2, Brescia, 1986.

Gambetti, Federico, *L'ultima leva: La scelta dei giovani dopo l'8 Settembre*, Bologna, 1996.

Garibaldi, Luciano, *Le soldatesse di Mussolini*, Milan, 1995.

Gariglio, Bartolo (ed.), 'Vita religiosa nella seconda guerra mondiale', *Mezzosecolo* 10, 1993.

Garrone, Alessandro Galante, *I miei maggiori*, Milan, 1984.

Gasco, Anna (ed.), *La guerra alla guerra: Storie di donne a Torino e in Piemonte tra il 1940 e il 1945*, Turin, 2007.

Gay Rochat, Donatella, *La resistenza nelle valli Valdesi 1943–44*, Turin, 1969.

Gerosa, Guido, *Le compagne*, Milan, 1979.

Gillette, Aaron, 'The origins of the Manifesto of Racial Scientists', in *Journal of Modern Italian Studies*, 9, 2010.

Ginzburg, Leone, *Scritti*, Turin, 1964.

Ginzburg, Leone, *Lettere del confino 1940–43*, ed. Luisa Mangoni, Turin, 2004.

Giovana, Mario, *La resistenza in Piemonte: storia del CLN regionale*, Milan, 1962.

Giovana, Mario, *Torino: la città e i signori 'FIAT'*, Milan, 1977.

Giovana, Mario, *Le nuove camicie nere*, Turin, 1996.

Giua, Lisetta, *E andata così*, Palermo, 2004.

Giua, Michele, *Ricordi di un ex-detenuto politico 1935–43*, Turin, 1945.

Giuliani, Fulvia, *Donne d'Italia: le ausiliarie nella RSI*, Rome, 1952.

Givardi, Luisa, 'Il partigiano imputato: Sentenze contro i partigiani piemontesi 1946–60', *Mezzosecolo* 12, 1978.

Gobetti, Ada, *Diario Partigiano*, Turin, 1956.

Gobetti, Ada, & Benedetto Croce, 'Carteggio 1928–52', *Mezzosecolo* 7, Turin, 1987–9.

Golin, Laura, *La storia dell'Olivetti ai tempi di Adriano*, Thesis, Venice, 2009.

Grazia, Victoria di, *The Culture of Consent: Mass organisation of leisure in fascist Italy*, Cambridge, MA, 1981.

Grazia, Victoria di, *How Fascism Ruled Women: Italy 1922–45*, Berkeley, 1992.

Grimaldi, U. Alfassio, & Marina Addis Saba, *Cultura a passo romano*, Milan, 1983.

Griner, Massimiliano, *La 'Banda Koch': Il reparto speciale di polizia 1943–44*, Turin, 2000.

Griner, Massimiliano, *La 'pupilla del Duce': La legione autonoma mobile Ettore Mutti*, Turin, 2004.

Guerrini, Martina, *Donne contro: ribelli, sovversive, antifasciste*, Milan, 2003.

Guidetti Serra, Bianca, *Primo Levi, l'amico*, Turin, 1987.

Guidetti Serra, Bianca, *Compagne*, Vols 1 & 2, Turin, 1997.

Guidetti Serra, Bianca, *Bianca la rossa*, Turin, 2009.

Helstosky, Carol F., 'Fascist Food Policies', *Journal of Modern Italian Studies* 9, 2004.

Hibbert, Christopher, *Mussolini: The Rise and Fall of Il Duce*, London, 1962.

Innocenti, Marco, *L'Italia del 1943: Come eravamo nell'anno in cui crollò il fascismo*, Milan, 1993.

Isnenghi, Mario, *Le guerre degli Italiani. Parole, immagini, ricordi 1848–1945*, Bologna, 2005.

Italia e la Gran Bretagna nella lotta di liberazione, Atti del Convegno di Bagni di Lucca Aprile 1975, Florence, 1977.

Kelly, Michael C., *The Failure of the Partisan Dream: Italian ex-partisans and post-liberation politics in Piedmont 1943–48*, PhD Thesis, Melbourne, 2004.

Kesselring, Field Marshal, *Memoirs*, London, 1953.

Klinkhammer, Lutz, *L'occupazione Tedesca in Italia 1943–45*, Turin, 1993.

Knox, McGregor, *Hitler's Italian Allies: Royal armed forces, Fascist regime and the war of 1940–43*, Cambridge, 2000.

Koon, Tracy H., *Believe, Obey, Fight: Political socialisation of youth in Fascist Italy, 1922–1943*, North Carolina, 1985.

Lazzero, Ricciotti, *Le SS Italiane*, Milan, 1982.

Lazzero, Ricciotti, *Le Brigate Nere*, Milan, 1983.

Legnani, Massimo, & Ferruccio Vendramini (eds), *Guerra: guerra di liberazione, guerra civile*, Milan, 1990.

Levi, Carlo, *Un'esperienza culturale e politica nella Torino degli anni trenta*, Turin (n.d.).

Levi, Fabio (ed.), *Le case e le cose: la persecutazione degli ebrei Torinesi 1938–45*, Turin, 1998.

Levi, Paolo Momigliano, & Ersilia Alessandrone Perona, *La presenza invisibile: Donne Guerra Montagna*, Florence, 2008.

Longo, Luigi, *Un popolo alla macchia*, Rome, 1947.

Luna, Giovanni de, *Storia del Partito d'Azione 1942–47*, Milan, 1982.

Luna, Giovanni de, *Le formazioni GL nella resistenza*, Milan, 1985.

Luna, Giovanni de, *Donne in oggetto: l'antifascismo nella società Italiana 1922–39*, Turin, 1995.

Luna, Giovanni de, & Marco Revelli, *Fascismo antifascismo: le idee, le identità*, Florence, 1995.

Lussu, Joyce, *L'uomo che voleva nascere donna*, Milan, 1978.

Lussu, Joyce, *Lotte, ricordi e altro*, Rome, 1992.

Macciocchi, Maria Antonietta, *La donna 'nera': Consenso femminile e fascismo*, Milan, 1976.

Macmillan, Harold, *War Diaries: Politics and War in the Mediterranean, January 1943–May 1945*, London, 1984.

Mafai, Miriam, *Pane nero: Donne e vita quotidiana nella seconda guerra mondiale*, Milan, 1987.

Maida, Bruno (ed.), *Guerra e società nella provincia di Torino*, Turin, 2007.

Maida, Bruno, *Prigionieri della memoria: Storia di due stragi della liberazione*, Milan, 2002.

Malan, Roberto, *Amici, fratelli, compagni: Memorie di un Valdese del XX secolo*, Cuneo, 1996.

Malgeri, Francesco, 'La chiesa di fronte al RSI', *Storia e memoria* No 2, Brescia, 1986.

Malvezzi, Piero, & Giovanni Pirelli (eds), *Lettere di condannati a morte della resistenza Italiana*, Turin, 1973.

Mangoni, Luisa, *Pensare i libri: La casa editrice Einaudi degli anni trenta agli anni sessanta*, Turin, 1999.

Marabotto, Giuseppe, *Un prete in galera*, Turin, 1964.

Marazio, Zelmira, *Il mio fascismo*, Baiso, 2005.

Marchesi, Luigi, et al., *Per la libertà: il contributo militare Italiano al servizio informazione alleato 8 Settembre 1943–25 Aprile 1945*, Milan, 1995.

Mastrogiovanni, Salvatore, *Un protestante nella resistenza*, Turin, 1962.

Matta, Tristano, 'La risiera di San Sabba', Italia 1939–45, in Anna Lisa Carlotti (ed.), *Storia e memoria*, Milan, 1996.

Meldini, Piero, *Sposa e madre esemplare*, Rimini, 1975.

Mercuri, Lamberto (ed.), *Intelligence: propaganda, missioni e 'operazioni speciali' degli alleati in Italia*, Rome, (n.d.).

'Missioni Alleate e Partigiani autonomi', Conference, Turin, 21–22 October 1978.

Morero, Vittorio (ed.) *La Chiesa Pinerolese durante la resistenza*, Pinerolo (n.d.).

Morgan, Philip, *The Fall of Mussolini: Italy, the Italians and the Second World War*, Oxford, 2007.

Motti, Lucia, & Marilena Rossi Caponeri (eds), *Accademiste a Orvieto: Donne e educazione fisica nell'Italia fascista 1932–43*, Perugia, 1996.

Munzi, Ulderico, *Donne di Salò: La vicenda delle ausiliare della Repubblica Sociale*, Milan, 1999.

Nasini, Claudia, *Una guerra di spie*, Trento, 2012.

Neri Serneri, Simone (ed.), *1914–1945: L'Italia nella guerra europea dei trent'anni*, Rome, 2016.

Oliva, Gianni, *La resistenza alle porte di Torino*, Milan, 1989.

Oliva, Gianni, *La resa dei conti, Aprile–Maggio 1945: Foibe, Piazzale Loreto e giustizia partigiana*, Milan, 1999.

Oliva, Gianni, *L'Italia del silenzio, 8 Settembre 1945: storia del paese che non ha fatto conti con il proprio passato*, Milan, 2013.

Ombra, Marisa, *La bella politica: La resistenza, 'Noi Donne', il femminismo*, Turin, 2009.

Ottolenghi, Massimo, *Per un pezzo di patria*, Turin, 2009.

Pansa, Gianpaolo, *L'esercito di Salò nei rapporti riservati della GNR 1943–44*, Milan, 1969.

Paoletti, Fiorella, *La resistenza 'dalla parte di lei'*, Thesis, Turin, 2012.

Parri, Ferruccio, *Sessant'anni di storia Italiana*, Bari, 1983.

Il Partito d'Azione e l'assistenza ai prigionieri alleati dall'8 Settembre 1943 all'agosto 1944, Rome, 1946.

Pavone, Claudio, *A Civil War: A History of the Italian Resistance*, London, 2014.

Peli, Santo, *Storia della resistenza in Italia*, Turin, 2006.

Perona, Gianni, 'Memoria di Lucilla Jervis', *Mezzosecolo* 12, 1997–8.

Perona, Gianni, & Barbara Berruti (eds), *Alpi in guerra 1939–45*, Chivasso, 2004.

Pesce, Giovanni, *Senza tregua: La guerra dei GAP*, Milan, 1967.

Petacco, Arrigo (ed.), *1943: giorno per giorno attraverso i bollettini del Comando Supremo*, Milan, 1993.

Peyrot, Bruna, *Resistere nelle valli Valdesi*, Turin, 1995.

Pflug, Maja, *Natalia Ginzburg*, Milan, 1997.

Pintor, Giaime, *Doppio diario 1936–43*, Turin, 1978.

Pizzardo, Tina, *Senza pensare due volte*, Bologna, 1996.

Ponzani, Michela, 'Trials of Partisans in the Italian Republic: the consequences of the elections of 18 April 1948', *Modern Italy* 16, 2011.

Ponzani, Michela, *Guerra alle donne partigiane, vittime di stupro, 'amanti del nemico'*, Torino, 2012.

Prearo, Antonio, *Terra ribelle 1943–45*, Turin, 1995.

Quatela, Antonio, *Hotel Gestapo: Milano Settembre 1943–Aprile 1945*, Milan, 2016.

Radeschi, Mina (ed.), *Frida Malan e il segno del suo tempo*, Turin, 2010.

Rainero, Romain H. (ed.), *I prigionieri militari Italiani durante la seconda guerra mondiale, Aspetti e problemi storici*, Milan, 1985.

Ravaioli, Viriana, *La partecipazione degli ebrei nella resistenza in Piemonte*, Thesis, Turin, 1997.

Ravera, Camilla, *La donna Italiana dal primo al secondo risorgimento*, Rome, 1965.

Renza, Francesca, *Letteratura della resistenza: protagoniste e paesaggio*, Thesis, Turin, 2005.

'La Resistenza Tacuita', Conference, 8 March 2004, Rome, 2006.

Revelli, Nuto, *La guerra dei poveri*, Turin, 1962.

Revelli, Nuto, *Il prete giusto*, Turin, 1998.

Rora 1943–45, Lavoro degli alunni.

Ruggero, Padre, *La testimonianza: carcere e resistenza*, Pinerolo, 2003.

Sacco, Marisa, *La pelliccia di agnello bianco: La gioventù d'azione nella resistenza*, Turin, 2008.

Salvadori, Massimo, *Resistenza e azione*, London, 1958.

Sasso, Chiara, & Massimo Molinero, *Una storia nella storia e altre storie*, Condove, 2000.

Schreiber, Gerhard, *La vendetta Tedesca 1943–45: Le rappresaglie Naziste in Italia*, Milan, 2000.

Schwarz, Guri (ed.), *Emanuele Artom: Diario di un partigiano ebreo, Gennaio 1940–Febraio 1944*, Turin, 2008.

Scurati, Antonio, *Il tempo migliore della nostra vita*, Milan, 2015.

Sebastian, Peter, *I servizi secreti speciali Britannici e l'Italia 1940–45*, Rome, 1986.

Secchia, Pietro, & Filippo Frassati, *La resistenza e gli alleati*, Milan, 1962.

Slaughter, Jane, *Women and the Italian Resistance*, Colorado, 1997.

Sprigge, Cecil, *Benedetto Croce: Man and Thinker*, Cambridge, 1952.

Stafford, David, *Mission Accomplished: SOE Italy 1943–45*, London, 2011.

Stille, Alexander, *Benevolence and betrayal: Five Italian Jewish families under Fascism*, London, 1992.

Storchi, Massimo, *Il sangue dei vincitori*, Rome, 2008.

Storchi, Massimo, in Philip Cooke & Ben H. Shepherd (eds), *European Resistance in the Second World War*, Barnsley, 2013.

Testori, Silvana, *Lotta partigiana e amnistia*, Thesis, Turin, 1980.

Thomson, Ian, *Primo Levi*, London, 2002.

Tognavini, Ivan, *Kesselring e le stragi nazifasciste*, Tuscany, 2002.

Tompkins, Peter, *A Spy in Rome*, London, 1962.

Tonizzi, M. Elisabetta, Nazisti contro i civili: le stragi in Italia 1943–45, *Storia e memoria*, Milan, No 1 Settembre 2001.

Torino 1938–45, Una guida per la memoria, Turin, 2000.

Tosca, Michele, *I ribelli siamo noi: Diario di Torino nella Repubblica Sociale Italiana*, Collegno (n.d.).

Trabucchi, Alessandro, *I vinti hanno sempre torto*, Turin, 1947.

Trabucco, Angela, *Resistenza in Val Chisone e nel Pinerolese*, Pinerolo, 1948.

Tranfoglia, Nicola, & Albertina Vittoria, *Storia degli editori Italiani*, Rome, 2000.

Trentin, Bruno, *Diario di guerra Settembre–Novembre 1943*, Rome, 2008.

Trentin, Silvio, *Il clero e la RSI. Annali della Fondazione Luigi Micheletti*, Brescia, 1986.

Treves, Benevenuta (ed.), *Tre vite: studi e memorie di Emilio, Emanuele, Ennio Artom*, Turin, 1954.

Tudor, Malcolm, *Prisoners and Partisans: Escape and Evasion in WWII Italy*, Newtown, 2006.

Tudor, Malcolm, *Special Force: SOE and the Italian Resistance 1943–45*, Newtown, 2004,

Turinetti, Elena, *Donne in carcere 1940–45*, Thesis, Turin, 2004.

Turinetti, Giuseppe, *Clero, guerra e resistenza nella diocesi di Torino 1940–45*, Omegna, 1996.

Uboldi, Raffaello, *25 Aprile 1945: I giorni dell'odio e della libertà*, Milan, 2004.

Vaccarino, Giorgio, Carla Gobetti & Romolo Gobbi (eds), *L'insurrezione a Torino*, Parma, 1968.

Vai, Elena, *La scia del sangue: Le repressioni Tedesche nella fase finale della guerra in Piemonte*, Thesis, Turin, 1997.

Valiani, Leo, *Tutte le strade conducono a Roma*, Florence, 1947.

Valiani, Leo, et al., *Azionisti Cattolici e comunisti nella resistenza*, Milan, 1971.

Veccho, Giorgio (ed.), *Le suore e la resistenza*, Milan, 2010.

Venturi, Franco, *Guerra partigiana*, Turin, 1954.

Venturoli, Cinzia, *La guerra sotto il sasso: Popolazione, Tedeschi, partigiani 1940–45*, Bologna, 1999.

Vermicelli, Gino, *La vita nelle formazioni partigiane*, Milan, 1994.

Viallet, Jean Pierre, 'Les vallées vaudoises, du Fascisme à la Resistance', in Ettore Passerin d'Entrèves (ed.), *Guerra e Resistenza nelle regioni alpini occidentali: 1940–45*, Milan, 1980.

Visani, Alessandro, 'Italian reactions to the racial laws of 1938 as seen through the classified files of the Ministry of Popular Culture', *Journal of Modern Italian Studies* 11, 2006.

Voltero Fin, Tino, *Resistenza partigiana nelle valle di Lanzo, nel Canavese e in Val di Susa*, Turin, 1994.

Wilson, Perry R., 'Saints and heroines: rewriting the history of Italian women in the Resistance', in T. Kirk & A McElligott (eds)., *Opposing Fascism*, Cambridge, 1999.

Wilson, Perry, *The Clockwork Factory: Women and Work in Fascist Italy*, Oxford, 1993.

Woolf, S. J., *The Rebirth of Italy 1943–50*, London, 1972.

Young, Allen, La missione Stevens e l'insurrezione a Torino. Atti di Convegno ISTORETO 1985

Zangrandi, Ruggero, *Il lungo viaggio attraverso il Fascismo*, Milan, 1962.

Zangrandi, Ruggero, *1943: 25 Luglio–8 Settembre*, Milan, 1964.

Notes

Preface

p. xix   'On the evening . . .' See Guidetti Serra, 1997.

p. xxii   'There were four women . . .' For Ada, see her *Diario Partigiano* 1956 and Alano 2016; for Bianca, *Bianca la rossa* 2009, *Primo Levi* 1987 and *Compagne* 1997; for Frida, Bouchard 2003 and 2005; for Silvia, Bonsanti 2004 and Fabbrini 2012.

p. xxiii   'Next day, she told . . .' Gasco (ed.), 2007, p. 139.

1: A Roman coup

p. 3   'Almost two years . . .' Good accounts of the coup against Mussolini are to be found in Bosworth 2002 and 2005; Hibbert 1962.

p. 4   'After three years . . .' See Revelli 1962.

p. 4   'Rome itself had just been . . .' See Bussoni 2013.

p. 4   'On 6 June . . .' Bosworth 2005, p. 492.

p. 6   'Before he left for . . .' Mafai 1987, p. 151.

p. 7   'And for the women . . .' For accounts of women's lives, see Grimaldi & Addis Saba 1983; Koon 1985.

p. 8   'In this authoritarian . . .' See Fraddosio 1989; Macciocchi 1976.

p. 9   'Boys, anti-feminist . . .' Meldini 1975, p. 42.

p. 10   'Duce! Duce! . . .' See Addis Saba 1973, 1988, 2005.

p. 10   'Pale, gaunt . . .' In *Critica Fascista* 1931, L'ideale della donna fascista

p. 10   'What mattered was . . .' Fraddosio 1989, p. 1150.

p. 10   'During the 1920s . . .' See Guerrini 2003.

p. 11   'Turin, with its . . .' *Il Ponte August–September 1949.*

p. 12   'Shortages of everything . . .' See Slaughter 1997.

p. 13   'Long before the war . . .' See D'Orsi 2000.

p. 13   'Ada's father . . .' For a full biography of Ada Gobetti, see Alano 2016.

p. 14   'But in Croce . . .' See *Mezzosecolo* 7 and 10.

p. 16   'For their part . . .' See Mangoni 1999; Einaudi 1988.

p. 18   'Bianca herself . . .' For an account of her life, see Guidetti Serra 2009.

p. 20   'It was there . . .' Angier 2002.

p. 21   'Searching for an animal . . .' Alano 2016, p. 108.

p. 22   'Then came Mussolini's . . .' For good accounts of wartime Turin, see Adduci 2003, 2014; Boccalatte, de Luna, Maida (eds) 1995.

p. 22   'Soon, Le Nuove . . .' See Turinetti 2004.

2: Interlude

p. 25   'In a report to . . .' Macmillan 1984, p. 219.

p. 26   'All over Italy . . .' see Etnasi 1966; Absalom 1991.

p. 26   'Since the term armistice . . .' Aga-Rossi 2000, p. 126.

p. 26   'An aide-memoire . . .' Delzell 1961, p. 248.

p. 27   'At 7.43 p.m. . . .' Petacco (ed.) 1993, p. 222.

p. 27   'There was a flicker . . .' Oliva 2013, p. 35.

p. 28   'The royal family . . .' See Bussoni 2013.

p. 28   'With no instructions . . .' See Klinkhammer 1993.

p. 28   'In just a few hours . . .' See Pavone 2014.

p. 28   'We had not expected . . .' See Young 1985.

p. 28   'Eisenhower spoke . . .' Letter to George Marshall 13 September 1943.

p. 29   'There was some fighting . . .' Zangrandi 1964, p. 528. For the collapse of Italy, see Collotti 1963; Isnenghi 2005; Bartoli 1983; Aga-Rossi 1985, 2000.

p. 29   'In Cephalonia . . .' Bosworth 2005, p. 508.

p. 29   '"Italy's fate" . . .' Collotti 1963, p. 99.

p. 31   'A song was composed . . .' See Davidson & Wright 1998.

p. 31   '"Their odyssey" . . .' L'Unità 15 September 1946.

p. 32   '"A little bloodshed" . . .' Aga-Rossi 2000, p. 53.

p. 33   'It took Foa . . .' See Foa 1991.

p. 33   'She told him . . .' See Giua 2004.

p. 34   'And they looked . . .' See Adduci 2003.

p. 35   'When the officers . . .' Fondo Allason, Centro Studi Gobetti Box F.

p. 36   'Not far away . . .' Trentin 2008, p. 75.

3: Bursting into life

p. 38   'That day, dozens . . .' Cooke (ed.) 1997, p. 62.

p. 39   'At the wheel was . . .' Ottolenghi 2009, p. 101.

p. 39   'All through the day . . .' See Bartoli 1983; Venturoli 1999.

p. 39   'The commanding officer . . .' Young 1985, p. 22.

p. 40   'The Alps that rise . . .' See Viallet 1980.

p. 40   'Years of unpopularity . . .' See Peyrot 1995.

p. 42   'Since the nineteenth century . . .' See Fabbrini 2017.

p. 43   'As news of . . .' See Malan 1996.

p. 43   'Frida Malan and Silvia . . .' See the biographies of Silvia Pons by Fabbrini 2012 and Bonsanti 2004; and of Frida Malan by Bouchard 2003.

p. 45   'One day after classes, as she . . .' Piera Egidi Bouchard interview with author. Also Frida Malan interview 1991 in ISTORETO, Turin.

p. 48   'Tutti politici . . .' see Diena (n.d.).

p. 50 'She, like Frida . . .' Matilde di Pietrantonio interview in ISTORETO 2 Februray 2005.

p. 51 'It was an explosive . . .' de Luna & Revelli 1995, p. 107.

p. 51 'As Agosti put it . . .' See Agosti & Bianco 2007.

p. 53 One evening the phone . . .' See Banfo & Bouchard 2014.

4: A war zone

p. 55 'In the autumn of . . .' Maida 2007, p. 52.

p. 55 'Towards the Latin . . .' Schreiber 2000, p. 39.

p. 55 'In the "total war" . . .' See Tonizzi 2001; Cooke 1997.

p. 55 'Every day, between . . .' Andrae 1995, p. 177.

p. 56 'What all agreed . . .' See Cerchia & Pandini 2008.

p. 56 'Only 36, 000 . . .' Pavone 2014, p. 55; see also Casadio 2004; Caruso 2004.

p. 57 'It had taken . . .' A very good account of Mussolini's rescue is to be found in Duggan 2012.

p. 57 'On their first . . .' Pavone 2014, p. 284.

p. 58 'To run his new . . .' Lazzero 1982, p. 13; see also Deakin 1962.

p. 61 'The Allies – behaving . . .' Aga-Rossi 1985, p. 113.

p. 62 'Anthony Eden and . . .' For accounts of British attitudes, see Ellwood 1985; Duggan 2012.

p. 62 'A Foreign Office report . . .' FO 893/369.

p. 63 'In July 1940 . . .' Sebastian 1986, p. 90.

p. 64 'While both the British and . . .' Salvadori 1958, p. 200.

p. 64 'With the first wave . . .' See Craveri 1980.

p. 66 'For the next twenty . . .' See Maida 2007; Adduci 2014; Caruso 2004.

p. 68 'The small town of Boves . . .' See Giovana 1962, 1996; Revelli 1962.

p. 70 'Further proof . . .' See Behan 2009.

p. 71 'Into them played . . .' *Il Ponte* January 1995.

p. 71 'Rather, it was a matter . . .' Falaschi 1976, p. 4.

5: Making lions

p. 73 'It seemed to her . . .' Bouchard 2003, p. 94.

p. 73 '"We had," wrote Roberto . . .' Malan 1996, p. 93.

p. 75 'A friend of Frida's . . .' See Boccalatte (ed.) 1998.

p. 78 'They came in shorts . . .' Zangrandi 1962, p. 12.

p. 78 'But lions can . . .' Pavone 2014, p. 172.

p. 78 '"We are" noted one . . .' See Schwarz 2008.

p. 82 'She was a woman . . .' Valiani 1947, p. 106.

p. 84 'Very few of the men . . .' See Neri Serneri (ed.) 2016.

p. 85 'The Partito d'Azione . . .' See Venturi 1954.

p. 85 'These friends, au . . .' Garrone 1984, p. 174.

p. 86 'There was talk of . . .' See Wilson 1999; Cooke (ed.) 1997.

p. 87 'After the general . . .' See Parri 1983.

p. 87 'As the autumn wore . . .' See Ellwood 1985; Craveri 1980; Young 1985.

p. 88 'A steady stream . . .' National Archives J/IT/7715.

p. 88 'The Allies made it . . .' Neri Serneri (ed.) 2016, p. 150.

p. 89 'It was no longer . . .' See Giovana 1962.

p. 89 'In the mountains . . .' Revelli 1962, p. 125.

6: The *piccoli geni*

p. 90 'But the racial laws . . .' For good accounts of Italy and anti-Semitism, see Levi 1998; Cavaglion 1994; Angier 2002; Thomson 2002; Arbib & Secchi 2011; Chiappano 2011.

p. 91 'One of Italian . . .' *Il Lambello* 10 June 1941.

p. 93 'Frida's particular . . .' See Treves (ed.) 1954; Cavaglion 1993.

p. 94 'where its Jewish community . . .' Levi, in *Mezzosecolo* 1993.

p. 96 'In November, General . . .' See Cerchia 2008; Pavone 2014.

p. 96 'A Piedmontese girl . . .' Marilda Musacchio interview with author.

p. 96 'By this stage . . .' See Klinkhammer 1993; Collotti 1963.

p. 97 'It was not, however . . .' See Favvetto 2017.

p. 98 'New Fascism was to . . .' See Innocenti 1993.

p. 98 'Hearing of the massacre . . .' Pavone 2014, p. 302.

p. 99 'many of these were boys . . .' Pansa 1969, p. 20.

p. 99 'Alongside the militia . . .' See Lazzero 1982, 1983.

p. 100 'Prince Valerio Julio Borghese . . .' See Gamba 1986.

p. 100 'Colombo's men . . .' See Griner 2004.

p. 101 'The water is cloudy . . .' 'Pioggia di Novembre' 1943.

p. 102 'She was continuing . . .' See Levi & Alessandrone Perona 2008.

p. 103 'In Susa, German . . .' See Berga 2003; Borgis (n.d.).

p. 104 'They decided that what . . .' See Bertolo 2009.

p. 105 'From the late 1930s . . .' See Cavaglion 2005.

p. 105 'proved little more welcoming . . .' By the end of the war, Switzerland had turned back 6,000 Jews trying to cross from Italy.

p. 105 'Though the Fascist . . .' Franzinelli 2007 p. 7, 2001 p. 174.

p. 107 'Emanuele had been . . .' See Schwartz 2008; also Schwartz interview with author.

p. 110 'Levi had never fired . . .' Thomson 2002, p. 139; see also Amsallem 2015.

7: A little woman

p. 112 'I am a woman . . .' *Sentinella Partigiana* 4 April 1945.

p. 112 'What had started . . .' For good accounts of women in the Resistance, see Bertolo 2014; Alloisio & Beltrami 1981; Gasco (ed.) 2007; Guidetti Serra 1997; Slaughter 1997; Fraddosio 1989, 1996; Addis Saba 1998; Bruzzone & Farina 1976.

p. 112 '"I hate neutrality" . . .' See Paoletti 2011.

p. 116 'Lisetta was busy . . .' See Giua 2004; also Anna and Lisabetta Foa interview with author.

p. 116 'What all would remember . . .' Bertolo 2014, p. 33.

p. 116 'They were instructed . . .' Etnasi (ed.) 1966, p. 251; see also di Grazia 1992.

p. 117 '"They work continually" . . .' Bravo 2005, p. 482.

p. 118 'A story did the rounds . . .' See Crain Metz 2013; Renza 2005.

p. 118 'As winter set in . . .' Diena (n.d.). p. 51.

p. 119 'One of the oldest . . .' See Ravaioli 1997.

p. 119 'Though small and frail-looking . . .' See Garrone 1984.

p. 121 'Turin, traditionally . . .' Aspetti dell'attività femminile 1962, p. 95.

p. 122 'Suor Giuseppina was round . . .' Felice Taglienti interview with author.

p. 123 'She found sick . . .' See Ruggero 2003.

p. 123 'The men were forbidden . . .' Chiavi 2006, p. 71.

p. 125 'But then he showed . . .' GDD founding charter, November 1943.

p. 126 'Turin was the perfect . . .' See Guidetti Serra 1997.

p. 126 'But their sense of . . .' See Alloisio et al. 1965.

p. 126 'Silvia had placed . . .' See Bonsanti 2004; Fabbrini 2012.

p. 127 'Was this shared "spirit" . . .' Bouchard 2003, p. 7.

p. 128 'They kept asking . . .' See Bertolo 2014.

p. 130 'These were Mussolini's . . .' See Fraddosio 1996; Garibaldi 1995; Munzi 1999.

p. 130 'She would be a little . . .' Cocco 1978, p. 307.

p. 132 'Describing the fever . . .' See Marazio 2005.

8: Heedless

p. 135 'In the middle of . . .' See Ellwood 1985.

p. 135 'Benedetto Croce . . .' see de Luna & Revelli 1995.

p. 136 'As Churchill told . . .' Telegram 23 January 1944; see also Young 1985.

p. 137 'The trial of the six . . .' Duggan 2012, p. 282; Farrell 2003, p. 443.

p. 138 'As traitors, the conspirators . . .' Chevallard 2005, p. 203.

p. 138 'Most of the Mussolini . . .' See Bosworth 2017.

p. 139 'i ragazzi di Salò . . .' Innocenti 1993, p. 178.

p. 139 'only those brave . . .' See GNR reports ISTORETO Caprioli 29 April 1944.

p. 139 'agnostic attendismo' . . . Pavone 2014, p. 83.

p. 140 'Though the Germans . . .' See Adduci 2014.

p. 140 'Every wall had become . . .' Caruso 2004, p. 66.

p. 141 'On 18 February . . .' See Boccalatte, de Luna & Maida (eds) 1995.

p. 141 '"We are expecting you" . . .' Franzinelli 2016, p. 252.

p. 142 'Fritz Sauckel . . .' Klinkhammer 1993, p. 194.

p. 142 'It was the first . . .' For good accounts of the strike, see Bertolo 2014; Adduci 2014; Guidetti Serra 1997.

p. 144 'Frida was there . . .' See Gay Rochat 1969; also interview with author.

p. 145 '"Neither the zeal" . . .' Cooke (ed.) 1997, p. 144.

p. 146 'Micki Cesan was . . .' Cesan interview with author.

p. 147 'Despite the ferocious . . .' Oliva 1989, p. 110.

p. 148 'an early casualty . . .' See Sasso & Molinero 2000.

p. 149 'But in Torre Pellice . . .' Bouchard 2005, p. 68.

p. 149 'A parish priest . . .' Morero (n.d.). p. 24.

p. 154 'Like Lombardini . . .' See Treves 1954; Floria 1995; Schwartz 2008.

p. 155 'the friends had written . . .' Angier 2002, p. 273.

9: The hunters and the hunted

p. 156 'That night, Perotti . . . Ceva 1964, p. 272.

p. 157 'At dawn on 5 April . . .' See Giovana 1962.

p. 157 'Matilde di Pietrantonio . . .' Gasco (ed.) 2007, p. 134.

p. 158 'Early April brought . . .' See Adduci 2003, 2014.

p. 158 'Italy's Jewish . . .' See Franzinelli 2001.

p. 159 'Towards the end of March . . .' Bosworth 2005, p. 498.

p. 159 'Giaime Pintor . . .' See Pintor 1978.

p. 159 'This was Leone . . .' Ginzburg 1964, p. xx, 111; See also Pflug 1997.

p. 161 'The Italian churches . . .' See Legnani & Vendramini (eds) 1990; Malgeri 1986.

p. 164 'He was an admirable . . .' Agosti & Bianco 2007, letter 16 June 1944.

p. 165 'All through the late . . .' For good accounts of partisan life, see Bianco 1954; Battaglia 1957, 1965; Boca 1966; Creonti 1973.

10: A lizard among the rocks

p. 167 'One day, Lombardini . . .' See Malan 1996.

p. 168 'For every active . . .' National Archives WO204/7319 22 June 1944.

p. 169 'Even the senior . . .' Oliva 1989, p. 182.

p. 172 'Records would later show . . .' See Pavone 2014.

p. 172 'As the months went by . . .' See Falaschi 1976.

p. 173 'Distribution of the written . . .' Gasco (ed.) 2007, p. 106.

p. 173 'They were urged . . .' National Archives WO204/7319 22 June 1944.

p. 175 'In the early days . . .' See Bersano Begey 1970.

p. 177 'In the middle of May . . .' Cesare Alvazzi interview with author.

p. 179 'Franco's sister Mila . . .' See Cavaglion 1994.

11: Nesting in kitchens

p. 181 'In April, 438 cities . . .' National Archives WO204/6311 Report on Piedmont.

p. 182 'Piero Calamandrei . . .' See Calamandrei 2015.

p. 182 'Palmiro Togliatti . . . ' See Delzell 1961.

p. 182 'What became known . . .' See Woolf 1972.

p. 183 'In any case, the part . . .' See Aga-Rossi 1985.

p. 184 'Rome now appointed . . .' See Craveri 1980.

p. 184 'Every stage . . .' Kesselring 1953, p. 227, 252; see also Andrae 1995; Vai 1997.

p. 186 'In Pinerolo . . .' Marilda Musacchio interview with author.

p. 187 'One of the stories . . .' See Bertolo 2014.

p. 188 'Italy's northern cities . . .' See Chevallard 2005.

p. 189 'Turin got the Ather Capelli . . .' See Lazzero 1982, 1983; National Archives WO204/6311.

p. 189 'Piedmont, Mussolini . . .' Chevallard 2005, p. 308.

p. 190 'In the Legione . . .' See Griner 2004.

p. 191 'Why "defence"? . . .' *Noi Donne* 27 April 1958.

p. 193 'A decision was taken . . .' See Ravera 1965; Etnasi (ed.) 1966.

12: Summer of Flames

p. 199 'For his part, Marcellin . . .' Bertolo 2009, p. 455.

p. 200 'Later, it would be said . . .' See Borgis (n.d.).

p. 201 'The battle for Triplex . . .' Young 1985, p. 162; see also Maida 2002.

p. 201 'Unable to move around . . .' Prearo 1995, p. 131.

p. 201 'Maria Gorlier . . .' See Bertolo 2014; Marabotto 1964.

13: Haunted by death

p. 205 'On the night of . . .' See Boccalatte 1998; Perona, *Mezzosecolo* 12

p. 207 '"I lose a dear" . . .' Letter 8 August 1944.

p. 207 'When he told Ada . . .' de Luna 1982, pp. xx, 111.

p. 207 'Towards the middle of . . .' Accounts of Bolaffi's life are to be found in his diaries (ed. Colombini) 2014 and in Bolaffi Benuzzi 2010.

p. 209 'A week later . . .' see Borgis (n.d.).

p. 210 'Agosti and his colleagues . . .' ISTORETO Bolaffi file G6.

p. 211 'The FIAT factory . . .' See Bertolo 2009.

p. 212 'The Germans had been . . .' See Vai 1997.

p. 213 'When General Cadorna . . .' See Fucci 1983.

p. 213 'The recently formed . . .' Aga-Rossi 2000, p. 172.

p. 215 'What he knew perfectly . . .' See Craveri 1980.

p. 216 'Here was clear proof . . .' *Il Ponte* January 2015.

p. 216 '"What did the Allies" . . .' See Cooke (ed.) 1997.

p. 217 'An early Allied . . .' National Archives HS 6/846 Donum.

p. 219 'Pietro Koch . . .' See Griner 2000; Liliana Cavani interviews on film ISTORETO.

p. 221 'They were also spending . . .' See Franzinelli 2001.

p. 222 'Then came an extraordinary . . .' See Giua 2004.

p. 225 'The next family to be . . .' See Diena (n.d.).

p. 227 'And a remarkable experiment . . .' See Davidson & Wright 1998.

14: Learning to live better

p. 231 'The orders that went out . . .' Battaglia 1957, p. 238.

p. 233 'Later, the partisans . . .' See Trabucchi 1947.

p. 233 'When partisans exploded . . .' Griner 2004, p. 177.

p. 234 'German reports spoke . . .' Lazzero 1982, p. 176.

p. 234 'The partisans, driven . . .' ISTORETO file C67.

p. 235 'As a secret memorandum . . .' National Archives WO 204/11958.

p. 236 'Plans to recruit . . .' See Collotti 1963.

p. 236 'This, as Agosti . . .' See Peli 2006.

p. 236 'No other European . . .' ISTORETO file G77.

p. 237 'Yet most of the women . . .' *Donne Fasciste* 14 July 1941.

p. 239 'The Italian industrialists . . .' Giovana 1977, p. 21.

p. 239 'As one woman . . .' Guidetti Serra 1997, p. 654.

p. 240 'A "Purge Commission" . . .' Kelly 2004, p. 141.

p. 240 'At the heart of . . .' National Archives HS 6/845 Political and Miliary Liaison.

p. 240 'The few that arrived . . .' Young 1985 p. 241.

p. 242 'Togliatti, determined . . .' Aga-Rossi 1985, p. 179.

p. 242 'All in all . . .' See Delzell 1961.

p. 244 'As for the *staffette* . . .' National Archives HS 6/846.

p. 245 'The man sent to . . .' Missioni Alleate 1978 Atti di Convegno.

p. 245 'His friends found . . .' Kelly 2004, p. 292.

p. 245 'From his hideout . . .' Giovana 1962, p. 179.

p. 247 'From the start . . .' Pavone 2014, p. 569.

p. 247 'With the northern . . .' See Adduci 2014; Bravo & Jalla 1986.

p. 248 'American reporters . . .' National Archives WO 204/6290.

p. 249 'Others had formed groups . . .' See Addis Saba 1998.

p. 249 'Women factory workers . . .' See Guidetti Serra 1997.

p. 251 'Suor Giuseppina . . .' Turinetti 1996, p. 17.

15: Mothers of the Resistance

p. 258 'No one in Grenoble . . .' National Archives HS 6/845 Political and Military Liaison.

p. 261 'In their hideouts . . .' Bonsanti 2004, p. 127.

p. 262 'The northern cities . . .' National Archives WO 204/6311.

p. 262 '"In the cities" . . .' See Giovana 1962, 1977.

p. 263 'Turin had turned into . . .' See Bravo & Jalla 1986.

p. 263 'An SOE agent . . .' National Archives WO 204/2610 Report on conditions in occupied Italy.

p. 264 'They also chronicled . . .' Adduci 2014, p. 241.

p. 265 'Reports were also going . . .' ISTORETO Relazioni dell'ufficio politico investigativo della GNR Scaffale C Busta 81.

p. 265 'The 650 men . . .' ISTORETO C77 GNR reports.

p. 265 'Anyone sporting . . .' Chevallard 2005, p. 383.

p. 267 '"the right to be full members" . . .' GDD leaflet Cuneo 1943.

p. 267 '"The mothers of the Resistance" . . .' Gobetti, in Addis Saba 1998.

p. 267 '"Because we were" . . .' See Gasco 2007.

p. 267 'The first free trade union . . .' Davidson & Wright 1998, p. 105.

16: Squashing the cockroaches

p. 271 'The wily and resourceful . . .' See Bertolo 2014.

p. 275 'But even he could sound . . .' Macmillan 1984, p. 724.

p. 276 'On liberation, he . . .' Tudor 2004 p. 39.

p. 276 'On another occasion . . .' See Oliva 1989, 1999.

p. 277 'Privately, Salvadori . . .' See Craveri 1980; Duggan 2012; Salvadori 1958.

p. 278 'Meanwhile, the Italians . . .' National Archives WO 204/10064.

p. 278 'A patronising tone . . .' National Archives WO 106/3965A.

p. 281 'All the leadership . . .' See Franzinelli 2001; Gamba 1986.

p. 284 'The Allies were on the . . .' See Davidson & Wright 1998.

p. 286 'In Turin, in a last frenzy . . .' See Pesce 1967.

p. 287 '"like the bursting of a giant" . . .' Stafford 2011, p. 293.

17: Insurrection

p. 289 'The liberation of Turin . . .' See Oliva 1999; Adduci 2014; Boccalatte, de Luna & Maida (eds) 1995; Uboldi 2004; Vaccarino, Gobetti & Gobbi 1968.

p. 292 'News came that Milan . . .' See Creonti 1973.

p. 292 'In the valleys, meanwhile . . .' Bolaffi 2014, p. 165.

p. 292 'The last woman to die . . .' See Floria 1995.

p. 293 'Apart from a few small . . .' See Borgis (n.d.).

p. 295 'Fifty special passes . . .' Gasco 2007, p. 223.

p. 297 'But Ada had not reckoned . . .' See Turinetti 2004.

p. 297 'Early on the 27th . . .' See Adduci 2014.

p. 299 'The last Germans too . . .' See Vai 1997.

p. 301 'Right up until . . .' good descriptions of Mussolini's capture are to be found in Duggan 2012; Bosworth 2002, 2017; Deakin 1962; Hibbert 1962.

p. 304 'Most of the northern . . .' See Maida 2002, 2007.

p. 307 'In the Hotel Svizzera . . .' National Archives WO 206/6373.

p. 308 'More and more people . . .' Revelli 1962, p. 260.

p. 310 'We sang and sang . . .' Guidetti Serra 1997, p. 24.

18: Bloodletting

p. 312 'but he was not able . . .' Vaccarino, Gobetti & Gobbi (eds) 1968, p. 303.

p. 312 'It was, wrote one man . . .' Giovana 1977, p. 11.

p. 314 'Buffarini Guidi, the Minister . . .' See Griner 2000, 2004.

p. 314 'Even Agosti . . .' Maida 2007, p. 90.

p. 315 'As the Fascists pulled . . .' Cocco 1978, p. 334.

p. 316 'Micki Cesan remembers . . .' Cesan interview with author.

p. 316 'The reaction of the northern . . .' Oliva 1999, p. 106.

p. 318 'At nine o'clock . . .' See Boccalatte, d'Arrigo & Maida (eds) 2006.

p. 320 'On 12 May . . .' National Archives WO 204/10063; see also Voltero Fin 1994.

p. 321 'As the weapons . . .' Dondi 1992, p. 472.

p. 321 'Later, the Allies . . .' Kelly 2004, p. 170.

p. 322 'On 1 June . . .' National Archives WO 204/6281 PWB.

p. 323 'Bolaffi had been difficult . . .' ISTORETO C63.

p. 323 'There was talk . . .' Farrell 2003, p. 459.

p. 324 'And it was widely . . .' Tudor 2004, p. 136.

p. 324 'What all agreed . . .' Fucci 1983, p. 15; National Archives WO204/10241.

p. 324 'By the time of the . . .' Cooke (ed.) 1997, p. 150; see also Storchi 2008.

p. 325 'The Italians could not quite . . .' Bosworth 2005, p. 534.

p. 326 'By early summer . . .' Pavone 2014, p. 495; see also Bedeschi (ed.) 1987.

p. 326 'The legacy of the war . . .' Venturoli 1999, p. 92; see also Cooke 2011.

p. 327 'As the prisoners of war . . .' See Rainero (ed) 1985.

p. 327 'And as the concentration . . .' L. Picciotto, Il libro della memoria, Milan, 1991 p. 27.

p. 328 'In June 1945 . . .' E. Ferrero, Primo Levi: La vita, le opere, Turin, 2007, p. 38.

p. 329 'Bianca always refused . . .' Guidetti Serra 2009, 1987.

19: A love of forgetting

p. 330 'Fascism had not destroyed . . .' C. Pavone, English History Review, Vol. 131, December 2016.

p. 331 'Who was there to lead . . .' Il Ponte January 1995.

p. 331 'True liberals and radicals . . .' See Foa 1991; 42.

p. 331 'The six parties within . . .' National Archives WO 204/6281 PWB.

p. 332 'Ferruccio Parri was appointed . . .' Pavone 2014, p. 705; Cooke 2011, p. 14.

p. 332 'Parri was further weakened . . .' See Delzell 1961.

p. 333 'In November, Parri . . .' See Foa 1999.

p. 333 'More important, perhaps . . .' See Foa, *Il Ponte* 1947.

p. 334 'What mattered was not . . .' See Aga-Rossi & Smith 2005.

p. 335 'Perhaps the greatest failure . . .' See Battaglia, 1962.

p. 335 'One immediate problem . . .' Tosca (n.d.), p. 48.

p. 337 'To make things worse . . .' See Zangrandi 1962.

p. 337 'One of them was Gino . . .' See Franzinelli 2001.

p. 338 'The judicial harassment . . .' Cooke 2011, p. 91.

p. 339 'An uncleansed former . . .' See Dunnage (ed) 1999.

p. 340 'As it turned out . . .' See Slaughter 1997.

p. 341 'We were, one woman . . .' Mafai 1987 p. 264.

p. 342 'In the huge spate . . .' See Addis Saba 1998; Longo 1947.

Afterword

p. 348 'They told each other . . .' Ombra 2009, p. 47.

Index

Achse, Plan, 56
Adami-Rossi, General Enrico, 31–2
Agnese (washerwoman), 114
Agnelli, Giovanni, 239–40, 309, 334–5
Agosti, Giorgio: survives, 24; joins Ada, 34–5; in Partito d'Azione, 49, 51–2, 85, 230, 240; as theoretician, 49, 74; on struggle against Fascism, 80; organises partisan bands, 83; political aims, 86, 166, 236, 333; in 'war cabinet', 102; and Ada's identification of Croce's grandson, 145; informs Lucilla Jervis of Willy's capture, 151; as political chief in Turin, 164, 178; manages money, 171; distributes underground publications, 173; Ada meets in Turin, 200; and Willy Jervis's imprisonment and death, 206–7; criticises Bolaffi, 210; sees partisans as allies of Anglo-Americans, 215; and Livio Bianco's falling morale, 231; on decline in morale and behaviour, 248; and Ada's mission to France, 257; and Bianco's replacing Duccio, 261; and ex-Fascist recruits to partisans, 270; and impending liberation, 279; near-apprehension, 281; commands police before liberation, 286; appointed police

commissioner in Turin, 308–10; orders executions of Fascists, 314; on Allied administration at war's end, 321; and post-war political corruption, 339; death, 347
Ajeta, Marchese, 63
Albarelli, Maia, 326
Alexander, General Harold, 20, 184, 198, 213, 228–9, 231, 233, 324
Allies: grand strategy, 25; Italian military campaign and advance, 26, 63, 89, 96, 181, 228, 237, 265, 284, 287; policy in governing Italy, 61–3, 87–8; send military advisers and agents to partisan groups, 88, 244; advance halted at Monte Cassino, 135; and reconstruction of Italy, 136; attitude to partisans, 145, 213, 274, 276; reduce strength in Italy for Normandy campaign, 184; invade south of France, 212; Psychological Warfare Branch, 213, 267, 277, 335; discontinue airdrops, 240; Resistance dependence on, 240–1; and Italian post-liberation political plans, 242; resume airdrops to partisans, 244, 274; recognise Italian women's role in Resistance, 267; and communist threat, 274; plans for liberation,

Allies: (*continued*)
277–8; breach Gothic Line, 282;
reach Piedmont, 307; take over
at war's end, 320–2; Screening
Commission in Piedmont, 324;
and administration of post-war
Italy, 332
Almirante, Giorgio, 333
Alpini, 42–3
Alta Italia, 241
Alvazzi, Cesare, 81–2, 177–8, 219,
234–5, 280–1, 323
Amay (hamlet), 108, 110
Amendola, Giorgio, 313
Anodera viaduct, 104
Antonicelli, Franco, 319
Anzio: Allied landings, 135
Ardeatine caves: massacre, 159,
161, 220, 338
Arduino, Antonio, xix
Arduino, Bruna, xix
Arduino, Gaspare, xix–xx
Arduino, Libera, xix–xx, 271
Arduino, Teresa, xix–xx
Arduino, Vera, xix–xx, 271
Artom, Emanuele (Eugenio Ansaldi):
asks Frida's help in hiding Jews,
45; and anti-Jewish measures,
93–4; as partisan, 106–8; keeps
daily diary, 107, 144, 146; as
political commissar, 107, 144; on
Italian defeat, 141; arrested and
tortured, 153–4, 206; death, 158,
167, 328, 344; collobarates with
Leone Ginzburg on paper, 178;
forced to reveal Willy Jervis's
name, 206
Artom, Emilio, 93, 108
Artom, Ennio, 93–4
Artom, Paolo, 344
Ather Capelli Brigade (Fascist),
189, 264
Audisio, Walter, 303
Auschwitz, 155, 194, 258

Bachi, Guido, 110–11
Badoglio, Marshal Pietro: forms
new government, 6, 24, 59–61,
136, 139; announces

continuation of war after
Mussolini's fall, 23; secret
negotiations with Allies, 24;
qualities, 25; inaction, 26–7, 30;
negotiates armistice, 26, 32;
popular opposition to, 26; flees
Rome, 27; frees political
prisoners, 32–3; opposition
groups reject, 84; ousts Fascists
from jobs, 86; rivalry with CLN
in Rome, 89; declares war on
Germany, 96; Togliatti agrees to
cooperate with, 182; flown to
Rome after liberation, 183;
differences with CLN, 330
Baili, La (underground paper), 172
Bardia, Anna Maria, 291
Bardonecchia, 322
Barone, Ines, 162
Battaglione Lupo (Fascist), 190
Begey, Dr Bersano, 175–6, 200
Bellini delle Stelle, Count Pier
Luigi, 303
Bellone, Sergio, 83
Ben Bella, Ahmed, 343
Bergamini, Admiral Carlo, 29
Bergen-Belsen, 285
Berlin: Soviets occupy, 294
'Bernardo' (*staffetta*), 281–2
Berne (Switzerland): Allied missions
in, 88
Bianco, Dante Livio: serves under
Duccio, 35; in Partito d'Azione,
50–2; as political theoretician,
74, 166, 236; sets up command
structure, 83, 85; friendship
with Venturi, 119; on adapting
to new conditions, 167; on
personal exhaustion, 231;
separation from wife, 251–2;
negotiates pacts with French
maquisards, 256; succeeds
Duccio as military commander,
261; disparages Fascists, 263; on
utilising converts, 270; known
to enemy, 279; prepares for
advance on Turin, 286; and
political reform, 310; killed in
climbing accident, 348

Bianco, Pinella, 85, 119, 125, 251, 279, 294, 300, 308
Black Brigades *see* Brigate Nere
black market, 142
Bolaffi, Stella, 208
Boccante, Gino, 337
Boetta, Lucia, 68–9, 216–18, 245, 271–2, 294, 331, 342
Bolaffi, Giulio: Ada meets, 207–10; qualities, 208, 323; in action, 209–10, 212, 224; meets Duccio, 209; gives revolver to Ada, 216; negotiates with Germans, 224; father's death, 225; and shortages, 230–1; and negotiations with French maquisards, 231, 255; Allied agent's dismissive view of, 244; on foreign agents in Piedmont, 248; and final battle plans, 286, 292; leads procession to lay wreaths for dead, 293; at liberation of Turin, 317–18; in dispute with French, 322–3; respect for Ada, 323
Bolaffi, Paolo, 208
Bono, Marshal Emilio de, 137
Bonomi, Ivanoe, 183–4, 213–14, 241, 243, 248, 275
Borello, 293–6, 300, 307
Borghese, Prince Valerio Julio, 100, 132, 338
Bosshammer, Friedrich, 158
Boves, 68–9, 162, 216
boys: in Fascist organisations, 141
Braccini, Paolo, 102, 156–8, 247
Braun, Eva, 313
Brigate Nere (Fascist force), 188–9, 196–7, 236, 264, 302, 314
Brindisi: Italy's second government in, 60
Britain: Mediterranean policy, 62; dislikes Italian national uprising, 88; attitude to partisans, 213, 275; ambivalent view of Italians, 323; *see also* Allies
Bussoleno (village), 198

Cadorna, General Raffaele, 184, 213, 240, 271, 274, 292

Calamandrei, Piero, 182
Calvino, Italo, 31, 234, 307, 346
Capelli, Ather, 158
Cappellani Neri (priests), 189
Cardon, Jenny Peyronel, 293, 316
Caretta, Dr, 262
Carletti, Cesarina, 129
Carnazzi, Cesare Augusto, 110
Carnia, 227, 229
Casablanca conference (January 1943), 24
Cataneo (lawyer), 53
Catholic Church: attitude to war and German occupation, 121; condemns excesses, 161; fears communist takeover, 273; and Fascism, 332; supports de Gasperi, 333; *see also* Vatican
Cavallero, General Ugo, 138
Centro Italiano Femminile, 267
Cesan, Micki, 16, 173, 316
Charvensod, Maria Daviso di, 125
Chevallard, Carlo, 37, 57, 181, 189, 227, 250, 289, 310, 313
Christian Democratic Party, 225, 339
Churchill, Winston: at Casablanca conference, 24; on Italian armistice, 26; condemns Mussolini, 62; on Italian campaign, 63; on Croce, 64; on inaction at Anzio, 135; on Badoglio, 136; on new Italian government, 183; and confusion in Italy, 275; at Yalta conference, 278; on 'iron curtain', 320; on effectiveness of partisans, 324
Cianetti, Tullio, 138
Ciano, Edda (Mussolini's daughter), 60, 137–8
Ciano, Count Galeazzo: demoted to Ambassador to Vatican, 3; and Mussolini's downfall, 6, 60; charged with conspiracy and executed, 136–8
Civitella, Val di Chiana, 185–6
Cold War, 320, 334
Collegno Rignon, Contessa Irene Provama di, 298

Colombo, Franco, 100, 190
Commando Piazza, 286
Committee of National Liberation
(CLN), 65, 135–6, 142–3, 183,
213, 278, 288, 330, 331–2
Committee of National Liberation
northern wing (CLNAI), 84–5,
108, 241, 274
Communists: Togliatti calls on to
join Resistance, 72; in coalition
against Badoglio's government,
84; strength, 143, 240; partisan
members, 165; and proposed
new Italian government, 182;
Togliatti launches new Party,
242; resist Western Allies' orders,
274; efficiency, 277; and Stevens'
intervention in liberation, 290;
US-British opposition to, 320; in
post-war politics, 330–2; attitude
to women, 341
Corallo, Virgilio and Eraldo, 257,
259–60, 266
Corpo Volontari della Libertà, 273
Craveri, Benedetta, 324
Craveri, Piero, 146, 324
Craveri, Raimondo, 65, 88, 145,
169, 215, 277, 324
Critica, La (magazine), 16
Croce, Benedetto: Ada's friendship
with, 14–16, 18, 345; followers,
16; and Ada's rooster story,
21–2; rescued by Allies, 64–5;
influence on Willy Jervis, 75; on
transitory Fascist rule, 135, 327;
on future of monarchy in Italy,
136; on killing of Gentile, 169
Croce, Elena, 14
Cueno, 35
Czechs: desert Germans to join
Resistance, 200

Dalton, Hugh, 63
Danneker, Theodor, 106
Darewski, Neville ('Major Temple'),
218, 245
Decima Mas (naval land unit),
100, 132, 291, 338
Dellera, Romano, 305

Delmastro, Sandro, 92, 102, 158,
247, 294, 344
Dennis, Major (English pilot),
81–2, 86, 102
Diena, Giorgio: relations and child
with Silvia, 20, 47–9, 74, 92,
101; joins Ada, 34–5;
background., 49; forms group,
74, 92–3; writes on future of
Partito d'Azione, 101; in 'war
cabinet', 102–3; Jewishness, 106;
studies trade unionism, 164; and
son Vittorio, 175, 308; plans
rescue of Momigliano, 179–80;
discusses liberation with Agosti,
261; political aims, 333
Diena, Marisa, 34–5, 47, 80,
118–19, 127–8, 142, 226–7,
229, 295
Diena, Paolo, 226–7
Diena, Sergio: death, 103
Difesa della Lavoratrice, La
(newspaper), 192
Dongo Treasure, 326
Donovan, William, 64–5
Dora, River, 80
Duccio (Tancredi Galimberti): calls
for popular rising, 35; in Partito
d'Azione war cabinet, 85, 102;
replaces Braccini as head of
Partito d'Azione formations,
164; plans for new society, 166;
Ada urges to unite Val de Susa
bands, 178; as commander in
chief for Piedmont Partito
d'Azione, 200, 230; Bolaffi
meets, 209; O'Regan meets,
217; arrested and killed, 246–7;
relations with Allied agents,
246; negotiates pact with French
maquisards, 256
Dulles, Allen W., 88, 213, 271
Dusi, Franco, 225

Eden, Anthony: contemptuous
attitude to Italians, 62, 87, 184,
229, 248
Eichmann, Adolf, 106
Einaudi, Giulio, 16

Eisenhower, General Dwight: commands Mediterranean campaign, 25; and Italian armistice, 27
Energie Nuove (magazine), 13
Espedita (concierge), 53, 129, 143, 178, 260
Esterina (Meana andlady), 203
Esther (Delmastro's fiancée), 108–9, 158, 294
Exilles: sabotage plan against bridge, 83; Germans fortify for final battle, 292

Falerno, Elsa, 326
Fallaci, Oriana, 114–15
Fascism: view of women, 7–8; ideology, 8–10; restored in Italy by Germans, 57–8; support for German occupation, 67; partisan opposition to, 79–80; women's resistance to, 113; women supporters, 130–2; and government of Italy after fall of Mussolini, 140; youth organisations, 141; reprisals against partisans, 149; demands Catholic support, 162; post-war Commission against, 183; terror organisations and practices, 188–90; and prospective liberation, 262–5; orders new restrictions, 263; post-war suppression of, 273–4; forces collapse on defeat, 285; defeated in Turin liberation, 289–90; in final fighting in Turin, 291, 296; supporters flee Turin, 299; suffer reprisals, 313–16; effect, 327, 330; sanctions against and amnesties, 335–7
Fascist Arditi, 234
Fascist Grand Council, 3, 5
Fascist Party: Verona Congress (November 1943), 98, 130
Fenestrelle (village), 195
Ferida, Luisa, 220, 314
FIAT (company): Turin factory, 11, 32; strikes, 97; partisans attack Susa factory, 211; leaders collaborate with Germans, 239; women worker reject conciliation, 240; factory and workers in final fighting in Turin, 297; Valletta defends role in war, 334–5; revived, 335; *see also* Turin
Fiordaliso, Villa, 138–9
Florence: liberated, 204, 228
Foa, Anna, 250, 3076
Foa, Massimo, 124
Foa, Vittorio: imprisoned, 18; freed and returned to Turin, 32–5; leaves Turin for Torre Pellice, 35, 50; in Partito d'Azione, 50–1; and formation of northern CLN, 84; engagement to Lisetta, 101–2; on Jews in Resistance, 107; in reorganised partisan movement, 164; negotiates with Operti, 170; plans rescue of Momigliano, 179; smoking, 219; and capture of Lisetta, 222–3; wishes Ada to become vice mayor of Turin, 255; and impending liberation, 279; Lisetta rejoins, 307, 307–8; and post-liberation administration, 310; on uncertain future, 331; political aims, 333
Foglia, Don, 82–3, 104, 121, 148
Fondelli, Countess Piera Gatteschi, 131, 315
Forces Françaises de l'Intérieur, 255
Fossati, Cardinal Maurilio, Archbishop of Turin, 121, 124, 148, 162–3, 202, 297, 346
Fossoli, near Carpi, 106, 154, 221
France: Allies invade south (Provence), 212, 231; Italian partisans seek contact with Maquis, 231–3; Ada leads mission to, 255–61; annexation plans in Piedmont, 322–3
Fronte della Gioventù, 261
Fronte Nazionale della Liberazione, 31, 65

Galimberti, Tancredi *see* Duccio
Galli, Luigi, 302
Garella, Giuseppe, 297–8
Garella, Pilado, 297–8
Gargagno, Lake Garda, 57
Garibaldi, Giuseppe, 84
Garibaldini (Communist groups), 107–8, 116, 118, 165, 198, 301
Garneri, Monsignor, 291, 306
Garzanti (publisher), 22
Gasperi, Alcide de, 242, 333
Gaulle, Charles de, 255–6, 323
Genoa: falls to partisans, 300
Gentile, Giovanni, 99, 169
Georgians: defect to partisans, 212
Germany: Italy's Pact of Steel with, 24; occupies Italy after collapse, 28–31, 34–5; attitude to Latin races, 55; lootings in Italy, 56, 263; controls Mussolini's puppet government (RSI), 60; reprisals and atrocities in Italy, 69–70, 96, 149–50, 184–8, 233–4; bombed, 97; returns men to Italy to act as instructors, 99; resists Allied advance in Italy, 181, 229; agents captured by partisans, 235; despises Italian military forces, 236; Italian captives in, 237–8; Allied advance in, 282; defeat in Italy, 284–5, 313; in final Turin and Piedmont fighting with partisans, 291, 297, 299; troops quit Turin, 299–300, 302, 305
Ghizzone, Rosa, xix-xx
Giannini, Guglielmo, 333
Ginzburg, Leone: qualities, 16–17; imprisoned, 18; freed and returned to Turin, 20, 32; marriage, 20; in penal exile, 49; advocates resistance, 52; optimism, 89; irreplaceable status, 159–60; captured, tortured and death, 160, 182, 344; clandestine acts, 178
Ginzburg, Natalia (*née* Levi): marriage to Leone, 20; relations with Lisetta Giua, 33; on

women's rebellion against Germans, 40; Silvia Pons and Giorgio Diena stay with, 49; returns to Turin, 343; on personal effect of Resistance, 344
Gioventù Cristiana, 43
Gioventù d'Azione (youth organisation), 228
girls: under Fascism, 10
Giua, Lisetta (*later* Foa): in Resistance, 32–5, 116; in Partito d'Azione, 50; engagement to Foa, 101–2; opposes Fascist recruitment of boys, 142; plans rescue of Momigliano, 179; capture, imprisonment and escape, 219, 221–3; gives birth to Anna, 250; and impending liberation, 279; carries messages, 295; returns home to baby, 308; on effect of Resistance activities, 348
Giua, Michele, 32
Giuliani, Fulvia, 130
Giunta Populare (Turin), 309
Giustizia e Libertà (anti-Fascist party), 17, 51
Globocnik, Odilo, 159
Gobetti, Ada: and killing of Arduino sisters, xxii; from Turin, 13; background and career, 14–15, 18; marriage, 14; relations with Croce, 14–16, 18; in Meana, 15, 105, 144, 177, 198–200, 203, 204, 218; remains in Turin during bombing, 21; remarries (Marchesini), 21; story of rooster, 21–2; and fall of Mussolini, 23; co-founds Partito d'Azione, 31; calls on Badoglio for peace, 34; and German control of Turin, 35; leadership, 35, 347; moves to mountains, 36; considers options, 37; advises Giorgio Diena, 47; in Partito d'Azione, 49; climbing, 52; agrees secret signals, 53;

friendship with Bianca, 54; and Allied rescue of Croce, 64; on political confusion in Italy, 66, 330–1, 339; plans resistance to Germans, 71; in Val di Susa, 80–3, 224; anxiety over Paolo, 83–4, 151–2, 202–3, 225, 232; and Major Dennis, 86; supports younger partisans, 101; winter activities, 101, 249; on Lisetta Giua, 102; holds back from group talks, 103; as active partisan, 112; on women partisans, 114; asked to recruit more women, 124, 126; house in Turin, 129; resists call-up of young men, 141–2; and round-ups, 143; identifies Croce's grandson, 145; wishes role recognised, 147; on death of Emanuele Artom, 158; on loss of friends and compatriots, 161, 182; political aims, 166, 178, 191, 333, 340, 344; manages money, 171; plans rescue of Momigliano, 179; on effect of liberation of Rome, 185; on confusion of civil war, 190; reorganises women's groups, 191, 198; meets Bolaffi, 207–9; told of Willy Jervis's death, 207; and Allied victories, 213; Lisetta visits after escape, 223; avoids Fascists and Germans, 224; visits Paolo's cabin, 225; disillusion with Allies' support, 230; travels to Milan, 232; requests money from Lancia industrialist, 239; accused by Marcellin, 241; on death of Duccio, 247; mission to France, 255, 257–61; status and appointments, 261; post-liberation plans, 265–6, 310–11; advances women's status, 266–9; as prospective vice mayor of Turin, 268, 272, 281; and ex-Fascist recruits to partisans, 270; meets Medici Tornaquinci, 272; and impending liberation, 279; alarmed by police call at home, 280; stopped and searched, 280–1; spills papers, 281; organises pre-insurrection for liberation of Turin, 282, 284; and final partisan actions, 286–7; sets up base in Borello, 293, 295–6, 300, 307; exhaustion at war's end, 301; organisation after liberation, 308; takes up post as vice mayor, 308–10, 331; praised after liberation, 317–18; on Bolaffi, 323; honoured, 342; on women's status and unequal pay, 342; later activities, 345, 347–8; death, 346; *Diario Partigiano*, 346, 348; *Giornale dei Genitori*, 347; *Storia del Gallo Sebastiano*, 22

Gobetti, Paolo: as Ada's son, xxii, 14; mother's fears for, 11–12, 83–4, 202–3, 225, 232; hiking in mountains, 21; hands out leaflets in Turin, 34; enthusiasm for resistance, 35, 82; in Susa with mother, 53; leads partisan sabotage group, 83–4; studies German insignia, 101; character, 105; in Meana, 105, 144; hides in bath, 143; avoids capture, 151–2; forms new partisan band, 178; acquires tommy gun, 210; plans to derail train, 218; names new band after Franco Dusi, 224–5; on missions to France, 231–2, 255, 258–60; becomes film director, 345

Gobetti, Piero (Ada's first husband), xxii, 13–14, 18, 54, 152, 347

Goebbels, Joseph, 137

Göring, Hermann, 29

Gorlier, Maria Teresa, 162–3, 201–2

Gothic Line (German line of defence), 229–30, 237, 247, 263, 265, 282

Gramsci, Antonio, 13, 75, 182
Grandi, Count Dino: plots
    Mussolini's downfall, 5
Graziani, Marshal Rodolfo, 58, 99
Graziella (Esterina's daughter),
    203–4
Greece: Resistance movement, 240
Grenoble, 257–9
Gruppi di Azione Patriottica
    (GAP), 86
Gruppi di difesa della donna e per
    l'assistenza ai combattenti della
    libertà (GDD), 124–5, 127–8,
    191, 232, 249, 266, 308, 340
Gruppi Universitari Fascisti (GUF),
    91
Gruppo Mobile Operativo, 270
Guardia Nazionale Repubblicana
    (GNR), 100, 139–40
Guidi, Guido Buffarini, 58, 156,
    220
gypsies: persecuted, 106

Hahn, Rudolf, 68
Hamilton, Major (of Grenoble),
    258
High Commission for Sanctions
    against Fascism, 335–6
Hitler, Adolf: deteriorating relations
    with Mussolini, 3; and collapse
    of Italy, 28–9; orders killing of
    all partisans, 55, 185; strategy
    in Italy, 56; and reinstallation of
    Mussolini, 57; Final Solution for
    Jews, 105; demands death
    sentence for Italian conspirators,
    137; orders arrest of Italian
    strikers, 143; orders retributive
    killings in Italy, 159; resists
    Allied advance in Europe, 237;
    orders death penalty for strikers,
    238–9; refuses capitulation in
    Italy, 285; suicide, 313

In Marcia (bulletin), 282
Intendenza, L' (partisan section),
    168
International Democratic
    Federation of Women, 345

Italia Combatte, 168, 228
Italia Libera, L' (clandestine paper),
    52, 89, 160, 172
Italian SS, 99–100, 149, 234, 236,
    273, 314, 328
Italy: mistrusted by Allies, xxvi;
    joins Axis powers in war, 3–4;
    military weakness, 4; wartime
    hardships, 4; industrial strikes,
    10, 12, 97; anti-Semitic laws
    (1938), 19, 45, 90; alliance with
    Germany, 24; and fall of
    Mussolini, 24; Allied military
    campaign and advance in, 26,
    63, 89, 96, 181, 228, 237, 265,
    284, 287; armistice with Allies,
    26–7; collapse and occupation
    by Germany, 28–31, 34–5;
    soldiers desert after German
    occupation, 39; resistance
    groups formed, 52, 77–8;
    killings by Germans, 55;
    German strategy in, 56; looted
    and despoiled by Germans, 56,
    263; puppet Fascist government
    under Germans, 58; deprivation
    of south, 61; communism in, 63;
    anti-Fascist groups offer support
    to Allies, 65; Allied view of,
    87–8, 136, 325; economy
    exploited by Germany, 97;
    workers rebel, 97–8; military
    and quasi-military units formed,
    100; and future of monarchy,
    135–6, 183; anti-Fascist
    congress (January 1944), 136;
    reconstruction, 136–7; anti-
    Mussolini conspirators tried,
    137; confused political
    administration, 139; anti-
    German industrial strikes,
    142–3; cities bombed by Allies,
    181; High Commission for
    Sanctions against Fascism, 183;
    new government after liberation
    of Rome, 183; post-liberation
    conditions, 183–4, 215–16, 310;
    men deported as slave labour to
    Germany, 199, 237–8, 327; gold

and equipment looted by Germans, 235; civil war, 236–7; military desertions, 236; post-liberation political plans, 241–3, 273; exceptionally cold winter (1944–5), 247–9; Fascist atrocities in, 263–4; Allies' plans for liberation, 277–8; uprising planned in north, 279; Allies take over at war's end, 320–1; casualties, 326, 327; effect of Fascism on, 326–7; post-war political confusion, 330–4; corruption in, 335, 338; *see also* partisans

Jackson, General Sir William, 287
Japan: Allies' war with, 320
Jervis, Giovanni, 75, 207
Jervis, Laura, 207
Jervis, Letizia, 75
Jervis, Lucilla, 75–6, 151, 205–7, 343
Jervis, Paola, 75, 206
Jervis, Willy: joins resistance group, 75–6, 85; liaises with Allies, 89; in Val Germanasca, 145; captured and imprisoned, 151, 205–7; shot and hanged, 205, 247, 328, 344; brokers weapons supply, 214; memorial plaque, 343
Jews: in Turin, 18; and Mussolini's anti-Semitic laws, 19, 45; persecuted and vilified in Italy, 90–6, 98, 159; Germans round up and kill, 95; and Final Solution, 105–6; flee to mountains and Switzerland, 105; join Resistance bands, 106, 328; imprisoned in Turin prison, 124; sent to Auschwitz and Bergen-Belsen, 155, 158; survivors return home after war, 327
Jodl, General Alfred, 96

Kesselring, Field Marshal Albert: command in Italy, 29; on treachery of Italians, 55;

strategy in Italy, 56, 70, 229; halts Allied advance, 135; and fall of Rome, 182; attitude to partisan activity, 184–5, 233; succeeded by Vietinghoff, 271; on danger of partisans, 324; death sentence commuted, 334
Koch, Pietro, 190, 219–22, 314

Lagen, Baron Dirk von, 22, 68
Lagen, Usci von, 158
Lambello, Il (newspaper), 91
Lambert, Erwin, 106
Lattes, Franco, 46
Legione Muti, 100
Levi, Anna Maria: Jewishness, 18, 92, 94–5; retreats to mountains, 108–9
Levi, Carlo: Jewishness, 18; climbing and skiing, 19–20; on life in Turin, 21; freed and returned to Turin, 32; on disarmament of Italian army, 37; *Christ Stopped at Eboli*, 18
Levi, Primo: in Jewish group, 91–3; moves to Milan, 94; flees to mountains, 95, 108, 110; on progress of war, 95; captured and detained, 110–11, 125, 154; sent to Auschwitz, 155; writes to Bianca from Auschwitz, 194–5; survives concentration camp and returns to Italy, 327; death (1987), 329; *The Drowned and the Saved*, 111, 329; *The Periodic Table*, 102
Lewis, Norman, 136
Leyers, General Hans, 56
Liberal Party, 331
Lombardini, Jacopo, 41, 52, 74, 78, 85, 153–4, 167, 196, 327, 344
Longo, Luigi, 275, 330

McCaffery, John, 88, 215, 244
Macmillan, Harold, 25, 61, 63, 136, 275, 323
Maestra, Vanda, 92, 94–5, 109–11, 125, 154–5, 327, 344

Maitland, General: takes over from Eisenhower in Italy, 63

Malan, Frida: attends funeral of Arduino sisters, xxiii–xxiv, 271; Resistance activities, xxiv, 19–20, 51, 66, 73, 144; friendship with Bianca Serra, 18; family in Torre Pellice, 41; friendship with Silvia Pons in Torre Pellice, 43; as secretary of Gioventù Cristiana, 43; birth and background, 44; character and ideals, 44–6; career, 46; Jewish friends, 90, 93, 96; supplies books to Emanuele Artom, 107; carries messages, 118; recruits women into Resistance, 126, 128; reaction to Emanuele Artom's death, 167; sees Lombardini in detention, 167; helps with underground press, 173; and emancipation of women, 191; arrested and released, 196–7; on solidarity among women, 239; on women's rights, 267; in Turin during final fighting, 295; political aims, 340, 344; honoured, 342; later activities and death, 346

Malan, Giulia, 43, 197

Malan, Gustavo, 44, 52, 73, 118, 172–3

Malan, Roberto: birth, 44; joins partisans, 46; organises resistance group, 52, 54, 73, 118, 145, 146; Paolo Gobetti joins, 144; negotiates exchange of prisoners, 149; and disciplinary measures, 169; threatened by Fascist, 196; intercedes for Fascist woman, 197; Willy Jervis names, 206; Allied agents' view of, 244

Marabotto, Don, 162–3, 201–2, 298

Marazio, Zelmira, 132, 237, 250

Marcellin (partisan band leader), 199–201, 241, 244

Marchesini, Ettore (Ada's second husband): Ada marries, 21; and German occupation of Turin, 34; in Meana, 36, 53, 105, 144, 203–4; helps escaped POWs, 82; works at Ente Italiano Radiofoniche, 86; winter activities, 101; and round-ups, 143; accompanies Ada to look for Paolo, 151–2; plots escape route from house, 178; establishes radio link, 200; on mission to France, 255, 257, 259–60

Maria José, Princess, 3

Marinelli, F.T., 99

Marinelli, Giovanni, 137–8

Marshall, Colonel (US army), 319

Marzabotto, 187

Mazzini, Giuseppe, 44

Meana, 53, 177, 198–200, 203–4, 218

Medici Tornaquinci, Aldobrando, 271–2, 278

Mediterranean: under Allied control, 25

Merlo, Ludovico, Carlo and Olivero, 316

Mezzasoma, Fernando, 58

Milan: falls to partisans, 292

Momigliano, Franco, 92, 155, 178–80, 328

Momigliano, Mila, 179

Momo (Marcellin's man), 200

Monte Cassino monastery, 135, 181, 213

Monti, Augusto, 17–18, 32, 93, 164, 268

Moroni, Edouardo, 238

Movimento Sociale Italiano, 333

Muro, Suor Giuseppina, 121–4, 129–30, 148, 202, 251, 297–9, 346

Mussolini, Benito: rule, xxvi, 3–4; convenes Fascist Grand Council meeting, 3, 5; and conduct of war, 4–5; decline, 5, 139, 236, 302; deposed and detained, 5–7, 22–3; view of women as limited,

7–8, 11; dominance, 9–10; purges, 13; anti-Semitic laws, 19, 90; hatred of Turin, 21; freed by Germans, 56–7; restored to head of Fascist government (RSI), 57–60, 98; calls up young for army and militia, 72, 77, 99; and repression of opposition, 98; collaborates with Hitler in Final Solution, 105; women supporters, 130–2; conspirators tried, 137–8; meets Ciano, 137; widens age bracket for compulsory military service, 140–1; and 'pacification' of Piedmont, 189; and capture of Don Marabotto, 202; proposes social contract, 238; Milan speech (December 1944), 250; and pre-liberation measures, 264; hopes to negotiate deal, 301; captured by partisans, 303; attempts flight, shot and body abused in Milan, 304; buried, 325; fate of papers and money, 326

Mussolini, Rachele, 6, 59, 137, 139, 302, 325
Mussolini, Vittorio, 138
Muti, Colonel Ettore, 7

Nachtigall, Operation, 201
Naples: resistance to Germans and reprisals in, 70, 97; disorder at liberation, 136–7
Nissim, Luciana, 92–3, 95, 109–11, 125, 154–5, 327–8
Noi Donne (newspaper), 192, 270, 343
Normandy: Allies invade (June 1944), 184
Nostra Bandiera, La (newspaper), 90
Nuova Realtà, La (publication), 194, 195, 300
Nuove, Le (prison), Turin: partisans and Jews imprisoned in, 120–4, 129, 251; Christmas celebrated

(1944), 251; at liberation of Turin, 297–8

Office of Strategic Services (OSS), 64, 145, 213, 215
Olivetti, Adriano, 75
Ombra, Marisa, 116
Operti, General Raffaello, 170–1
O'Regan, Captain Patrick, 217–18, 240–1, 276
Organizzazione della Resistenza Italiana (ORI), 64, 88
Origo, Iris, 228
Orlandi, Anna, 315
Orlandi, Luciana, 315

Pagliai, Pier Luigi, 172
Parri, Ferruccio: organises Resistance in north, 87, 88, 272; political aims, 88–9, 184, 273; visits Ada, 102; on inadequate support from Allies, 145; fights for independent Italy, 215–16; asks Allies to recognise 'Alta Italia', 241–2; captured by Germans, 243; on English view of war against Fascism, 243; accepts shooting of Fascist traitors, 247; arrested, 258, 261; freed, 271; creates single fighting force, 284; deplores death of Mussolini, 304; relations with Communist Longo, 330; appointed president of Italy, 332; resigns, 333, 335; accused of massacres, 338; praises women in Resistance, 339; and death of Bianco, 348
Partigiano Alpino, Il (underground paper), 172
partisans: shortages, 15, 168, 214; Salò government persecutes, 20; Allied agents parchuted to, 24, 145–6, 214, 244–6; sabotage activities, 83, 147–8; Allied military advisers join, 88; German offensive against, 103, 148–50, 234; women join, 112–13; numbers increase, 140,

partisans: (*continued*)
165, 270; dress, 146–7; Turin leaders captured, tried and executed, 156–7; negotiate exchanges of prisoners, 157–8, 170; unified and reorganised, 164–5, 168; composition, 165–6; disciplinary measures, 169–70; executions by, 169–70; money management, 171; attention to wounded and dead, 174–6, 200; medical practices and treatment, 175–6; Kesselring's policy on, 184–5; in summer of 1944, 198; Allied attitude to, 213–14, 244, 323–4; supplied from air drops, 214, 217–18, 244, 274; occupy and control areas in north, 227; Alexander orders to suspend operations for winter 1944–5, 229–31, 233; capture German agents, 235; dependence on Allies, 240–1; late successes in Turin, 265; prepare for liberation, 274; disarmed on liberation, 277; in final defeat of Germans in Italy, 284–6; last battles with Germans and Fascists, 291–2; capture Milan, 292; casualties, 292, 326; resent Allied control, 321; disillusion with post-war politics, 333; post-liberation reprisals declared criminal, 337–8; accused of being threat to society, 339; women honoured, 342

Partito d'Azione: founded, xxii, 31; in Resistance, xxv; Germans suppress, 35; Giorgio Diena as theorist for, 49, 101; activities, 50; and other resistance groups, 52, 165; military committee, 85; British view of, 89; and Jewish Resistance, 106–7; and Duccio, 164–5; groups reorganised, 164; women's section, 194; ends, 333

Passoni, Pier Luigi, 308

Pavese, Cesare, 32, 34

Pavia (Solaro's deputy), 306

Pavolini, Alessandro, 58, 188–9, 236, 264, 285, 302

Pavolini, Renato, 99

Pavone, Claudio, 326

Perone, Lorenzo, 194–5

Perotti, General Giuseppe, 163, 256–7

Petacci, Claretta: as Mussolini's mistress, 4; flees to north on Mussolini's downfall, 6; in Salò, 59; in d'Annunzio's villa, 138–9; attempts flight with Mussolini and shot, 302–4

Piedmont: Resistance in, xxvi, 74, 89; opposition to Fascism, 12; Alpini (special troops) in, 42; as secondary front for Germans, 66; casualties and destruction, 147, 317, 326; partisan groups unified, 163; partisan numbers, 165, 198, 270; post-liberation political aims, 184; Mussolini demands to be pacified, 189; in summer of 1944, 198–201; German anti-partisan methods in, 233; and plans for liberation, 279; liberation, 282, 287, 289, 307; final battle plans, 286; post-liberation reprisals, 316; Allied Screening Commission in, 324; women granted equal pay, 341–2

Pietrantonio, Matilde di, 119, 157, 294, 347

Pillo (Paolo Gobetti's friend), 177, 257, 259

Pintor, Giaime, 103, 159

Pioniere, Il (underground paper), 173

Pizzoni, Alfredo, 171

Pons, Enrico, 47, 49

Pons, Lily, 47, 49

Pons, Silvia: attends funeral of Arduino sisters, xxiv; in Resistance, xxv, 66; from Turin, 13; medical training, 20; relations and child with Giorgio Diena, 20, 47–9; friendship with

Frida Malan in Torre Pellice, 43, 46; beauty and character, 47; birth and background, 47; mother's suicide, 49; career, 50; in Partito d'Azione, 50; on partisan bands in Val Pellice, 53; Jewish friends, 90; as *staffetta*, 101; recruits women into Resistance, 126, 128; medical practices with partisans, 175, 177; plans rescue of Momigliano, 179–80; on emancipation of women, 191, 267; writings and poetry, 192, 249, 295, 300, 347; and death of Paolo Diena, 225–6; in winter of 1944–5, 249; calls on more women to join partisans, 270; in final fighting, 293; calls on Ada in Borello, 300; returns to Torre Pellice, 308; political aims, 340, 344; honoured, 342; later career, decline and death, 347

Pons, Vittorio, 126, 175

Potsdam Conference (August 1945), 325

Pound, Ezra, 7

Prearo, Antonio, 52

Predappio, 325

press (underground), 171–3

Preziosi, Giovanni, 106, 158

prisoners of war (Allied): in hiding, 89, 102; smuggled into Switzerland, 102; numbers and fortunes, 324n

Prospero, Giacomo (Ada Gobetti's father), 13

Protani, Emanuele, 309

Rahn, Rudolf, 60, 238

Rappresaglie Anti-Partigiani (RAP), 270

rastrellamenti (round-ups), 143, 151–3, 156, 175, 195, 205, 229, 270, 305

Repubblica Sociale Italiana (RSI), 60, 80, 98, 106, 235

Ricci, Renato, 58, 99, 139

Rivoluzione Liberale (magazine), 13

Roatta, General Mario, 25, 31

Rocca, Agostino, 97

Rollier, Eric, 50

Roma (Italian battleship), 29

Rome: bombed, 4; surrenders to Germans, 28; liberated, 182; Protocols of (1944), 242; trade union congress (December 1944), 267

Rommel, General Erwin: commands in northern Italy, 29, 37; strategy in Italy, 56

Roosevelt, Franklin D.: at Casablanca conference, 24; on Italian armistice, 26; demands elimination of Fascism, 61; at Yalta conference, 278

Rora (village), 96

Rosenberg, Alfred, 56

Rosselli, Carlo, 51

Roveda, Giovanni, 268, 308

Ruffino, Virginia and Felicita, 291

Ruggero, Padre, 251

Sacerdote, Emma, 119

Sacerdote, Ugo, 119

Salerno: Allied landing at, 27

Salmoni, Alberto: and Bianca Serra, 19, 53, 92, 115; eagerness to begin sabotage, 54; joins Giorgio Diena's group, 74; supports Jewish cause, 91–2, 106; takes Le Nuove prison in Turin, 298; marries Bianca, 331

Salò: restored Fascist government in, 57–9, 98, 121, 139, 161–2, 264; offers amnesty to partisans, 230; ineffectiveness, 235, 238; troops in Turin, 299

Salvadori, Max, 276–7, 314

San Marco Division (Fascist), 285

Sauckel, General Fritz, 56, 99, 142

Schlemmer, General Johann, 300

Schmidt, Lieut. Alois, 66, 68

Schuster, Cardinal Alfredo Ildefonso, 222, 233, 249, 285, 302

Serra, Alberto (Bianca's son): on Bianca's 'existential anguish', 18; in Torre Pellice, 72; in Meana, 152; and emancipation of women, 191; plans to derail train, 218; missions to France, 231–2, 255, 260

Serra, Bianca Guidetti: and killing of Arduino sisters, xxii ; in Resistance, xxv, 19–20, 51, 66, 71, 147; from Turin, 13; background and career, 18–19; as Catholic, 18; character and qualities, 18; climbing and skiing, 19; joins Ada, 34; considers options, 36; in Meana, 53; friendship with Ada, 54; *nom de guerre* (Nerina), 72; returns to Torre Pellice, 72; works full-time for Communist Party, 72; Jewish friends, 90, 92–3; on anger in factories, 98; in mountains with Ada, 101; as guerrilla leader, 103; supplies Emanuele Artom with books, 107, 153; arrested and escapes, 111; learns of arrest of Amay partisans, 111; recruits women into Resistance, 126, 128; helps with underground press, 173–4; taken by Germans in Fenestrelle, 195; rides on Ettore's bicycle handlebars, 219; visits Paolo Gobetti's cabin, 225; on solidarity among women, 239; on missing Allied airdrops, 240; in winter of 1944–5, 249; promotes women's understanding of civic duties, 267–8; and pre-insurrection strike in Milan, 282–3; gives final instructions to Bergman rubber factory workers, 287; on Silvia's fearlessness, 300; visits Levi on return from concentration camp, 328; Levi sends chapter of *The Drowned and the Saved* to, 329; marries Alberto, 331; on Togliatti's anti-Fascist amnesty, 337; on post-liberation political corruption, 339; political aims, 340, 344; leads strike for equal pay for women, 341; honoured, 342; later activities and death, 346; *Compagne*, 346

Serra, Bruno, 257
Serra, Carla, xxii, 18, 22
Serra, Fabrizio, 346
Sicily: Allies invade and occupy, 5; Mafia in, 332
Siegel (SS officer), 123, 251, 297–8
SIR, 265
Skorzeny, Otto, 57
Socialist Party, 331
Solaro, Giuseppe: role in Turin, 67; tries partisans, 156; on enemy in cities, 262; and Fascist collapse in Turin, 286; in final fighting in Turin, 291, 296, 298–9; captured and executed, 305–7, 313
Solaro, Rosetta, 120
Soviet Russia: view of Italy, 63, 275; advance in Europe, 97, 136, 265; releases Italian POWs, 327; as prospective enemy of Allies, 334
Special Operations Executive (SOE): formed, 63–4; Italian policy, 87
Speer, Albert, 56
Spinelli, Gigliola (*later* Venturi), 119–20, 223, 331
staffette: role, xix, 79; links with Piedmont partisans, 84; and women's role as partisans, 113–14, 117–20, 218; word meaning, 113–14; members captured and executed, 168; negotiate for goods, 168; and medical practices, 175; overlooked by Allied agents, 244; Duccio supports, 246; and liberation, 261; in final partisan actions, 286; work for Ada, 293; in liberated Turin, 295; restricted in Turin victory parade, 318–19; casualties, 326

Stalin, Josef, 183, 278
Stalingrad: falls (January 1943), 24
Stampa, La (newspaper), 131
Stefano (partisan youth), 203
Stella Rossa (band), 187
Stellina (partisan brigade), xxii, 209–10, 286, 318, 322–3
Stevens, Lieut. Col. John Melchior, 245–6, 275–7, 287–8, 290, 296, 300, 312, 331–2
Sunrise, Operation, 334
Susa, 292–3; see also Val di Susa
Switzerland: Allied prisoners of war smuggled into, 102; Jews flee to, 105

Tamburini, Tullio, 220
Temple, Major see Darewski, Neville
Testori, Renato, 216, 331
Teta (of Meana), 198, 203
Thures (village), 162
Tipografia Alpina, 172
Togliatti, Palmiro, 72, 182, 184, 242, 303, 332–3, 336–7, 339
Tomassetti, Cleonice ('Nice'), 187–8
Tompkins, Peter, 248
Torre, Ada della, 94–5, 125, 180
Torre Pellice (Waldensian village), 41–4, 50, 72–4, 149, 292; underground press, 172
Trabucchi, General, 275, 277, 319, 342
Trentin, Bruno, 36
Triplex, 200–1
Truman, Harry, 323
Turin: women partisans killed, xix–xxii; bombed by Allies, 11–12, 21, 26, 182, 275; wealth, 11; industrial strikes, 12, 142, 239; anti-Fascist movements, 17, 21; Jewish community, 18; violence at Mussolini's fall, 22–3; Germans control, 34–5, 37, 53, 66–8; Italian cavalry regiment rescued and escape, 38; looting, 38–9; German suppression in, 39–40; evacuees move to mountains to escape bombing, 43; devastation, 65; Fascist support for German rule in, 67–8; divided, 70–1; Catholic Church in, 121; prison, 121–4, 129, 251; women recruited by Resistance, 126; resistance groups formed, 151; bicycles banned, 190; industrial leaders conspire in, 239; make-do inventiveness, 263; Fascist militia in, 264; and plans for liberation, 279; liberated, 282–4, 287, 289–90, 307; final fighting, 291, 293–9; Germans and Fascists leave, 299–300, 302; Fascists leave snipers after liberation, 304–5, 308–9; post-liberation administration, 308–9; post-liberation conditions, 310; Allies enter, 312; casualty numbers, 312, 317; standing-down parade, 318–19
Tuscan Committee of National Liberation, 228

Umberto, Crown Prince (later King Umberto II), 136, 183, 318
Unione Donne Italiane, 267, 340
United States: view of Mussolini and Italians, 62–3, 323; attitude to Italian moves to liberation, 275
Uomo Qualunque, L' (anti-party), 333

Val Chisone, 201
Val d'Aosta, 108, 322
Val di Susa, 80–1, 198–9, 201
Val Germanasca, 144–5
Val Pellice, 51
Valenti, Osvaldo, 220, 314
Valiani, Leo, 88–9
Valletta, Vittorio, 239–40, 287, 334
Vatican: refuses to recognise Mussolini's Salò government, 59, 121; silence over persecution of Jews, 106; see also Catholic Church

VE Day (8 May 1945), 20
Venturi, Franco, 119, 331
Vernon (of Allied Psychological
  Warfare Branch), 259
Verona Congress (November
  1943), 98, 130
Viale, Don Raimondo, 315–16
Victor Emmanuel III, King of Italy:
  joins Axis powers in war, 3;
  relations with Maria José, 3;
  and Mussolini's downfall, 6; and
  Italy's surrender, 24; Allies' view
  of, 25; disparaged by USA, 25;
  flees Rome, 27–8; clings to
  power, 59–60; under Allied
  control, 61; declares war on
  Germany, 96; refuses abdication,
  136–7; abdicates, 182
Vienna, Congress of (1943), 105
Vietinghoff, General Heinrich von,
  271
Viganò, Renata, 114

Waldensian Church, 40–1, 43, 161
Waldensian valleys, 41–3; German
  reprisals in, 53
White Russians: work for
  Germans, 103
winter (1944–5), 247–9, 258
Wolff, General Karl: commands SS
  in Italy, 56; controls Mussolini,
  60; moves to crush Resistance,
  148, 234; unleashes Operation
  Nachtigall, 201; negotiates with
  Dulles, 271; deal with Cadorna,
  292; arrested, 313, 334;
  post-war fortunes, 334
women: under Fascism, 7–8,
  10–11; anti-Fascist, 10, 113;
  active in strikes, 12; rebel
against German occupation, 40,
  112; new life in Resistance,
  78–9, 168; adopt new
  independent role, 113–18,
  125–6, 191–2, 237, 249; flirt
  with German soldiers, 116;
  mistreated by Germans, 120; in
  Turin prison, 124; recruited into
  Resistance, 126–9; Fascist
  supporters, 130–2; consort with
  Fascists and Germans, 170–1;
  promised vote, 183, 237; do not
  desert, 237; support strike
  action, 239–40; numbers in
  GDD, 249, 266; protests in
  winter 1944–5, 249; Ada
  promotes emancipation, 266–7;
  finally given vote, 272; in Turin
  liberation insurrection, 283–4;
  casualties, 291, 293, 312, 339;
  Fascist auxiliaries and
  collaborators punished and
  executed, 315–16; excluded
  from victory parades, 318–19,
  340; praised for role in war,
  339–40; constitution grants
  equality, 340; marriages and
  babies, 341; status belittled,
  341; overlooked in memoirs and
  accounts of Resistance, 342–3;
  partisans honoured, 342

Yalta conference (February 1945),
  278

Zerbino, Valerio Paolo: role in
  Turin, 67; tries partisans, 156;
  appointed 'Extraordinary
  Commissioner', 264
Zimmermann, General Paul, 97, 103